Language Files

Language Files

Materials for An Introduction to Language

Compilers of the Fourth Edition

Carolyn McManis
Deborah Stollenwerk
Zhang Zheng–Sheng

Editors of Previous Editions

Annette S. Bissantz
Keith A. Johnson
Carol Jean Godby
Rex Wallace
Catherine Jolley
Deborah B. Schaffer
John W. Perkins
F. Christian Latta
Sheila Graves Geoghegan

Advocate Publishing Group
7516 Slate Ridge Boulevard
Reynoldsburg, Ohio 43068

ISBN 0-89894-040-0

Illustrations by J. Howard Noel and Tom Staselavage
Cover Design by Mary Gillespie

10 9 8 7 6 5 4 3 2 1

Printed in the United States of America

PREFACE TO THE FOURTH EDITION

The *Language Files* began as a collection of handouts and readings which the OSU Graduate Teaching Associates and faculty members felt were particularly useful in teaching our introductory undergraduate course, 'Introduction to Language'. Originally, we used this book as a supplement to widely used texts. Having undergone successive revisions, however, we feel that it is sufficiently versatile to be used as a primary text. The *Files* is not simply a collection of exercises in phonetics, phonology, morphology, and historical linguistics that could be found in any traditional linguistic workbook. It has grown to include a variety of linguistic materials: (1) expositions of key linguistic concepts and definitions (such as *arbitrariness*), (2) information on topics not standardly found in textbooks (such as kinesics, sex differences, prescriptive grammar, and computational linguistics), (3) 'handouts' to accompany class lectures or tapes*, (4) field projects (such as dialect surveys), and (5) practical material (such as how to write an answer to an essay question).

Among our goals as editors of this 4th edition of the *Files* has been the desire to continue the trend towards creating a more self-contained text. Towards this end we have added introductory files to each section. These new files add cohesiveness to each section, defining the pertinent subfield of linguistics and important concepts related to that subfield as well as explaining the presence of subsequent files in the section. We have also added files and sections to fill in informational gaps:

2	Anthropological Linguistics
3	Speech and Writing
12	The Birds and the Bees
16	Computers and Language
21	The Sapir-Whorf Hypothesis
22	Language Origins
53	Arbitrariness in Language
71	Meaning Relationships
72	Semantic Compostition
94	The Acquisition of Morphology and Syntax
97	Adult Language Processing
107	Syntactic Change
131	Some Causal Factors in the Formation of American English Dialects
141	Social Variation: Two Case Studies

Along with these additions we have revised numerous files, adding informational material as in File 41 (Phonological Processes), including more exercises as in File 35, (Exercises in Description), modifying exercises as in File 58, (Morphology Problems), making corrections as in some of the data of File 103, (The Comparative Method). Another major change has been to reorganize the files, creating new sections, dividing and reapportioning existing sections, and rearranging the internal order of sections. Finally, we have created an index to aid students in locating important linguistic terms across files.

An undertaking of this size requires the efforts of many people. Thus, we would like to thank all of those who have, both in the past and present, contributed to the creation and revision of the *Files*. Arnold Zwicky is responsible for the original concept of the *Files* and is among its first authors. Sheila Geoghehan in 1977 assembled the first collection which has been revised by John Perkins (1978), F. Christian Latta (1978), Jean Godby, Rex Wallace, and Catherine Jolley (1982), and Annette S. Bissantz and Keith Johnson (1985). Numerous people, students and faculty members at OSU and other universities, have contributed to the writing of the *Files,* and we are very grateful for their help. For this 4th edition we would particularly like to thank Cathy Callaghan, Wayne Cowart, Dave DeHilster, Tom Ernst, Mike Geis, Brian Joseph, Joyce Powers, Katherine Welker and Arnold Zwicky for their contributions in

---

* A set of cassette tapes is available from Advocate Publishing Company to accompany the following files: 171 (Ten Commonly Spoken Languages), 85 (Conversation), 135 (American Dialects), 124 (Kiro), 125 (Gullah), and 143 (Matched Guises).

writing new files and giving consultational help. In addition we would like to thank the staff of the Advocate Publishing Group. Unfortunately, it is not possible to mention all of the names of those colleagues at other universities who have kindly offered corrections and suggestions for revisions over the years, but we are nonetheless grateful for their contributions.

Carolyn McManis
Deborah Stollenwerk
Zhang Zheng-Sheng
Linguistics Department
The Ohio State University

ACKNOWLEDGEMENTS:

The author and publishers are grateful to the following sources for permission to reprint material appearing in:

File 12: from Fromkin, Victoria and Rodman, Robert, "The Birds and the Bees" from *An Introduction to Language* 2nd Edition, Holt, Rinehart and Winston, NY; chpt. 3, pp. 41-45.

File 13: from "How Nim Chimpsky Changed My Mind," reprinted from *Psychology Today Magazine,* Copyright 1981 Ziff-Davis Publishing Company.

File 22: from *"Language Origins",* selected excerpts from Fromkin and Rodman, chpt. 2, pp. 18-25

File 31: A list of phonetic symbols and English words, *Ibid.,* chpt. 4, pp. 61-63.

File 32: A diagram of a saggital section from *Language: Introductory Readings* (3rd Edition), Clark, Virginia P.; Escholz, Paul A.; and Rosa, Alfred F. St. Martin's Press, Inc. NY; pp. 283 in Callary's *Phonology.*

File 45: from Cowan, William and Rakusan, Jaromira, *Source Book for Linguistics* (1980), Carleton University, Ottawa, Canada; Gleason, H.A. *Workbook in Descriptive Linguistics* (1955), Holt, Rhinehart & Winston, NY; Ladefoged, Peter, *Preliminaries to Linguistic Phonetics* (1971) The University of Chicago Press, Chicago; and Pearson, Bruce L., *Workbook in Linguistic Concepts* (1977) Alfred A. Knopf, NY; Akmajian, Demers and Harnish, *Linguistics: An Introduction to Language and Communication,* MIT Press, Cambridge, MA.

File 58:from Cowan, William and Rakusan, Jaromira, *Source Book for Linguistics* (1980) Carleton University, Ottawa; Gleason, H.A., *Workbook in Descriptive Linguistics* (1955), Holt, Rinehart and Winston, NY; Nida, Eugene A., *Morphology: The Descriptive Analysis of Words* (1949) Ann Arbor, The University of Michigan Press; and Pearson, Bruce L. *Workbook in Linguistic Concepts* (1977) Alfred A. Knopf, NY.

File 71: adapted from unpublished material by William Baedecker and Thomas Ernst and used with their kind permission.

File 91: A diagram of a brain from "Language and the Brain," Geschwind, Norman, *Scientific American,* 226.4: pp. 76-83.

File 92: from "Table. 4.1. Developmental Milestones in Motor and Language Development," from *Biological Foundation of Language* (1967), Lenneberg, Eric H.; John Wiley and Sons, Inc., pp. 128-30.

File 96: from *Psychology and Language* by Herbert H. and Eve V. Clark, Copyright 1977 by Harcourt Brace Jovanovich, Inc. Reprinted by permission of the publisher.

File 101: A tree diagram of Indo-European languages from *Principals and Methods for Historical Linguistics* (1979), Jeffers, Robert J. and Lehiste, Ilse; The MIT press, Cambridge, MA.; p. 29

File 104: from *Introduction to Historical Linguistics* (1972), Arlotto, Anthony, Houghton Mifflin Co., Boston; *Introductory Workbook in Historical Phonolgy* (1974), Columbus, Frederick, Slavica Publishers Inc., Cambridge, MA.; *Sourcebook for Linguistics* (1980), Cowan, William and Rakusan, Jaromira, Carleton University, Ottawa, Canada; *Workbook in Linguistic Concepts* (1977), Pearson, Bruce L., Alfred A, Knopf, NY.

File 109: from *Problems in the Origin and Development of the English Language,* Algeo, John and Pyles, Thomas, copyright 1966 by Harcourt Brace Jovanovich, Inc. Reprinted by permission of the publisher.

File 111: from "The Indo-European Origin of English" by Watkins, Calvert, *The American Heritage Dictionary of the English Language,* Copyright 1978 by Houghton Mifflin Company, by permission of *The American Heritage Dictionary of the English Language.*

TABLE OF CONTENTS

INTRODUCTION:
OBJECTIVES
AND GOALS

COURSE OBJECTIVES

The main thing we want you to draw from this course is a broad understanding of human language: what it is, what it's used for, and how it works. It's not a purpose of this course to teach you to speak or write better, but the course should enable you to recognize an uninformed statement about language when you hear it. Five years after this course is over, after you may have forgotten all the definitions and phonetic symbols you learned in it, we hope the course will have left you with a sharper ear for language, a deeper understanding of its nature, and a livelier interest in all its manifestations.

The more immediate objectives of this course are:
1. To lead you to examine your own linguistic beliefs and attitudes.
2. To make you aware of both the diversity of language systems and their fundamental similarities.
3. To give you a reasonable taste of most of the subfields of linguistics: phonetics, phonology, morphology, semantics and syntax; synchronic and diachronic linguistics; psycholinguistics and sociolinguistics.
4. To equip you with some tools and techniques for linguistic analysis and give you some practice in using these to arrive at organizing principles of a language.
5. To acquaint you with the basic concepts necessary to further pursue linguistic studies, if you wish to.

GENERAL CONCEPTUAL GOALS

Below is a list of some very general principles of human language that will be explained and illustrated throughout this course. Though the full significance of these characteristics won't be apparent to you at the beginning of the course, they are the underlying themes of many of the lectures you will hear and the assignments you will read.

1. Every language is enormously *complex*.
2. Despite this enormous complexity, every language is *systematic*, often in ways that are hidden, not obvious, and surprising. (General statements of the systematic relationships in a language are called *rules*.)
3. Not only is language systematic, but it is systematic *on many levels*, from the system of sounds to the organization of discourses.
4. This systematicity is sometimes *hard to see*, for at least two reasons:
   (a) the very complexity of language obscures the patterns and regularities;
   (b) in actual speech, there are hesitations, errors, changes in midstream, interruptions, confusions, and misunderstandings.
5. Language *varies* systematically from person to person, area to area, situation to situation. There is variation at every level of structure. Much of it is unconscious.
6. Languages are *diverse*, often astonishingly so. There are surprising differences in the way different languages are organized.

7. Despite this diversity, there are a great many *universal* properties of languages: there are characteristics shared by all languages and, also, characteristics no language can have.

8. Some properties of a language are *arbitrary*, in the sense that they cannot be predicted from other properties or from general principles.

9. Speech is almost entirely *unconscious*, so that it is not easy for speakers of a language to reflect on it; although we speak according to a great many complex rules, we are no more conscious of them than we are of the principles that govern ball-throwing or bicycle-riding.

10. The *attitudes* that people hold about language and other languages, or about their speech and other people's, can be very different from the *facts* about them. These attitudes make an important field of study on their own.

11. *Speech* is primary to *writing* in many important ways.

12. Although children *learn* their first language, they cannot really be said to be *taught* it; they intuit the rules of their language from what they hear, plus certain implicit assumptions about what language is like.

13. All languages *change* as time passes, again systematically, whether speakers desire change or not; often they are not aware of it.

14. Linguists try to give accounts of the properties of a language that are both as *precise* and as *complete* as possible.

15. In particular, they try to say what is common to all languages and how languages can differ.

THERAPEUTIC GOALS

People have all sorts of beliefs about language and languages, only some of which have been supported by the research of linguists. One of the incidental functions of this course is to correct misconceptions about language and languages. Some of these misconceptions are harmless, others are not — some of these beliefs could lead you to spend a great deal of time trying to change things that can't be changed or don't need fixing; and some can be used as instruments of prejudice against various groups. Here is a random, unorganized list of *misconceptions*. Look the list over carefully. Some of them you'll readily perceive as misconceptions (and be able to explain why they're misconceptions). Others you may see as misconceptions without really being able to explain why. And still others you'll probably agree with. You may wish to refer to this list as the course progresses. At the end of this course, we hope you'll be able to look at this list and be able to provide a cogent explanation of the misconception.

1. Writing is more perfect than speech.
2. Women generally speak better than men.
3. There are 'primitive' languages with only a few hundred words.
4. French is a clearer and more logical language than English or German.
5. People from the East Coast talk nasally.
6. Homosexuals lisp.
7. People who say *Nobody ain't done nothin'* can't think logically.
8. Swearing degrades a language.
9. Kids need to study for years in school to learn to speak their language properly.
10. Some people can pick up a language in a couple of weeks.
11. It's easier to learn Chinese if your ancestry is Chinese.
12. American Indians all speak dialects of the same language.
13. Some words, like *sapphire*, are naturally more beautiful than others, like *runt* or *stupid*.
14. The only reasonable way to arrange words in a sentence is to start with the subject and follow with the verb.
15. English is a simpler language than Latin and Greek.
16. Every language distinguishes singular nouns from plural nouns by an ending in the plural.
17. The only ways deaf people can communicate are by writing, by reading lips, and by spelling out English with their fingers.
18. People all over the world indicate 'yes' or 'no' by the same gestures of the head that we use.
19. Many animals have languages much like human languages.

20. You can almost always recognize Jews and Blacks by the way they talk.
21. Correct spelling preserves a language.
22. International relations would get better if everyone spoke the same language.
23. Japanese, Chinese, and Korean are dialects of the same language.
24. The more time parents spend teaching their children English, the better their children will speak.
25. There were once tribes of American Indians that had no spoken language but relied solely on sign language.
26. Sloppy speech should be avoided whenever possible.
27. Eskimos don't have a general word for snow, therefore they can't think abstractly.
28. The more words you know in a language, the better you know the language.
29. Nouns refer to people, places, or things.
30. *It's me* is ungrammatical, bad English and ought to be avoided by educated speakers of English.

INTRODUCTION: MAJOR SUBFIELDS OF LINGUISTICS

Listed below are some of the major subfields of linguistics and the aspect of language with which each is especially concerned.

Anthropological Linguistics: the study of the interrelationship between language and culture (particularly in the context of non-Western cultures and societies).

Applied Linguistics: the application of the methods and results of linguistics to such areas as language teaching; national language policies; lexicography; translation; and language in politics, advertising, classrooms, courts, and the like.

Historical Linguistics: the study of how languages change through time; the relationships of languages to each other.

Morphology: the study of the way in which words are constructed out of smaller meaningful units.

Neurolinguistics: the study of the brain and how it functions in the production, perception and acquisition of language.

Phonetics: the study of speech sounds; how they are articulated (articulatory phonetics); their physical properties (acoustic phonetics); how they are perceived (auditory/perceptual phonetics).

Phonology: the study of the sound system of language; how the particular sounds used in each language form an integrated system for encoding information and how such systems differ from one language to another.

Pragmatics: how the meaning conveyed by a word or sentence depends on aspects of the context in which it is used (such as time, place, social relationship between speaker and hearer, and speaker's assumptions about the hearer's beliefs).

Psycholinguistics: the study of the interrelationship of language and cognitive structures; the acquisition of language.

Semantics: the study of meaning; how words and sentences are related to the (real or imaginary) objects they refer to and the situations they describe.

Sociolinguistics: the study of the interrelationships of language and social structure, linguistic variation, and attitudes toward language.

Syntax: the study of the way in which sentences are constructed; how sentences are related to each other.

INTRODUCTION: SPEECH AND WRITING

It is a very widely held misconception that writing is more perfect than speech. To many people, writing somehow is more correct and more stable, whereas speech can be sloppy, corrupted and easily susceptible to change. Some people even go so far as to identify language with writing and regard speech as a secondary form of language used imperfectly to approximate the ideals of the written language.

One of the basic tenets of modern linguistics, however, starts with the diametrically opposed assumption that speech is primary and writing is secondary. The most immediate manifestation of language is speech and not writing. Writing is simply the representation of speech in another physical medium. Thus, writing is a secondary representation of thought. Spoken language encodes thought into a physically transmittable form, while writing, in turn, encodes spoken language into a physically preservable form. Writing is a two-stage process. All units of writing, be it letters or characters, are based on units of speech, i.e. sounds and syllables. When linguists study language, they take the spoken language as their best source of data and their object of description, except in instances of dead languages like Latin for which there are no speakers. Whatever we say in this course about language, we will also assume that it is the spoken language that we are concerned with. Ideally, we should be giving our examples in audio form, but due to technical reasons, we will use the conventional orthographic form instead, with the understanding that it is always the spoken form that is intended.

There are various reasons to think that speech is primary and writing is secondary. The most important ones are the following:

1. Writing is a later historical development of mankind than spoken language. Current archeological evidence indicates that writing was first utilized in Sumeria about 6000 years ago. (Sumeria is in modern-day Iraq.) The Sumerians probably devised written characters for the purpose of maintaining inventories of livestock and merchandise. As far as physical and cultural anthropologists can tell, spoken language has probably been used by humans for hundreds of thousands of years.

2. Writing does not exist everywhere that spoken language exits. This seems hard to imagine in our highly literate society. But the fact is that there are even today many communities in the world where a written form of language is not used. In fact, the majority of the earth's inhabitants are illiterate, though quite capable of spoken communication. The reverse, however, is not true---no society uses only a written language with no spoken form.

3. Writing must be taught, whereas spoken language is acquired automatically. All children naturally learn to speak the language of the community in which they are brought up. They acquire the basics of their native language before they enter school, or even if they never attend school. Writing systems vary in complexity, but regardless of their level of sophisitication, they all must be taught.

What then gives rise to the misconception that writing is more perfect than speech? There are a number of reasons:

1. The product of writing is usually more aptly worded and better organized, containing fewer grammatical mistakes, hesitations and incomplete sentences than are found in speech. This 'perfection of writing' can be explained by the fact that writing is the result of deliberation, correction and revision while speech is the spontaneous and simultaneous formulation of ideas; writing is therefore less subject to the constraint of time than speech.

2. Writing is intimately associated with education and educated speech. Since the speech of the educated is more often than not set up as the 'standard language', writing is associated indirectly with the 'correct', standard, varieties of language. However, the association of writing with the standard variety is not a necessary one, as evidenced by the attempts of contemporary writers to

transcribe faithfully the speech of their characters. (Mark Twain's *Huckleberry Finn* and John Steinbeck's *Of Mice and Men,* for example.)

3. Speech is ephemeral and transient, but due to its physical medium, writing lasts and can be preserved for a very long time. Spelling does not seem to vary from individual to individual or from place to place as easily as pronunciation does. Thus writing has the appearance of being more stable. But this is not a necessary feature of writing either. Spelling does vary, as exemplified by the differences between the British and the American ways of spelling *gray* and words with the *-ize, -ization* suffixes. (British has *grey* and *-ise* and *-isation*.) Writing could also change if it were made to follow the changes of speech. The fact that people at various times try to carry out spelling reforms amply illustrates this possibility. (*Through* is changed to *thru* to reflect the changed pronunciation more closely.)

INTRODUCTION: WHAT DO YOU KNOW WHEN YOU KNOW A LANGUAGE?

Knowing a language differs from using that knowledge. Many people consider 'knowing a language' to be the ability to speak that language well. We will not be considering knowledge of a language in exactly this light. We will be after something a little deeper; that is, what linguists refer to as *linguistic competence*. Your linguistic competence is your (mostly unconscious) knowledge of the rules of a language. This competence differs in significant ways from *linguistic performance*, which is your actual speech behavior.

If you listen to a conversation between native speakers of a language, you will notice (and probably be quite surprised) that their speech is peppered with false starts, hesitations, slips of the tongue, and ungrammatical sentences. They are all part of *linguistic performance*. Many linguists focus their attention on *competence*, though performance, including errors, provides important clues to what is "in" a speaker's competence.

As you read through the following discussion compare each of these aspects of linguistic competence with your own view of "knowing a language". Many of these aspects have probably escaped your consideration before. Remember that much of language is unconscious. A very important part of this course will be getting you to consider aspects of language that you have never thought about before.

THE SOUND SYSTEM (PHONOLOGY)

Part of your competence has to do with the phonology of the language. When you hear or attempt to learn a foreign language, you become acutely aware that other languages have sounds that English does not have — for example the French *r*, Spanish or French *p*, the clicks of some African languages, the German *ü* and *ö* vowels, and the tones of languages like Chinese. When we run across foreign sounds we replace them with English sounds. Thus, in English we usually say *Bach* with a final *k* (in German it's [×]) and we say *h* or *ch* for the first sound in *Chanukah* (Hebrew [×]), and *h* or *j* for the first sound in *junta* (Spanish [×]). Can you think of other substitutions we have made?

You also know what sequences of sounds are possible in different positions. For names like *Ptah* or *Ptolemy* people usually crop the *p* or insert a vowel between the *p* and the *t*. There is nothing inherently difficult about this cluster and it occurs in many English words, though not initially: *apt, captive, lapped*. You can find other examples of this type of thing by listening to newscasters trying to pronounce foreign names and places.

An even more dramatic demonstration of your inherent knowledge of possible sound sequences appears when you consider *Jumbles* and *Scrambles* from the newspapers. (These are actually concerned with unscrambling letters though the same principles apply.) For example, *gisnt* has five letters. There are 5! (5 x 4 x 3 x 2 x 1 = 120) possible arrangements of these letters. When you do a *Jumble*, however, you rarely consider many of the possibilities: you've probably already grouped *n* and *g* as *ng*, put the one vowel somewhere in the middle and put *s* and *t* together in *st*. You don't even think of beginning words with *ng*, *gt*, or *gs* or ending them with *gnt* or *tn*, or even *gn* (this does occur, but it's rare and pronounced as *n*). What allows you to skip these possibilities? Your inherent knowledge of what is a possible sequence of sounds in the English language.

MORPHOLOGY

Speech consists of continuous utterances. Often there are no physical breaks between words. Yet we can break utterances down into words without difficulty. For example, (a) can be broken down into (b), but no speaker would break it down into (c). Consider the Navaho sentence (d), which means the same thing as (a). Just as breaking down (a) is a relatively simple matter for us, breaking down (d) is a straightforward matter for a speaker of Navaho.

- a) hewenttotownonhishorse
- b) he went to town on his horse
- c) *hew enttot ow nonh ishor se
- d) kintakgoobilo'oolloozh
  kintakgoo bil o'oolloozh

Words function in different ways and it is possible to determine what function a word has even when its meaning is somewhat obscure.

- e) Lewis Carroll: *Through the Looking Glass*,
  from *The Jabberwocky*
      'Twas brillig, and the slithy toves
      Did gyre and gimble in the wabe
- f) Anthony Burgess: *A Clockwork Orange*
      The gloopy malchicks scattered razdrazily
      to the mesto.

Without too much difficulty, you will be able to identify the functions of the unfamiliar words in (e) and (f). For example, *slithy* must be an adjective modifying *toves*, a plural noun.

SYNTAX

You can recognize well-formed — that is, grammatical — sentences:

- a) *You up pick at o'clock will eight.
- b) *I will picks you up at eight o'clock.
- c) I will pick you up at eight o'clock.

Only (c) is grammatical: (a) is 'word salad' and (b) violates the English rule of subject-verb agreement. (The '*' is used to indicate that a sentence is ungrammatical.)

There is an important difference between the grammaticality of a sentence — is it structurally well-formed? — and semantic well-formedness — does it make sense? Below, (d) is structurally well-formed but semantically odd. Compare (d) through (g).

- d) I just saw a unicorn playing a concerto
      on his horn.
- e) *Colorless green ideas sleeps furiously.
- f) Colorless green ideas sleep furiously.
- g) *Green furiously colorless sleep ideas.

Both (d) and (f) are grammatical; they are also semantically peculiar.

SEMANTICS

Part of your linguistic competence has to do with your ability to determine the meaning of sentences. But your competence goes beyond this. You can determine when a sentence has more than one meaning.

- a) Jack rolled over Jill.
- b) Mary threw up her lunch.
- c) Visiting martians can be a nuisance.
- d) I saw her duck.

You also know when different sentences mean the same thing.

- e) John is an unmarried male.
- f) John is a bachelor.
- g) The car bumped the truck.

h) The truck was bumped by the car.

Above, (e) and (f) are synonymous pairs, as are (g) and (h). In addition, (g) and (h) are syntactically related (one is the passive of the other), while (e) and (f) are not.

STYLES OF SPEECH

You also understand the contexts or situations in which different styles of language may be used. To demonstrate this, match the following sentences to the situations in which you could use them; you should also have no trouble deciding which matches are appropriate and which are inappropriate.

	Sentence		Situation
_____ 1.	Pardon me, but would you mind opening the window please?	a.	Doing homework with your girl/boy friend.
_____ 2.	Open the window, will ya buddy?	b.	Babysitting your snotty younger brother.
_____ 3.	Open the window **now**.	c.	Meeting with the dean in his/her office
_____ 4.	Gee, it's hot in here.	d.	Sitting in a bus next to a man dressed in work clothes.

These feelings are just a part of the attitudes you have about how and when different forms of speech are used and about the people who use them. Consider the following sentences: what is your reaction to the people who would use them and what non-language factors do you think influence your attitudes?

Nobody ain't done nothin'.
This unseemly incident was unfortunately perpetrated by members of our own organization.
See the cute doggie go bow-wow at the nasty man?
My shirt needs cleaned.
A heart attack you'll give me with your careless driving.

INTRODUCTION: PRESCRIPTIVE VS. DESCRIPTIVE RULES OF GRAMMAR

Many people associate the idea of rules in a language with those they learned in a grammar course. These rules, laid out for them by teachers and grammarians over the course of the last three or four centuries, pertain mainly to syntax and vocabulary usage. They usually take the form:

> Use X when . . .
> Don't use X when . . .
> Never say X.

These are what linguists call *prescriptive rules*. They *prescribe* a standard of usage. However, this standard is appropriate only to a specific variety of language—a fairly formal one. Think of some of the prescriptive rules you know:

Use 'shall' when using the first person ('I' or 'we'); use 'will' with second or third person ('you,' 'he, she, it' and 'they'.)

> RIGHT: I shall go tomorrow.
> WRONG: I will go tomorrow.

Never use *not* with *hardly, scarcely, neither, never, none, no one, nobody,* or *nothing.* These words, combined with *not* form a DOUBLE NEGATIVE, which is incorrect English.

> RIGHT: I can hardly lift that box.
> WRONG: I can't hardly lift that box.

> RIGHT: I don't have anything. I have nothing.
> WRONG: I don't have nothing.

Never split an infinitive.

> RIGHT: To enhance revenues further, the company has agreed to new marketing techniques.
> WRONG: To further enhance revenues, the company has agreed to new marketing techniques.

Never end a sentence with a preposition.

> RIGHT: From where do you come?
> WRONG: Where do you come from?

Now try to remember when you were taught these common prescriptive rules. You probably started learning them in grade school, and continued on through your college composition course. But the fact is that when you began to learn these rules, you *already* spoke your native language intelligibly. The existence of prescriptive rules or your knowledge of them didn't *improve* your ability to communicate your thoughts and ideas. Prescriptive rules serve only to mold your spoken and written English to some standard norm.

Linguists are interested not in prescriptive rules but rather in the unconscious rules we apply when we speak. Regardless of what dialect or style we employ when we speak, we follow certain rules. These rules were never taught to us as native speakers of a language, and often they don't correspond to the prescriptive rules we learned in school. In fact, they may vary from style to style, dialect to dialect. A linguist is interested in determining exactly what these rules are and in describing them. Thus, they are called *descriptive rules*. Let's look at some descriptive and prescriptive rules to see how they differ.

Let's look at some descriptive and prescriptive rules to see how they differ.

Prescriptive Rule	*Descriptive Rule*
It's wrong to use *ain't*.	Joe uses *ain't* as the negative form for *be*, as in *I ain't going*, *He ain't a truck driver*, etc.

| It's not correct English to end a sentence with a preposition. | Sue uses sentences that end with prepositions, as in *Who are you with?* or *Where did you come from?* |
| It's wrong to use two modal verbs in a single clause. | Bob uses *I might could go* to mean it is possible that he would be able to go. |

Notice that the prescriptive rules make a value judgement about the correctness of an utterance and try to force a usage that aligns with one formal norm. Descriptive rules, on the other hand, accept the patterns a speaker actually uses and tries to account for them. Descriptive rules allow for different varieties of a language; they don't ignore a construction simply because a prescriptive grammarian doesn't like it.

So, if prescriptive rules are not based on actual use, how did they arise? Many of these rules were literally created by someone. During the seventeenth and eighteenth centuries, scholars became preoccupied with the art, ideas, and language of ancient Greece and Rome. The Classical Period was regarded as a golden age and Latin as the perfect language. The notion that Latin was somehow better or purer than contemporary languages was strengthened by the fact that Latin was strictly a written language and had long ceased to undergo the changes natural to spoken language. John Dryden's preoccupation with Latin led him to write: "I am often put to a stand in considering whether what I write be the idiom of the tongue . . . and have no other way to clear my doubts but by translating my English into Latin." For many writers of the seventeenth and eighteenth centuries the rules of Latin became, whenever remotely feasible, the rules of English. Several of the above rules are a result of this phenomenon.

Speakers of English have been ending sentences with prepositions freely since the beginning of the Middle English period (about 1100). There are even some instances of this construction in Old English. Speakers who attempt to avoid this often sound stilted and stuffy. The fact that ending sentences with prepositions is perfectly natural in English did not stop John Dryden from forbidding it because he found it to be non-Latin. Unfortunately, his rule has been with us ever since.

Since the early Middle English period, English has had a two-word infinitive composed of 'to' plus an uninflected verb (e.g., 'to win'). English speakers have always split this two-word infinitive by inserting words (usually adverbs) between the 'to' and the verb (e.g., 'to quickly hide'). There have been periods in English literary history when splitting infinitives was very fashionable. However, 18th century grammarians noticed that Latin infinitives were never split. Of course, it was impossible to split a Latin infinitive because it was a single, inflected word (e.g., *describere* 'to describe'). But that fact did not prevent the prescriptive grammarians from formulating another rule of English grammar.

The double negative rule has a different source. In Old and Middle English, double and triple negatives were common, and quadruple negatives existed. By Shakespeare's time, however, the double negative was rarely used by educated speakers, although it was still common in many dialects. In 1762, Bishop Lowth attempted to argue against the double negative by invoking rules of logic: ". . . two negatives in English destroy one another or are equivalent to an affirmative." Of course, logic and language are different systems, and there are many languages (e.g. modern French and Spanish) in which double negatives are required for grammaticality. Certainly no one misunderstands the English-speaking child who says, "I don't want no milk." But Lowth ignored the fact that it is usage, not logic, that must determine the rules of a grammar.

It is somewhat surprising that rules which do not reflect actual language use should survive. There are several reasons for this. First, they provide a standard of English that is accepted by most speakers; adherence to prescriptive rules allows the speaker to be understood by the greatest possible number of individuals. A set of standard rules is also necessary for students learning English (or any other language) as a second language. Imagine the chaos if there were no guidelines for learning English (or Spanish, or German, or Russian, etc.). Thus they serve a very useful purpose for language teachers and learners as well. Finally, and most importantly, there are *social* reasons for their existence. Non-standard dialects are still frowned upon by many groups and can inhibit one's progress in society. The existence of prescriptive rules allows a speaker of a non-standard dialect to learn the rules of the standard dialect and employ them in appropriate social circumstances. This does *not* mean, however, that these judgements are *linguistically* valid. The idea that one dialect of a language is intrinsically better than another is simply false; from a linguistic point of view all dialects are equally good and equally valid. To look down on non-standard dialects is to exercise a form of social prejudice.

INTRODUCTION:
ANIMAL COMMUNICATION

. . . one night, just as the Doctor was going to bed after a hard day's work with his new book on oceanography, a member of the Badgers' Tavern knocked on the door asking to see him. He said he had a terrible toothache and wanted the Doctor, if he would, to look at it at once. This, of course, the Doctor did. He was very clever at animal dentistry.

"Ah!" said he. "You've broken a corner off that tooth. No wonder it hurts. But it can be fixed. Open your mouth a little wider, please . . . .That's better — why, how curious! Did I ever fill any teeth for you before?"

"No," said the badger. "This is the first time I've come to you for treatment of any kind. I'm very healthy."

"But you have gold in your teeth," said the Doctor. "How did that come there if you haven't been to a dentist?"

"I'm sure I don't know," said the badger. "What is gold?"

"Look, I'll show you in the mirror," said the Doctor. "Stubbins, give me that hand glass, will you, please?"

I got it and brought it to the Doctor, who held it in front of the badger's face while he pointed to a place in his teeth with a small instrument.

"There," said John Dolittle, "you see that yellow metal sticking between your teeth? That's gold."

"Oh!" said the badger, peering into the mirror, very pleased with his own handsome reflection. "I and my wife were digging a hole out by Dobbin's Meadow and we chewed up a whole lot of that stuff. That's what I broke my tooth on."

(Hugh Lofting, 1925, *Doctor Dolittle's Zoo*)

As children, we heard about Dr. Dolittle's extraordinary ability to talk to animals. Not only did he talk to them, but they talked back to him. Many of us, as adults, are still convinced that we can talk with animals, particularly those of us with pets. "When I tell Kitty to get off the kitchen table, she does." "Three barks from Fido means he wants to go outside." While we are certainly able to communicate with our pets, the question arises as to whether we actually "talk with" them.

Before we can answer the above question, we need to consider what "to talk with" means. On the most basic level, it means that we communicate with each other. One way that we can represent this communication is by means of the Message Model.

SENDER	CHANNEL	RECEIVER
MESSAGE SOURCE ⟶	///////// SIGNAL ///////// ⟶	DESTINATION

THE MESSAGE MODEL

According to the Message Model, one communicator, the sender, thinks up some information at the source, then transmits that information through a signal. The receiver picks up the signal at the message destination and then decodes it. The sender and the receiver can exchange positions, and the signal can be manifested in a variety of forms: chemical emission, gesture, sound, . . .On a more technical level, "talk with" means that we have a sender and a receiver and we exchange messages through the medium of sound, more specifically language. When we communicate with our pets, we really do not talk with them as they do not use language to communicate messages back to us, and they may not even function as a sender at all. The question then arises as to whether animals talk with each other. Certainly, we know that they communicate. Honeybees, for example, tell each other where food sources are located. Dolphins can communicate their emotional states. Are they, however, using language to communicate with each other? The answer depends on what we consider language to be. Are language and communication equivalent, or is language somehow special?

The files in this section deal with the fundamental question: What is language? File 11 presents a set of features which have been posited to define language as opposed to communication. File 12 presents the details of various animal communication systems as a contrast to our human form of communication. Finally, File 13 describes a number of the attempts done to teach animals how to use language. Even if animals do not use language for their own communication systems, scientists have tried to show that they have a capacity for language. Some have run experiments in hopes of discovering the neurological structures necessary for language. Others have attempted to demonstrate that humans are unique in being the only creature with the capacity for language. Finally, some have done these experiments in order to ''talk with'' another species: ''It is lonely being the only language-using species in the universe. We want a chimp to talk so that we can say: 'Hello, out there. What's it like, being a chimpanzee?' '' (Roger Brown, 1970, 'The First Sentences of Child and Chimpanzee')

ANIMAL COMMUNICATION SYSTEMS: TRUE LANGUAGE?

A basic question pondered at some time or other by all human language users is whether any other species also has a real language. Certainly other species have forms of communication, but "communication" is not synonymous with "language". No known animal uses a language in the wild, but animals do communicate with each other in systems called signal codes. A true language differs from a signal code in terms of several essential features.

LANGUAGE FEATURES
COMMUNICATION SYSTEMS have

1. **A Mode of Communication:** The mode of communication may be vocal-auditory as in human and most animal systems, or visual as in sign language and many other animal systems (e.g. bees), or tactile, or even chemical (e.g. moths).
2. **Semanticity:** The signals in any communication system have meaning. Without this feature, the system would consist merely of noise (in the technical sense of a meaningless jumble).
3. **Pragmatic Function:** All systems of communication serve some useful purpose(s), from helping the species to stay alive to influencing others' behavior in some way (as in TV commercials).
4. **Interchangeability (reciprocality):** Humans can both send and receive messages (both speak and listen), but not all animals can. For example, the moth (Bombyx Mori) uses a chemical communication system. When the female is ready to mate, she secretes a chemical which males can trace back to her. The males themselves cannot secrete this chemical; they can only be receivers. Certain fish also lack interchangeability.
5. **Traditional Transmission:** Humans have certain innate abilities which allow us to learn a language when exposed to one. While the ability itself is innate, humans must learn the symbols. In most organisms, the actual signal code itself is innate, a matter of instinct, but in a few systems, including certain bird songs and chimpanzee signals, some of the signals seem to be instinctive while others are learned. Humans, of course, must learn all the signals of their language.

A TRUE LANGUAGE has, in addition to the above, all of the following characteristics:

6. **Productivity:** With language, humans have the ability to produce and understand any number of messages that have never been said before and which may express ideas that have never before been expressed.
7. **Displacement:** With language, humans have the ability to communicate about something which is distant in space and/or time. We can talk about the color red when we are not actually seeing it, or we can talk about a friend who lives in another state when he is not with us. Furthermore, we can talk about a class we had last year, or the class we will take next year.
8. **Arbitrariness:** With language, the relationship between a symbol and its meaning, if it is arbitrary, cannot be figured out by logic or rationale. The word "cat", for example, does not sound like a cat or represent a cat in any logical way. We know that the word "cat" symbolizes the furry creature that many of us have for a pet because we have learned that word as native English speakers. If we were French, the word would be "chat" and if we were Russian it would be "koshka". When a symbol is arbitrary, then, there is nothing inherent in it that designates its meaning. It must be learned. Most animal systems, however, are iconic (directly represent their meaning) — for instance a bird's distress call.

SIGNAL CODES VS. LANGUAGE

Some of the signal codes used by animals may exhibit one or more of the features described above, but only to a limited degree. For example, the dance of the honeybees has limited displacement — it communicates information about the location of a distant food source seen in the recent past — and parts of the dance are arbitrary, though others are representational. The bee's system is not completely productive since they cannot, for example, convey information about vertical distance or direction. Most signal codes consist of a small, finite number of discrete signals, often concerned with essentials of survival such as food, danger, or reproduction. These systems lack a mechanism for introducing new signals: they are *closed* communication systems. Thus when the animal is confronted with a novel situation, it has no way to communicate about that situation (an obvious disadvantage for the best chances of survival).

Language, in contrast, must have all of the language features to be considered language. Without one or more, it would simply be a signal code.

ANIMAL COMMUNICATION:
THE BIRDS AND THE BEES

The birds and animals are all friendly to each other, and there are no disputes about anything. They all talk, and they all talk to me, but it must be a foreign language, for I cannot make out a word they say.

MARK TWAIN,
Eve's Diary

Most animals possess some kind of "signaling" communication system. Among the spiders there is a complex system for courtship. The male spider, before he approaches his lady love, goes through elaborate gestures to inform her he is indeed a spider and not a crumb or a fly to be eaten. These gestures are invariant. One never finds a "creative" spider changing or adding to the particular courtship ritual of his species.

A similar kind of "gesture" language is found among the fiddler crabs. There are forty different varieties, and each species uses its own particular "claw-waving" movement to signal to another member of its "clan." The timing, movement, and posture of the body never change from one time to another or from one crab to another within the particular species. Whatever the signal means, it is fixed. Only one meaning can be conveyed. There is not an infinite set of fiddler crab "sentences." Nor can the signal be "broken down" into smaller elements, as is possible in any utterance of human language.

The "language" of the honeybees is far more complex than that of the spiders or fiddler crabs. When a forager bee returns to the hive, if it has located a source of food it does a dance which communicates certain information about that source to other members of the colony.

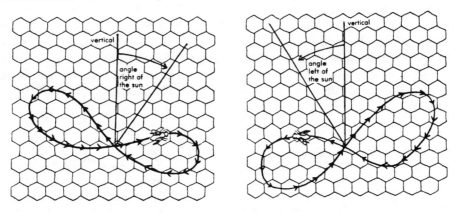

Figure 1 The sickle dance. In this case the food source is 20-60 feet from the hive.

The dancing behavior may assume one of three possible patterns: *round, sickle,* and *tail-wagging.* The determining factor in the choice of dance pattern is the distance of the food source from the hive. The round dance indicates locations near the hive, within twenty feet or so. The sickle dance indicates locations at an intermediate distance from the hive, approximately twenty to sixty feet. The tail-wagging dance is for distances that exceed sixty feet or so.

In all the dances the bee alights on a wall of the hive and literally dances on its feet through the appropriate pattern. For the round dance, the bee describes a circle. The only other semantic information imparted by the round dance, besides approximate distance, is the quality of the food source. This is indicated by the number of repetitions of the basic pattern that the bee executes, and the vivacity with which it performs the dance. This feature is true of all three patterns.

To perform the sickle dance the bee traces out a sickle-shaped figure-eight on the wall. The angle made by the direction of the open end of the sickle with the vertical is the same angle as the food source is from the sun. Thus the sickle dance imparts the information: approximate distance, direction, and quality (see Figure 1).

The tail-wagging dance imparts all the information of the sickle dance with one important addition. The number of repetitions per minute of the basic pattern of the dance indicates the precise distance: the slower the repetition rate, the longer the distance (see Figure 2).

The bee's dance is an effective system of communication, capable, in principle, of infinitely many different messages, and in this sense the bee's dance is infinitely variable, like human language. But unlike human language, the communication system of the bees is confined to a single subject, or thought. It is frozen and inflexible. For example, an experimenter forced a bee to walk to the food source. When the bee returned to the hive, it indicated a distance twenty-five times farther away than the food source actually was. The bee had no way of communicating the special circumstances or taking them into account in its message. This absence of *creativity* makes the bee's dance qualitatively different from human language.

The bee's dance does give us a chance to illustrate another very interesting property that every natural language of the world possesses, as already discussed in Chapter 1. We called this property the **arbitrariness** of the linguistic sign. In every system of communication that has a semantic system, each basic unit has two aspects, the **form** and the **meaning**. In the case of human language, the form is the actual string of sounds that make up the unit's pronunciation. Its meaning, or linguistic meaning, is of course determined by whatever language it belongs to. The sound and the meaning are like the head and tail of the same coin — distinct but inseparable. An example taken from the English language is the word *tree*. The linguistic form is the string of sounds *t-r-ee*; the linguistic meaning is the concept "tree." The same concept or meaning is expressed by different sounds in other languages. To take an example that does not involve language, consider a red traffic signal. The form is the physical object, a red light. The meaning is "stop — danger."

When we say that the linguistic sign is arbitrary, we mean that there is no connection between the linguistic form and its corresponding linguistic meaning. There is no connection between the sounds of the word *tree* and the concept "tree." Likewise there is no connection between a red light and the notion "stop — danger." The relationship in this case is a cultural matter. In all human languages the relationship between the sounds and meanings of the overwhelming majority of words is an arbitrary one.

What about the bees' dance? What are the forms of the sign, and to what meanings do they correspond? Are the relationships arbitrary or nonarbitrary? Consider the tail-wagging dance. One linguistic form is the vivacity of the dance, with a corresponding meaning "quality of food source." The relationship is clearly arbitrary, for there is nothing inherent about vivaciousness that indicates good or bad quality. In fact, we have been careful not to say whether more vivacity indicates a greater or lesser quality source of food. Because the relationship is arbitrary, there is no a priori way of telling.

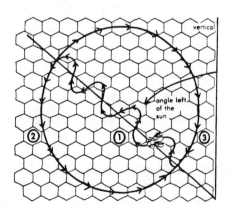 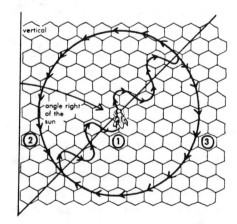

Figure 2 The tail wagging dance. The numer of times per minute the bee dances a complete pattern (1-2-1-3) indicates the distance of the food source.

What about distance? The question here is more complicated. Remember that the slower the repetition rate, the greater the distance. On the surface this relationship may seem arbitrary, but let's use a little physics to reword the relationship: The longer it takes to complete the basic pattern, the longer it will take a bee to fly to the source. Thus we see that this sign is in some sense nonarbitrary. Similarly, the direction-determining aspect of the dance is perfectly nonarbitrary.

It should be remembered, however, that there are many communication systems, other than language, which contain signs that are arbitrarily related to the meanings they stand for. "Arbitrariness" is not enough to make a system a language in the sense of human language.

We have talked about the "language" systems of the spiders, the crabs, and the bees. What about the birds? It is known that the songs of certain species of birds have definite meanings. One song may mean "let's build a nest together," another song may mean "go get some worms for the babies," and so on. But the bird cannot make up a new song to cope with a new situation.

Two French scientists have studied the songs of the European robin. They found that the songs are very complicated indeed. But, interestingly, the complications have little effect on the "message" which is being conveyed. The song which was studied was that which signaled the robin's possession of a certain territory. The scientists found that the rival robins paid attention only to the alternation between high-pitched and low-pitched notes, and which came first didn't matter at all. The message varies only to the extent of expressing how strongly the robin feels about his possession and how much he is prepared to defend it and start a family in that territory. The different alternations therefore express "intensity" and nothing more. The robin is creative in his ability to sing the same thing in many different ways, but not creative in his ability to use the same "units" of the system to express many different "utterances" all of which have different meanings.

Bird songs, then, seem to be no more similar to human language than are the movements of the spider, the claw-waving of the crab, or the dancing of the bees. All these systems are "fixed" in terms of the messages which can be conveyed. They lack the creative element of human language.

A study of higher animals also reveals no "language" systems that are creative in the way human language is. Wolves use many facial expressions, movements of their tails, and growls to express different degrees of threats, anxiety, depression, and submission. But that's all they can do. And the sounds and gestures produced by nonhuman primates, the monkeys and apes, show that their signals are highly stereotyped and limited in terms of the messages which they convey. Most importantly, studies of such animal communication systems reveal that the basic "vocabularies" produced by either sounds or facial expressions occur primarily as emotional responses to particular situations. They have no way of expressing the anger they felt "yesterday."

Descartes pointed out more than three hundred years ago that the communication systems of animals are qualitatively different from the language used by humans:

> *It is a very remarkable fact that there are none so depraved and stupid, without even excepting idiots, that they cannot arrange different words together, forming of them a statement by which they make known their thoughts; while, on the other hand, there is no other animal, however perfect and fortunately circumstanced it may be, which can do the same.*

Descartes goes on to state that one of the major differences between humans and animals is that human use of language is not just a response to external, or even internal, emotional stimuli, as are the grunts and gestures of animals. He warns against confusing human use of language with "natural movements which betray passions and may be . . . manifested by animals."

All the studies of animals communication systems provide evidence for Descartes' distinction between the fixed stimulus-bound messages of animals and the linguistic creative ability possessed by the human animal.

ANIMAL COMMUNICATION: HOW NIM CHIMPSKY CHANGED MY MIND BY HERBERT TERRACE

". . . there was no attraction for me in imitating human beings; I imitated them because I needed a way out, and for no other reason. . . . And so I learned things, gentlemen. Ah, one learns when one has to; one learns when one needs a way out; one learns at all costs."

"A Report to an Academy"
—Franz Kafka

In Kafka's short story, a chimpanzee explains how the gift of language made him feel human. For the past decade, a number of psychologists have been presenting evidence that real apes have acquired this gift. According to their reports, more than a dozen chimps, two gorillas, and an orangutan have learned extensive vocabularies in one or another visual language. Even more intriguing are claims that the apes have mastered a fundamental aspect of human language: the ability to create sentences.

How persuasive is the evidence for such claims? The researchers themselves have been clearly positive about their conclusions, which have been the focus of much discussion both in scientific journals and in the popular press.

According to Beatrice and R. Allen Gardner, who trained a female chimp named Washoe in American Sign Language (ASL), "the results of Project Washoe presented the first serious challenge to the traditional doctrine that only human beings have language." David Premack, who trained a juvenile female chimp, Sarah, to use a series of plastic chips representing words, has reported that "Sarah comprehended (and in a few cases produced) sentences formed by a process more demanding than that of combining phrases." And Duane Rumbaugh, who taught another female chimp, Lana, to communicate with symbols displayed on a computer terminal and called lexigrams ("Yerkish"), has argued: "Apes spontaneously string word units (signs, lexigrams) together. Additionally, they learned prescribed grammatical rules for ordering strings, thereby demonstrating at least elementary syntactical ability."

If these claims are valid, I might agree with Penny Patterson of Stanford University, whose experience in teaching sign language to a gorilla named Koko led her to declare that "language is no longer the exclusive domain of man." After a five-year research project of my own, however, I am skeptical about such pronouncements. When I began my study with a male chimp called Nim Chimpsky, I hoped to demonstrate that apes can, indeed, form sentences. I wanted to go beyond the anecdotal evidence reported by other studies and show that grammatical rules are needed to describe many of an ape's utterances.

Initially, the regularities I observed in thousands of Nim's communications in sign language suggested that he was, in fact, using a grammar. However, after analyzing videotapes of his "conversations" with his teachers, I discovered that the sequences of words that looked like sentences were subtle imitations of the teacher's sequences. I could find no evidence confirming an ape's grammatical competence, either in my own data or those of others, that could not be explained by simpler processes.

The sentence and the word are the two basic features of human language that separate it from other forms of animal communication. In contrast to the fixed character of most animal sounds, the word is flexible in meaning. Many species of birds, for instance, sing one song when in distress, another when courting a mate, and still another when asserting territorial rights. It does not appear possible to teach birds to produce different songs in these situations.

But human language is most distinctive because of its use of the sentence. A sentence expresses a particular meaning with a set of words and phrases that stand in a particular grammatical relationship to one another. Unlike words, whose meaning can be learned one by one, most sentences are not learned individually. Instead, children master grammatical rules that allow new meanings to be created by arranging or inflecting a set of words, or by substituting one word for another. Having mastered a few subject-verb-object sequences, such as *John hit Bill*, a child readily produces other subject-verb-object sequences without explicit training, such as *Bill hit John, John ate the apple, Bill chased the cat*, and so on. Psychologists, psycholinguists, and linguists agree that knowing a human language entails knowing a grammar. How else can one account for a child's ultimate ability to create an indeterminate number of meaningful sentences from a finite number of words?

In their first efforts to determine whether chimpanzees have similar capabilities, researchers quickly discovered that the chimps could not reproduce spoken language. These failures might be explained by anatomical limitations of the chimpanzee's vocal tract: it is incapable of producing the broad range of sounds that consitute spoken human language. That is one reason why experimenters attempted to teach them visual languages such as Yerkish and ASL.*

Washoe, Sarah, and Lana each acquired vocabularies of more than 100 words in their respective languages. Their trainers interpreted these words as they would corresponding words in human languages: names of people, objects, actions, attributes, and various relationships. In more recent studies, other apes have acquired similar vocabularies. Penny Patterson recently reported that Koko has acquired a vocabulary of more than 400 signs of ASL.

The words learned by each of these apes were symbolically arbitrary, in the sense that it was not generally possible to infer their meanings from their form. In Sarah's language, for example, the word *apple* is a nonsense geometric form on a red background. In ASL, *apple* is made by pressing the knuckle of the index finger into the cheek and twisting forward.

Apes can undoubtedly master larger vocabularies and learn them at a faster rate than, say, dogs. However, a dog who learns some arbitrary posture in order to beg, or responds to his master's command to sit, also demonstrates that it can understand arbitrary words. There is virtually no evidence, though, that domestic animals can produce sequences of the "words" they have been taught, at least not in any systematic manner.

Given that apes have been observed to produce sequences such as *Washoe more eat, water bird, Mary give Sarah apple, please machine give Lana apple*, it is natural to ask whether such sequences were generated by a grammar. It is difficult to answer this question, if for no other reason than that linguists have yet to devise a decisive test of whether a sequence of words constitutes a sentence. Even if an animal produced such a sequence, we could not conclude that it was a sentence. A well-known hypothetical experiment shows why:

Imagine a monkey who has not been taught anything about language pressing the keys of a typewriter in a random manner. Some small fraction of what it types might make sense to an English-speaking reader. In theory, the monkey's typing could even include a phrase or a sentence written by Shakespeare. It is gratuitous to attribute grammatical competence to a monkey because of a few chance responses on its typewriter. When viewed in the larger perspective of the monkey's total output, meaningful sequence is seen as a chance utterance.

Another way to perform this experiment is to train the monkey to produce specific sequences in order to obtain a reward. Monkeys, pigeons, and chimpanzees can readily learn such tasks. So can human beings, as when they learn to dial a phone number.

What is important to recognize about variations of the monkey-at-the-typewriter experiment is that neither the symbols nor the relationships between the symbols have specific meanings. Although the words and word order may be meaningful to an English speaker, they may be meaningless to the animal producing them.

This is not to say that Sarah and Lana did not understand how to use certain symbols in order to obtain a piece of apple. That they clearly could do. What is at issue is whether the chimps related the symbols to their nonverbal understanding of why they were given the food. In sentences like *Mary give Sarah banana* or *machine give Lana Coke*, that understanding does not appear to be based on a perception of the symbols *Mary* and *machine* as subjects, of *give* as a verb, and of *Sarah* and *Lana* as indirect objects. The only symbols that Sarah and Lana varied systematically were the names of the rewards they sought to obtain: *Coke, banana, movie*, and so on. If Sarah and Lana did not know the meanings of the first three symbols of the sequences they produced, it is erroneous to suppose that they understood the relationship between the symbols. Yet it is just that type of knowledge that would allow one to regard Sarah's and Lana's sequences as sentences rather than as a sequence of three nonsense symbols *A, B,* and *C,* and one meaningful symbol *X.*

Washoe combined many of her signs without being trained specifically to do so, producing sequences such as *more drink* and *open hurry*. When shown a swan for the first time by Roger Fouts, her main trainer, Washoe signed *water bird*. Since such combinations were not learned by rote training and Washoe was not required to make any of them, Fouts and the Gardners interpreted them as elementary sentences.

That conclusion seems premature, for a number of reasons. One is a flaw in the Gardners' system of recording data. With one minor exception, they recorded Washoe's combinations in only one order: in most cases, this was the order that would be followed in English. But that was not necessarily the order in which she signed. Thus, the

---

*It is estimated that ASL is used by more than 500,000 deaf and hearing people in the United States alone. This makes ASL the fourth most frequently used language in the country (after English, Spanish, and Italian). Recent research on sign language shows that it can express any concept or idea that can be expressed in spoken language. Other distinct sign languages exist in many countries: England, France, Israel, China, and Japan, to name a few.

combinations *more drink* and *drink more* were both recorded as instances of *more drink*. Since Washoe learned that either *more* or *drink* would be rewarded, it is not surprising that both signs occurred in the same utterance. But *more* and *drink* may not be related grammatically.

Typically, Washoe had to be drilled about the names and attributes of things in her environment. Her response to *what that?* was usually a name; to the question *color that?*, she would respond with an attribute. For answering correctly, the chimp was rewarded with tidbits of food, hugs, brief bouts of tickling, and signed praise. From the account of the occasion when Washoe signed *water bird*, there is no way of knowing why she made these signs. When asked *what that?* in the presence of a swan, she may have first responded *water*. If that was not what the trainer had in mind, it is reasonable to expect that, as a result of previous vocabulary drills, she would then have signed *bird*, which was also appropriate to the situation.

Even if Washoe's signs were not evoked by questions, one cannot conclude that she created a new meaning by combining the signs *water* and *bird* in a novel manner. Before doing so, it would be necessary to know if she combined other adjectives and nouns in the same way; for example, *red* and *crayon*, or *big* and *doll*. Without such information, there is no way of knowing whether *water* and *bird* are unrelated signs, each appropriate to its context, or a "true" (adjective plus noun) construction.

To decide whether a signing ape can create a sentence, it is necessary to have a record of *all* its utterances during a study. The investigator must look for evidence that a grammatical rule, such as sign order, was used to communicate different meanings. For example, how frequently did *more* precede the names of a variety of objects and actions when the chimp seemed to want more? How frequently did adjectives precede or follow nouns? Without a thorough record, we are left with only anecdotal examples of an ape's ability to create sentences—which may not have much more credibility than a passage from Shakespeare typed by a monkey.

The goal of Project Nim, which I started in 1973, was to collect and analyze a large corpus of a chimpanzee's sign combinations. The subject of the study was an infant male chimpanzee who was born at the Oklahoma Institute for Primate Studies. I chose the name Nim Chimpsky in honor of the well-known linguist who has argued that language is innate and unique to the human species. (Of course, I also had in mind the irony that would result if Nim could, indeed, create sentences.)

Nim was one week old when he was flown to New York in December 1973. He lived initially in a researcher's home in Manhattan, and later with three of his teachers in a university-owned mansion in the Riverdale section of the Bronx. Nim became the sole student in a small classroom I designed for him in the psychology department at Columbia University. The classroom allowed his teachers to focus his attention more easily than they could in his home. It also provided good opportunities to introduce him to many activities conducive to signing, such as looking at pictures, drawing, and sorting objects.

At home, Nim was treated like a young child. He slept on a loft bed in his own room and was toilet trained by the age of two and a half. My purpose was not to make Nim into a middle-class chimpanzee, but rather to provide him with as many opportunities to sign as possible. Situations in which Nim liked to behave as his teachers did—by dressing, helping to prepare meals, or cleaning up the house—provided natural opportunities for learning signs.

Nim formed particularly close attachments to certain members of the project. I maintained a strong and continuous bond with him throughout the project. During the first 18 months, Stephanie LaFarge, the experienced chimp mother with whom he lived, was the central person in his life. Following his move to Riverdale, he became closely attached to Laura Petitto, an outstanding teacher who supervised his care at home and in the Columbia classroom. After Laura left, when Nim was 34 months old, he became closely attached to two other resident teachers, Bill Tynan and Joyce Butler.

During the four years he lived in New York, Nim was taught by more than 60 volunteer teachers, as we were unable to pay enough to keep a small group of skilled, permanent caretakers. At least six people were needed to work with Nim, since it was hard for any one of them to sustain the energy needed to focus his attention and anticipate his reactions for more than five or six hours a day; also, every hour spent with Nim required at least an hour of preparation and record keeping. Because of Nim's emotional reactions to the many changes in personnel, it became increasingly difficult to command his attention.

Both at home and in the classroom, Nim's teachers kept careful chronological records of what he signed. During each session, the teacher dictated into a cassette recorder as much information as possible about Nim's signing and the context of that signing. A one-way window in a wall of the classroom and a concealed opening below that window allowed the project members to observe and videotape Nim and his teachers without being seen. The videotapes proved to be invaluable, enabling us to reevaluate Nim's performance and to look at details that took too long for teachers to describe during the limited time they had available for dictating.

Nim learned to express 125 signs during the 44 months of the project. Two of the most interesting ones were the signs for *angry* and *bite*, which he often displayed to a person he was about to attack while exhibiting a clear warning of aggression—his lips drawn back to expose his teeth, his hands raised over his head, and his hair standing on end. Having signed *angry* or *bite* in these situations, however, the physical expressions of Nim's anger subsided. If this observation can be confirmed with other chimpanzees, an important use of human language will have been duplicated by apes: expressing an emotion through symbols rather than physical acts.

Nim learned to sign *dirty* when he needed to use the toilet. He also learned that this sign had a reliable effect on his teachers' behavior: the teacher interrupted whatever he or she was doing and took him to the bathroom. On many occasions, Nim signed *dirty* right after he had been taken to the bathroom. At other times, he signed it and then showed no interest in using the toilet. The misuse of *dirty* was often accompanied by a slight grin and an avoidance of eye contact. Typically, it occurred when Nim did not want to cooperate with his teacher or was given a new teacher. Like a child saying, "I need to go to the bathroom" when he or she doesn't have to go, Nim used the sign *dirty* to manipulate his teachers' behavior.

Other apes have also learned to use the sign *dirty* to express a need to use the toilet. Indeed, it is claimed that both Washoe and Koko have signed *dirty* as an expletive. Washoe signed *dirty* in the presence of a macaque monkey she did not like, and *dirty Roger* when Roger Fouts refused to take her for a walk. Koko signed *you dirty bad toilet* when she was unjustly accused of having damaged a doll.

Fouts and Penny Patterson have interpreted this use of the word as evidence that apes are capable of cursing. However, a simpler explanation suffices: notice that each presumed use of *dirty* as an expletive occurred in trying situations and that the sign *dirty* was a reliable way, actually the most reliable way, to get the teacher to remove the ape from those situations.

During a two-year period, Nim's teachers recorded more than 20,000 of his utterances that consisted of two or more signs. Almost half were two-sign combinations, of which 1,378 were different from one another.

One characteristic of Nim's two-sign combinations led me to believe they were primitive sentences. In many cases, Nim used particular signs in either the first or the second position, no matter what other sign he combined it with. For example, *more* occurred in the first position in 85 percent of the two-sign utterances in which *more* appeared (such as *more banana, more drink, more hug,* and *more tickle*). Of the 348 two-sign combinations containing *give*, 78 percent had it in the first position. There were 946 instances in which a transitive verb (such as *hug, tickle, give*) was combined with *me* and *Nim*, and in 83 percent of them, the transitive verb occurred in the first position.

These and other regularities in Nim's two-sign utterances were the first demonstrations of a reliable use of sign order by a chimpanzee. By themselves, however, they do not justify the conclusion that they were created according to grammatical rules. Nim could have simply imitated what his teachers were signing, although at first such an explanation seemed doubtful—for a number of reasons. Nim's teachers had no reason to sign many of the combinations Nim had produced. Nim asked to be tickled long before he showed any interest in tickling his teacher; thus, there was no reason for the teacher to sign *tickle me* to Nim. Likewise, Nim requested various objects by signing *give + x* (*x* being whatever he wanted) long before he began to offer objects to his teachers. More generally, all of Nim's teachers had the clear impression that his utterances typically contained signs that we had never used with him.

Other explanations of the regularities of Nim's two-sign combinations were possible. But the statistical analyses showed that they did not result from Nim's preferences for using particular signs in the first or second positions of two-sign combinations. And the sheer number of Nim's combinations—and the regularities in them—makes implausible the hypothesis that Nim, like a monkey at a typewriter, was combining signs at random.

The more I analyzed Nim's combinations, the more certain I felt that I was on solid ground in concluding that they were grammatical and that they were comparable to the first sentences of a child. It was not until Nim was returned to Oklahoma Institute for Primate Studies (when our funds ran out) that I became skeptical of that conclusion. Ironically, it was my newly found freedom from data-collecting and from teaching and looking after the chimp that allowed me and other members of the project to examine Nim's use of sign language more thoroughly.

What emerged from our new analyses was a number of important differences between Nim's and a child's use of language. One of the first facts that troubled me was the absence of any increase in the length of Nim's utterances. During the last two years that Nim was in New York, the average length of his utterances fluctuated between 1.1 and 1.6

signs. That performance is like what children do when they *begin* combining words.

As children get older, the average length of their utterances increases steadily. This is true both of children with normal hearing and of deaf children who sign. After learning to make utterances relating a verb and an object (*eats breakfast*), the child learns to link them into longer utterances relating the subject, verb, and object (*Daddy eats breakfast*). Later, the child learns to elaborate these utterances into statements such as *Daddy didn't eat breakfast*, or, *When will Daddy eat breakfast?*

Despite the steady increase in the size of Nim's vocabulary, the mean length of his utterances did not increase. Although some of his utterances were very long, they were not, as a rule, very informative. Consider, for example, his longest, which contained 16 signs: *give orange me give eat orange me eat orange give me eat orange give me you.* While a child's longer utterances expand upon the meanings of shorter utterances, this one does not. Furthermore, the maximum length of a child's utterances is related very reliably to their average length. Nim's showed no such relationship.

The most dramatic difference between Nim's and a child's use of language was revealed in a painstaking analysis of videotapes of Nim's and his teacher's signing. A doctoral dissertation written by Richard J. Sanders, one of his teachers, showed that Nim's signing with his teachers bore only a superficial resemblance to a child's conversations with his or her parents. What is more, only 12 percent of Nim's utterances were spontaneous—that is, 88 percent were preceded by a teacher's utterance. A significantly larger proportion of a child's utterances is spontaneous. But even if there were no differences in spontaneity, there were differences in creativity.

As a child gets older, the proportion of utterances that are full or partial imitations of his or her parents' language decreases from less than 20 percent at 21 months to almost zero by the time the child is three years old. When Nim was 26 months old, 38 percent of his utterances were full or partial imitations of his teacher's. By the time he was 44 months old, the proportion had risen to 54 percent.

As children imitate fewer of their parents' utterances, they begin to expand upon what they hear their parents say. At 21 months, 22 percent of a child's utterances add at least one word to the parent's prior utterance; at 36 months, 42 percent are expansions of the parent's prior utterance. Fewer than 10 percent of Nim's utterances recorded during 22 months of video-taping (the last 22 months of the project) were expansions. Like the mean length of his utterances, this value remained fairly constant.

The videotapes showed another distinctive feature of Nim's conversations that we had been unaware of. He was as likely to interrupt his teacher's signing as not. In contrast, children interrupt their parents so rarely that interruptions are all but ignored in studies of their language development. A child learns readily what one takes for granted in a two-way conversation: each speaker adds information to the preceding utterance and each speaker takes turns in holding the floor. Nim rarely added information and showed no evidence of turn-taking.

None of the features of Nim's discourse—his lack of spontaneity, his partial imitation of his teacher's signing, his tendency to interrupt—had been noticed by any of his teachers or by the many expert observers who had watched Nim sign. Once I was sure that Nim wasn't imitating what I signed *precisely*, I had felt that it was less important to record the teachers' signs than it was to capture as much as I could about his signing: the context and specific physical movements, what hand he signed with, the order of his signs, and their appropriateness.

We found in our photographs examples of situations in which the teacher's signs had prompted Nim's signs. A careful examination of the series on page 71, which was suggested by the results of our discourse analysis, revealed that Nim's teacher was signing *you* while Nim was signing *me*; she was signing *who* while he was signing *cat*. Because these were the only four photographs taken of this discourse, we cannot specify just when the teacher began her signs. It is not clear, for example, whether the teacher signed *you* simultaneously or immediately prior to Nim's *me*. It is, however, unlikely that the teacher signed *who?* after Nim signed *cat*.

I have reason to believe that prompting by the teacher also influenced Washoe's signing. Indeed, the only two films about the Gardners' work with Washoe support the idea that prompting has played a much greater role in "conversations" with chimpanzees than previously recognized. In a "Nova"-produced film, "The First Signs of Washoe," Beatrice Gardner signs *what time now?* and Washoe interrupts to sign *time eat, time eat*. A longer version of the same exchange, shown in the second film, "Teaching Sign Language to the Chimpanzee Washoe," began with Gardner signing *eat me, more me*, after which Washoe gave her something to eat. Then she signed *thank you*—and only then asked *what time now?* Washoe's response *time eat, time eat* can hardly be considered spontaneous, since Gardner had just used the same signs and Washoe was offering a direct answer to her question.

The potential for misinterpreting an ape's signing because of inadequate reporting is made plain by another example in both films. Washoe is conversing with her teacher, Susan Nichols, who shows the chimp a tiny doll in a cup. Nichols points to the cup and signs *that*; Washoe signs *baby*. Nichols brings the cup and doll closer to Washoe, allowing her to touch them, slowly pulls them away, and then signs *that* while pointing to the cup. Washoe signs *in* and looks away. Nichols brings the cup with the doll closer to Washoe again, who looks at the two objects once more, and signs *baby*. Then, as she brings the cup still closer, Washoe signs *in*. *That*, signs Nichols, and points to the cup; *my drink*, signs Washoe.

Given these facts, there is no basis to refer to Washoe's utterance—*baby in baby in my drink*—as either a spontaneous or a creative use of "in" as a preposition joining two objects. It is actually a "run on" sequence with very little relationship between its parts. Only the last two signs were uttered without prompting from the teacher. Moreover, the sequence of the prompts (pointing to the doll, and then pointing to the cup) follows the order called for in constructing an English prepositional phrase. In short, discourse analysis makes a chimpanzee's linguistic achievement less remarkable than it might seem at first.

In his discussion of communicating with an animal, the philosopher Ludwig Wittgenstein cautions that apparent instances of an animal using human language may prove to be a "game" that is played by simpler rules. Nim's and Washoe's use of signs suggests a type of interaction between chimp and trainer that has little to do with human language. Nim's and Washoe's signing appears to have the sole function of requesting various rewards that can be obtained only by signing.

First, the teacher tries to interest the chimp in some activity such as looking at a picture book, drawing, or playing catch. Typically, the chimp tries to engage in such activities without signing. The teacher then tries to initiate signing by asking questions such as *what that? what you want? whose book?* and *ball red or blue?*

The more rapidly the chimpanzee signs, the more rapidly it can obtain what it wants. It is therefore not surprising that the chimp frequently interrupts the teacher. From the chimpanzee's point of view, the teacher's signs provide an excellent model of the signs it is expected to make. By simply imitating a few of them, often in the same order used by the teacher, and by adding a few "wild cards"—general purpose signs such as *give, me, Nim*, or *more*—the chimpanzee may well produce utterances that appear to follow grammatical rules. What seems like conversation from a human point of view is actually an attempt to communicate a demand (a nonconversational message) as quickly as possible.

It might be argued that Nim and Washoe had the potential to create sentences but did not do so because of motivational rather than intellectual limitations. Perhaps Nim and Washoe would have been more motivated to communicate in sign language if they had been raised by smaller and more consistent groups of teachers, thus sparing them emotional upheavals. Quite possibly a new project, administered by a permanent group of teachers who are fluent in sign language and have the skills necessary for such experiments, would prove successful in getting apes to create sentences.

The personnel in the new project would have to be on guard against the subtle and complex imitation that was demonstrated in Project Nim. Requiring proof that an ape is not just mirroring the signs of its teachers is not unreasonable; indeed, it is essential for any researcher who seeks to determine, once and for all, whether apes can, like humans, create sentences. Nor is it unreasonable to expect that in any such experiment, ape "language" must be measured against a child's sophisticated ability. That ability still stands as an important definition of the human species. Much as I would have preferred otherwise, a chimpanzee's "Report to an Academy" remains a work of fiction.

INTRODUCTION: ANTHROPOLOGICAL LINGUISTICS

A construction worker flicks a lighted match into an open sewer filled with water — and methane gas — touching off an explosion and resultant fire. Another person tosses a cigarette butt into an empty gasoline can and the results are identical — explosion and fire. Do generalizations about the words *empty* (inert, therefore harmless) and *water* (non-combustible) have any influence on our (perhaps largely unconscious) view of the world? (For further discussion of this, see File 21.)

The English language has one, all-inclusive word for precipitation in the form of frozen-water crystals — i.e. *snow* — making no distinction between falling snow, snow on the ground, blowing snow, etc. By contrast, Eskimo uses different terms for such perceptually distinct types of snow yet has no all-inclusive, generic term for snow. Aztec generalizes even more than English, having only one, generic term for *cold* and *ice* as well as *snow*. Is Eskimo more complex than English or Aztec? Are Aztec and Eskimo deficient in abstract terms? Or are differences among the three cultures manifested in aspects of language?

Analysis of such phenomena lies within the domain of the subfield of linguistics known as anthropological linguistics. This field of study examines the interrelationship between language on the one hand and culture and thought on the other. How are the differences between cultures and world-views manifested in languages? How much influence is exerted upon our culture or our view of the world by our language and vice versa? These are the sorts of questions to which anthropological linguists seek answers and the sorts of issues which are examined in File No. 21 in a discussion of Benjamin Whorf's theory of linguistic relativism.

Whorf, through his analysis of Hopi (a southwestern U.S Indian language) found that world-views vary among cultures, and, moreover, that aspects of a culture's view of the world are manifest in language. Western cultures, for example, somehow conceptualize three desks, three chairs, three plants and three days as the same; that is, desks, chairs, plants and days are all seen as separate entities that can be counted. However, if we look a little more closely we realize that desks, chairs and plants are objects which can be gathered together into the same room. Days, however, are units of time which must be experienced separately. They clearly cannot be found together — for the existence of one day precludes the concurrent or simultaneous existence of all other days. Western (or Standard Average European (SAE) languages reflect this view, however, in that days are as countable as desks.

The Hopi, on the other hand, do not view days as separate entities to be counted but rather as a recurrence of the same entity, although slightly older, slightly altered. The Hopi language reflects this view by reserving a special kind of adverb to mark such units of time, and a different type of marker for entities which can be counted.

Anthropological linguists study language to gain greater understanding of both the language, itself, and other matters as well — e.g. culture, thought, social structure, etc. — and are particularly interested in non-Western (non-IndoEuropean) languages like American Indian, Southeast Asian or African languages. The principle method used by anthropological linguists is the **field method.** This method utilizes a technique known as elicitation for gathering speech samples from a respondent. A commonly-used method for eliciting data, especially with a monolingual speaker, is to simply point at objects, thereby eliciting the names of these objects from the respondent. This can produce inaccurate results, however, if the object at the end of the pointed finger is misinterpreted by the respondent — e.g. the linguist may point to what he interprets as his *chin,* and the respondent offers the term for *jaw.* The optimum situation is when the respondent is monolingual but a bilingual speaker is available to serve as interpreter. Data is gathered on such semantic catagories as kinship terms, color terms, plant terms, body parts and religious terms (among others). Dictionaries and entire grammars of languages can be compiled by this method as well as reconstruction of proto-languages.

Before actually eliciting speech samples, however, the linguist does as much homework as possible by gathering ethnographic information on, for example, the history of the people, social structures, customs and mores, taboo words and topics, etc. This homework can prevent future headaches. One such case where not enough ethnographic information was obtained involved a linguist who pointed to a series of objects (e.g. tree, rock, body parts) in an elicitation session. His efforts resulted in the elicitation of the same word for each point of his finger — the word for *finger.* It seems that in this particular culture, the technique for pointing involves the use of the lower lip instead of the index finger.

Until the late 1950s, linguistics in the United States was essentially anthropological linguistics, even though European linguists were becoming more theory-based. It was this brand of linguistics (i.e. anthropological) which became the springboard for modern theoretical linguistics in this country — largely through the work of such American Structuralists as Leonard Bloomfield, Franz Boas (known as the father of American Indian language study), Edward Sapir (a student of Boas) and Benjamin Whorf (a student of Sapir).

Since the 1960s, although theoretical linguistics (the study of language for its own sake rather than for understanding of other matters) has dominated the discipline, the work of the anthropological linguist continues. In this country, work has begun on the analysis of mission records of extinct or nearly extinct languages, and linguists continue to study such Amerindian languages as Costanoan, Pomo, and Lake Miwok, and reconstruct proto-languages for Amerindian language families. Bible translators are at work translating the Bible into hundreds of non-Western languages and, in the process, compiling grammars and dictionaries. Moreover, institutes for the study of many non-Western languages exist all over the world.

Finally, as Robbins Burling notes in **Man's Many Voices** (1970:3), *"It has probably been excellent strategy to limit attention to the internal organization of language and to set aside for a time any serious concern for its context. Nevertheless, anyone who has a broad interest in the role of language must sooner or later be drawn to see language in a much wider perspective and to try to understand how language and its setting interact."*

ANTHROPOLOGICAL LINGUISTICS: THE WHORF HYPOTHESIS

It is commonly assumed that language simply reflects culture. The hectic pace of American life, for instance, is shown in the numerous metaphors involving verbs of action, such as *"catch a train"* and *"grab a bite to eat."* The Whorf Hypothesis (or the hypothesis of linguistic relativism) is the contrary proposition; namely, that the world view of a culture is subtly conditioned by the structure of its language. Westerners, for example, tend to divide reality into things and actions (or events). If we look closely at these two categories, we note that what we classify as *"things"* are nouns in our language, and *"actions"* or *"events"* turn out to be verbs. An example is *"lightning,"* which many of us unconsciously consider a thing, although physically it is closer to an action or an event.

Linguistic relativism is at least two centuries old in Europe. It is prominent in the writings of the eighteenth-century German philosopher Johann G. Herder and the nineteenth-century German philosopher-linguist Wilhelm von Humbolt, although these two scholars were more concerned with the emotional and spiritual realms than the metaphysical.

In the early twentieth century, Franz Boas and his student Edward Sapir did extensive research on American Indian languages. They both stressed the unconscious connections between language and culture and the great diversity of linguistic structure in New World languages.

Benjamin Lee Whorf was professionally neither an anthropologist nor a linguist. He was born in 1897, studied chemical engineering at the Massachusetts Institute of Technology, and worked as a fire prevention expert for the Hartford Fire Insurance Company. His interest in linguistics stemmed from problems in interpreting the Bible. His work in fire prevention made him keenly aware of the consequences of unconsidered action. Workers tended to be cautious around full gasoline drums, but might smoke or throw cigarette stubs around *"empty"* gasoline drums, which were even more dangerous because they were full of explosive vapor. In another case, a workman threw a lighted match into a partially-covered pool of waste water. Evolving gases over the pool ignited, and the fire spread to an adjoining building. Perhaps these workers associated *"empty"* with inertness, and *"water"* with non-combustibility.

Whorf suspected that the relationship between language and world view went far beyond word association and involved the structure of the language. He met Edward Sapir in 1928 and came to know many of the Yale Circle linguists during the 30's. He made contact with a Hopi Indian living in New York City and started eliciting data on the language, spoken by Pueblo Indians living in Arizona.

Whorf's great contribution to the hypothesis of linguistic relativism was his attempt to work out the interrelationship between language and world view of a non-Western group, and to compare it with the "Standard Average European" (SAE) world view and linguistic categories. In English, and SAE language, we apply plurality and cardinal numbers to both spatial and temporal entities. We say *"ten days"* and *"ten men."* Yet physically, they are quite different. It is possible to place ten men in an objective group, but not *"ten days," "ten steps forward,"* or *"ten strokes on a bell."* Physically, such events are cyclical rather than spacial, but our language predisposes us to place them in an imaginary mental group.

A Hopi could not say *"they stayed ten days"* because time is expressed by adverbs rather than count nouns in Hopi. A Hopi would say *"they left after the tenth day."* *"Ten days"* is not viewed as a collection of different days, but as successive appearances of the same day. The same is true of *"years"* and other temporal units.

The fact that *"days"* and other time periods are count nouns in SAE languages predisposes us to regard time as linear and segmentable. This attitude is reinforced by our tense system, in which past, present, and future are obligatory categories. We think of ourselves as on a point (the present) moving on the *"line of time,"* which extends indefinitely into the past and future. The past is irrevocably behind us, whether an event occurred ten minutes or ten million years ago. In addition, each of us carries his or her own *"imaginary space,"* the realm of dreams, hopes, and wishes, which are assumed to have no direct effect on the external world.

The Hopi recognize no *"imaginary space."* If one holds a mental image of a corn plant, it will have a direct effect on that plant. If the thought is wholesome, its growth will be helped. If the thought is destructive, the plant might wither. Consequently, the Hopi emphasize preparing for an event, whether it is a rabbit hunt or a ceremonial rain dance. This will include private prayer and meditation, as well as collective positive thinking designed to store up power and ward off the effects of any ill wishes.

Hopi verbs lack the tense system so common in SAE languages. The primary distinction indicated by Hopi verbs concerns whether the action takes place in the Objective (Manifested) Realm or the Subjective (Unmanifest) Realm. The Manifested Realm includes everything that is concretely in existence. This comprises the recent past (no suffix on Hopi verbs) and the edge of the present that has just emerged, for which Hopi verbs take the inceptive suffix *-va*. The Realm of the Unmanifest includes everything mental (thoughts, wishes, striving, dreams, possibilities) as well as events remote in space and time, the mythological past, the edge of the present about to emerge, and the whole of the future. Corresponding Hopi verbs take the expective suffix (*-ni* and variants). Examples include the following:

wari	"is running, ran"
wárik-ni	"will run"
wárik-nì-qa	"a possible runner"
tewá̧-ni	"(I) will see, would have seen"

If we contrast the Hopi system with SAE, we note that the SAE, *"present"* is split between the Manifested and the Unmanifested Realms. Only a portion of the SAE past, the recent past of *"real space,"* occupies the Hopi Manifested Realm. All the rest is in the Unmanifest, which is not thought of unreal, but intensely real and potent, the source of all change in the Manifested Realm. The following schematic diagrams illustrate the differences between the SAE and the Hopi treatment of space and time, according to Whorf.

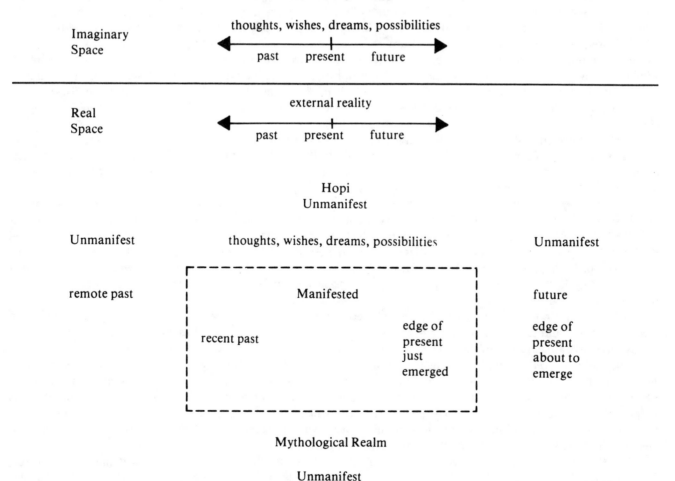

The Hopi lack a concept of time as linear progression. They substitute the notion of *"becoming later" ("latering"),* through which items in the Manifested Realm undergo growth, development, and change. The source of this change, the Unmanifest, is thought to be already vibrantly present among us, working out its effects. An analogy not used by Whorf would be a supersaturated solution (corresponding to the Unmanifest) precipitating crystals (corresponding to the Manifested). The Hopi tend to be unconcerned with exact dates and records, which are so important in Western society. Whatever has happened still is, but in an altered form. We should not record the present, but treat it as *"preparing."*

Whorf wrote articles on such diverse groups as the Shawnee, the Chinese, and the Mayan. His early death in 1941 prevented him from synthesizing his ideas on language and culture into a textbook.

The validity of the Whorf Hypothesis remains in question. Some scholars have questioned Whorf's analysis of the Hopi world view of space and time, suggesting that Whorf was simply projecting his ideas from the Hopi grammatical structure, which would make his statements circular. Other scholars have stated that Whorf's perception of the general Pueblo world view was highly accurate.

The Whorf Hypothesis is difficult to test. In one study, E. H. Lenneberg and J. M. Roberts describe an experiment in which a group of English speakers and a group of monolingual Zuni speakers were presented with diverse colors ranging between yellow and orange. The English speakers, who have two basic color terms for this range, were highly consistent in naming the colors, whereas the Zuni, who have a single term encompassing yellow and orange, made no consistent choice of names. These results support the Whorf Hypothesis.

A similar experiment with Quechi subjects on the blue-green area of the spectrum (for which Quechi has a single term) showed that speakers tended to perform groupings based on criteria apart from their lexicon. These findings would tend to negate the Whorf Hypothesis.

A *"strong"* view of linguistic relativism (one not espoused by Whorf) would claim that world view is almost totally dependent upon language, and that it is possible to greatly modify public attitudes by forcing changes in language. The error of this assumption becomes apparent when one examines the results of past substitutions, such as *"underprivileged,"* or *"disadvantaged"* for *"poor"* and *"retarded"* for *"dull"* or *"stupid."* In time, the substitutions acquire most of the unpleasant connotations of the original term. We can only eliminate such connotations by eliminating (if possible) the undesirable situations. It may be good to encourage change in language while working for social reform, but we must remember that language alone cannot serve as a mechanism for social betterment.

There are additional ways to test weaker forms of the hypothesis of linguistic relativism. One would be an investigation of non-Western cultures speaking languages with elaborate tense systems. In what ways are speakers preoccupied with time? Another avenue of research is comparison of the Hopi with another Pueblo culture speaking an unrelated language. There has been too much speculation concerning the Whorf Hypothesis and not enough data gathering to test it.

Sources for "The Whorf Hypothesis"

Andre von Wattenwyl and Heinrich Zollinger, "The Color Lexica of Two American Indian Languages, Quechi and Misquito:
A Critical Contribution to the Application of the Whorf Thesis to Color Naming,"
International Journal of American Linguistics 44 (1). 56-68 (1978).

Benjamin Lee Whorf, "The Hopi Language," 59 pp. (1935, unpublished).
Language, Thought, and Reality: Selected Writings of Benjamin Lee Whorf,
The MIT Press, Cambridge, Massachusetts (1956)

ANTHROPOLOGICAL LINGUISTICS: LANGUAGE ORIGINS

For millennia, "scientific" experiments have reportedly been devised to verify particular theories of language origin. In the fifth century B.C. the Greek historian Herodotus reported that the Egyptian Pharaoh Psammetichus (664-610 B.C.) sought to determine the most primitive "natural" language by experimental methods. The monarch was said to have placed two infants in an isolated mountain hut, to be cared for by a servant who was cautioned not to utter a single word in their presence on pain of death. The Pharaoh believed that without any linguistic input the children would develop their own language and would thus reveal the original tongue of man. Patiently the Egyptian waited for the children to become old enough to talk. According to the story, the first word uttered was *bekos*. Scholars were consulted, and it was discovered that *bekos* was the word for "bread" in Phrygian, the language spoken in the province of Phrygia (the northwest corner of modern Turkey). This ancient language, which has long since died out, was thought, on the basis of this "experiment," to be the original language.

Whether James IV of Scotland (1473-1513) had read the works of Herodotus is not known. According to reports he attempted a replication of Psammetichus's experiment, but his attempt yielded different results. The Scottish children matured and "spak very guid Ebrew," providing "scientific evidence" that Hebrew was the language used in the Garden of Eden.

Two hundred years before James's "experiment," the Holy Roman Emperor Frederick II of Hohenstaufen was said to have carried out a similar test, but without any results; the children died before they uttered a single word.

Other proposals were put forth. The belief that all languages originated from a single source is found in Genesis: ". . .the whole earth was of one language, and of one speech." The Tower of Babel story attempts to account for the diversity of languages. In this, and in similar accounts, the "confusion" of languages *preceded* the dispersement of peoples. (According to some Biblical scholars, *Babel* derives from the Hebrew *bilbel,* meaning "confusion"; others say it derives from the name Babylon.) Genesis continues: "Therefore is the name of it called Babel; because the Lord did there confound the language of all the earth: and from thence did the Lord scatter them abroad upon the face of all the earth."

A legend of the Toltecs, given by the native Mexican historian Ixtlilxochitl, also explains the diversity of languages by a similar account: "... after men had multiplied, their languages were confused, and not being able to undertand each other, they went to different parts of the earth."

A study of the history of languages does indeed show that many languages develop from a single one, as will be discussed in later chapters. But in these attested cases the "confusion" comes *after* the separation of peoples. Any view which maintains a single origin of language must provide some explanation for the number of language *families* which exist. The Bible explains this as an act of God, who at Babel created from one language many, all of which would eventually become individual multilanguage families. The monogenetic theory of languages — the single-origin theory — is related to a belief in the monogenetic origin of man. Many scientists today believe, instead, that man arose in many different places on earth. If this is the case, there were many proto-languages, out of which the modern language families developed.

The idea that the earliest form of language was imitative, or "echoic," was reiterated by many scholars up to recent times. According to this view, a dog, which emits a noise that (supposedly) sounds like "bow-wow" would be designated by the word *bow-wow*. To refute this position one need merely point to the small number of such words in any language and, in addition, to the fact that words alone do not constitute language.

A parallel view states that language at first consisted of emotional ejaculations of pain, fear, surprise, pleasure, anger, and so on. This theory — that the earliest manifestations of language were "cries of nature" that man shared with animals — was the view proposed by Jean Jacques Rousseau in the middle of the eighteenth century. According to him, both emotive cries and gestures were used by man, but gestures proved to be too inefficient for communicating, and so man invented language. It was out of the natural cries that man "constructed" words.

Rousseau's position was essentially that of the *empiricists,* who held that all knowledge results from the perception of observable data. Thus, the first words were names of individual things and the first sentences were one-word sentences. General and abstract names were invented only later, as were the "different parts of speech," and more complex sentences. Rousseau stated this in the following way: The more limited the knowledge, the more extensive the dictionary.... General ideas can come into the mind only with the aid of words, and the understanding grasps them only through propositions.

It is difficult to understand his reasoning. How was man able to acquire the ability for abstract thought through his use of concrete words if he was not, from the very beginning, equipped with special mental abilities? But, according to Rousseau, it is not man's ability to reason which distinguished him from animals (the view held by the earlier French philosopher Descartes); rather, it is his "will to be free." According to Rousseau, it is this freedom which led to the invention of languages. He did not explain how this freedom permitted speakers to associate certain sounds with certain meanings and to construct a complex system of rules which permitted them to construct new sentences. Rousseau based some of his ideas on the assumption that the first languages used by humans were crude and primitive languages "approximately like those which the various savage nations still have today." It is interesting that this man, who spent his life fighting inequality, should espouse such a position. Just one year after Rousseau's treatise, Suessmilch, arguing against Rousseau and in favor of the divine-origin theory, maintained the equality and perfection of all languages.

Almost two hundred years after Rousseau suggested that both the "cries of nature" and gestures formed the basis for language development, Sir Richard Paget argued for an "oral gesture theory":

> *"Human speech arose out of a generalized unconscious pantomimic gesture language — made by the limbs and features as a whole (including the tongue and lips) — which became specialized in gestures of the organs of articulation, owing to the human hands (and eyes) becoming continuously occupied with the use of tools. The gestures of the organs of articulation were recognized by the hearer because the hearer unconsciously reproduced in his mind the actual gesture which had produced this sound."*

It is difficult to know exactly how the tongue and lips and other vocal organs were used as "pantomimic gestures." But it is of interest that there are a number of scholars today who accept a "motor theory of speech perception" which is a sophisticated version of Paget's last statement.

The view that human language developed out of an earlier gestural communication system is found in the current publications of Gordon Hewers. He does not claim, however, that this was the only system utilized, but points to the cases where gestures are used where speech cannot be used (as for the deaf) or where speech is not feasible (under noisy conditions or where unknown languages are being spoken).

Another hypothesis concerning the development of human languages suggests that language arose out of the rhythmical grunts of men working together. The Soviet aphasiologist A. R. Luria accepted this view in 1970:

> *"There is every reason to believe that speech originated in productive activity and arose first in the form of abbreviated motions which represented certain work activities and pointing gestures by which men communicated with one another .... Only considerably later, as shown by speech paleontology, did verbal speech develop. Only in the course of a very long historical period was the disassociation of sound and gesture accomplished."*

One of the more charming views on language origin was suggested by Otto Jespersen. He proposed a theory stating that language derived from song as an expressive rather than a communicative need, with love being the greatest stimulus for language development.

Just as with the theories of the divine origin of language, many of these proposals in support of the idea that man invented language, or that it arose in the course of man's development — whether out of the cries of nature, the vocal mimicry of gestures, the songs of love, or the grunts of labor — are inconclusive. The debate is unsettled and it continues.

Despite the earlier "bans" on speculation regarding the origin of human language, the interest in this question has been rekindled. Two scholarly societies, the American Anthropological Association and the New York Academy of Sciences, held forums to review recent research on the topic (in 1974 and 1976). Research being conducted in various disciplines is providing data which were unavailable earlier and which are directly related to the development of language in the human species.

Scholars are now concerned with how the development of language is related to the evolutionary development of the human species. There are those who view language ability as a difference in degree between humans and other primates, and those who see the onset of language ability as a qualitative leap. The linguists who, in their evolutionary approach, take a "discontinuity" view believe that language is species specific, and among these linguists there are those who further believe that the brain mechanisms which underlie this language ability are specific to language, rather than being a mere offshoot of more highly developed cognitive abilities. This latter view holds that all humans are innately or genetically equipped with a unique language learning ability or with genetically determined, specifically linguistic, neurological mechanisms. Such linguists agree with the earlier views of Herder.

In trying to understand the development of language, scholars past and present have debated the role played by the vocal tract and the ear. The linguist Philip Lieberman suggests that "nonhuman primates lack the physical apparatus that is necessary to produce the range of human speech." He links the development of language with the evolutionary development of the speech production and perception apparatus. This, of course, would be accompanied by changes in the brain and the nervous system toward greater complexity. Lieberman's view implies that the languages of our human ancestors of millions of years ago may have been syntactically and phonologically simpler than any language known to us today. This still begs the question, however, because the notion "simpler" is left undefined. One suggestion is that his primeval language had a smaller phonetic inventory. But the reconstructed shape of the Neanderthal vocal tract (which Lieberman and the Yale anatomist Edmund Crelin constructed, based on fossil remains) on which this hypothesis is based has been questioned: E. L. Du Brul points out that if the Neanderthal vocal tract was as reconstructed, he would not have been able to open his mouth, let alone speak.

Certainly one evolutionary step must have resulted in the development of a vocal tract capable of producing the wide variety of sounds utilized by human language, as well as the mechanism for perceiving and distinguishing them. That this step is insufficient to explain the origin of language is evidenced by the existence of mynah birds and parrots, which have this ability. Their imitations, however, are merely patterned repetitions.

Human language utilizes a fairly small number of sounds, which are combined in linear sequence to form words. Each sound is reused many times, as is each word. Suessmilch pointed to this fact as evidence of the "efficiency" and "perfection" of language. Indeed, the discreteness of these basic linguistic elements — these sounds — was noted in the earliest views of language.

Children learn very early in life that the continuous sounds of words like *bad* and *dad* can be "broken up" into descrete segments. In fact, children that know these two words may on their own produce the word *dab,* though they have never heard it before. Mynah birds can learn to produce the sounds *bad* and *dad,* but no bird could ever produce the sound *dab* without actually hearing it.

On the other hand we also know that the ability to hear speech sounds is not a necessary condition for the acquisition and use of language. Humans who are born deaf learn the sign languages which are used around them, and these are as "creative" and complex as spoken languages. And deaf children acquire these languages in the same way as hearing children do — without being taught — by mere exposure.

Our curiosity about ourselves and our most unique possession, language, has led to numerous theories about language origin. There is no way at present to "prove" or "disprove" these hypothesis, but they are of interest for the light they shed on the nature of human language.

ANTHROPOLOGICAL LINGUISTICS: SOUND SYMBOLISM

Sound symbolism refers to a non-arbitrary connection between sound and meaning. In other words, sounds and combinations of sounds may have some kind of meaning in themselves in addition to their arbitrary use in the words of a particular language. There are two ways we can find evidence about this phenomenon.

First, if there is anything at all to sound symbolism, experimentation should show that speakers perceive something consistent about like sounds or combinations. This experimentation should also give us some indication of what it is that's consistent. We would also expect that a direct sound-meaning connection would be *universal*; that is, the connection would be the same for speakers of any language. Second, languages themselves should provide evidence that like sounds have something "in common" in the meanings they are used to convey. If sound symbolism can be shown to exist (either as a widespread or limited phenomenon), then this second type of evidence may be able to help us to understand a great deal more about the way languages use sound to symbolize meaning — about the extent of arbitrariness (convention) in language.

EXPERIMENTS IN SOUND SYMBOLISM

What are your judgments in the following test? (pronounce according to English spelling).

Put the pairs in the order heavier-lighter.
1. lat — loat   _____   _____
2. foon — feen   _____   _____
3. mobe — meeb   _____   _____
4. toos — tace   _____   _____
5. fleen — feen   _____   _____
6. seeg — sleeg   _____   _____
7. poas — poat   _____   _____
8. toos — tood   _____   _____

In a real experiment, the pairs would be listened to (*not* read) and a single judgment (for example, 'heavier') made by indicating 1 (first word) or 2 (second word), depending on which was perceived to be heavier. Experiments like this one have shown that on a nearly universal scale the single difference in sound between the members of a pair will be judged to make a difference in meaning. Even when nonsense words are used, subjects show agreement (sometimes as high as 80 percent) on what the difference between pairs of words is.

Agreement is higher when there is some feature of the sound or its production which is appropriate to the meaning judgment being made. For example, the vowels have been shown to be judged as meaning *smaller* if they are (1), in the *front* of the mouth rather than the back, and (2) produced with the tongue *higher* in the mouth rather than lower. This suggests that we connect a sound's "meaning" to the experience of its production.

MEANINGS AND SOUNDS

The most obvious thing to notice is that sound symbolism is *not* a basic principle for expressing meaning in English (or any other language, for that matter). In terms of sound *bead* differs from *beet* exactly the same way as *bed* differs from *bet*. But in meaning, the difference between *bead* and *beet* shares nothing with the difference between *bed* and *bet*. Also, *bead* and *bed* have two sounds exactly the same, differing only in the vowel. Sound symbolism would require that they share the "meanings" of these sounds. But they certainly don't share any meaning that can be pinned on *b* and *d*. *Bed* is much more closely related to *couch* (which shares no sounds with *bed*), than it is to *bead*. It appears, then, that the sounds of English do not have their own meaning, but serve only to make words *different*. It is these words that have the meaning.

However if we take a closer look at English, we find that there *are* some groups of words that share a part of their meaning *and* sounds as well. Look at the following lists:

A	B	C	D
ba*sh*	*fl*y	*sn*out	flick*er*
cra*sh*	*fl*ing	*sn*eeze	tott*er* (teet*er*)
fla*sh*	*fl*ash	*sn*oop	wav*er*
ma*sh*	*fl*ip	*sn*iff	.
.	*fl*imsy	.	.
.	.	.	.
.	.	.	.

What meaning do the members of each list share (very generally)? Can you find exceptions to these (that is, words with the italicized sounds in the same position but not having the right meaning)? With some thought you certainly can. This shows that *sound symbolism* is a very limited part of our language.

We can also show quite easily that the sound symbolisms found in English are not universal. The word for "flash" in Arabic sounds like "bark". A French "sneeze" is *éternuement*. "Waver" in German is *wanken*. Each language has its own subsets of sound-symbolized words.

Sound symbolism then is a definite human ability, but one which is not found as a principal basis to speech. It seems to be an independent process which has its most prominent effect in language which is used for its own sake, that is, in poetry and literature.

> The fleeing raven flew from leaf to leaf
> But none would hold his weight.

INTRODUCTION:
PHONETICS

Although in principle languages can employ various modes besides sounds to convey meaning, such as visual signals in the case of sign language, it remains true that human languages are mostly spoken. Sound is used to communicate meaning. The spoken character of human languages may not be an accident. Some theorists have claimed that using the vocal apparatus for language freed the human hands to engage in other activities and thus had survival value in the evolution of the race. It is interesting that people all over the world adopted spoken language, but sign language is only used in special circumstances. Speech sounds then are very important for human languages. The study of speech sounds is *phonetics.*

To communicate meaning by sound, a whole chain of activities is involved. First of all, meaning is encoded into sounds which are produced by the speaker by using the mouth, tongue, lips, and other articulatory organs. They are transmitted through the air to reach the hearer and are then perceived by the hearer through auditory processes, finally being translated back into meaning. The study of speech sounds then involves three aspects: how the sounds are produced, how they are transmitted and how they are perceived. The study of the production of speech sounds constitutes *articulatory phonetics;* the study of the transmission and the physical properties of speech sounds, i.e. intensity, frequency and duration, constitutes *acoustic phonetics;* the study of the perception of speech sounds constitutes the study of *auditory phonetics.*

The study of articulatory phonetics has had the longest history among the three sub-branches of phonetics, probably due to the fact that it is relatively easy to observe articulatory processes. In the 19th century, articulatory phonetics was already fairly developed. In the popular musical *My Fair Lady,* based on Bernard Shaw's play *Pygmalion,* the eccentric professor, Higgins, was actually modeled after the then prominent phonetician Henry Sweet. But acoustic phonetics has developed only in the last few decades. In contrast to articulatory phonetics, acoustic phonetics relies on the heavy use of sophisticated instruments in a way that is similar to the study of acoustics in physics. The most important instrument so far, the spectrograph, was invented only in the 40's. Among the three branches of phonetics, auditory phonetics is the least understood aspect, due to gaps in the understanding of human neurology and perception.

The study of articulatory phonetics has three subparts. First, we study the articulation, i.e. production, of speech sounds. Second, we describe the sounds in a way that is understood by other linguists in the field. Third, we classify sounds according to the properties they have. The files from 31 through 36 deal with the first two aspects, by way of the exposition of the concepts and procedures involved and a set of exercises to provide hands-on experience. File 31 explains the inadequacies of English orthography in the representation of speech sounds. A set of phonetic symbols are introduced which aim at representing each sound by one symbol and using each symbol to represent one sound. Files 32 and 33 deal with consonants and vowels, respectively. In these two files, we first describe the physiology of the production of speech sounds in general. Then the consonant and vowel sounds in English are discussed in detail, along with a classification according to the properties of these sounds. Files 34 through 36 are three collections of exercises. File 34 is a set of sagittal section identification exercises, which aim at familiarizing you with the vocal configurations involved in producing various speech sounds. File 35 is a set of exercises in the description of speech sounds by using classificatory labels denoting phonetic properties of sounds. File 36 is a set of exercises in transcription. It includes both transcribing English words using the newly learned phonetic alphabet and reading passages and words written in the phonetic alphabet. File 37 discusses natural classes. File 38 gives a brief introduction to acoustic phonetics.

PHONETICS: ENGLISH ORTHOGRAPHY AND PHONETIC TRANSCRIPTION

As you have probably noticed, our English spelling systems often fails to represent in an unambiguous way the sound of words. For example, in the two lists below, the italicized letters represent the same sounds.

    (1) *to too two* thr*ough* cl*ue* sh*oe* s*ui*t c*ou*p

    (2) s*ea* s*ee* sc*e*ne rec*ei*ve th*ie*f am*oe*ba mach*i*ne *A*esop

Notices also that the same spelling can represent different sounds:

    (3) d*a*me d*a*d f*a*ther c*a*ll sof*a* m*a*ny

    (4) *ch*arter *ch*aracter

    (5) *ou*t thr*ou*gh t*ou*gh

    (6) *s*ign plea*s*ure re*s*ign

    (7) pleasure re*a*d

    (8) *th*in *th*en

A combination of letters may represent only one sound:

    (9) *ch*aracter tou*gh th*ough d*ea*l p*h*ysics

And sometimes a combination of sounds is represented by a single letter:

    (10) e*x*it a*x*e

And sometimes letters represent no sound at all:

    (11) thou*gh* of*t*en bom*b* mak*e* *p*neumonia

    In order to avoid these problems when discussing the sounds of languages (not just English), it is advantageous to use a phonetic alphabet. In such an alphabet each symbol represents only one sound, and each sound is represented by just one symbol. In a phonetic alphabet, there is a one-to-one correspondence between sounds and symbols. Phonetic symbols are written within square brackets, [ ], to distinguish them from letters or words written in an ordinary spelling system (orthography).

The phonetic alphabet we will be using is given below. The symbols are listed on the left and examples of words including the sounds represented by these symbols are given on the right. The italic parts of the spelling correspond to the symbols. You can see the problems with English orthography discussed above very well from these correspondences.

CONSONANTS
SYMBOLS   EXAMPLES

p   *p*at ta*p* *p*it s*p*it ti*p* hiccou*gh* a*pp*le am*p*le
     *p*rick *p*laque a*pp*ear

b   *b*at ta*b* am*b*le *b*rick *b*lack *b*u*bb*le

m   *m*at ta*m* s*m*ack a*m*nesia a*m*ple E*mm*y ca*m*p
     co*mb*

t   *t*ap pa*t* s*t*ick men*t*or *pt*erodac*t*yl scen*t*ing
     kiss*ed* kick*ed* stuff*ed*

d   *d*ip ca*d* *d*rip guar*d* sen*d*ing men*d*er lov*ed*
     cur*ed* robb*ed* batt*ed*

n   *n*ap ca*n* s*n*ow *kn*ow *mn*emonic a*n*y pi*n*t
     *gn*ostic desig*n* *pn*eumatic sig*n* thi*n*

k   *k*it *c*at *ch*arisma *ch*aracter sti*ck* *c*riti*qu*e anti*c*
     *c*lose me*ch*anic ex*c*eed o*ch*er

g   *g*uard bur*g* ba*g* o*g*re a*g*nostic lon*g*er desi*g*nate
     Pittsbur*gh*

ŋ   si*ng* lo*ng* thi*n*k fi*n*ger si*ng*er a*n*kle (the sound
     represented by the *n* in *think* is not produced in the
     same way as that represented by the *n* in *thin;* say the
     two words to yourself and notice that the tongue
     gestures are different)

f   *f*at *f*ish *ph*iloso*ph*y *f*racture *f*lat *ph*logiston
     co*ff*ee ree*f* cou*gh* com*f*ort

v   *v*at do*v*e ri*v*al gra*v*el an*v*il ra*v*age

s   *s*ap *s*kip *s*nip *ps*ychology pa*ss* pat*s* pack*s*
     democra*c*y *s*cissors fa*s*ten de*c*eive de*s*cent
     *s*clerosis *ps*eudo rhap*s*ody pea*c*e pota*ss*ium

z   *z*ip ja*zz* ra*z*or pad*s* ki*ss*es *X*erox *x*ylophone
     de*s*ign la*z*y mai*z*e lie*s* physic*s* pea*s*
     magne*s*ium

θ   *th*igh *th*rough wra*th* *th*istle e*th*er wrea*th* *th*ink
     mo*th* arithme*t*ic Me*th*uselah tee*th* Ma*tth*ew

ð   *th*e *th*eir *th*en wrea*the* la*the* mo*th*er ei*th*er
     ra*th*er tee*the*

š   *sh*oe *sh*y mu*sh* mar*sh* mi*ss*ion na*t*ion fi*sh*
     gla*ci*al *s*ure deduc*t*ion Ru*ss*ian logi*c*ian

ž   mea*s*ure vi*s*ion a*z*ure rou*ge* (for those who do not
     pronounce this word with the same ending sound as in
     judge) ca*s*ualty deci*s*ion Carte*s*ian

č   *ch*oke *ch*urch ma*tch* fea*t*ure ri*ch* lun*ch*
     righ*t*eous consti*t*uent

ǰ   *j*udge mi*dg*et *G*eorge ma*g*istrate *j*ello *g*elatine
     re*g*ion resi*d*ual

l   *l*eaf fee*l* *l*ock ca*ll* pa*l*ace sing*le* mi*l*d p*l*ant
        pu*l*p app*l*aud

r   *r*eef fea*r* *r*ock ca*r* Pa*r*is singe*r* p*r*une ca*r*p
        fu*r*l c*r*uel

y   *y*ou *y*es pla*y*ing f*eu*d *u*se

w   *w*ith s*w*im mo*w*ing q*u*een

ʍ   *wh*ich *wh*ere *wh*at *wh*ale (for those dialects that do
        not pronounce *witch* and *which* the same)

h   *wh*o *h*at re*h*ash *h*ole *wh*ole

ʔ   bo*tt*le bu*tt*on La*t*in glo*tt*al (only for the dialect
        whose speakers substitute for the '*t* sound the sound
        which occurs between the vowels as in *uh-uh)*

VOWELS
SYMBOLS   **EXAMPLES**

i   b*ee*t b*ea*t w*e* s*ee* s*ea* rec*ei*ve k*ey* bel*ie*ve
        am*oe*be p*eo*ple C*ae*sar vasel*i*ne f*ie*nd
        mon*ey* lil*y*

ɪ   b*i*t cons*i*st *i*njury mal*i*gnant b*i*n

e   b*a*te b*ai*t r*ay* prof*a*ne gr*ea*t *ai*r *ei*ght g*au*ge
        r*ai*n r*ei*gn th*ey*

ɛ   b*e*t ser*e*nity rec*e*ption s*ay*s gu*e*st d*ea*d s*ai*d

æ   p*a*n *a*ct l*au*gh *a*nger l*a*boratory (American
        English) comr*a*de r*a*lly

u   b*oo*t wh*o* s*e*wer d*u*ty thr*ou*gh p*oo*r t*o* t*oo*
        t*w*o m*o*ve L*ou*

ʊ   p*u*t f*oo*t b*u*tcher c*ou*ld

ʌ   b*u*t t*ou*gh am*o*ng *o*ven d*oe*s c*o*ver fl*oo*d

o   b*oa*t g*o* b*eau* gr*o*w th*ou*gh t*oe* *o*wn *o*ver
        mel*o*dious

ɔ   b*ou*ght c*au*ght wr*o*ng st*a*lk c*o*re s*a*w b*a*ll
        *au*thor *a*we

a   p*o*t f*a*ther p*a*lm c*a*r s*e*rgeant h*o*nor h*o*spital
        mel*o*dic

ə   sof*a* *a*lone princip*a*l sc*ie*nce tel*e*graph symph*o*ny
        ros*e*s diffic*u*lt s*u*ppose mel*o*dy mel*o*di*ou*s
        want*e*d kiss*e*s th*e* f*a*ther b*i*rd h*e*rd w*o*rd f*u*r
        want*e*d, vis*io*n, tel*e*vis*io*n

ˌ   (written underneath unstressed, syllabic n, m,
      r, or l) button, chicken, kitten,
      bottom, butter, water, little, bottle

DIPTHONGS
SYMBOLS   **EXAMPLES**

ay   b*i*te s*igh*t b*y* d*ie* d*ye* St*ei*n *ai*sle ch*oi*r liar
       *i*sland h*eigh*t s*i*gn

aw   ab*ou*t br*ow*n d*ou*bt c*ow*ard

oy   b*oy* d*oi*ly

The words in (1) above would use the same phonetic symbol [u] for the italicized vowel sound.

(1a) [tu   tu   tu   θru   θru   klu   šu   sut   ku]

The italicized vowel sound in   (2) above is transcribed with [i]:

(2a) [si   si   sin   risiv   θif   əmibə   məšin   isap]

The vowel *sounds* would be represented by different phonetic symbols:

(3a) [dem   dæd   fašr   kɔl   sofə   mɛni]

Consider also:

(4a) [čartr̩   kɛrəktr̩]

(5a) [awt   θru   tʌf]

(6a) [sɔyn   plɛžr̩   rizayn]

(7a) [plɛžr̩   rid]

(8a) [θɪn   ðɛn]

A combination of phonetic symbols always represents a combination of sounds — there are no "silent" phonetic symbols (compare (9) and (11) above).

(9a) [kɛrəktr̩   tʌf   ðo   dil   fɪzɪks]

(11a) [ðo   ɔfn̩   bam   mek   nəmonya]

A combination of sounds will be represented by a combination of phonetic symbols:

(10a) [ɛksɪt   (or   ɛgzɪt)   æks   ]

EXERCISES

PART I

Below are some groups of words. Considering one group at a time, pronounce the words (as many times as necessary) and compare the *sounds* that the italicized letter(s) in each word stands for. (*Ignore the rest of the word.*) Are all 5 sounds in the 5 words *the same*? If so, write "All the same." Find one other word that includes this same sound. Are four of the sounds the same and one different? Are three of the sounds the same and two different? If so, put an 'X' beside the two words whose relevant sounds don't match those of the other three. For these groups find one other word that has the same sound that's included in the word(s) that you marked with an 'X'. Find one word with the same sound that's included in the unmarked words, too.

Remember: sameness or difference in spelling is irrelevant. Don't be misled!

1. *sh*rink	3. *c*ut	5. smoo*ch*ing	7. tac*t*
bi*sh*op	p*u*t	smu*dg*e	walk*ed*
na*ti*on	st*u*dy	*g*enerous	wait*ed*
spe*ci*al	t*ou*ch	le*g*end	rac*ed*
spla*sh*	*j*uggle	*J*une	logg*ed*
2. *th*umb	4. plea*s*ure	6. supp*o*se	8. si*ng*er
bo*th*	televi*s*ion	t*o*	ra*ng*
e*th*er	fi*sh*ing	s*u*per	fi*ng*er
o*th*er	a*z*ure	br*oo*m	belo*ng*
*th*at	fla*sh*er	y*ou*	gi*ng*er

PART II

Consider *only* the vowel sounds represented by the italicized letters in the words below. How many different italicized vowel sounds are there altogether? Place the words in groups according to the sounds of their italicized letters (same sound, same group). There may be "groups" with only one member.

r*y*e	prof*a*nity
s*i*bling	s*u*per
d*o* (Do you want to come?)	h*ey*
supp*o*se	*a*verage
I	*a*ble

PART III

Which of the letters in the following words are silent, and which combine with another letter to represent a single sound?

listen, cough, autumn, graph, thistle, who, wrinkle, unique

PHONETICS: ARTICULATION AND DESCRIPTION OF ENGLISH CONSONANTS

English speech sounds are formed by modifying in some way the stream of air which is forced out of the lungs through the oral and/or nasal cavities; sounds created using this type of air flow are said to be made by using a *pulmonic egressive airstream mechanism* (other airstream mechanisms are possible but will not be discussed here).

Consonants, unlike vowels, are speech sounds produced with a narrowing of the *vocal tract* which is sufficient to prevent them from functioning as *syllable nuclei* (the nucleus is the "heart" of the syllable, carrying stress, loudness, pitch information and usually consisting of a vowel). When describing consonants it is necessary to provide information about three different aspects of the articulation of the consonant.

1. Is it voiced or voiceless?
2. Where is the sound produced?
3. How is the sound produced?

Each of these will be discussed in turn.

STATE OF THE GLOTTIS

As you know, humans have a *larynx* (voicebox) at the top of the *trachea* (windpipe). Within the larynx are *vocal folds* or *vocal cords* (although they are not really cords). In the diagram below the front of the throat is uppermost

LARYNX

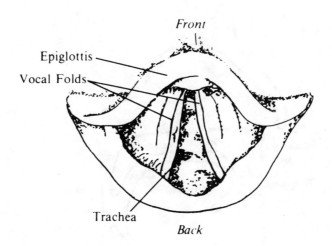

Front

Epiglottis

Vocal Folds

Trachea

Back

(compare this to the sagittal section below). The epiglottis is a flap of tissue which attaches at the front of the larynx and can fold down and back to cover and protect the vocal folds, which are stretched horizontally along the open center of the larynx. These folds are attached together to a cartilage at the front of the larynx but are separated at the back; by bringing the two free ends together the opening between the folds, called the *glottis,* can be closed, and when the folds are wide open the glottis has roughly the shape of a triangle, as can be seen in the diagram. (The ringed section shown between the vocal folds is actually the front wall of the trachea, extending downward below the larynx.)

The vocal folds can be relaxed so that the flow of air passes freely. The folds may also be held close together so that they *vibrate* as air passes through. If you make a [s] (draw it out) your vocal folds are relaxed. When you make a [z] (again, draw it out), you will feel a vibration. This vibration is due to the vibration of the vocal folds. Sounds made with the vocal folds vibrating are called *voiced* sounds. Sounds made without such vibration are said to be *voiceless*. The italicized sounds in the following pairs of words differ only in that the sound is *voiceless* in the first word of each pair and *voiced* in the second. (It is important that you don't whisper when articulating these words; whispering has the effect of eliminating vocal fold vibration).

(a) [f] *f*at	(b) [θ] *th*igh	(c) [s] *s*ip	(d) [š] dilu*t*ion
[v] *v*at	[ð] *th*y	[z] *z*ip	[ž] delu*s*ion
(e) [č] ri*ch*	(f) [p] *p*at	(g) [t] *t*ab	(h) [k] *k*ill
[ǰ] ri*dge*	[b] *b*at	[d] *d*ab	[g] *g*ill

The first thing it is necessary to say about a sound when providing an articulatory description, then, is whether it is *voiced* (the vocal folds are vibrating) or *voiceless* (no vocal fold vibration).

POINT OF ARTICULATION

It is also necessary to tell where the sound is produced in the vocal tract; that is, to give the sound's *point of articulation*. When reading about each of the following points of articulation, refer to the diagram below.

SAGITTAL SECTION

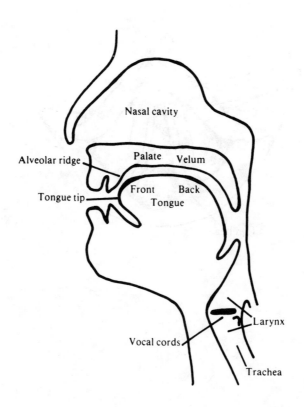

Bilabial — bilabial sounds are made with both lips. There are five such sounds possible in English: [p]*p*at, [b] *b*at, [m] *m*at, [w] *w*ith, and [ʍ] *wh*ere (present only in some dialects).

Labio-dental — labio-dental consonants are made with the lower lip against the upper front teeth. English has two labio-dentals [f] as in *f*at and [v] as in *v*at.

Interdental — interdentals are made with the tip of the tongue between the front teeth. There are two interdental sounds in English: [θ] *th*igh and [ð̌] *th*y.

Alveolar — just behind your upper front teeth there is a small ridge called the alveolar ridge. English makes seven sounds at or near this ridge: [t] *t*ab, [d] *d*ab, [s] *s*ip, [z] *z*ip, [n] *n*oose, [l] *l*oose, and [r] *r*ed.

Palatal — if you let your finger glide back along the roof of your mouth you will note that the anterior portion is hard while the posterior portion is soft. Sounds made near the hard part of the roof of the mouth are said to be *palatal*. English makes five sounds in the palatal region: [š] lea*sh*, [ž] mea*s*ure, [č] *ch*urch, [ǰ] *j*udge, [y] *y*es.

Velar — the soft part of the roof of the mouth behind the hard palate is called the *velum*. Sounds made near the velum are said to be *velar*. There are three velar sounds in English: [k] *k*ill, [g] *g*ill, and [ŋ] si*ng*.

Glottal — the space between the vocal folds is the glottis. English has two sounds made at the glottis. The first is easy to hear: [h] as in *h*igh and *h*istory. The second is called a glottal stop and it is written phonetically as [ʔ] (a question mark without the dot). This sound occurs before each vowel sound in *uh-oh* (see below under *stops*).

MANNER OF ARTICULATION

Besides telling whether or not a sound is voiced or voiceless and giving the sound's point of articulation, it is necessary to describe a sound's *manner of articulation*, that is, *how* the airstream is modified by the vocal tract to produce the sound. The manner of articulation of a sound depends on the degree of closure of the articulators (how close together or far apart they are).

Stops — stops are made by totally obstructing the airstream. Notice that when you say [p] and [b] your lips are closed together for a moment, stopping the air flow. [p] and [b] are *bilabial stops*. [b] is a *voiced bilabial stop*. [t], [d], [k], and [g] are also stops. How would you describe each?
Example: [d] — voiced alveolar stop.

The glottal stop, [ʔ], is made by momentarily closing the vocal folds. The expression *uh-oh* has a [ʔ] before each vowel. If you stop half-way through *uh-oh* and hold your articulators in position for the second half, you should be able to feel yourself making the glottal stop. (It will feel like a catch in your throat.) Nasal consonants are also stops; see below.

Fricatives — fricatives are made by forming a nearly complete stoppage of the airstream. The opening through which the air escapes is so small that *friction* is produced (much as air escaping from a punctured tire makes a "hissing" noise). [š] is made by almost stopping the air with the tongue near the roof of the mouth. It is a *voiceless palatal fricative*. How would you describe each of the following? [f], [v], [θ], [ð], [s], [z], and [ž]?
Example: [v] — voiced labio-dental fricative.

Affricates — an affricate is made by briefly stopping the airstream completely and then releasing the articulators slightly so that friction is produced. (Affricates can be thought of as a combination of a stop and a fricative.) English has only two affricates: [č] and [ǰ]. [č] is a combination of [t] (a voiceless alveolar stop) and [š] (a voiceless palatal fricative), and so may be thought of as having two points of articulation (alveolar for [t] and palatal for [š]); however, for descriptive purposes we will use only the point of its release, and describe [č] as a voiceless palatal affricate. [ǰ] is a combination of [d] and [ž]. How would you describe [ǰ]?

Nasals — notice that the velum can be raised or lowered. If it is *lowered*, as it is during normal breathing and during nasal sounds, then the air stream can escape out through the nasal cavity as well as through the unobstructed oral cavity. When the velum is raised against the back of the throat (pharynx) no air can escape. The sounds [m], [n] and [ŋ] are produced with the velum lowered and a complete obstruction in the oral cavity. They are said to be *nasals* or *nasal stops*, since the oral cavity is completely obstructed, as for the oral stops. [m] is made with the velum lowered and a complete obstruction of the air stream at the lips. For [n], the velum is lowered and the tongue tip pressed against the aveolar ridge. [ ] is made with the velum lowered and the back of the tongue stopping the air stream in the velar region. In English, all *nasals* are voiced. Thus [m] is a *voiced bilabial nasal (stop)*; the only difference between [m] and [b] is that the velum is lowered for the articulation of [m], but raised for the articulation of [b]. How would you describe [n]? [ŋ]?

Liquids — when a liquid is produced there is a closure formed by the articulators, but it is not narrow enough to cause friction. [l] in *leaf* is produced by resting the tongue on the alveolar ridge with the airstream escaping around the *sides* of the tongue. Thus it's a *lateral liquid*. Liquids are usually voiced in English: [l] is a *voiced alveolar lateral liquid*. There is a great deal of variation in the ways speakers of English make *r*-sounds; most are voiced and articulated in the alveolar region, and a common type also has the tip of the tongue curled back to make a *retroflex* sound. For our purposes [r] in *red* may be considered a *voiced alveolar retroflex liquid*.

Nasals and liquids are classified as consonants. However, they sometimes act like vowels in that they can function as syllable nuclei. Listen to the liquids and nasals in the following words: pri*sm*, but*ton*, bot*tle*, and but*ter*. In these words the second syllable consists only of a syllabic nasal or liquid. That is, the nasals and liquids are functioning as syllables. In order to indicate the syllabic character of these nasals and liquids, a ',' is placed below the phonetic symbol. The final *m* of *prism* would be transcribed [m̩] and likewise [n̩], [l̩], and [r̩] for *button, bottle,* and *butter,* respectively.

Glides — glides are made with only a slight closure of the articulators. In fact, if the vocal tract were any more open you would produce a vowel sound. [w] is made by raising the back of the tongue toward the velum while rounding your lips at the same time; it is thus classified as a *voiced bilabial glide*. (Notice the similarity in the way you articulate [w] in *woo* and the [u] vowel in this word: the only change is that you open your lips a little more for [u].) [ʍ] is produced just like [w], but it is voiceless. [y] is made with a closure in the palatal region. It is a *voiced palatal glide*. (Notice the similarity of [y] and [i] in *ye*.)

The following chart of the consonants of English can be used for easy reference. To find the *description of a sound* locate the sound on the chart. Look to the left under "State of Glottis": this will tell you whether or not the sound is *voiced, positive voi*, or *voiceless, negative voi*. Then look above the sound and see what vertical column it is in: this will tell you the sound's point of articulation. Finally look to the far left and see what horizontal row it is in: this will tell you its manner of articulation. Locate [ð], for example. It is in the *positive voi* row under State of Glottis. Thus it is voiced. Look above [ð]. It is in the vertical column marked *interdental*. Looking to the far left you see it is a fricative. [ð], then, is a *voiced interdental fricative*.

You can also use the chart to find a sound with a particular description by essentially reversing the above procedure. If you wanted to find the *voiced palatal fricative*, first look in the fricative row, then under the palatal column, and locate the symbol in the row marked *positive voi*: this is [ž].

The chart can also be used to find classes of sounds, for example, all the alveolars: simply read off all the sounds under the alveolar column. Or, all the stops: simply read off all the sounds in the stop row.

You should familiarize yourself with the chart so that you can easily recognize the phonetic symbols. Remember, too, that we are talking about **sounds** and **not letters**.

Manner of Articulation	State of Glottis	Bilabial	Labio-dental	Inter-dental	Alveolar	Palatal	Velar	Glottal	Sample Words
Stop	-voi	p			t		k	ʔ	pill, rill / kill, _uh_oh
	+voi	b			d		g		bill, dill / gill
Fricative	-voi		f	θ	s	š		h	fat, thin, sip, shin, hill
	+voi		v	ð	z	ž			vat, then, zip, measure
Affricate	-voi					č (+š)			chip, church,
	+voi					ǰ (dž)			gyp, judge
Nasal	+voi	m			n		ŋ		simmer, sinner, singer
Lateral Liquid	+voi				l				leak, look
Retroflex Liquid	+voi				r				reek, rook
Glide	+voi	w				y			witch, you
	-voi	ʍ							which

Notes: The abbreviation [+voi] designates *voiced* consonants, while [-voi] refers to *voiceless* ones. When the nasal stops and liquids are used as syllabic sounds, they are transcribed with a short vertical stroke [ˌ] under them, e.g. *bottom* [bɑdm̩], *button* [bʌʔn̩], and *turtle* [tɹdl̩].

PHONETICS: ARTICULATION AND DESCRIPTION OF ENGLISH VOWELS

Vowels are the most sonorant (intense) and most audible sounds in speech. They usually function as syllable nuclei, and the consonants that surround them often depend on the vowel for their audibility. (E.g., in *pop*, neither [p] has much sound of its own; the [p]'s are heard mainly because of the way they affect the beginning and end of the vowel.)

We will need to describe vowels in terms of different features from those we use for consonants. Vowels are sounds produced with a relatively open vocal tract, so they actually do not have a point of articulation (place of constriction) or a manner of articulation (type and degree of constriction), and they are almost always voiced.

Vocal cord vibration (voicing) is the sound source for vowels. The vocal tract above the glottis acts as a resonator affecting the sound made by the vocal cords. The shape of this resonator determines the quality— [i] vs. [u] vs. [a], etc.—of vowel.

We can change the shape of the vocal tract, and thus change vowel quality, in various ways.

1. we can raise or lower the body of the tongue,
2. we can advance or retract the body of the tongue,
3. we can round the lips or not,
4. and we can make these movements with a tense or a lax gesture.

Each of these features will be discussed in turn.

1. TONGUE HEIGHT

If you repeat to yourself the vowel sounds of *seat, set, sat*—transcribed [i], [ɛ], [æ]—you will find that you naturally open your mouth a little wider as you change from [i] to [ɛ], and then a little wider still as you change from [ɛ] to [æ]. These varying degrees of openness correspond to different degrees of tongue height: high for [i], mid for [ɛ], and low for [æ].

High vowels like [i] are made with the front of the mouth less open because the tongue body is raised, or high. The high vowels of English are [i, u, ɪ, ʊ] as in *leap, loop, lip, look*. Conversely, low vowels like [æ] in *sat* are pronounced with the front of the mouth open and the tongue lowered. [æ, a], as in *cat, cot*, are the English low vowels. Mid vowels like [ɛ] in *set* are produced with an intermediate tongue height; in English, these mid vowels include [e, ɛ, ʌ, ə, ɔ, o] as in *bait, bet, but, about, caught, boat*.

2. TONGUE ADVANCEMENT

Besides being held high or mid or low, the tongue can also be pushed forward or pulled back within the oral cavity. For example, in the high *front* vowel [i], the body of the tongue is raised and pushed forward just under the hard palate. The high *back* vowel [u] in *boot*, on the other hand, is made by raising the body of the tongue in the back of the mouth—toward the velum. The tongue is advanced or pushed frontward for all the front vowels, [i, ɪ, e, ɛ, æ], as in *see, Mick, take, Fred, back*, and retracted or pulled back for the back vowels [u, ʊ, o, ɔ, a], as in *you, look, so, soft, doc*. Central vowels require neither fronting nor retraction of the tongue.

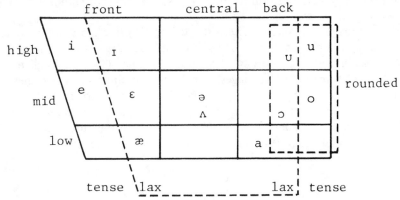

LIP ROUNDING

Vowel quality also depends on lip position. When you say the [u] in *two*, your lips are rounded. For the [i] in *tea*, they are unrounded. English has four rounded vowels:[u, ʊ, o, ɔ], as in *you, could, go, wrong*. All other vowels in English are unrounded. In the vowel chart, the rounded vowels are enclosed in a dotted-line rectangle.

In some American dialects, [ɔ] and [a] are pronounced the same, as in *caught* and *cot*, or *Don* and *dawn*. If you say these pairs the same, you probably use the unrounded vowel [a] in these words.

TENSENESS

Vowels that are called *tense* are produced with an extra degree of muscular effort. Lax vowels lack this extra effort. For example, *tense front* vowels are made with a stronger or more extreme tongue fronting gesture than lax front vowels, which are produced with a weaker fronting movement: compare tense [i] in *meet* with lax [ɪ] in *mitt*, or tense [e] in *late* with lax [ɛ] in *let*. *Tense rounded* vowels are made with stronger or tighter lip rounding than their lax counterparts: compare tense [u] in *boot* with lax [ʊ] in *put*.

Now we can consider some sample descriptions of English vowels:

[i], as in *beat*, is high, front, unrounded, and tense.
[ɔ], as in *caught,* is mid, back, rounded, and lax.
[a], as in *cot*, is low, back, unrounded, and lax.
[ʌ], as in *cut*, is mid, central, unrounded, and lax. (Note central vs. mid)
[e], as in *cake*, is mid, front, unrounded, and tense.

How would you describe each of the following English vowels? Specify height, advancement, rounding, and tenseness.

[ɪ], as in *bit*
[o], as in *boat*
[ɛ], as in *bet*
[u], as in *boot*
[æ], as in *cat*
[ʊ], as in *could*

DIPHTHONGS

At this point, we still have not described the vowel sounds of some English words—e.g., *hide, loud, coin*. Unlike the simple vowels described above, the vowels of these words are *diphthongs*, two-part vowel sounds consisting of a vowel and a glide in the same syllable. If you say *eye* slowly, concentrating on how you make this vowel, you should find that your tongue starts out in the position for [a] and moves toward the position for the vowel [i] or the palatal glide [y].[1] This diphthong, which consists of two articulations and two corresponding sounds, is written with two symbols: [ay], as in [hayd] *hide*. To make the vowel of *loud*, the tongue and the lips start in position for [a] and move toward the position for [u] or [w], so this dipthong is written [aw], as in [lawd] *loud*.[2] In the vowel of *coin*, the movement is from [o] position toward position for [i] or [y], so the vowel of *coin* is written [oy], as in [koyn][3].

It is worth noting that although we usually write just [e] or [o] for the vowel sounds of *stay* or *go*, these vowels are usually pronounced as diphthongs in English—that is, they are actually pronounced with a following glide, as [ey] and [ow], as in [stey] and [gow]. The [ey] and [ow] of English are thus a bit different from the plain [e] and [o] of some other languages, like French or Spanish, where these vowels are produced without glides (e.g. French *été* or *beau*, Spanish *mesa* or *boca*). (When we try to speak these languages, we are inclined to use our English [ey] and [ow] instead of [e] and [o], and this sounds funny to speakers of those languages—we have a foreign accent. Of course, the reverse occurs when they use plain [e] and [o] in English. This is one example of the many small details that contribute to what we call accents.)

FOOTNOTES

¹ If you have a hard time perceiving this as two sounds, try laying a (clean) finger on your tongue and saying 'eye.' This should help you feel the upward tongue movement.

² Some speakers have [ɔ] as the starting-point of this diphthong:[ɔw].

³ The positions of the vocal organs for [y] and [w] are very close to the positions for [i] and [u], respectively. So diphthongs are often written with two vowels instead of vowel plus glide: [ay], [oy] and [aw] can be written [ai̯], [oi̯] and [au̯]. The ˯ mark under the second vowel of a diphthong indicates that this vowel doesn't make a separate symbol, as a vowel usually would. ([au] would be the way to write *ahh-ooh!* and [au̯] would be the way to write *ow!).*

PHONETICS: SAGITTAL SECTION EXERCISES

EXERCISES

The following exercises are designed to help you become more familiar with the shapes of the vocal tract connected with the production of different speech sounds. For each drawing presented below there is only one sound of English which could be produced by a vocal tract positioned as shown; you are to figure out which sound is represented (either by referring to the descriptions of different sounds or by experimenting with your own vocal tract) and write the phonetic symbol for that sound between the brackets below the appropriate drawing. Note that voicing is shown by wavy lines at that point in the throat where the larynx should be, while unvoiced sounds are represented by two straight lines at that point; also, the tense-lax distinction for vowels is not shown. The first drawing in three of the rows is labelled to start you off.

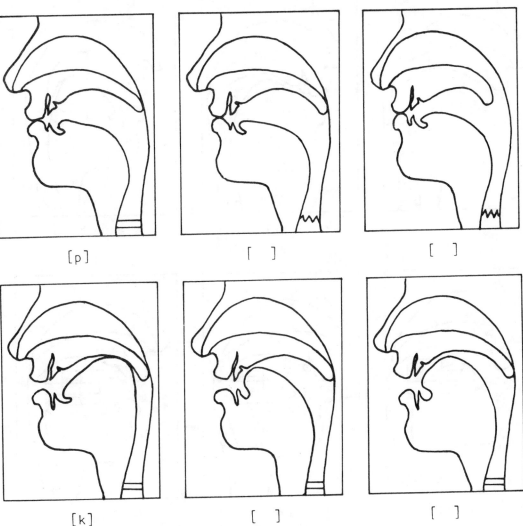

[p]   [　]   [　]

[k]   [　]   [　]

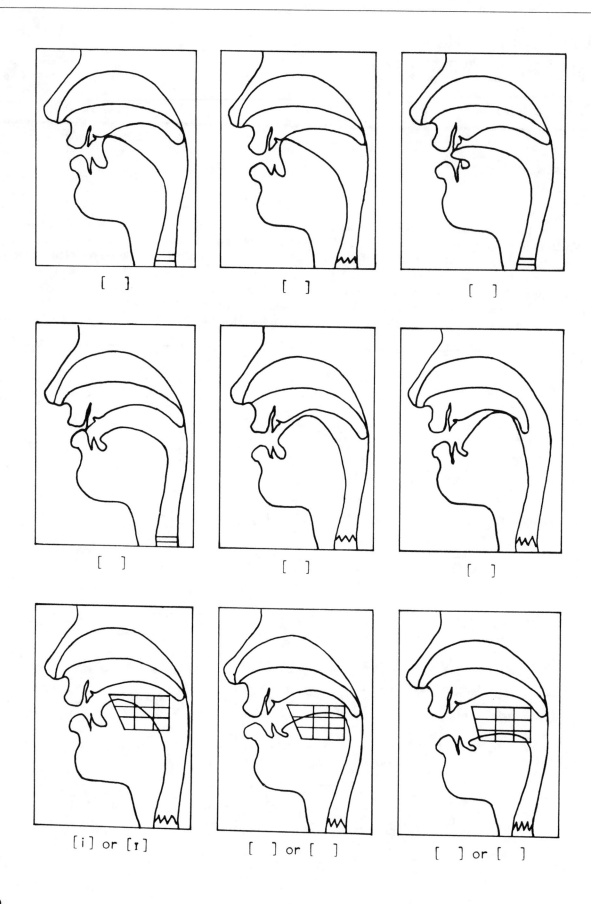

[ ]

[ ]

[ ]

[ ]

[ ]

[ ]

[i] or [ɪ]

[ ] or [ ]

[ ] or [ ]

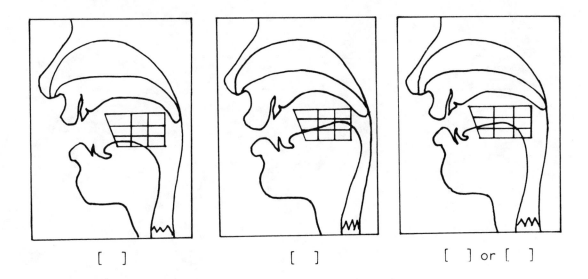

[　]   [　]   [　] or [　]

PHONETICS: EXERCISES IN DESCRIPTION

1. Underline all the sounds below that are voiced:

[l], [s], [v], [h], [w], [r], [z], [k], [b], [t]

[p], [o], [f], [d], [g], [i], [m], [θ], [ʔ], [ð]

2. Group the sounds above, according to their places of articulation, into the categories below: (there may be sounds that do not fit any of the categories; there may also be categories that none of the sounds fit)

    a. alveolar sounds   [   ]
    b. velar sounds   [   ]
    c. bilabial sounds   [   ]
    d. glottal sounds   [   ]
    e. palatal sounds   [   ]

3. Group the following vowels into the categories provided below:

[o], [ɪ], [ɛ], [æ], [ʌ], [a], [i], [ə], [e], [ɔ]

    a. high vowels: [   ]
    b. tense vowels: [   ]
    c. rounded vowels: [   ]
    d. mid back vowels: [   ]
    e. central vowels: [   ]
    f. low front vowels: [   ]

4. Identify the following sounds on the basis of their articulatory descriptions:

    a. high front tense unrounded   [   ]
    b. mid back lax rounded   [   ]
    c. low back lax unrounded   [   ]
    d. mid front lax unrounded   [   ]
    e. voiced labio-dental fricative   [   ]
    f. voiceless palatal affricate   [   ]
    g. voiced velar nasal   [   ]
    h. voiceless glottal fricative   [   ]
    i. voiced interdental fricative   [   ]
    j. voiced palatal fricative   [   ]
    k. voiced alveolar lateral liquid [   ]

5. Provide articulatory descriptions for the following sounds:

    a. [ɛ]
    b. [o]
    c. [a]
    d. [æ]
    e. [z]
    f. [n]
    g. [č]
    h. [ŋ]
    i. [g]
    j. [f]
    k. [s]

6. Give the phonetic symbol and the articulatory descriptions for the first and the last sound of each of the following words:

	symbols	descriptions
soothe	first sound	
	last sound	
gym	first sound	
	last sound	
cough	first sound	
	last sound	

PHONETICS: TRANSCRIPTION PRACTICE

Transcribe the following words into our phonetic alphabet:

1. lose	9. breathe	17. dove (the bird)
2. loose	10. circus	18. hour
3. mustache	11. patient	19. rhythm
4. cough	12. hue	20. price
5. though	13. thing	21. touch
6. vision	14. prays	22. clapped
7. said	15. move	23. moist
8. breath	16. wove	24. pushed

Give the conventional spelling for the following phonetically transcribed words:

1.[rič]	5.[rat]	9.[baks]
2.[rɪč]	6.[rut]	10.[kloð]
3.[rɪǰ]	7.[krɔld]	11.[gres]
4.[rot]	8.[sel]	12.[buti]

Which of the following phonetic transcriptions are actual English words? Circle the real ones.

[swit]	[shut]	[čild]	[stuk]	[trad]
[sɪpd]	[θɛm]	[falw]	[strʌgl̩]	[left]

    These transcripts below represent the pronunciation of a particular speaker on a particular occasion and thus may differ from your own pronunciation of the same passage in certain minor details, but this should not cause you any difficulty in reading the transcription. Passages 1 through 8 are by Woody Allen (*Without Feathers*); passage 9 is from the poem "Language" by Jack Spicer. Punctuation marks are included in the last passage for clarity's sake.

1. [dʌbz æskt hɪz brʌðr̩ wʌt ɪt wʌz layk ɪn ði ʌðr̩ wr̩ld n̩d ɪz brʌðr̩ sɛd

   ɪt wʌz nat ənlayk klivlənd]

2. [itr̩n̩l nʌθɪŋnɛs ɪz oke æz lɔŋ æz yr̩ drɛst fr̩ ɪt]

3. [ɪf yu ar sɪkstin ɔr ʌndr̩ tray nat tə go bɔld]

4. [ænd sun ǰobz pæšč̩rz drayd ʌp n̩d ɪz tʌŋ klivd tu ðə ruf əv ɪz mawθ

   so hi kud nat pronawns ðə wr̩d fræŋkɪnsɛns wɪθawt gɛtɪŋ bɪg læfs]

5. [mʌni ɪz nat ɛvriθɪŋ bʌt ɪt ɪz bɛtr̩ ðæn hævɪŋ wʌnz hɛlθ]

6. [ðə græshapr̩ pled ɔl sʌmr̩ wayl ði ænt wr̩kt n̩ sevd wɛn wɪntr̩ kem ðə

   græshapr̩ hæd nʌθɪŋ bʌt ði ænt kəmplend əv čɛst penz]

7. [ðə sæfayr wʌz ərɪǰənəli ond bay ə sʌltn̩ hu dayd ʌndr mɪstɪriəs srkəmstænsəz
    wɛn ə hænd rɪčt awt əv ə bol əv sup hi wʌz itɪŋ n̩ stræŋgl̩d hɪm]

8. [ðə gret ro ɪz ə mɪθəkl̩ bist wɪθ ðə hɛd əv ə layən ŋ ðə badi əv ə layən
    bʌt nat ðə sem layən]

9. [mæləs əfɔrθɔt. ɛvri sawnd yu mek mekɪŋ myuzɪk. tʌf lɪps. ǰɪs ɪz no
    naytəŋgel. no badiz wæksən ɪmɪǰ brnd. onli bəliv mi. lɪŋgwɪstɪks
    ɪz dəvaydɛd layk grevz mɪθaləǰi əv mɪθaləǰiz, ə trɪpl̩ gadəs mɔrfaləǰi
    fənaləǰi, ænd sɪntæks.]

PHONETICS:
NATURAL CLASSES

In studying phonetics we have noticed that sounds may be described by listing their articulatory features (voicing, place and manner of articulation for consonants, and tongue height, tongue advancement, tenseness, and roundness for vowels). Thus, [t] is described as a voiceless, alveolar stop consonant and [a] is described as a back, low, lax, unrounded vowel. This system of description lends itself quite handily to the description of natural classes (or groups) of sounds.

Natural classes are groups of sounds in a language which share some articulatory or auditory feature(s). In order for a group of sounds to be a natural class it must include *all* of the sounds that share a particular feature or group of features, and not include any sounds that don't. Thus, when we refer to the natural class of voiced stops in English, we mean all of the sounds which are voiced stops in English and no sounds that are not (i.e., [b, d, g]).

Describing sounds in terms of natural classes makes it possible to state generalizations concerning (1) the sound systems of human languages (e.g., the possible sequences of sounds that can occur together, which sounds will be modified when next to some other sound, etc.); (2) dialect variation; (3) changes in the pronunciation of borrowed words; (4) the acquisition of language by children; (5) rules for rhyming in poetry; (6) processes of sound change over the history of a language. All of these things are easier to understand when we understand what natural classes are.

WHAT IS NATURAL?

What makes one group of sounds a natural class while another group of sounds (perhaps with the same number of members) is not a natural class? What is it that makes a natural class natural?

Consider two groups of sounds: [p, t, k] and [p, l, w] . The first of these two groups is a natural class, the second isn't. Notice that [p, t, k] all share the feature of voicelessness and that they are all oral stops (as opposed to nasal stops /m, n, ŋ/ and glottal stop). In fact these three sounds are the set of all sounds in English that have both the features *voiceless* and *oral stop*. The sounds in [p, l, w] on the other hand, have no feature in common (except that they are all consonants, and obviously [p, l, w] is not the set of all consonants in English). Thus, [p, t, k] is a natural class because it is the set of all sounds in English which are voiceless, oral stops. [p, l, w] on the other hand, is not a natural class because the only feature they all have in common (consonant) describes a much larger set of sounds. We might say that [p, l, w] is a subset of the natural class of consonants in English, but it is certainly not a natural class itself.

FEATURES USED TO DESCRIBE NATURAL CLASSES

All of the features used in files 32 and 33 to describe individual sounds can also be used to describe natural classes. For example, in English the vowels [i, e, o, u] are all tense vowels (and there are no other tense vowels in English). Because these vowels share the feature tense they are members of the natural class of tense vowels in English. Likewise, the consonants [k, g, ŋ] are all described as velar consonants (and they are the only velar consonants used in English), thus they constitute the natural class of velar consonants in English.

In talking about groups of sounds we must use a few features in addition to those used to describe the individual sounds. For example if you look at the consonant chart in File 32 you will notice that the only labiodental consonants in English are the fricatives [f] and [v], while the bilabial fricative slots are left empty. In many situations it is advantageous to refer to [f] and [v], and [p] and [b] as belonging to the same natural class. For this purpose we use the feature *labial*. In other words, the fact that all of these sounds are produced with a lip gesture means that they all share the feature *labial,* and are thus grouped together in a natural class. This natural class is used by English speakers. For example, for most speakers of English the sound [w] does not occur after the consonants [m, b, p, f, v]. As a result, *mwoast, *pwell, *bwint, *fwallow,* and *vwoot* are not possible English words. If we had noticed that [m, b, p, f, v] share the feature *labial* (and are thus members of the same natural class) we would have no simple way to account for the fact that speakers of English treat the sounds as if they were all the same in some way.

Some of the additional features used in describing natural classes focus on a similarity in sound quality. Up till now we have been saying that sounds are members of a natural class because they are similar in some aspect of their production. It is also the case that sounds may be grouped together by speakers because of a similarity in the way they sound. An example of a natural class based on an auditory feature is the class of *sibilant* consonants in English. Normally a noun is made plural in English by adding the suffix '-s.' This suffix is pronounced in three different ways depending on the last sound in the noun to which it is added. If the noun ends with a voiced sound the phonetic form of the plural suffix is [z]. If the noun ends in a voiceless sound the phonetic form of the plural suffix is [s]. Notice, however, that the form of the suffix indicating plural for words like *riches, bushes, kisses, garages, rouges,* and *mazes* is [əz] rather than [z] or [s]. The group of sounds which end these words are the consonants [č, š, s, ǰ, ž, z]. Note that these sounds differ with respect to voicing, place, and manner of articulation. They do, however, have an auditory property in common: they all have a high pitched hissing sound quality. These sounds form the natural class of *sibilant* consonants in English. It's important to realize that the feature sibilant refers to a real property that is shared by all of the sounds in this natural class. Also, the feature makes it possible to state a generalization.

(1) //+plural// ⟶ [əz] /after a sibilant consonant
(2) //+plural// ⟶ [əz] /after[č, š, s, ǰ, ž, z]

In rule 1 we state that one phenomenon (plurality realized as [əz]) occurs in one situation (after a sibilant consonant). In rule 2, on the other hand, we state that the one phenomenon occurs in six different situations (after [č] , after [š] , etc.). The formulation in 2 makes no mention of any common property of the sounds involved and thus treats them as if they were a random collection of sounds with no relation to each other. Thus natural classes make it possible to state generalizations.

Another feature used to describe natural classes divides consonants into two groups—*obstruents* and *sonorants*. Obstruents are produced with an 'obstruction' of the air flow. The sounds in this category are stops, fricatives, and affricates. Sonorants on the other hand are consonants produced with a relatively open passage for the air flow. Sonorant consonants include nasals, liquids and glides. Thus, the class of labial obstruents in English is [p, f, b, v], while the class of labial consonants includes[p, f, b, v, m, w]. As we will see in the phonology section of *Language Files*, being able to divide consonants into obstruents and sonorants is quite useful in stating phonological rules.

The simplest kind of natural class is one in which all of the members share *one* particular feature. For example the natural class of velar consonants in English are all of those sounds in English that are produced with an obstruction of the vocal tract at the velum (i.e.[k, g, ŋ]). The natural class of high vowels are all of those vowels described using the feature high ([i, ɪ, u, ʊ]). Another way that natural classes can be designated is by indicating more than one feature that all of the members of the class have. So, for instance, the high, tense vowels of English are [i, u], the natural class of voiceless sibilants in English is[č, š, s], and so on. Notice that by adding to the number of features used to define the natural class we reduce the number of members in the class. In general it is true that a natural class defined by few features will be larger than one defined by many features.

CONCLUSION

In this file we have shown that a natural class is a group of all the sounds in a language which share some articulatory or auditory feature (s). We have used the features *consonant/vowel, labial, sibilant, obstruent/sonorant,* as well as the features used to describe individual consonants and vowels to describe natural classes.

EXERCISES

I. List the members of the following natural classes of English sounds.

    1. Alveolar Stop Consonants

    2. Labial Sonorant Consonants

    3. Velar Oral Stop Consonants

    4. Interdental Fricative Consonants

5. High Tense Vowels

6. Low Vowels

7. Bilabial Obstruent Consonants

8. Voiced Sibilant Consonants

II. Describe the following natural classes of English sounds.

1. [p, b]

2. [w, y]

3. [r, l]

4. [i, e, o, u]

5. [f, s, š, h, θ]

6. [n, r, l]

III. Consider the following paragraphs and answer the questions about natural classes.

1. Some American English speakers (largely in the Midwest and North) pronounce [ɛ] and [ɪ] the same in words like *then, Kenny, pen, Bengals, gem, Mencken, Remington,* and *temperature.* What natural class of sounds follows these vowels?

2. At a certain point of a child's language development, she might pronounce certain words as follows: *love* [lʌf], *God* [gat], *rub* [rʌp], *big* [bɪk]. What natural class of sounds is being affected? What is happening to this natural class of sounds?

3. The English indefinite article is 'an' [æn] rather than 'a' [ʌ] before words like *apple, onion, icicle, evening, eagle,* and *honor.* What natural class of sounds begins the words of this list?

4. Some Midwestern American speakers in casual speech drop the unstressed vowel in the first syllable of words like *police, believe, parade, Columbus, pollution, terrific,* and *collision,* but do not drop it in words like *detective, dependent, majestic,* or *pedantic.* What natural class of sounds follows the unstressed vowel in the first syllable in this first group of words?

5. You may have noticed that the discussion of the plural suffix in this file was not exactly correct. The three rules which were given are:

//plural// ⟶ [z] /after a voiced sound
//plural// ⟶ [s] /after a voiceless sound
//plural// ⟶ [əz] /after a sibilant consonant

These rules are in conflict with one another. Notice that *rich* ends in a voiceless sound (and thus fits the description for rule two), and it also ends in a sibilant consonant (as required for rule three). How would you have to revise the first two rules to account for the fact that some of the sibilant consonants referred to in the third rule are voiced and some of them are voiceless?

PHONETICS:
ACOUSTIC PHONETICS OVERVIEW

"One of the main difficulties of studying speech is that sounds are so fleeting and transient. As each word is uttered it ceases to exist. The sounds can, it is true, be recalled, either by repeating the words, or by using recording instruments such as the gramophone. But in both these cases it is another event that is happening. It is a copy of the original sound, not the sound itself."

Peter Ladefoged, *Elements of Acoustic Phonetics*, 1962.

It may be that the reason the study of language has historically tended to focus on written language rather than spoken language is the fact that written messages are fairly permanant, while spoken messages cease to exsist as they are being produced. It seems that the study of spoken language runs the risk of being nothing but a series of debates about what a language user actually said (did he say [a] or [ã]? etc.) With the written language there can be no debate about what someone said, just about what was meant by what was said. Yet, it is the contention of linguists that written language is a *secondary* manifestation of the human language ability, while spoken language is the *primary* form of language. Thus, linguists place themselves in the position of having to study language in spite of the fact that it is nard sometimes to pin down just exactly what a language user said.

In this file we will examine some of the speech sounds that have been discussed in this section of Language Files, but instead of approaching the sounds in terms of their production we will consider the acoustic characteristics of these speech sounds. Through advances in technology it has become possible to conquer the fleeting and transitory nature of speech, at least to some degree. In this file we will discuss a small sampling of the results of applying technology to the study of speech.

SIMPLE SOUND WAVES

Before we look at speech sounds it is important to understand something of the nature of simple sound waves. Sound waves, unlike letters on a page, are not permanent things but rather are disturbances in air set off by a movement of some sort. One kind of movement which can set off a sound wave is vibration such as that produced by violin strings, rubber bands and tuning forks. In this kind of sound wave a vibrating body of some sort sets the air molecules surrounding it into vibration. In order to understand how this happens you must realize that air molecules are like people in a crowded elevator—they try to keep a comfortable distance from each other.

There are two physical phenomena resulting from this tendency for equidistance which make it possible for sound waves to move through the atmosphere. The names of these phenomena are *compression* and *rarefaction*. In compression air molecules are crowded together more than they normally are. In rarefaction air molecules are spread further apart than they normally are. Because there is a tendency for air molecules to remain equidistant from each other, whenever they are placed in compression or rarefaction a certain instability is set up. There is a tendency for compressed molecules to move away from each other. Likewise, when air is rarefied there is a tendency for the molecules to get closer to each other.

When a string of a guitar is vibrating it causes a sound wave in the following way. As the string moves, it compresses the molecules in its way. These molecules move away from the string, but in the process get closer to other molecules, causing compression. The chain reaction involving compression and a return to a rest state is illustrated in Figure 1.

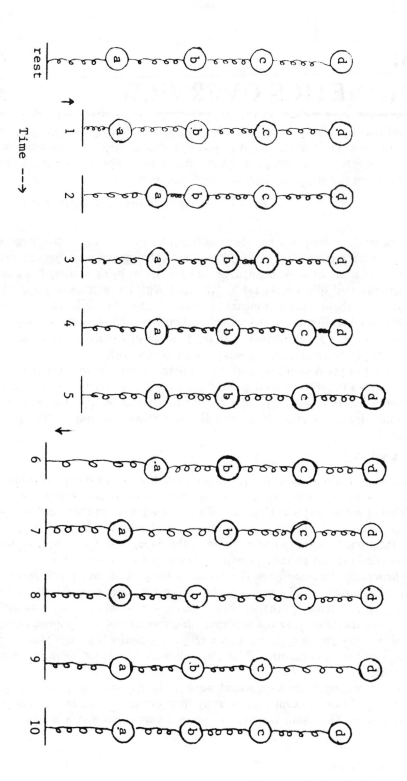

Figure 1. Movement of a string and the consequent movement of air molecules.

At time 1 the string gets closer to molecule (a) than it would be in a rest condition. This movement of the string creates a state of compression between the string and molecule (a) (this state is illustrated as a compressed spring for sake of illustration. Of course there aren't really little springs connecting air molecules.) At time 2 molecule (a) has moved away from the string (thus relieving the pressure between them), but in the process (a) has become closer to (b) than normal. This state of compression is relieved when (b) moves away from (a), but by moving away from (a), (b) becomes closer to (c), creating compression between them, and so on.

Of course a vibrating guitar string does not move in just one direction. Thus, starting at time 6 in the diagram we see illustrated the effect of the return movement of the guitar string. As the string moves away from (a) a state of rarefaction is created between the string and (a). This causes (a) to move toward the string which in turn creates rarefaction between (a) and (b). (b) then moves toward (a) as a result of the rarefaction between them. This movement causes a state of rarefaction between (b) and (c), which causes (c) to move toward (b), which in turn causes rarefaction between (c) and (d), and so on.

Notice from the diagram that molecule (d), although not in direct contact with the vibrating string, vibrates (moves up and down) at the same rate (up for 5 counts and down for 5 counts). Thus, when the string vibrates at a particular frequency air molecules which are some distance from the string will also vibrate at that frequency.

If the cycle which is illustrated in figure 1 is repeated at a rate of about 440 times per second (and we assume that the string moves smoothly from up to down rather than jumping from one extreme to the other as in the diagram) we will hear a musical tone called 'A above middle C.' If we plot the movement of air molecules in such a sound in a way that's similar to the plot in Figure 1 the resulting plot looks like Figure 2.

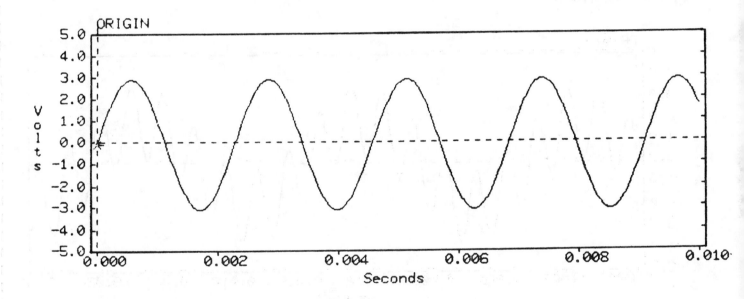

Figure 2.   'A' 440 sine wave.

You can think of Figure 2 as a plot of the movement (vertical axis) of one air molecule across time (horizontal axis). Compare Figure 2 with the movement of (d) in Figure 1. When air molecules vibrate at rates from 20 to 20,000 times per second the vibration is perceived as sound. It is interesting to note, however, that we don't really use this whole range for speech. In fact, the highest frequency that can be transmitted by a telephone is 3,500 cycles per second.

COMPLEX SOUND WAVES

You should realize that our discussion of sound waves up to this point has been very simplified. In fact, simple sound waves such as those discussed in the previous section are not produced by guitar strings, *or* by human vocal cords.

It's really not very difficult to understand why simple sound waves could not be produced by a guitar string. In figure 1 we illustrated the effect of the movement of one point of a guitar string. When we look at the vibration of the whole length of the string it becomes clear that a simple wave cannot result. Figure 3 shows the vibrating string with the amount of movement greatly exaggerated.

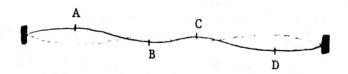

Figure 3. Complex vibration of a string,
from Ladefoged (1962) Fig. 3.2.

From this figure you can see that the string vibrates in one way at A, another way at B, another way at C, and in yet a different way at D. The result of the simultaneous vibration of parts of the string in different ways is a complex wave such as that in Figure 4.

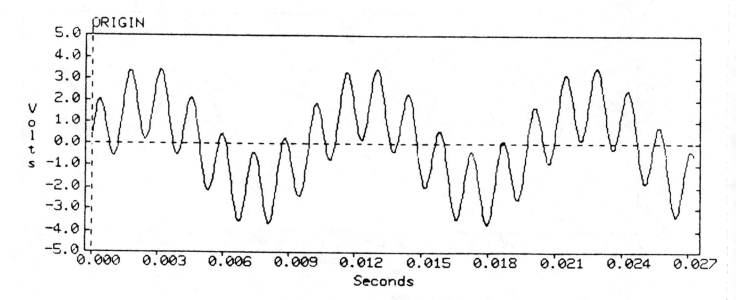

Figure 4. A complex wave.

Complex waves can be viewed as the combination of a number of simple waves in the same way that the complex pattern of vibration illustrated in Figure 5 can be seen as the combination of several simpler patterns of vibration.

Thus, the wave pictured in Figure 4 may be analysed as having the following simple wave components.

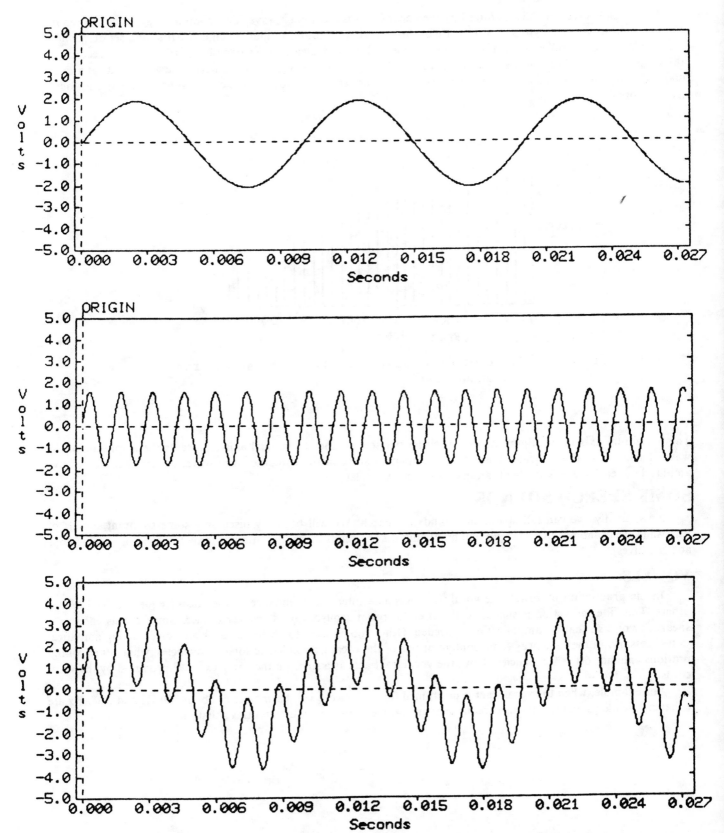

Figure 5. Two simple waves combine to form a complex wave.

The sound wave which is produced by the vocal cords is a complex wave. This complex wave is composed of a *fundamental* wave which vibrates at the rate of the vocal cord vibrations, and which is the first of a set of *harmonic* waves which are multiples of the fundamental. Thus, if the fundamental wave completes 100 cycles per second then the second harmonic wave will vibrate at the rate of 200 cycles per second, the third harmonic will vibrate at a rate of 300 cycles per second and so on. The complex wave generated by the vocal cords can be represented in a histogram as in Figure 6.

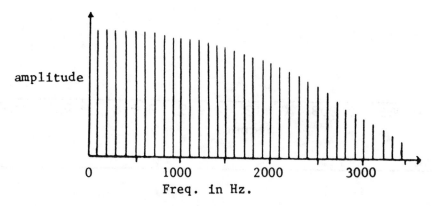

Figure 6.   The complex vocal wave.   Each line stands for one
component wave.

The horizontal axis in this figure stands for cycles per second and the vertical axis represents the amplitude of the wave. Each line in the diagram stands for a component wave in the complex vocal wave. Notice that the relative amplitude of each wave is smaller than that of the one to its left.

SOME SPEECH SOUNDS

Now, finally, we can talk about the sounds of speech. We will begin by discussing some sonorant sounds of English (vowels and nasals). Then we will briefly discuss the acoustic manifestation of some English obstruents (stops and fricatives).

VOWELS

In the production of vowels the vocal tract acts as a filter which enhances some vocal frequencies and damps others. This filtering action is similar to the effect of room acoustics on a speaker's voice. Some rooms enhance a speaker's voice so that no amplification is needed. Other rooms seem to absorb a speaker's voice making amplification necessary. In the same way some configurations of the vocal tract enhance some frequencies, while other configurations enhance other frequencies. Thus, the vocal tract acts as a filter on the complex wave produced by the vocal cords.

For example, when the vocal tract is positioned for the vowel [i], harmonics at about 300 Hz and 2300 Hz are enhanced, while harmonics at other frequencies are damped. Figure 7 illustrates this situation.

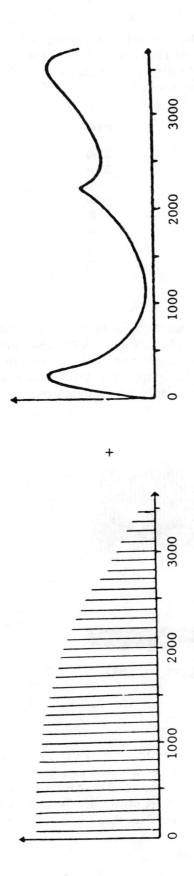

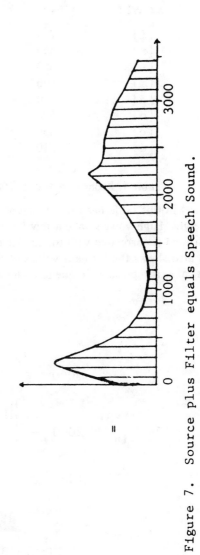

Figure 7. Source plus Filter equals Speech Sound.

In this figure we see the complex wave which is generated by the vocal cords (labeled 'source,' see also Figure 6) and the filtering configuration of the vocal tract adding together and resulting in the sound wave which is heard as [i]. The peaks in the filter function are called *formants* and they differ depending on the quality of the vowel. The following table lists the formant frequencies for eight American English vowels.

VOWEL	F1	F2	F3
[i]	280	2250	2890
[ɪ]	400	1920	2560
[ɛ]	550	1770	2490
[æ]	690	1660	2490
[a]	710	1100	2540
[o]	590	880	2540
[ʊ]	450	1030	2380
[u]	310	870	2250

Table 1. From Ladefoged (1982), p. 176.

Each vowel in this table has three formant values. Notice that the value of the first formant (F1) is correlated with vowel height. High vowels have a low F1 value while low vowels have a high F1 value. Similarly, the value of the second formant is correlated with tongue advancement. Front vowels have higher F2 values than do back vowels.

Figure 8 also shows the formant values of the vowel [i] but in this figure the horizontal axis represents time while the vertical axis represents frequency. This type of representation is called a spectrogram.

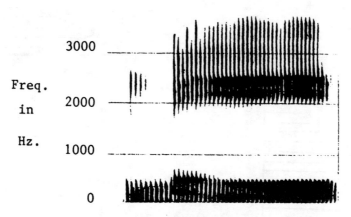

Figure 8. Spectrogram of [mi].

NASALS

In the production of nasal consonants, the oral tract is closed as if producing a stop consonant but the velum is lowered allowing air to escape out of the nose. In acoustic terms then the nasal passage serves as the filter for the vocal source in addition to the oral tract. Consequently, nasal consonants all have nasal formants which reflect the resonating characteristics of the nasal passage. The nasal formants are usually at 250, 2500, and 3250 Hz. Place of articulation information for nasal consonants is encoded in the same way that it is for oral stop consonants, so we will now consider the acoustic manifestation of these stop consonants.

STOPS

Most of the important information for stop consonants in English is encoded either as formant transitions in vowels or as a delay in the onset of voicing of the vowels. For the sake of simplicity we will discuss only word initial stops although much of what will be said also applies to stops in other positions.

The acoustic information that lets us know what *place of articulation* was used in producing a stop is really a part of the vowel which follows the stop. In the production of a stop-vowel sequence such as [da] we don't instantaneously move the tongue from the alveolar ridge (where the stop is produced) to a low back tongue position. Rather, the tongue slides from its position for the stop to the vowel position. So, there are points in time when the tongue is in transition from the consonant articulation to the vowel articulation. Thus, at the first part of the vowel sound the formants are in transition toward their usual values for the vowel. Figure 9 is a spectrographic analysis of the syllable [dan]. Notice the movement of the formants in between the silence of the consonant and their steady state values in the vowel.

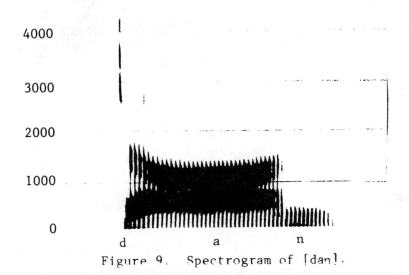

Figure 9. Spectrogram of [dan].

For aveolar consonants the transition of the second formant starts at about 1700-1800 Hz. In bilabial stops the second formant starts at a relatively low frequency and goes up to the appropriate value for the vowel. With front vowels the second formant for velar stops starts higher than it needs to be for vowels and thus moves down to the value of the following vowel. With back vowels the transition from vowel into velar consonant starts at a lower value (about 900 Hz.)

The main acoustic cue for *voicing* in English word initial stop consonants is called VOT. This stands for Voice Onset Time. In producing voiceless stop consonants we delay in starting the voicing of the vowel for about 50 milliseconds. In other words, we release the stop closure and then hold the vocal cords open for five one-hundredths of a second and then allow the vocal cords to start vibrating for the vowel. The measure of this delay in the onset of voicing is called voice onset time. For voiced stops in English the VOT value is very small, and voiced stops in some languages have negative VOT values which means that voicing starts before the stop is released. While the vocal cords are being held apart in the delay of voicing for voiceless sounds air from the lungs rushes out.

FRICATIVES

Fricatives involve a type of sound that we have not explicitly dealt with up to this point. Basically, the difference between the noise used in vowels and the noise used for fricatives is that the sound in vowels is *periodic* (i.e., it involves the repetition of a relatively stable wave form), while the sound in fricatives is *aperiodic* (it involves random movement of air molecules). In Figure 10, notice that during vowels there is a regular repetition of a wave form (vertical stripes) while in the segment labeled [s] no such periodicity exists.

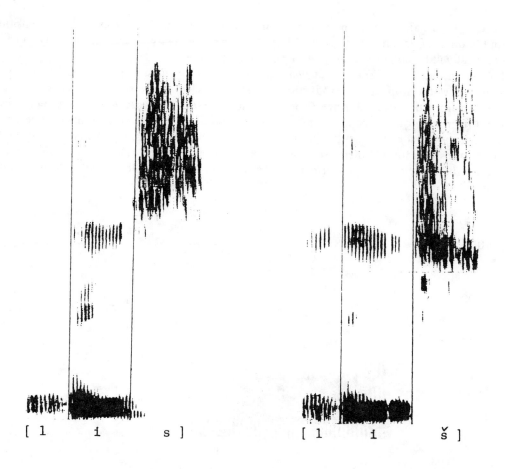

Figure 10. Spectrograms of 'lease' and 'leash'

The main differences between fricatives (in acoustic terms) are relative *frequency*, thus [s] is higher pitched than [š], *amplitude*, so [š] is louder than [f], and *duration* (e.g. in English [s] is longer than [z]). As with stop consonants the transition of the vowel from consonant position to vowel position is used by listeners to determine the place of articulation.

Finally, some sounds combine both periodic and aperiodic sound. These are the voiced fricatives. They involve voicing (which is periodic), combined with frication (which is aperiodic).

CONCLUSION

In this file we have investigated the nature of simple and complex sound waves. We then noticed that vowels and nasals can be described acoustically as the result of combining the complex wave caused by the process of voicing with the filtering action of the oral (or nasal) tract. We then noticed that stop consonants are distinguished from each other by virtue of the transitions from consonant position to vowel position and by their relative voice onset times. Finally, we discussed the aperiodic nature of the fricative consonants and some acoustic dimensions which keep the different fricatives separate from each other.

SOURCES AND FURTHER READING

Ladefoged, Peter. (1962) *Elements of Acoustic Phonetics*. Chicago: Univ. of Chicago Press.

Ladefoged, Peter. (1982) *A Course in Phonetics*. 2nd ed. New York: Harcourt Brace Jovanovich, Inc. Chapter 8.

INTRODUCTION: PHONOLOGY

We saw in the previous section that phonetics is the subfield of linguistics concerned with the description of speech sounds. The subfield known as *phonology* is concerned with how these sounds are systematically organized in a language, how they are combined to form words, how they are categorized by, and interpreted in, the minds of speakers. Put simply, phonology is the study of the sound patterns of language, how speech sounds are grouped by speakers to effect communication. For example, it is a fact of English that the sound sequence [ps] never occurs at the beginning of a word — although it can occur word-medially as in [kæpsul] 'capsule' or word-finally as in [tæps] 'taps'. (Notice that a word like **psychology**, although spelled with initial ps-, is pronounced with [s] word-initially.

While phonetics is concerned with the physical properties of speech sounds, phonology deals with the abstract, or psychological, level of sounds, the level at which speech sounds are stored in our minds. For example, the **t** of **top** is phonetically realized as the aspirated [tʰ], the **t** of **stop** as the unaspirated [t], and (in American English) the **t** of **kitten** as the glottal stop [ʔ]. Phonetically, these are three distinct sounds. However, virtually any native speaker would interpret all three sounds as simply a /t/ — i.e. they are stored in the mind of the speaker as merely a /t/. Such linguistic knowledge is largely unconscious. Speech sounds at this abstract level are called *phonemes* while those at the concrete or phonetic level are known as *allophones,* this distinction being the subject of File 43.

When the speech sound as stored in our minds like the /t/ above, differs from the physical sound as it is spoken, like the [t] of **kitten**, it is because the /t/ has undergone an alteration. We say that the /t/ has been changed to a [ʔ] by the application of a type of rule known as a *phonological process*. There are various types of phonological processes and various reasons for their occurrences; these are examined in File 41.

In studying language it is important to distinguish between phonemes and allophones because this distinction is an important fact about language. Since phonemes exist only in the mind of the speaker — i.e. phonemes are never actually spoken — how does one discover what the phonemes of a language are? To ask the speaker these questions would prove unfruitful since, as stated earlier, this is a largely unconscious knowledge. Instead, the linguist performs what is known as a *phonemic* analysis. File 44 presents a method for doing phonemic analysis while File 45 presents a series of graded phonemic analysis problems offering opportunity for practice.

Finally, not all languages have the same sound systems or permit the same combinations of sounds in words. For example, the sound system of English does not contain the voiceless velar fricative /x/ that is found in German (e.g. in the word Bach /bax/) and, while English does not permit word-initial [ps] sequences, a language such as Greek does; in fact words like **pseudo, psyche,** and **psychiatrist** are borrowed from Greek. File 46 discusses some of the various restrictions on sound combinations in language and touches briefly on sound substitutions as a motivation for foreign accents.

PHONOLOGY: PHONOLOGICAL PROCESSES

The study of phonetics gives ample support for one potentially disastrous conclusion: there is tremendous variability in human speech. In fact, no two pronunciations of a word are ever exactly the same, even when given successively by the same speaker on the same occasion. But if this is so, how are we able to communicate vocally at all? Part of the reason is that each language selects an inventory of sounds which is a subset of the set of physically possible sounds. Further, each language sets limits on what can count as a production of one of these sounds and on what can count as a possible sequence of sounds. Phonetic variation in language is constrained, or systematic. Phonology is the study of the systems of sounds and sound combinations in language.

If we listen carefully to our own pronunciations and the pronunciations of others, we can observe that there is often a difference between the way we actually pronounce sounds and the way we think of them or store them in long-term memory. In some cases, the difference between the sound as we remember it and the sound as we actually pronounce it can be noticed easily. For example, we think of the word 'can' /kæn/ as having a final /n/ sound, and in many of our pronunciations 'can' does indeed end with an [n]. But if we listen carefully, we find that the final sound is often [m] when 'can' comes before a word that begins with a bilabial sound, as in:

'I can play'	[ay kæm ple]
'I can be there'	[ay kæm bi ðer]
'I can make it'	[ay kæm mek ɪt]

Or the final sound may be pronounced [ŋ] if 'can' precedes a word that begins with a velar sound, as in:

| 'I can come' | [ay kæŋ kʌm] |
| 'I can go' | [ay kæŋ go] |

In our mental processing of language, we change final [ŋ]'s like the one in 'can' by applying a kind of rule called a *phonological process*. This process changes the /n/ so that it matches the following sound in point of articulation.

PHONEMIC AND PHONETIC FORMS

In the above example, the sound as stored may sometimes differ from the sound as spoken. We can describe this situation by saying that each word (or each morpheme) has a basic underlying *phonemic form* which we store in our mental dictionary, and that this phonemic form may be changed by phonological processes to become the phonetic form. (We write the phonemic form in //'s and the phonetic form in []'s). This can be expressed with a diagram:

/kæn bi/	The *phonemic form*
↓	
PROCESSES	undergoes phonological processes to become
↓	
[kæm bi]	the *phonetic form*

This is what happens in speaking. In listening, we have to read the diagram from bottom to top: we perceive the phonetic form, and we send it backwards through the phonological processes until we obtain a phonemic form that matches an appropriate form in our mental dictionary.

WHY THERE ARE PHONOLOGICAL PROCESSES

Phonological processes apply to alter the phonemic forms of words in various ways.

A. Some processes make sequences of sounds *easier to pronounce*. When we say [kæm bi] instead of [kæn bi], we make two bilabial sounds in a row (using a single lip gesture) instead of making an alveolar [n] and then a bilabial [b] (with two different gestures). The substitution of [m] for [n] contributes to ease of pronunciation.

B. Processes can also make individual sounds *easier to perceive*. For example, when we pronounce a word with a final [p], [t], or [k] very emphatically, we sometimes release the stop in an exaggerated way, with a small puff of air (called aspiration) following the release: e.g., 'I'm   [nat^h]   going!'

C. Some processes *adjust the timing* of sounds to maintain a steady rhythm in speech. For example, there is some tendency in English to prefer words and phrases in which stressed and unstressed syllables alternate—like 'elevator operator.' To help us achieve this, there is a process in English that allows us to make a syllabic [r] or [l] non-syllabic when it is one of two consecutive unstressed syllables, so

/ǰɛnrl̩/ 'general' becomes   [ǰɛnrl]   , and

/wɪglɪŋ/ 'wiggling' becomes   [wɪglɪŋ]

KINDS OF PHONOLOGICAL PROCESSES

There are several different kinds of phonological processes which fulfill the functions sketched above.

METATHESES are processes which re-order sounds. Example: In some dialects /æskt/ 'asked'———[ækst] and /prəskrɪpšən/ 'prescription'———[pərskrɪpšən].

ASSIMILATIONS are processes which make two adjacent sounds more alike with respect to some feature. Example: in part A of the preceding section, we say that /n/ is assimilated to the bilabial place of articulation of the following /b/ and thus becomes [m]. Another example: In English, a vowel that occurs before a nasal sound becomes nasalized, so   /sʌm/ 'some' → [sʌ̃m]   , and   /bænd/ → [bæ̃nd]

DELETIONS are processes which eliminate a sound. Examples: /h/ is optionally deleted at the beginning of unstressed syllables in English, e.g. /hi hændɛd hr hiz hæt/ may become [hi hændɛd r̩ ɪz hæt]. It may be that deletions are simply total assimilations of all the features of a sound to those of its context, so that the sound just disappears. In the example here, /h/ assimilates to the nonaspiration and voicing of its context, so nothing is left of it.

Both assimilations *and* deletions make sequences of sounds easier to pronounce. Thus, they are usually allowed to apply more freely in unstressed syllables, or in casual speech styles.

DISSIMILATIONS are processes which make two adjacent sounds less alike with respect to some feature. Example: The fricative /θ/ optionally becomes nonfricative (that is, it becomes the stop [t]) after other fricative consonants: /fɪfθ/ 'fifth' ——→ [fɪft], or /sɪksθ/ 'sixth' ——→ [sɪkst].

INSERTIONS are processes which add a sound. Example: Between a nasal and a voiceless fricative, a voiceless stop with the same point of articulation as the nasal is inserted:

/hæmstr̩/   [hæmpstr̩] ——→ 'hamster'

/dæns/   [dænts] ——→ 'dance'

/strɛŋθ/   [strɛŋkθ] ——→ 'strength'

Dissimilations and insertions may actually contribute to ease of articulation, but they also function to preserve information and make sounds easier to perceive. While they may eliminate some phonetic difficulty, they always do so by emphasizing a phonetic property of the individual sound that is being changed. In the examples above, when /θ/ becomes [t], it becomes more different from the adjacent fricative by acquiring a more extreme consonantal constriction, thus emphasizing the tongue-tip activity involved in /θ/-production. The stop-insertion process avoids the difficulty of getting from a nasal articulation to a voiceless-fricative articulation (which requires that the speaker release the stop closure of the nasal and raise his velum at precisely the same moment), but it does so by emphasizing the stop quality of the nasal consonant.

SOME EXAMPLES OF OPTIONAL PHONOLOGICAL PROCESSES

The following are some examples of specific phonological processes that apply in most dialects of American English. We call them optional processes because they may apply or not apply in an individual's speech. Optional processes are responsible for variation in speech: we can pronounce /kæn bi/ as [kæm bi] or as [kæn bi], depending on whether the n-assimilation process is applied or not. Whether an optional process applies or not depends on the speaker's dialect, the style he's using, the rate at which he's speaking, and, to some extent, his personal preference (but remember that the application of processes is for the most part entirely unconscious).

FLAPPING: Alveolar stops /t, d/ become flaps [D] after a stressed vowel and before an unstressed syllable.

E.g.,   'writer' /ráytr/ ⟶ [ráyDr]
        'rider'   /ráydr̩/ ⟶ [ráyDr̩]

> **ALVEOLAR ASSIMILATION:** Alveolar stops /t, d, n/ take on the same point of articulation as a following stop. That is, they become labial before a labial stop, or velar before a velar stop. (This is the same process we started out talking about with [kæn bi] and [kæm bi].)
>
> E.g.,   'could be' /kʊd bi/ ⟶ [kʊb bi]
>   'could go' /kʊd go/ ⟶ [kʊg go]
>
>   'might be' /mayt bi/ ⟶ [mayp bi]
>   'might go' /mayt go/ ⟶ [mayk go]
>
>   'can be'   /kæn bi/ ⟶ [kæm bi]
>   'can go'   /kæn go/ ⟶ [kæŋ go]
>
> **H-DELETION:** /h/ is deleted in unstressed syllables.
> E.g., 'He handed her his hat.' /hi hǽndɛd hr̩ hɪz hǽt/ ⟶ [hi hǽndɛd r̩ ɪz hǽt]

(Note that this is not the same process as the famous h-deletion of the London Cockney dialect, which also deletes [h] in stressed syllables: [i ǽndɛd r̩ ɪz ǽt]).

> **GLOTTAL STOP INSERTION:** /ʔ/ is optionally inserted before a stressed vowel at the beginning of a word.
> E.g., 'It's awful!' /ɪts ɔ́fl/ ⟶ [ɪts ʔɔ́fl]
> (In Cockney dialects, /h/ is inserted in the same place: [ɪts hɔ́fl].)

> **PALATALIZATION:** This is an assimilation process where a sound becomes palatal when it occurs in the vicinity of a palatal sound. Consider the phrase 'did you' /dɪdyu/ which in casual or rapid speech becomes [dɪǰyu]. The [d] assimilates to the point of articulation of the following palatal glide by becoming the palatal affricate [ǰ].
>
>   The palatal glide is not the only sound to condition a palatalization. Certain vowels, generally front and non-low (like [i] and [e]), will do as well because of their approximation to the palatal point of articulation. Consider the word *chide* which in an earlier period of English was [ki:dan]. Later, the [k] became palatalized to [č] because of the influence of the following [i] — thus, [či:dan].

The processes described here may apply whenever their specifications are met. When a /t/ appears in the appropriate environment, we can flap it or not, as we choose. But there are some phonological processes that must apply whenever their specifications are met.

SOME EXAMPLES OF OBLIGATORY PHONOLOGICAL PROCESSES

Obligatory phonological processes are those that always apply in the speech of all speakers of a language (or dialect)—regardless of style, or rate, or individual preference. The differences that obligatory processes make in our speech often seem very subtle or difficult to hear because we are not used to listening for them, but they are an important part of our native accent. Our application of these processes makes us sound like native speakers of English.

Here is an example: The words 'eight' /et/ , 'wide' /wayd/ , and 'ten' /tɛn/ end in the alveolar stops /t, d, n/: [et] , [wayd], [tɛn] . But when these words are given a /θ/ suffix, as in 'eighth,' 'width,' and 'tenth,' the /t, d, n/ are no longer articulated at the alveolar ridge. Instead, the stop closure is made with the tongue against the teeth. The stop is assimilated to the following interdental fricative in all pronunciations of these words. Notice that the dental stops [t̪, d̪, n̪] still sound like or count as /t, d, n/, even though they are physically different from the usual pronunciations [t, d, n].

There are many more examples of obligatory processes. Here are a few others:

> **VOWEL NASALIZATION:** A vowel becomes nasalized before a nasal sound, e.g. /bænd/ 'band' ⟶ [bæ̃nd].

Remember that the difference between the sound as we store it in memory and the sound as we pronounce it may seem subtle. We think of the vowel in 'band' as the same as the vowel in 'bad' and we apparently store these two sounds as the same— /æ/—in long-term memory. But in fact the vowel of 'band' is always nasalized [æ̃], while the vowel of 'bad' is always non-nasalized [æ] .

ASPIRATION: A voiceless stop becomes aspirated when it is the first sound in a stressed syllable.
E.g., 'top' /tap/ ⟶ [tʰap] .

Again, we think of the /t/ in 'top' as the same as the /t/ in 'stop,' but in fact the /t/ in 'top' is followed by a brief period of voicelessness (sometimes this can be felt as a puff of air) following the release of the /t/. The /t/ in 'stop' is never pronounced with aspiration; the /t/ in 'top' always is.

LIQUID DEVOICING: A liquid (/r/ or /l/) becomes voiceless when it occurs after a voiceless obstruent such as /p/ or /s/, e.g. 'slob'/slab/ ⟶ [sl̥ab] or 'price' /prays/ ⟶ [pr̥ays]. This is an assimilation process whereby the liquid is becoming more like the preceding voiceless obstruent by becoming voiceless. (Remember that liquids, like all sonorants, are voiced.)

VOWEL LENGTHENING: A vowel becomes long before a voiced consonant.

E.g., 'robe'   /rob/ ⟶[roːb]
    'bed'   /bɛd/ ⟶[bɛːd]
    'pig'   /pɪg/ ⟶[pɪːg]

Compare the following words, which do not undergo such lengthening:

    'rope'   /rop/ ⟶ [rop]
    'bet'   /bɛt/ ⟶[bɛt]
    'pick'   /pɪk/ ⟶[pɪk]

Here too, we think of the vowels of 'rope' and 'robe' as the same (and also those of 'bet' and 'bed', and 'pick' and 'pig') — even though there is a consistent, measurable, and in fact quite audible difference in their duration.

PHONOLOGY:
PHONOLOGICAL PROCESSES:
PROBLEMS

Identify the process which operates on each word below and indicate whether this process is **optional** or **obligatory**.

1) 'winter' /wɪntr̩/———⟩[wɪnr̩] in certain dialects.
2) 'little' /lɪtl̩/——— ⟩[lɪDl̩]
3) 'fifty' /fɪfti/———⟩[fɪti]
4) 'play' /ple/———⟩[pl̥e]
5) 'store' /stɔr/———⟩[stɔ:] in certain dialects of the East and South.
6) 'wash' /waš/———⟩[warš̩]in some dialects.
7) 'leave' /liv/———⟩[li:v]
8) 'teeth' /tie/———⟩[tʰ iθ]
9) 'tedious' /tidiəs/———⟩[tɪǰəs]
10) 'stamp' /stæmp/———⟩[stæ̃mp]

The problems below involve the operation of a phonological process. Identify the process and determine the environment (sounds) that conditions the change. (HINT: It is helpful to make a list of the sounds that precede and follow the sound in question and then look for natural classes or make generalizations.)

1) In the speech of some New Yorkers, the following process operates. Study the data below. Then identify the process and state the environment in which it occurs.

'marry' /mæri/———⟩[mæri]
'there' /ðɛr/———⟩[ðɛ:]
'story' /stɔri/———⟩[stɔri]
'cared' /kɛrd/———⟩[kɛd]

'answer' /ænsər/———⟩[ænsə:]
'court' /kɔrt/———⟩[kɔt]
'stores' /stɔrz/———⟩[stɔ:z]
'large' /larj/———⟩[la:ǰ]

2) What process is illustrated below? What is the conditioning environment?

'O.S.U.' /oɛsyu/———⟩[oɛšyu]
'postulate' /pastyulet/———⟩[pasčyulet]
'negotiate' /nəgosiet/———⟩[nəgošiet]
'emaciated' /imesieDəd/———⟩[imešieDəd]

PHONOLOGY: THE VALUE OF SOUNDS: PHONEMES

DISTINCTIVE AND NONDISTINCTIVE SOUNDS

A list of all sounds in a language does not give us information about a very important aspect of the sound structure of a language: the values that these sounds have to its native speakers. In every language, certain sounds are considered to be the 'same' sound, even though they may be phonetically distinct. For example, native speakers of English consider the *l* in *lay* to be the same sound as that in *play*, even though the former is voiced and the latter voiceless. And if you ask a native speaker of English how many different sounds are represented by the italicized letters in the words *p*in, *b*in, and *sp*in, he will probably say "two," grouping the aspirated [pʰ] of 'pin' and unaspirated [p] of 'spin' together. Though [pʰ] and [p] are phonetically different sounds, native English speakers overlook this difference.

A native speaker of Hindi could not overlook this difference. To a speaker of Hindi, [pʰ] is as different from [p] as [pʰ] is from [b] to our ears. The difference between aspirated and unaspirated stops must be kept in mind by Hindi speakers because their language contains many words that are phonetically identical, except that one word will have an aspirated stop where the other has an unaspirated stop:

[kʰʌl]	'wicked person'
[kʌl]	'yesterday'
[kapi]	'copy'
[kapʰi]	'ample'
[pʰʌl]	'fruit'
[pʌl]	'moment'
[bʌl]	'strength'

A native speaker of English can ignore the difference between aspirated and unaspirated stops because aspiration will never make a difference in the meanings of words. If we hear someone say [tæp] and [tæpʰ] we may recognize them as different pronunciations of the same word *tap*, not as different words. Because of the different ways in which [p], [pʰ] and [b] lead to meaning distinctions in English and Hindi, these sounds have different values in the phonological systems of the two languages.

In general, speakers will attend to phonetic differences between two sounds only when the sounds have the ability to change the meaning of a word. Such sounds are said to be *distinctive*. One way to determine whether two sounds in a language are distinctive, is to identify a *minimal pair*—a pair of words that differ by a single sound in the same position, have different meanings, but are otherwise identical. For example, [tʰæp] and [tʰɪp] constitute a minimal pair in English, in which [æ] and [ɪ] contrast. Thus [æ] and [ɪ] are distinctive sounds in English. [pʰul] and [bul] constitute a minimal pair in Hindi, contrasting [pʰ] and [b]; [pʰul] and [pul] are also a minimal pair in Hindi. But notice that there are no English minimal pairs involving [pʰ] and [p]. These two sounds are never distinctive in English.

Consider another example in which two languages make different distinctions using the same set of sounds. In English it is possible to find minimal pairs in which [l] and [r] are contrasted: *leaf* [lif], *reef* [rif]; *lack* [læk], *rack* [ræk]. However, [l] and [r] are never distinctive in Korean:

[param]	'wind'
[irɨm]	'name'
[pal]	'foot'
[mal]	'horse'

As these examples demonstrate, minimal pairs can never be found for [r] and [l] in Korean because they do not appear in the same positions in words: [r] appears only between two vowels, while [l] does not appear in this position. And this observation about the distribution of [r] and [l] is not merely a property of these isolated examples, but is true of *all* Korean words containing these sounds. Observations of this sort play an important role in determining which sounds are considered to be 'the same' by a native speaker.

PHONEMES AND ALLOPHONES

So far, we have shown that some phonological information cannot be extracted from a list of the sounds in a language. Yet it is important for a native speaker to distinguish between distinctive and nondistinctive sounds because they don't have equivalent values in a phonological system. Linguists attempt to characterize this 'extra' information by grouping the sounds in the phonetic inventory into classes. Each class contains all of the sounds which a native speaker considers to be 'the same' sound. For example, [p] and [pʰ] in English would be members of the same class. But [p] and [b] are members of different classes because they are distinctive. A class of sounds which are identified by a native speaker as the same sound is called a *phoneme*. The members of these classes, or the actual phonetic segments produced by a native speaker, are called *allophones*. In the above example, [p] and [pʰ] are allophones of the phoneme *p*.

By giving a description like this, linguists attempt to show that the phonological system of a language has two levels. The more concrete level involves the physical reality of phonetic segments. But phonemes are something more abstract. Note that when sounds are grouped into classes to identify phonemes, it is necessary to appeal to psychological notions like meaning. This is no accident, because phonemes *are* psychological units of linguistic structure.

To emphasize this point, linguists sometimes describe phonemes as the form in which we 'think of' sounds and store them in our memory. It makes sense to remember words in terms of phonemes rather than phonetic segments because it is much more efficient to store a single form of a word rather than multiple forms. And a single representation contains exactly what we have learned when we memorize a word. For example, when we attempt to memorize a word like *path*, we notice that it begins with a *p*, not an *s* or a *j*. But we need not learn as a particular fact about this word that the *p* must be aspirated; this is done 'automatically' whenever the word is pronounced.

The first sound in a word like *path* is pronounced when the brain sends signals to the articulatory organs to produce a phonetic realization of the phoneme *p*—or, in everyday terms, to make the *p*-sound. [pʰ], an allophone of the phoneme *p*, is the product of these instructions. Since phonemes are psychological concepts, they are not directly observable in a stream of speech. Only allophones of phonemes are.

The phoneme is a unit of linguistic structure which is just as significant to the native speaker as the word or the sentence. Native speakers reveal their knowledge of phonemes in a number of ways. When an English speaker makes a slip of the tongue and says [či ken] for *key chain*, thereby reversing [č] and [k], he has demonstrated that [č] functions mentally as a single unit, as does [k]. Recall from phonetics that this is not the only way to conceptualize [č]: it is phonetically complex, consisting of [t] followed immediately by [š]. Yet since [č] represents the pronunciation of a single phoneme in English, no native speaker would make an error which would involve splitting up its phonetic components; you will never hear [ti kšen] as a slip of the tongue.

Knowledge of phonemes is also revealed in spelling systems. For example, English does not have separate letters for [pʰ] and [p]; they are both spelled with the letter *p*. The same point can be made about alveolar and velar *l*, oral and nasal vowels, and long and short consonants. Examples like these show that the English spelling system ignores the differences in pronunciation that don't result in meaning distinctions. For the most part, the English spelling system attempts to provide symbols for phonemes, not phonetic segments. In general, alphabetic writing systems tend to be phonemic rather than phonetic, though they achieve this goal with varying degrees of success.

PHONEMES AND PHONOLOGICAL PROCESSES

Why should a single phoneme have more than one pronunciation? If the phoneme is *p*, why not say [p], rather than [pʰ]? Or if the phoneme is [æ], why not say [æ] rather than [æ̃], as we do in words like [kæ̃n] *can*?

Phonological processes are responsible for the fact that we pronounce sounds differently from the way we store them in our memory. Phonological processes make the substitutions that 'distort' our stored representations of sounds. They do this either (a) to make sequences of sounds easier to pronounce—as when vowels become nasalized before nasalized consonants or (b) to make sounds easier to perceive—as when voiceless stops are aspirated at the beginning of a stressed syllable.

Recall that phonological processes change single phonetic features. For example, voicing assimilation changes voicing, leaving all of the features for manner and place of articulation intact. Likewise, vowel nasalization changes only nasality, and does not affect vowel height, backness and rounding. Because phonological processes change single phonetic features, phonemes and their phonetic realizations are assumed to be basically similar. This means that no language would have a phoneme *p* pronounced as [a] and [s]. There is simply no phonological process that would ever 'convert' *p* into sounds as different as these. For the same reason, the variant pronunciations of a phoneme share most phonetic properties.

Distribution of Speech Sounds

To find out which sounds make a difference in meaning or which are thought of by a native speaker as the same sound, it is important to look at where these sounds occur and how they function in a language; that is, to discover what the phonemes of a language are, we want to know their distribution.

There are two types of distribution — **overlapping** and **complementary**. Overlapping environments are identical environments. In the words 'time' /taym/ and 'dime' /daym/, consider the sounds [t] and [d]. [t] occurs word-initially and before [ay]; [d] occurs word-initially and before [ay], as well. In other words, [t] and [d] occur in the same environment; their environments overlap. Because of this overlap, one cannot predict that [t] will occur in the same position X but [d] in position Y. (This is the fundamental difference between overlapping and complementary distribution. Complementary distribution is entirely predictable.)

Sounds that occur in overlapping environments can either be **contrastive** (make a difference in meaning) or occur in **free variation** (interchangeable with *no* difference in meaning). Let's consider 'time' /taym/ again. If a [d] is substituted for the [t], the result is *dime* [daym], clearly a new word with a distinct meaning. Therefore, because these sounds serve to contrast words, to create a difference in meaning, they are said to be **contrastive**. Clearly considered by a native speaker as distinct sounds, they are seperate phonemes, as well.

One way to determine if two (or more) sounds are separate phonemes is to identify minimal pairs (or sets). These are words that are phonetically the same except for one corresponding segment and they have different meanings — as in the following:

'time'	[taym]
'dime'	[daym]
'rhyme'	[raym]
'lime'	[laym]

In this set we can determine that /t/, /d/, /r/ and /s/ are separate phonemes and in contrastive distribution because they cause a meaning contrast.

Now consider the phrase **not ready**. In careful or emphatic speech, a native speaker might articulate **not** in this phrase with a word-final [t] — as in [natrɛdi]. But in casual or rapid speech, the glottal stop is more common — thus, [naʔrɛdi]. Notice that both the [t] and [ʔ] occur after [a] and before [r]. Their environments are identical; their environments overlap. However, notice also that while there are two pronunciations of this utterance there is no difference in meaning. In fact, the native speaker perceives [ʔ] and [t] as the *same sound*. Therefore, the distinction between these two sounds (relative to this utterance) is *not* contrastive. Rather, they are said to be allophones of the same phoneme /t/, occuring in **free variation**; that is, they occur in the same phonetic environment (in this case, between [a] and [r]) but there is no difference in meaning. They are interchangeable. With this type of distribution (free variation), as with contrastive distribution, it cannot be predicted which one will occur in any given utterance.

Sounds may also occur in **complementary distribution** — i.e., one allophone can be found in a position where the other(s) cannot occur and vice versa. Sounds in complementary distribution, as in free variation, are *not* contrastive; they do not create a difference in meaning. Rather, as in free variation, they are allophones of the same phoneme. However, complementary distribution differs from free variation in that 1) the allophones do *not* occur in the same phonetic environment and 2) we *can* predict which one will occur at any given utterance of a relevant word. In other words, the distribution of one allophone is the complement of the distribution of the other(s).

Consider the words *pit* [pʰɪt] and *spit* [spɪt]. In *pit* the [p] is aspirated while in *spit* it is unaspirated. (This difference may seem extremely minute in English but in other languages like Hindi the presence or absence of aspiration alone makes a meaning difference.) [pʰ] will never occur in the position following the [s] of *spit;* likewise, [p] will never occur word-initially in a word like *pit*. These allophones, then, are said to be in complementary distribution and are, therefore, allophones of the same phoneme /p/.

PHONOLOGY: HOW TO SOLVE PHONOLOGY PROBLEMS

Because phonemes are important units of linguistic structure, linguists must have a general method for identifying them in all languages. But the task of distinguishing separate phonemes from allophones of the same phoneme is not always straightforward. For one thing, the set of phonemes differs from language to language, thus requiring a different analysis for each language. Moreover, phonemes are psychological units of linguistic structure and are not physically present in a stream of speech. As a result, it is not possible to identify the phonemes of a language simply by taking physical measurements on a sample of language. And it is not always easy to identify phonemes by investigating a native speaker's intuitions, since the minute phonetic details on which decisions about phonemes are made are often precisely those which he is not accustomed to noticing.

To get around these problems, linguists have developed an objective procedure by which the phonemes of a language can be discovered through examination of a set of words written in narrow phonetic transcription. This procedure involves making observations about patterns of sounds.

1. *Phonemes make distinctions in meaning.* If two sounds are members of separate phonemes, minimal pairs can be found. For example, the minimal pair *led* and *red* is evidence that *l* and *r* are members of separate phonemes in English. But if two sounds are allophones of the same phoneme, minimal pairs should not exist.

2. *The allophones of a phoneme are not a random collection of sounds, but are a set of sounds which have the same psychological function.* Accordingly, allophones of the same phoneme should be systematically related to one another:

    a. They share many phonetic properties.

    b. It is possible to predict which allophone will appear in a word on the basis of general phonetic principles.
It is important to emphasize here what the procedure for identifying the phonemes of a language attempts to accomplish. By analyzing the patterns of sounds which are *physically* present, it is possible to draw conclusions about the *psychological* organization of a language, which is not directly observable.

HOW TO DO A PHONEMIC ANALYSIS

Though a phonemic analysis can be performed successfully on any language, it is easiest to begin with a problem based on English, since we already know in effect what the solution is. Look over the data given below in narrow phonetic transcription:

pʰɾ̥e	kʰɾ̥æb	rigen
gre	pʰɪr	rif
	bræwn	
	fɾ̥æt	

Limiting our attention to the sounds [r] and [ɾ], we attempt to answer the following question: are these sounds members of separate phonemes, or allophones of the same phoneme? (Of course, native speakers of English intuitively know that they are allophones of the same phoneme. The procedure for doing a phonemic analysis should produce the same answer, *without* appealing to the intuitions of native speakers.)

Step 1. Following the flow chart on the following page, the best way to start a phonemic analysis is to look for minimal pairs. If minimal pairs are present in the data we know immediately that the difference between [r] and [ɾ] distinguishes between words, that they are different phonemes. However, examination of the above list reveals that there are no minimal pairs involving [r] and [ɾ]. (Note, however, that a minimal pair does exist for [p] and [g] — [pʰre] and [gre], thus we can conclude that [pʰ] and [g] *do* belong to separate phonemes.)

Since there are no minimal pairs for [ɾ] and [r], it is reasonable to assume that they can be allophones of the same phoneme. However, this assumption must be *proven* by showing that the distribution of [ɾ] and [r] is predictable by general phonetic principles. If so, they should be in complementary distribution, and should be related to one another by a phonological process. In contrast, the disribution of separate phonemes is always random.

PHONEMIC ANALYSIS FLOW CHART

1. Look for minimal pairs

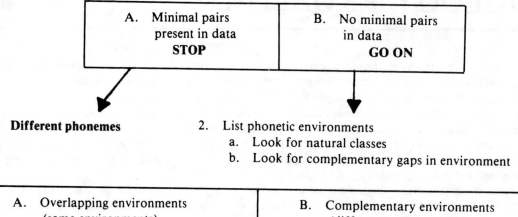

| A. Minimal pairs present in data **STOP** | B. No minimal pairs in data **GO ON** |

Different phonemes

2. List phonetic environments
   a. Look for natural classes
   b. Look for complementary gaps in environment

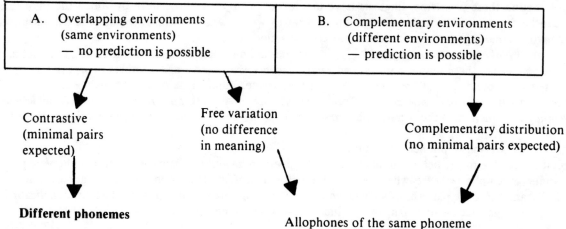

| A. Overlapping environments (same environments) — no prediction is possible | B. Complementary environments (different environments) — prediction is possible |

Contrastive (minimal pairs expected)

Free variation (no difference in meaning)

Complementary distribution (no minimal pairs expected)

Different phonemes

Allophones of the same phoneme

At step 1, remember that minimal pairs are pairs of words which are phonetically the same with the exception of one segment in a corresponding position and which have different meanings. For example, the word *'pin'* /pɪn/ and *'bin'* /bɪn/ constitute a minimal pair in English which shows that /p/ and /b/ are separate phonemes in English.

At step 2, when you are trying to determine if two sounds are separate phonemes or allophones of the same phoneme, make a list of the sounds that occur before and after the sounds in question. Then look for similarities among the list of sounds to see if there is a natural class which conditions the occurrence of either of the sounds.

Step 2. To show that the distribution of [ɹ] and [r] is predictable, we proceed to step 2 and make a list of the phonetic environments in which each sound occurs.

a. [r̥] appears after [pʰ]—as in [pʰr̥ə]
after [kʰ]—as in [kʰr̥æb]
after [f]—as in [fr̥æt]

b. [r] appears after [g]—as in [gre]
after [b]—as in [bræwn]
at the beginnings of words—as in [rɪf]
at the ends of words—as in [pʰɪr]

This is the set of observations upon which the entire phonemic analysis is based.

3. Once you have collected the list of phonetic environments for each sound, it is necessary to make two types of generalizations:

a. *Look at the environments to find natural classes.* [r̥] is preceded by [pʰ], [kʰ] and [f], all of which are voiceless consonants. This generalization permits us to simplify the description of the environment for [r̥]: instead of listing each sound separately, it is now possible to say simply:

[r̥] appears after voiceless consonants

Now look at the environment in which [r] appears. Are there any natural classes? Yes and no. Certainly [b] and [g] are voiced consonants, but the set which includes [b], [g], the beginnings of words and the ends of words does not form a natural class. Thus the critical observation to make here is that there is no *single* natural class in which [r] can be found.

b. *Look for complementary gaps in the environments.* So far, we have shown that [r̥] appears after voiceless consonants, while [r] appears in an apparently random set of environments. Yet it is possible to make one more critical observation. [r] does not appear in the environments in which [r̥] appears—after voiceless consonants. Moreover, [r̥] does not appear where [r] does; there is no [r̥] after voiced consonants and at the beginnings and ends of words. Since the environments for [r̥] and [r] have systematic and complementary gaps, we say that [r̥] and [r] are in *complementary distribution*.

*If there are no complementary gaps, if sounds occur in overlapping or identical environments, then they are different phonemes.

On the basis of observations made in Step 2, it is possible to identify the phonetic motivation which results in the alternation between [ɹ] and [r]. Since [ɹ] always follows voiceless consonants, this looks like a case of voicing assimilation. Likewise, [r] is always voiced when it follows voiced consonants.

In Steps 1 and 2 we described the distribution of [ɹ] and [r]. We now have good reason to believe that they are allophones of the same phoneme because there are no minimal pairs and it is possible to predict their appearance on the basis of a phonological process. The remaining task is to identify the phoneme of which [ɹ] and [r] are allophones. In doing this, we are finally making the leap from observable phonetic reality to unobservable psychological reality.

The procedure for identifying the phoneme involves finding the *basic* and the *restricted* allophone. This is also done on the basis of observations about the environments in which [ɹ] and [r] appear. Recall that the environment for [ɹ] constitutes a single natural class (voiceless consonants), and a single phonological process (voicing assimilation). These facts are enough to justify the claim that the voiceless environment distorts the pronunciation of the 'r' and *causes* it to be voiceless. Because [ɹ] can be described as a product of its phonetic environment and appears *only* in this environment, it is said to be *restricted*.

Consider now the environment for [r]. It is *not* a single natural class. Voiced consonants and the beginnings and ends of words are all distinct phonetic environments which might be expected to affect a sound in different ways. Yet [r] is phonetically identical in all of these contexts. This indicates that the environments in which [r] appears *do not* distort its pronunciation. A sound which appears unchanged in more than one distinct phonetic environment is called the *basic allophone*. It is assumed to be the closest approximation of the mental 'sound' which we somewhat sloppily call 'r' in everyday speech. As a result, the name of the basic allophone is adopted as the name of the phoneme.

Phonemes are written between slanted lines, as a reminder that they represent a level of linguistic structure which is distinct from that of the phonetic segment. Thus the solution to the problem we have been concerned with can be summarized as:

/ r / ⟶ [ρ̥] after voiceless consonants

⟶ [r] after voiced consonants
at the beginnings of words
at the ends of words

This diagram says that the phoneme / r / is pronounced [ρ̥] before voiceless consonants and as [r] in the other environments listed.

SOME POTENTIAL TROUBLE SPOTS

The procedure outlined in the previous section will work for any language for which reliable phonetic transcriptions exist. However, beginners are often confused by a few very legitimate questions.

1. If you discover that no minimal pairs exist for two sounds, isn't it possible to conclude automatically that they are allophones of the same phoneme? No. It is still necessary to show that the sounds are in complementary distribution, since allophones are *predictable* variant pronunciations of the same phoneme.

Consider what happens if you make a decision too soon. Using the data presented at the beginning of the previous section, suppose you wanted to know if [g] and [f] are allophones of the same phoneme. Since there are no minimal pairs, it might seem reasonable to conclude that they are. But a careful examination of the data reveals that this is the wrong conclusion. Listing the data and the relevant environments, you get:

for [g]:

  data [gr e] [r i gen]
  generalization: [g] appears between vowels and at the beginnings of words

for [f]:

  data [r i f] [f̥ æt]
  generalization: [f] appears at the beginnings and ends of words.

There are no generalizations to make about where [g] and [f] occur. Since there is no single natural class in the environments for either [g] or [f], no phonological process can be responsible for their distribution. And they are not in complementary distribution because both can appear at the beginnings of words.

In general when *no generalization* can be made about where a group of sounds can occur, it is possible to conclude that they are members of separate phonemes. A conclusion based on such a demonstration is just as valid as showing that minimal pairs exist. This alternative way of showing that sounds are members of separate phonemes is useful because it is not always possible to find minimal pairs for all distinctive sounds. For example, there are no minimal pairs involving [ž] and [h] in English. But they belong to separate phonemes because they share few phonetic properties, and no phonological process determines where they can occur.

The range of tests for identifying phonemes can be broadened somewhat by the existence of *near-minimal pairs*—which are like minimal pairs, except that they differ by an additional sound whose presence has no influence on the critical sounds. For example, *hurt* [hᵊrt] and *bird* [bᵊrd] are near-minimal pairs involving [h] and [b]. We are justified in saying that [h] and [b] are members of separate phonemes because no conceivable phonological process would permit only [h] at the beginnings of words ending in [t], and only [b] at the beginnings of words ending in [d].

To summarize, separate phonemes and allophones of the same phoneme can be distinguished by the following properties:

Separate phonemes:
1. They may be phonetically dissimilar.
2. Their distribution cannot be predicted on the basis of general phonetic principles.
3. Minimal pairs can usually be found.

Allophones of the same phoneme:
1. They are phonetically similar.
2. Their distribution can be predicted by phonetic principles.
3. Minimal pairs can *never* be found.

2. When describing the environment in which a sound appears, how do you know where to look? In the problem we solved in the previous section, we considered only the sounds which *preceded* [ρ̥] and [r]. This is certainly not the only possibility. In fact, identifying environments is the trickiest part of doing a phonemic analysis.

Since there are many logically possible environments to consider, the task is made easier by eliminating all of those except the most plausible. This can be accomplished by using strategies like the following:

a. *Formulate hypotheses about the allophones.* Investigation of the world's languages has revealed that some sounds are more common than others. For example:

(a) Voiced nasals and liquids are more common than voiceless ones.

(b) Oral vowels are more common than nasal vowels.

(c) Consonants of normal duration are more common than long consonants.

(d) 'Plain' consonants are more common than those with secondary articulations like velarization, palatalization and labialization.

On the basis of these generalizations, it is possible to speculate that if an uncommon sound appears in a language, it is probably a restricted allophone. But these tendencies should be used only as a guide for forming hypotheses, not as a basis for jumping to conclusions, since some languages exhibit exceptions. For example, nasal and oral vowels are separate phonemes in French.

b. *Keep in mind that allophonic variation results from the application of phonological processes.* Once you have a hunch about the restricted allophone, check the environment in which it appears for evidence of a phonological process. This may involve looking in more than one place until you have discovered a reasonable candidate. In the problem in the previous section, we were guided by the knowledge that voicing differences in consonants are often caused by voicing assimilation, and that voicing assimilation frequently occurs in consonant clusters. Since /r/ is the second member of all of the clusters given, we concluded that the consonant preceding it constituted the relevant environment.

PHONOLOGY: PHONEMIC ANALYSIS PROBLEMS

This file is designed to give you practice in doing phonemic analysis at the beginning, intermediate, and more advanced levels. The instructions to each problem are somewhat different in each case, so read them carefully before proceeding. However, each problem requires that you follow the step-by-step procedure for doing a phonemic analysis outlined in the previous file. The problems are designed to introduce you to problems involving minimal pairs, complementary distribution, and free variation. (A linguist making a phonemic analysis of an unknown language would of course examine *hundreds* of words in order to be sure to have enough data to find the relevant minimal pairs, complementary distributions, etc. But to save you time, the data in the problems below has been very carefully selected to give you *all* the relevant information you will need to answer the questions asked in a very small set of words. The same applies to all the phonology problems you will be asked to solve in this course.)

I. Beginning Problems

I.1 English

In the following dialect of English there is a predictable variant [ʌy] of the diphthong [ay]. (a) What phonetic segments condition this change? (b) What feature(s) characterize the class of conditioning segments?

[bʌyt]	bite	[fʌyt]	fight	[taym]	time
[tay]	tie	[bay]	buy	[tʌyp]	type
[rayd]	ride	[rʌys]	rice	[naynθ]	ninth
[rayz]	rise	[fayl]	file	[fayr]	fire
[rʌyt]	write	[lʌyf]	life	[bʌyk]	bike

I.2 Burmese

The following Burmese data, transcribed phonetically, contain both voiced and voiceless nasals. The latter are indicated by a small circle placed under the symbol. Voiced and voiceless nasals are in complementary distribution and, therefore, are allophones of the same phoneme. State the contexts in which voiced and voiceless nasals occur.

1.	[mi]	'five'		8.	[m̥i]	'to lean against'
2.	[mwey]	'to give birth'		9.	[m̥wey]	'fragrant'
3.	[myiʔ]	'river'		10.	[m̥yayʔ]	'to cure'
4.	[ne]	'small'		11.	[n̥ey]	'slow'
5.	[nwe]	'to bend flexibly'		12.	[n̥wey]	'to heat'
6.	[ŋa]	'five'		13.	[ŋ̥a]	'to lend property'
7.	[ŋouʔ]	'stump (of tree)'		14.	[ŋ̥eʔ]	'bird'

1.3   Tamil

In the following words determine the distribution of [p] and [b]. Are they in complementary distribution? Are they allophones of the same phoneme or different phonemes? State the distribution.

Now look at [k] and [g]. Do they follow the same pattern that [p] and [b] do? How about [ʈ] and [ɖ] (retroflex alveolar stops) and [t̪] and [d̪] (dental alveolar stops)? Try stating a general rule that will describe the distribution of all of these consonants.

[pal]	'tooth'	[id̪ɨ]	'this'
[abayam]	'refuge'	[ad̪ɨ]	'that'
[kappal]	'ship'	[kaʈʈi]	'knife'
[saabam]	'curse'	[kuɖi]	'jump'
[kaakkaay]	'crow'	[paʈʈɨ]	'ten'
[mugil]	'cloud'	[paaɖam]	'foot'
[ʈuukkɨ]	'carry, lift'	[idam]	'place'
[ʈugil]	'veil'	[káatpaadi]	'name of a town'
[t̪attɨ]	'plate'	[pattɨ]	'silk'
[pad̪ɨ]	'lie down'		

I.4   Russian

Determine in the following Russian data whether [a] and [a>] (> indicates that the vowel is backed) are allophones of the same phoneme or if they are in contrast as separate phonemes. If they are separate phonemes, provide evidence for your claim. If they are in complementary distribution, pick one sound as the basic sound and give the conditioning phonetic contexts for its allophones. Remember that [ɫ] is a velarized [l].

1. [atəm]   'atom'

2. [dva]   'two'

3. [dar]   'gift'

4. [mas̡]   'ointment'

5. [m̡atə]   'mint'

6. [pa>ɫ]   'he fell'

7. [da>ɫ]   'he gave'

8. [pa>ɫkə]   'stick'

9. [ukra>tə]   'she stole'

10. [bra>ɫ]   'he took'

[s̡] is a palatalized voiceless dental fricative;
[m̡] is a palatalized voiced bilabial nasal.

I.5   Sindhi

Determine the phonemic status of [p], [pʰ] and [b]. That is, are the three sounds different phonemes or allophones of the same phoneme? Is the relationship between the sounds the same as in English? Why or why not?

1 [pʌnu]   'leaf'

2 [vʌǰu]   'opportunity'

3. [s̆ʌki]   'suspicious'

4. [gʌdo]   'dull'

5. [dʌru]   'door'

6. [pʰʌnu]   'snake hood'

7 [tʌru]   'bottom'

8. [kʰʌto]   'sour'

9. [bʌǰu]   'run'

10. [bʌnu]   'forest'

11. [bʌc̆u]   'be safe'

12. [ǰʌǰu]   'judge'

I.6 Finnish

Examine the pairs of sounds [s], [z] and [d], [t]. Are [s] and [z] different phonemes, are they in complementary distribution, or are they in free variation? Determine the same information for [d] and [t]. Give evidence for your conclusions. Also, there is one *near minimal* pair—which pair is it?

1. [ku:zi]   'six'
2. [kadot]   'failures'
3. [kate]   'cover'
4. [katot]   'roofs'
5. [kade]   'envious'
6. [ku:si]   'six'

7. [li:sa]   'Lisa'
8. [madon]   'of a worm'
9. [maton]   'of a rug'
10. [ratas]   'wheel'
11. [li:za]   'Lisa'
12. [radan]   'of a track'

I.7 Tojolabal

Determine whether plain [k] and glottalized [k'] are allophones of a single phoneme, in free variation, or in contrast as separate phonemes. Support your answer with specific examples. (Hint: Don't forget that near minimal pairs can be as convincing as minimal pairs.)

1. [kisim]   'my beard'
2. [cak'a]   'chop it down'
3. [koktit]'   'our feet'
4. [k'ak]   'flea'
5. [p'akan]   'hanging'
6. [k'a?əm]   'sugar cane'

7. [sak]   'white'
8. [k'iši n]   'warm'
9. [skuču]   'he is carrying it'
10. [k'uut es] 'to dress'
11. [snika]   'he stirred it'
12. [?ak']   'read'

I.8 Totonac

Examine the pairs of vowels [i , i̥], [a , ḁ], and [u, u̥]. Are voiced and voiceless vowels in Totonac in contrast, in free variation, or in complementary distribution? If the sounds are in complementary distribution, pick one sound as the basic sound and give the phonetic contexts for its allophones (note that [¢] is an alveolar affricate).

1. [¢apsḁ]   'he stacks'
2. [¢ilinksḁ]   'it resounded'
3. [kasitti̥]   'cut it'
4. [kuku̥]   'uncle'
5. [ɬkakḁ]   'peppery'
6. [miki̥]   'snow'

7. [snapapḁ]   'white'
8. [stapu̥]   'beans'
9. [šumpi̥]   'porcupine'
10. [ɬa:qhu̥]   'you plunged'
11. [tihasɬi̥]   'he rested'
12. [tukšɬi̥]   'it broke'

II. Intermediate
II.1   German
Examine the voiceless velar fricative [x] and the voiceless palatal fricative [ç] in the German data below. Are the two sounds in complementary distribution or are they in contrast? If the sounds are allophones of the same phoneme, pick one sound as basic and determine the phonetic contexts of its allophones.

1.	[axt]	'eight'		6.	[ɪç]	'I'
2.	[bux]	'book'		7.	[εçt]	'real'
3.	[lɔx]	'hole'		8.	[laxən]	'to laugh'
4.	[ho:x]	'high'		9.	[lεçʌln]	'to smile'
5.	[rauxən]	'to smoke'		10.	[raɪçən]	'to reach'

II.2   Korean
Determine whether [s], [š], and [z] are all allophones of the same phoneme or if any of them are in contrast. If they are all members of the same phoneme, state the distribution of the allophones and pick one as the basic sound of the phoneme. [ɯ] is a high back unrounded vowel.

1.	[šihap]	'game'		8.	[šilsu]	'mistake'
2.	[šipsam]	'thirteen'		9.	[šiɱho]	'signal'
3.	[inza]	'greetings'		10.	[paŋzək]	'cushion'
4.	[yʌŋzučɯŋ]	'receipt'		11.	[šesušil]	'washroom'
5.	[son]	'hand'		12.	[sɔm]	'sack'
6.	[sosʌi]	'novel'		13.	[sæk]	'color'
7.	[us]	'upper'				

II.3 Old English

In Old English, [f] and [v], [h] and [x], [n] and [ŋ] were in complementary distribution. Based on the following data, what is the distribution?

1.	[brɪŋgan]	'to bring'	11.	[lʊvʊ]	'love'	
2.	[drɪŋkan]	'to drink'	12.	[mannes]	'man's'	
3.	[fæst]	'fast'	13.	[mo:na]	'moon'	
4.	[fi:fta]	'fifth'	14.	[ni:xsta]	'next'	
5.	[fɔlk]	'folk'	15.	[nixt]	'night'	
6.	[fɔnt]	'font'	16.	[no:n]	'noon'	
7.	[ha:t]	'hot'	17.	[ɔffrian]	'to offer'	
8.	[hlo:θ]	'troop'	18.	[ɔvnas]	'ovens'	
9.	[hlyxxan]	'to laugh'	19.	[ru:x]	'rough'	
10.	[θʊŋgɛn]	'full grown'	20.	[lɛŋgan]	'to lengthen'	
			21.	[hrævn]	'raven'	

II.4 Persian

How many different phonemes do the various [r]'s shown in the data represent? If they are different phonemes, give the pairs of forms which show this. If they are allophones of one (or two) phonemes, state the rules for their distribution. Which one would you choose to represent the phonemic form, and why?

	[r̃] voiced trill			[ř] voiced flap	
1.	[ær̃teš]	'army'	13. [ahaři]		'starched'
2.	[far̃si]	'Persian'	14. [bær̃adær̃]		'brother'
3.	[qædr̃i]	'a little bit'	15. [berid]		'go'
4.	[r̃ah]	'road'	16. [biræng]		'pale'
5.	[r̃ast]	'right'	17. [bořos]		'hairbrush'
6.	[r̃æng]	'paint'	18. [cera]		'why?'
7.	[r̃iš]	'beard'	19. [darid]		'you have'
8.	[r̃uz]	'day'	20. [širini]		'pastry'

	[r̥̃] voiceless trill			[r̥̃] voiceless trill	
9.	[ahar̥̃]	'starch'	21. [car̥̃]		'four'
10.	[axær̥̃]	'last'	22. [ceȷur̥̃]		'what kind?'
11.	[behtær̥̃]	'better'	23. [hær̃towr̥̃]		'however'
12.	[ænar̥̃]	'pomegranate'	24. [šir̥̃]		'lion'

III. Advanced

III.1 Greek

Examine the sounds [×, k, c, ç̧]—[×] is a voiceless velar fricative, [ç̧] is a voiceless palatal fricative, and [c] is a voiceless palatal stop. What of these sounds are contrastive and which are in complementary distribution? State the distribution of the allophones.

1.	[kano]	'do'		10.	[kori]	'daughter'
2.	[xano]	'lose'		11.	[xori]	'dances'
3.	[ç̧ino]	'pour'		12.	[xrima]	'money'
4.	[cino]	'move'		13.	[krima]	'shame'
5.	[kali]	'charms'		14.	[xufta]	'handful'
6.	[xali]	'plight'		15.	[kufeta]	'bonbons'
7.	[ç̧eli]	'eel'		16.	[oç̧i]	'no'
8.	[ceri]	'candle'		17.	[oci]	'2.82 pounds'
9.	[ç̧eri]	'hand'				

III.2 Igbirra

Examine the sounds [e] and [a]. Do they appear to be separate phonemes or allophones of the same phoneme? If the two sounds are in complementary distribution, give the conditioning environments for the allophones.

1.	[mezi]	'I expect'		5.	[mazɪ]	'I am in pain'
2.	[meze]	'I am well'		6.	[mazɛ]	'I agree'
3.	[meto]	'I arrange'		7.	[matɔ]	'I pick'
4.	[metu]	'I beat'		8.	[matʊ]	'I send'

PHONOLOGY: SUBSTITUTIONS AND PHONOTACTICS

I. SOUND SUBSTITUTIONS

Not all sound systems are the same, as we discovered in conducting phonemic analyses of different languages. Some languages have fewer or more phonemes and/or allophones than English does, and we can detect this when we hear non-native speakers of English pronounce English. For instance, French speakers pronounce English *this* [ðɪs] as [zɪs] and *thin* [θɪn] as [sɪn]. The reason for this mispronunciation is that the phonemic inventory of French does not contain / ð / or / θ / so French speakers substitute the nearest equivalent sounds, the fricatives / z / and / s /, which are in their phonemic inventory.

These are known as *sound substitutions*, a process whereby sounds that already exist in the language are used to replace sounds that do not exist in the language when borrowing or trying to pronounce a foreign word. Another familiar example comes from German, a language that has the sound [x], a voiceless velar fricative. English, of course, lacks this sound, though we do have a voiceless velar stop [k]. Most speakers of English substitute [k] for [x] in a German word like *Bach* [bax], producing [bak]. Another example of the same substitution is the way Americans pronounce the German word *lebkuchen* [ˌlebkuxən] 'a Christmas cookie' as [ˌlebkukən]. Some English speakers, striving for a more "Germanlike" pronunciation will pronounce the word as [ˌlebkuhən] which is still incorrect. Why do you suppose an English speaker might substitute [h] for [x]?

II. PHONOTACTICS

In every language there are restrictions on the kinds of sounds and sound sequences possible in different positions in words (particularly at the beginning and end), restrictions which can be formulated in terms of rules stating which sound sequences are possible and which are not. Restrictions on possible combinations of sounds are known as *phonotactic constraints*. Languages generally prefer Consonant (C) first, Vowel (V) second type syllable structure, but not all languages allow a syllable to begin with more than one consonant. For instance, English allows up to three consonants to start a word, provided the first is [s], the second [p], [t] or [k] and the third [l], [r], [y], or [w] (see below), and has a wide variety of types:

V	'oh'	CV	'no'	CCV	'flew'	CCCV	'spree'
VC	'at'	CVC	'not'	CCVC	'flute'	CCCVC	'spleen'
VCC	'ask'	CVCC	'ramp'	CCVCC	'flutes'	CCCVCC	'strength'
VCCC	'asked'	CVCCC	'ramps'	CCVCCC	'crafts'	CCCVCCC	'strengths'

Other languages, however, do not have such a large number of syllable structures, as can be seen by examining the following lists:

Hebrew	Japanese	Hawaiian	Indonesian
CV	V	V	V
CVC	CV	CV	VC
CVCC (only	CVN (N =		CV
at the end of	nasal stop		CVC
a word)			

Notice that this means that Hebrew does not have any initial consonant clusters and that Indonesian clusters only in the middle of words; that is, there are no clusters initially or finally. Hawaiian does not permit clusters in any position.

We can investigate examples of restrictions on consonant sequences in more detail by considering some in a language we know very well—English. To start with, any consonants of English may occur initially (at the beginning) in words except for two: [ž] and [ŋ]. While some speakers *do* pronounce these sounds in borrowed words such as "Jacques" and "Nguyen," no native English word begins with them. A large number of two consonant combinations also occur, with a stop or fricative being followed by a liquid or glide:

[br] 'bring'	[gl] 'glean'	[my] 'music'	[kw] 'quick'
[θr] 'three'	[fl] 'fly'	[hy] 'humor'	[sw] 'sweet'

In addition, [s] can also be followed by voiceless and nasal stops (as in *stay, small*) and by [f] and [v] in a small number of borrowed words (*sphere, svelt*, etc.). [š] can be followed by a nasal stop or a liquid, but only [šr] is a cluster native to English (e.g. *shrink*). The others are present only in borrowings from Yiddish and German (*schlemiel* 'klutz', *Schwinn, schnook* 'turkey').

III. BORROWING AND ACCENTS

If a language has severe restrictions on its phonotactics, the restrictions will apply to every word in the language, native or not. Therefore, just as languages substitute familiar sounds for non-familiar ones, languages also seek to overcome problems of borrowing a foreign word which violates their phonotactics. For instance in English, two stops cannot come at the beginning of words, nor can stop plus nasal combinations. So, in order to more easily pronounce the foreign words *Ptolemy* and *gnostic*, English speakers simply drop the first consonant and pronounce the words [taləmi] and [nostɪk] respectively.

There are different ways of handling phonotactic problems: Japanese and Finnish provide us with instructive examples. Japanese and Finnish only allow the CV-type syllable, with a few exceptions. When borrowing a foreign word that violates the CV structure, the two languages must force it somehow to fit. CCV, CVC, etc. must be forced into a CV framework. There are two ways to do this. One is to drop or delete the extra consonant(s); the other is to add or insert vowels to separate the consonants. Finnish opts for deletion. In loanwords, Finnish drops the first of a series of consonants that do not conform to its phonotactics. Thus Germanic *strand* (CCCV-Nasal-C) ends up as *ranta* 'beach' (CV-Nasal-CV) in Finnish, and *glass* becomes *lasi*. Note also the addition of a final vowel to avoid a consonant in syllable final position.

The other way to break up consonant clusters is used by Japanese. Japanese inserts vowels into the cluster. A sequence of consonants CCC will end up looking like this: CVCVCV. The insertions are rule-governed, meaning that the insertion always works the same and we can predict the shape of new words in the Japanese lexicon (e.g. recent English loanwords in the language). The vowel [u] is inserted, except after [t] and [d]. Notice the sound substitutions made by Japanese for English:

l → r	ɛ → e	ə → a
v → b	ɪ → i	æ → (y)a
θ → s	ɔ → o	Vr → V̄
č → z	u → u	

Furthermore, the nasals [m] and [n] are allowed syllable finally. So, for example, when the English term *birth control* was borrowed into Japanese, it became *bāsu-kontorōru*.

[bərθ]	[kəntrol]
[bāsu]	[kontorōru]

The [u] in *bāsu* and the last [u] in *kontorōru* are inserted to keep the word-final syllables from ending in a consonant. The second [o] in *kontorōru* is inserted to prevent [t] and [r] from being together.

We can conclude by observing that substitutions by non-native speakers and strategies for handling phonotactic constraints both result in foreign accents, as well as very different looking words after having been borrowed into another language. A Spanish speaker does not pronounce *student* as [ɛstudənt] because he doesn't know any better, but because the consonant clusters *st-*, *sk-*, and *sp-* never occur in Spanish without being preceded by a vowel — e.g. *'estudiante'* 'student', *escuela* 'school', *espalda* 'shoulder'.

EXERCISES

1. Consider the stop/fricative plus liquid/glide initial clusters described in section 2. Name one such cluster which does not occur in English as far as you can tell. Then make up a nonsense word beginning with that cluster and say whether you think that word would ever be likely to be added to English.

2. We've seen above that two stops cannot begin a word; can they **end** a word, and if so, are there any restrictions on what kinds of stops can occur together? Be very careful not to let *spelling* influence your answer.

3. Think of some 3-consonant final clusters other than those mentioned in section I and give an example of an English word for each.

4. Some clusters in English which cannot occur either initially or finally *can* occur medially, because the consonants belong to two separate syllables (for example, [dp] in *bedpan*). Think of other medial clusters which cannot occur initially or finally, with examples.

5. Based on the information given in this File on Japanese borrowing, guess the English sources of the following Japanese words. (NOTE: [o] is used in place of [u] after [t] and [d].

firumu
daburu
puraido

Now try to predict the form of English loanwords in Japanese.

bust   speed
drive   friend
desk   picnic
biscuit   girl

6. An Ohio State student from Puerto Rico asked several of her American friends to a party she was giving the following weekend. As a means of attracting them, she told her friends that she was going to have a big [kɛk]. Discussing the invitation later, the American students could not decide whether their hostess was to have a *keg* or a *cake* at her party. Why were the students confused? How could you explain the mispronunciation if the Puerto Rican student were trying to say *cake*? How about *keg*?

7. During the Cambodian incursion in the early 1970s there was a lot in the news about capital city Phnom Penh. Most newscasters pronounced the name incorrectly as [pənam pɛn]. Why? How is this different from the pronunciation of *gnostic* or *Ptolemy*?

8. *Sri Lanka*, an island country off the coast of India, is usually pronounced incorrectly by English speakers as [šri lanka]. Can you give a reason for this mispronunciation? Also, why does the English speaker substitute [š] rather than something else?

PHONOLOGY: IMPLICATIONAL LAWS

In the study of phonetics you may have noticed that human languages use a wide variety of sounds. In spite of this variety some sounds are more common than others. Thus while it is true that almost all human languages use the stop consonants [p] and [t] and the vowel [a], very few languages use pharyngeal fricatives (the throat clearing sounds used in Arabic), voiceless vowels (like in whispered speech), and clicks (*tsk, tsk!* and horse calling sounds are American examples). So, [p], [t], and [a] are very *common* in languages while pharyngeal fricatives, voiceless vowels, and clicks are very *uncommon* sounds. The purpose of this file is to explain why some sounds are more common than others. Before attempting an explanation, however, we will make four observations concerning common and uncommon speech sounds.

OBSERVATIONS
SOUND INVENTORIES

The first observation concerning common and uncommon speech sounds has to do with the inventories of sounds in languages. The observation is basically this—if a language uses an uncommon sound, one of its more common counterparts will also be used. Two parts of this statement need clarification.

First, when we say that a language *uses* a sound we mean that that sound is in the inventory of distinctive sounds in the language. Distinctive sounds are the sounds used in a language to distinguish one word from another. Different languages have different inventories of distinctive sounds.

The second part of the statement that needs clarification is the phrase 'one of its more common counterparts.' This phrase refers to the fact that there tends to be a common sound associated with each uncommon sound which is just like the uncommon sound except for one or two features. For instance, the common counterpart of a voiceless vowel is a voiced vowel of the same tongue height, tongue advancement, lip rounding, and muscular tension. Likewise the common counterpart of a voiceless pharyngeal fricative is a voiceless velar fricative.

In the following chart we present some (relatively) uncommon sounds and their (relatively) more common counterparts.

UNCOMMON	COMMON
ḁ	a
ã	a
x	k
x	s
s	t
θ	t
ð	d
θ	s
ð	z

So, uncommon sounds differ from their common counterparts in only one or two features. Notice that [x] (voiceless velar fricative) has two counterparts— [k] and [s]. [k] is a voiceless velar *stop* so it differs from [x] by only one feature, and [s] is a voiceless *alveolar* fricative so it too differs from [x] by only one feature. [θ] and [ð] are in a similar relation. [θ] differs from [s] in terms of *place* of articulation interdental versus alveolar), and it differs from [t] in terms of *manner* of articulation (fricative versus stop) and in terms of place.

One other thing to notice about this chart: [s] appears both as a common sound (as opposed to [θ]) *and* as an uncommon sound (as opposed to [t]). This illustrates the fact that by using common and uncommon to designate the sounds in an implicational law we do not mean an *absolute* standard such as that a certain percentage of the world's languages use the sounds involved. Rather, common and uncommon are used in a *relative* way. In other words, [s] is uncommon *in relation to* [t], and common in relation to [θ]. In terms of an absolute sense of common versus uncommon [s] would surely count as a common sound, but [s] is relatively less common than [t] and therefore is uncommon in relation to [t].

Now, back to the observation. We have said that if a language uses (includes in its inventory of distinct sounds) an uncommon sound, one of its more common counterparts will also be included in that language's inventory of distinct sounds. In terms of the chart presented above what this means is that any language that uses [a] will also use [a], and any language that uses [ã] will also use [a], any language that uses [x] will also use [k̥], and so on. This type of observation is called an implicational law because the presence of the uncommon sound *implies* that the common sound will also be used in the language. Of course the implication cannot be reversed. In other words, just because English uses the sound [k] does not imply that we also use [x]. So, the presence of [x] in a language implies the presence of [k] in that language, while the presence of [k] doesn't tell you anything about whether there is a [x] used in that language.

Implicational laws can be stated for natural classes of sounds rather than just for individual pairs as in the chart above. So, for instance, the class of voiceless consonants is *relatively* more common than voiced consonants. In other words, if a language makes use of voiced stops it will also make use of voiceless ones, but the reverse implication does not work. Thus, there are some languages that have only voiceless stops. So, the presence of voiced stops *implies* the presence of their voiceless counterparts, while the presence of voiceless stops does not imply the presence of voiced ones.

Another implicational law that can be stated in terms of a natural class of sound is that the presence of fricatives in a language implies the presence of homorganic stops (stops with the same place of articulation) in that language. Thus, if a language uses an [s] then it also uses a [t].

FREQUENCY AND DISTRIBUTION

So far we've just been talking about one kind of observation that has been made concerning implicational laws, namely that the implicational laws state generalizations about the kind of inventory of sounds which can be used by a language.

The second observation concerning implicational laws is that they are not only generalizations concerning inventories of sounds, but also are related to the *degree* to which sounds will be used in a particular language and the *range of distribution* of the sounds in the words of the language. Thus, even if a language makes use of a pharyngeal fricative, this uncommon sound will be used in fewer words than will the more common alveolar fricative. In other words, the pharyngeal fricative will have limited usage compared with the velar fricative. Common sounds also have a *wider distribution* within a language. So, for instance, Cantonese Chinese has both stops and fricatives in its inventory of sounds, but fricatives may occur in only one spot in the syllable (as the first sound) while stops have wider distribution: they occur both syllable initially and syllable finally.

An English example of the limited usage and limited distribution of uncommon sounds has to do with the 'th' sound [ð]. [ð] can be classified as uncommon because it is relatively rare in the languages of the world and anyplace [ð] occurs [z] can also occur. If you try to think of words that have [ð] you will probably find that your list is limited to grammar words ('this,' 'that,' 'those,' 'them,' 'they' . . .) and a few other words ('either,' 'lathe'). Compared with the number of words that use [z] (the more common counterpart of [ð]) it is obvious then that [ð] has limited use in English. It is also interesting that [ð] occurs as the last sound in English words less often than [z]. Compared to the distribution of [z], [ð] has a limited distribution.

ACQUISITION OF SOUNDS

Another type of observation which is related to the implicational laws has to do with the order of the *acquisition* of sounds. This observation is that children acquire the use of common sounds before they acquire the use of uncommon sounds. As a result, children who have not yet mastered the complete sound inventory of their native language will substitute common sounds when trying to say uncommon sounds. Thus when a little girl says [t^{h}ek u] for 'thank you' she is replacing the relatively uncommon [θ] with [t^h] (a much more common sound). This is an indication that the child has not yet acquired the use of [θ] while [t] is readily available for use. When the language development of a child is followed from babbling through maturity a characteristic order of acquisition appears. This order in the acquisition of sounds is relatively constant for children around the world, no matter what language they are learning. Once again the implicational laws capture a generalization about language—namely, that the acquisition of a relatively uncommon sound implies that its more common counterpart has already been acquired.

SOUND CHANGE

The last type of observation which is related to implicational laws has to do with *language change*. This observation is that uncommon sounds tend to be less stable than common ones. Thus, in the course of language change, if any sound is going to be lost, it will be an uncommon one rather than its more common counterpart. An illustration of this feature of implicational laws can be drawn from the history of English. In the Old English pronunciation of the word 'knight' there was a velar fricative [x] in the position of the silent 'gh.' During the development of English, this velar fricative was lost (so 'knight' now rhymes with 'quite'). In fact, all instances of the velar fricative sound (as in 'height,' 'sight,' 'fight,' 'might' and so on) were lost. English speakers just stopped using velar fricatives altogether, so now we find it hard to learn how to say them when we are trying to learn a language like German. This observation fits in with the implicational law that says that fricatives are less common than stops. Therefore the fricative [x] is less stable and more likely to be lost than the corresponding stop consonant [k].

EXPLANATION

At this point we can summarize what we have observed about common and uncommon speech sounds: (1) the presence of an uncommon sound in a language implies that its more common counterpart will also be present, (2) uncommon sounds have limited usage and distribution in the languages that do make use of them, as compared with common sounds, (3) the use of common sounds is acquired before the use of uncommon ones, (4) uncommon sounds tend to be less stable than common ones, and are thus more likely to be lost or changed over time.

We might be tempted to say that the implicational laws (for instance, [k] is more common than [x]) are themselves the explanations of the observations in 1-4. Thus, we might say that [x] is more likely to be lost in language change than is [k] because [k] is more common than [x]. Or we might want to say that [k] is acquired by children before [x] because [k] is more common than [x]. This type of explanation is, however, circular. The circularity stems from the fact that we distinguished between common and uncommon sounds by pointing out the observations in 1-4. In other words, we are saying the [k] is more common than [x] because the observations in 1-4 are true of [k] relative to [x], then we are turning around and saying that the observations in 1-4 are true of [k] relative to [x] because [k] is more common than [x].

EASE OF PRODUCTION

The alternative to this circular form of explanation is to explain the observations in 1-4 (and thus the implicational laws) in terms of the communicative nature of language. It is important to realize that when people use language, their goal (generally speaking) is to communicate—that is, to successfully transmit a message from a speaker to a hearer. Focussing on the function of language leads us to the question, "What sounds are most useful for transmitting a message from speaker to hearer?" First of all, notice that if a sound is difficult to produce, speakers will be somewhat inconsistent in pronouncing it, and this inconsistency will result in confusion on the part of the hearer. To avoid being misunderstood, speakers may avoid words with difficult sounds (limited usage) and if enough speakers avoid a difficult sound it may disappear from the language entirely (language change). Of course, sounds that are difficult to produce (such as fricatives with the delicate control of muscles involved in their production) are not likely to be mastered by children before easier sounds are. As you can see, there are at least some instances where the observation that sound 'X' is more common than sound 'Y' is directly tied to the fact that sound 'X' is easier to produce than sound 'Y'. Thus, [k] is more common than [x] because stops are easier to produce than are fricatives. Alveolar fricatives are more common than pharyngeal fricatives because the tip of tongue is more agile than the back of the tongue, hence alveolar consonants are easier to say than are pharyngeal ones. Thus ease of production is an explaination of at least some of the implicational laws.

EASE OF PERCEPTION

Another way to answer the question, "What sounds are most useful for transmitting a message from speaker to hearer?" focuses on the hearer's point of view. From this point of view it is reasonable to suppose that if a sound blends into the surrounding sounds too much, its distinctive qualities may become difficult to hear. So, for example, if Morse code were made up of long dashes and no-so-long dashes, or dots and somewhat-shorter dots, rather than dots and dashes, it would be difficult to use. In the same way, the consonants and vowels which make up syllables are most usable when they are quite different from each other. So, the kind of syllable which is most useful in transmitting messages in language is composed of *maximally distinct* consonants and vowels. By maximally distinct, we mean that the consonant has very few qualities in common with the vowel and the vowel is likewise very different from the consonant. The value of maximally distinct carriers of information is obvious when we think about Morse code. If you can't tell the difference between dots and dashes then not much communication can take place. In the same way, if you can't tell the difference between consonants and vowels, then communication using language is likely to be very inefficient also.

Perhaps a couple of examples of the ways that consonants can be more vowel-like, or vowels can be more consonant-like are in order. One implicational law that we noticed is that the use of voiced consonants in a language implies the use of voiceless ones (thus voiceless consonants are more common than voiced ones). The natural explanation for this implicational law is that voiceless consonants have fewer qualities in common with vowels than do voiced consonants, thus, in syllables of consonants and vowels, voiceless consonants are perceptually more salient (or noticeable) than voiced ones. A way that vowels can be less consonant-like is to be pronounced with the mouth wide open, as in the vowel [a]. Because consonants are made by obstructing the vocal tract in some way, a vowel that is pronounced with the mouth wide open will be more distinct from surrounding consonants than will be a vowel like [i] or [u] which is pronounced with the mouth somewhat closed. It just so happens that there is an implicational law corresponding to this distinction between [i], [u], and [a]. The presence of a closed vowel ([i], [u]) implies the presence of an open vowel ([a]). Thus, syllables with maximally distinct consonants and vowels are easier to perceive than syllables with consonants and vowels that resemble each other, and therefore some implicational laws exist for the sake of the listener—to make language easier to perceive.

CONCLUSION

In this file we have seen that although there is a great variety in the sounds which can be employed in language, there are universal tendencies (1) to restrict the inventory of sounds to certain common sounds, (2) to restrict the degree of utilization and distribution of uncommon sounds in languages that do use them, (3) to acquire common sounds earlier than uncommon ones, and (4) for uncommon sounds to be unstable in the face of language change. We have also shown that these observations concerning common and uncommon sounds are related to the ease of production and ease of perception of those sounds, and that the implicational laws can be explained by assuming that people are using language in order to communicate, and that this produces a need for efficiency which leads to the use of easily produced and perceived sounds.

DISCUSSION QUESTION

1. Uncommon speech sounds are, nevertheless, speech sounds. There are languages that use them. Are the languages that use uncommon speech sounds harder than ones that don't? Are there any languages that don't use uncommon speech sounds at all?

INTRODUCTION
MORPHOLOGY

Despite the difficulty in its definition, the *word* is perhaps the linguistic unit most familiar to us. As one linguist aptly remarked, 'it is the kind of thing which a child learns to say, which a teacher teaches children to read and write in school, which a writer is paid for so much per thousand, which a clerk in a telegraph office counts and charges so much per, the kind of thing one makes slips of the tongue on, and for the right or wrong use of which one is praised or blamed.'[1]

Not surprisingly, the study of the word has had a long history. People have studied the origin and history of words for centuries. This kind of study is called *etymology*. Dictionary making has also been a time-honored practice in literate societies. The compiling of a dictionary is called *lexicography*. Etymology and lexicography, however, are not the only disciplines which study words. *Morphology,* a branch of linguistics, also studies words. But it is not the same as etymology and lexicography.

What is morphology then? *Morphology* is the study of how words are structured and how they are put together from smaller parts. One way in which morphology differs from etymology is that it looks at the word at a particular point in time, not focusing on the historical aspects as etymology does. An important way in which morphology differs from dictionary making is that it does not simply record and list the usages of words one by one, but tries to uncover the underlying principles in creating words. It attempts to give the rules, morphological rules, used in forming all the words in a language, including possible but nonoccurring words. These rules should thus license the creation of novel words such as those by Lewis Carroll,* but should rule out things like *lyhappy,* as native speakers of English recognize the former as possible words, but the latter as impossible ones. In doing so, morphology describes the native speaker's morphological competence. This part of competence includes the ability to recognize words as being well-formed or ill-formed, and the ability to come up with new creations based on existing patterns.

Specifically, in the morphological section of this course we address the following questions: What are the building blocks of words? What is the relationship between the meanings of these building blocks and the way they are pronounced? How are the building blocks put together to form words? What is the structure of complex words? How do languages differ in the structure and formation of words?

Despite the popular notion that the word is the smallest meaningful unit, the smallest unit with meaning is actually the *morpheme*. A word may be made up of several morphemes. File 51 discusses the problem of identifying morphemes in complex words and how to classify them according to their form and function in word and sentence formation. File 52 follows up the discussion by providing a set of exercises in identifying morphemes in English words.

The relationship between the meaning and the pronunciation of a morpheme is arbitrary, except in the cases of onomatopoetic words and sound symbols. It is this property of human languages that sets them off from instinctive communicative signals by other animals. Arbitrariness in language also allows languages to change and vary as they do. File 53 discusses this important fact of human language.

Words are not only analyzable but they also have internal structures according to which their components are related to each other. File 54 argues against the view that morphemes are like 'beads on a string' and are only ordered linearly with respect to each other.

File 55 surveys the various ways to put together morphemes to form words in the world's languages. File 56 looks at some of the ways to form words in English.

In contrast to File 55 and 56, which deal with synthesis, File 57 explains the procedure of morphological analysis. Given a string of sounds from an unfamiliar language, how can we analyze it into words and then component morphemes? A general procedure is given in the file, as well as some cautionary notes, which will help guard against having what you know about English interfere with your analysis of another language. File 58 is a set of morphological analysis problems.

File 59 contrasts morphological types of the worlds' languages. It shows that languages differ greatly with respect to the complexity of words, the way meaning distinctions are encoded in morphemes and how these morphemes are realized in form.

* In his well-known "Jabberwocky."
Note[1]: Y.R. Chao (1968): A Grammar of Spoken Chinese. University of California Press. p. 136

A morpheme is the minimal linguistic unit which has a meaning or grammatical function. Although many people think of words as the basic meaningful elements of a language, many words can be broken down into still smaller units, called *morphemes*. In English, for example, the word *ripens* consists of three morphemes: *ripe* plus *en* plus *s*. *-En* is a morpheme which changes adjectives into verbs: *ripe* is an adjective, but *ripen* is a verb. *Ripens* is still a verb: the morpheme *-s* indicates that the subject of the verb is third person singular and that the action is neither past nor future.

Those morphemes which can stand alone as words are said to be *free morphemes*, e.g. *ripe* and *artichoke*. Those which are always attached to some other morpheme are said to be *bound*, e.g. *-en, -s, un-, pre-* (see below).

Notice that the term *morpheme* has been defined as "a minimal unit of *meaning* or *grammatical function*" to show that different morphemes serve different purposes. Some morphemes derive (create) new words by either changing the meaning (*happy* vs. *unhappy*, both adjectives) or the part of speech (syntactic category, e.g. *ripe*, an adjective, vs. *ripen*, a verb) or both. These are called *derivational morphemes*. Other morphemes change neither part of speech nor meaning, but only refine and give extra grammatical information about the already existing meaning of a word. Thus, *cat* and *cats* are both nouns and have the same meaning (refer to the same thing), but *cats*, with the plural morpheme *-s*, contains the additional information that there are more than one of these things. (Notice that the same information could be conveyed by including a number before the word — the plural *-s* marker then would not be needed at all.) These morphemes which serve a purely grammatical function, never creating a different word, but only a different *form* of the same word, are called *inflectional morphemes*.

Both derivational and inflectional morphemes are bound forms and are called *affixes*. When they are attached to other morphemes they change the meaning or the grammatical function of the word in some way, as just seen; when added to the beginning of a word or morpheme they are called *prefixes*, and when added to the end of a word or morpheme they are called *suffixes*. For example, *unpremeditatedly* has two prefixes (one added to the front of the other) and two suffixes (one added to the end of the other), all attached to the word *meditate*.

In English, the derivational morphemes are either prefixes or suffixes, but the inflectional morphemes are all suffixes. There are only eight of them in English.

The Inflectional Suffixes of English

Base	Suffix	Function	Example
wait	-s	3rd p sg present	She wait*s* there at noon.
wait	-ed	past tense	She wait*ed* there yesterday.
wait	-ing	progressive	She is wait*ing* there right now.
eat	-en	past participle	Jack has eat*en* all the Oreos.
chair	-s	plural marker	The chair*s* are set around the table.
chair	-'s	possessive	The chair*'s* leg is broken.
fast	-er	comparative adj or adv	Billy Jean runs fast*er* than Bobby.
fast	-est	superlative adj or adv	Valerie is the fast*est* runner of all.

50-1

119

Below are listed four characteristics which separate inflectional and derivational affixes:

Inflectional Morphemes:

1. Do not change meaning or part of speech, e.g. *big* and *bigger* are both adjectives.

2. Typically indicate syntactic or semantic relations between different words in a sentence, e.g. the present tense morpheme *-s* in *waits* shows agreement with the subject of the verb (both are third person singular).

3. Typically occur with all members of some large class of morphemes, e.g., the plural morpheme *-s* occurs with most nouns.

4. Typically occur at the margins of words, e.g., the plural morphemes *-s* always come last in a word, as in *baby-sitters* or *rationalizations*.

Derivational Morphemes:

1. Change meaning or part of speech, e.g. *-ment* forms nouns, such as *judgment*, from verbs, such as *judge*.

2. Typically indicate semantic relations within the word, e.g. the morpheme *-ful* in *painful* has no particular connection with any other morpheme beyond the word *painful*.

3. Typically occur with only some members of a class of morphemes, e.g., the suffix *-hood* occurs with just a few nouns such as *brother*, *neighbor*, and *knight*, but not with most others, e.g., *friend, daughter, candle*, etc.

4. Typically occur before inflectional suffixes, e.g., in *chillier*, the derivational suffix *-y* comes before the inflectional *-er*.

There is one more distinction between types of morphemes which it can be useful to make. Most morphemes have *semantic content*, that is, they either have some kind of independent, identifiable meaning or indicate a change in meaning when added to a word. Others serve only to provide information about *grammatical function* by relating certain words in a sentence to each other (see 2 under inflectional morphemes, above). The former are called *content morphemes*, the latter are called *function morphemes*. In English, all roots and derivational affixes are content morphemes, while inflectional affixes and such "function words" as prepositions, articles, pronouns, and conjunctions are function morphemes.

Many people confuse morphemes with syllables. A few examples will show that the numbers of morphemes and syllables in a word are independent of each other. *Ripe* is one morpheme which happens to consist of a single syllable. *—s*, however, is not even a syllable, though it is a morpheme. *Ripens* is a two syllable word composed of three morphemes, while *syllable* is a three syllable word composed of only one morpheme.

Morphemes are pairings of sounds with meanings. Some morphemes have one sound as their phonetic representation, e.g., [i] in *lucky* or [e] in *asexual*. Some morphemes consist of one syllable, e.g., [ən] in *unable* or [pri] in *preview*. Other morphemes are *polysyllabic* (have more than one syllable), e.g., *language, banana, Mississippi*, and the suffix *ity* in *sanity*.

Sometimes different morphemes have the same phonetic representations, as in *ear* (for hearing) and *ear* (of corn). The same is true of affixes, e.g., the plural, possessive, and third person singular suffixes can all sound alike. There is a morpheme *in-* that means "not", e.g., *inoperable* or *intolerable*, and another *in-* that means "in", e.g., *intake* or *inside*. This same sequence [ɪn] is only part of the morpheme in [ˌtwɪn]. In the same way the [t] in [mɪst] can be either the past tense marker in *missed* or just part of the word *mist*, without any special morphemic content of its own.

Some morphemes have more than one phonetic representation depending on which sounds precede or follow them, but all meaning the same thing and serving the same purpose. For example, the phonetic representation of the plural morphemes is either [s] *cats*, [z] *dogs*, or [əz] *churches*. Each of these three different phonetic shapes is said to be an *allomorph* of the same morpheme. The plural, possessive, and third person singular morphemes all have three allomorphs apiece. Can you think of other morphemes which have more than one phonetic representation?

120

MORPHOLOGY: EXERCISES IN ISOLATING MORPHEMES

1.   The following words are made up of either one or two morphemes: isolate them and decide for each if it is free or bound, what kind of affix is involved, and (where applicable) if it is inflectional or derivational.

cats	catsup	succotash	entrust
unhappy	milder	bicycle	signpost

2.   Divide the words below into their component morphemes and identify the nature of the morphemes as in 1. Warning: Words may consist of one, two or more than two morphemes.

comfortable	reconditioned	thickeners
Massachusetts	unidirectional	rationalization

3.   The following words all involve morphemes whose forms are changed in some way when they become part of a word including other morphemes; some of these changes are only in the spelling, while others involve pronunciation changes as well. Identify all morphemes and give their isolated forms: then for those which change say whether spelling changes or pronunciation as well.

Example: babies — baby: free morpheme; -s bound inflectional suffix
Only the spelling of *baby* changes.

monstrous	undeniable	laziness
fatalities	divisible	fixation

4. In each group of words below, two words have a different morphological structure than the others: one has a different type of suffix, and one has no suffix at all. Identify the word that has no suffix and the word whose suffix is different from the others. Isolate the suffix that the remaining two words share and give its type (as in 1) and function.

a. rider	b. tresses	c. running	d. tables
colder	melodies	foundling	lens
silver	Bess's	handling	witches
actor	guess	fling	calculates

5.   In each group of words that follows, identify the parts of speech of the stems and the parts of speech of the whole words.

a. government	b. fictional	c. calmest
speaker	childish	lovelier
contemplation	colorful	sillier

6. From the examples given for each of the following suffixes determine: (i) the part of speech of the expression with which the suffix combines and (ii) the part of speech of the expressions formed by the addition of the suffix.

    a. *-ify: solidify, intensify, purify, clarify, rarefy*

    b. *-ity: rigidity, stupidity, hostility, intensity, responsibility*

    c. *-ize: unionize, terrorize, hospitalize, crystallize, magnetize*

    d. *-ive: repressive, active, disruptive, abusive, explosive*

    e. *-ion: invention, injection, narration, expression, pollution*

    f. *-less: nameless, penniless, useless, heartless, mindless*

MORPHOLOGY: ARBITRARINESS IN LANGUAGE

We have defined morpheme as the minimal linguistic unit with meaning. For instance, we say that 'tip' is a morpheme because it has meaning, but the component phonemes /t/, /ɪ/ and /p/, though capable of distinguishing meaning, do not have meanings themselves. It is only when the phonemes are combined in a certain way that we have the morpheme 'tip'. Other possible combinations of the three phonemes may either give a different morpheme, for example 'pit' or no morphemes at all. 'ipt' and 'itp' and 'tpi' and 'pti' are not morphemes of English and have no meaning at all.

Where do the meanings of morphemes come from, if the component phonemes do not have meanings of their own? There are two possible answers to this question. Either we say that the meanings of morphemes are inherently connected with the way they are pronounced or that the relationship between the meanings of morphemes and their pronunciation is arbitrary. The first answer will entail that given the way a morpheme sounds, it has to have a certain meaning while the latter view will mean that a given sound sequence just happens to be associated with a certain meaning. Another consequence that follows from the first position is that the same meaning will have to be expressed by the same sounds in different languages and *vice versa* while for the second position the same meaning can well be expressed by different sounds in different languages.

Both of the two positions outlined above were actually taken by the Greek philosophers, who were very concerned with the nature of language. The first position, which argues for the inherent connection between meanings and forms, was held by the 'nature' school, which tries to relate the sounds of words directly to reality. The second position, opting for the accidental character of the relation between forms and meanings, was maintained by the 'convention' school, who argued that if there is anything that enables a stable meaning to be associated with a sequence of sound, it is the social convention within a speech community and not some sort of inherent connection.

For the 'nature' school, onomatopoetic words and sound symbolisms of various kinds are the best supporting evidence for their theory. In every language, there are invariably some morphemes that try to imitate sounds in nature. In English, for example, we have the morpheme 'cuckoo', which imitates the sound of the cuckoo bird. In morphemes like these, the relationship between the meaning and the sound is undoubtably quite direct. In many languages, there are also morphemes that more abstractly suggest some physical characteristics by the way they sound. These are sound symbols. In English, for example, words beginning with *fl-* like *fly, flee, flow, flimsy, flick, fluid,* all suggest quickness and lightness. Poets use sound symbols to their advantage. In the poem *'The Raven'* by Edgar Allen Poe, for example, quite a few words with *fl-* are used to conjure up the raven's flighty image. Onomatopoetic words and sound symbols are *iconic,* to a greater or lesser extent.

The fact is, however, that onomatopoetic words and sound symbolisms are relatively rare in any language. How about the majority of morphemes? The 'nature' school tried to relate these other morphemes to the more iconic morphemes. A lot of effort was spent on the etymology of words. But however far we go back and however many stories we can tell of the evolution of words, most of the words in the vocabulary are bound to be unaccounted for in this way. Therefore, modern linguists will generally agree with the 'convention' school and say that the relation between the meaning of morphemes and the way they are pronounced is largely arbitrary, and conventional, rather than iconic. It remains for us to joke about the unfortunate fictional character who still thinks the pronunciation of 'water' is the most natural way and indeed the only way to refer to the substance H_2O. But what are the different pieces of evidence we have for the arbitrariness of language apart from the scarcity of onomatopoetic and sound symbolic words? Let us summarize them below:

1. First of all, knowledge of foreign languages tells us that the same meaning can be expressed with different sounds in different languages. What is 'water' in English is 'eau' in French, 'Wasser' in German and 'šuy' in Mandarin Chinese. On the other hand, the same sequence of sounds can mean different things in different languages. Approximately the same sounds that we use for 'women' mean 'we' or 'us' in Mandarin Chinese. Therefore, the relationship between a morpheme's form and its meaning cannot be inherent.

2.   Even in the same language, we may use several different morphemes to express the same meaning. We have synonyms. 'Bucket' and 'pail' may refer to the same thing and yet sound very different. On the other hand, the same sound sequence can be used to express different meanings. We have homonyms. For example [nayt] 'knight/night' [flawr]'flower/flour' and [b æ ŋk] 'financial institution/riverside', to name just a few.

3.   The pronunciations of words change over the course of time. From the spelling of words such as 'wrong', 'knight', 'know', we know that the pronunciations for these words must have had the initial 'w', 'k' sounds and the 'g' sound at some point in the history of English. Suppose that the original pronunciations reflect the meaning inherently. How can we maintain this inherent connection when the pronunciation changes without necessary concomitant changes in the meaning? The relationship between the form and meaning of a morpheme has to be arbitrary to allow sound changes.

4.   Even the onomatopoetic words are arbitrary to some extent. When different languages imitate the same sound, say, the sound of a rooster, they have to make use of their own linguistic resources. Different languages admit different sound combinations. So even the same sound in nature may have to be imitated differently in different languages. The rooster says [kakədudḷ-du] in English but [kukuku] in Mandarin Chinese. If there were an inherent connection between the meaning and the form of a morpheme, we would expect the same meaning to be represented by the same sounds. Hence the strongest evidence for the 'nature' school is seriously weakened. To give more examples of the arbitrariness in onomatopoetic words, we list eleven natural sounds below which are represented with onomatopoetic words in eight languages. The similarity between them is expected, both due to the onomatopoetic nature of them and the possibility of borrowing between related languages like English and German, French and Spanish, Hebrew and Arabic. But the variation is also great.

Sound	English	German	French	Spanish (Chilean)	Hebrew	Arabic	Mandarin (Chinese -- Taiwan)	Japanese
1. Dog barking	[bɔw-wɔw] or [wuf-wuf]	[vaw-vaw]	[wah-wah]	[waw-waw]	[haw-haw]	[ʕaw-ʕaw]	[wãw-wãw]	[wã-wã]
2. Rooster crowing	[kak-ə-dudḷ-du]	[kikaʀiki]	[kokoʀiko]	[kikiʔiki] or [kokořoko]	[kukuʀiku]	[kukuriku]	[kuku]	[kokekoko]
3. Cat purring	[miaw]	[miaw]	[miaw]	[mɪaw]	[miaw]	[maw-maw]	[mɔaw]	[niaw]
4. Cow lowing	[mu:]	[mu]	[mø:]	[mu]	[mu]	[ʕu:]	[m:³⁻¹ₗ*]	[mo:mo]
5. Sheep bleating	[ba:]	[mɛ:] or [bɛ:]	[be:]	[bɛ:]	[mɛ̃:mɛ̃:]	[maʔ:]	[mɛ̃:mɛ̃:]	[mã:mã:]
6. Bird chirping	[twit-twit]	-	[kwikwi]	[pip-pip]	[tswits-tswits]		[čiči]	[čiči]
7. Bomb exploding	[bum]	-	[bʀum] or [vʀum]	[bum]	[bum]	-	[bõm]	[baŋg]
8. Sound of laughing	[ha-ha]	[hɔ-ha]	[ha-ha]	[xa-xa]	[ha-ha]	[qah-qah]	[ha-ha]	
9. Sound of sneezing	[ačʰu]	-	[ačum]	[ačʰu] or [ači]	[apčʰi]	[ʕats]	[hačũ:]	[hakšu]
10. Sound of something juicy hitting a hard surface	[splæt]	[pač]	[flæk]	-	[flox]	-	[pyak]	[pḷšapišạ]
11. Sound of a clock	[tɪk-tak]	[tɪk-tɪk]	[tɪk-tak]	[tɪk-tak]	[tɪk-tak]	[tɪktɪk]	[tɪktɔk]	[čɪkwtakw]

*Buffalo cow

MORPHOLOGY: THE HIERARCHICAL STRUCTURE OF WORDS

There are two important facts about the ways in which affixes join with their expressions. First, the expressions with which a given affix may combine normally belong to the same part of speech. For example, the suffix *-able* attaches freely to verbs, but not, for example, to adjectives or nouns; thus, we can add this suffix to the verb *adjust, break, compare,* and *debate,* but not to the adjectives *asleep, lovely, happy,* and *strong,* nor the nouns *anger, morning, student,* or *success.* Second, the expressions resulting from the addition of a given affix to some word or morpheme also normally belong to the same part of speech. For example, the expressions resulting from the addition of *-able* to a verb are always adjectives; thus *adjustable, breakable, comparable,* and *debatable* are all adjectives. An important consequence of these two facts is that in the formation of a word, the affixes aren't just strung together all at once; instead, they are put together step by step. That is, the internal structure of words is *hierarchical.*

To see this, consider the adjective *reusable* (as in *HandiWipes are reusable!*). This adjective consists of three morphemes: the free morpheme *use* and the derivational affixes *re-* and *-able.* As was noted above, *-able* is a suffix which joins with a verb to form an adjective:

(I)	Verb	+	*-able*	=	Adjective
	adjust				*adjustable*
	break				*breakable*
	compare				*comparable*
	debate				*debatable*
	lock				*lockable*
	use				*usable*

The prefix *re-*, on the other hand, joins with a verb to form a new verb:

(II)	*re-*	+	Verb	=	Verb
			adjust		*readjust*
			appear		*reappear*
			consider		*reconsider*
			construct		*reconstruct*
			decorate		*redecorate*
			use		*reuse*

These facts allow us to see that the word *reusable* is formed in two steps: first, the prefix *re-* joins with the verb *use* to form the verb *reuse,* as in (II); second, the suffix *-able* attaches to the verb *reuse* to form the adjective *reusable,* just as it attaches to the verb *adjust* to form the adjective *adjustable* in (I). These steps in the formation of *reusable* can be schematically represented by means of a tree structure:

Notice that *reusable* cannot be regarded as the result of adding the prefix *re-* to the word *usable.* A little consideration reveals why this is so: since *use* is a verb, *-able* may attach to it to form the adjective *usable,* as in (I); but because *usable* is an adjective, *re-* cannot join with it, since *re-* only joins with verbs. Thus, our understanding of how the affixes *re-* and *-able* combine with other morphemes allows us to conclude that the verb *reuse,* but not the adjective *usable,* is a step in the formation of the adjective *reusable.*

125

Interestingly, some words are ambiguous (i.e. have more than one meaning) because their internal structure may be analyzed in more than one way. Consider, for example, the word *unlockable*: this could mean either 'not able to be locked' or 'able to be unlocked.' If we consider the bound morphemes in this word very carefully, we can see why this ambiguity arises.

In English, there are not one but two prefixes *un-*: the first combines with an adjective to form a new adjective, and means simply 'not';

(III) *un-*₁	+	Adjective	=	Adjective
	able			*unable* 'not able'
	aware			*unaware* 'not aware'
	happy			*unhappy* 'not happy'
	intelligent			*unintelligent* 'not intelligent'
	lucky			*unlucky* 'not lucky'

The second *un-* combines with a verb to form a new verb, and means 'to do the reverse of.'

(III) *un-*₂	+	Verb	=	Verb
	do			*undo* 'to do the reverse of doing'
	dress			*undress* 'to do the reverse of dressing'
	load			*unload* 'to do the reverse of loading'
	lock			*unlock* 'to do the reverse of locking'
	tie			*untie* 'to do the reverse of tying'

Because of these two different sorts of *un-* in English, *unlockable* may be analyzed in two different ways. First, the suffix *-able* may join with the verb *lock* to form the adjective *lockable*, as in (I); *un-*₁ may then join with this adjective to form the new adjective *unlockable*. This way of forming *unlockable* is schematized in the following tree structure:

Since *un-*₁ just means 'not', this tree structure represents the meaning 'not able to be locked.'

The second way of forming *unlockable* is as follows. The prefix *un-*₂ joins with the verb *lock* to form the verb *unlock*, as in (IV); the suffix *-able* then joins with this verb to form the adjective *unlockable*. This manner of forming *unlockable* is represented by the following tree.

Since *un-*₂ means 'to do the reverse of', as in the verb *unlock* 'to do the reverse of locking', this tree represents the meaning 'able to be unlocked.'

Exercise: Draw tree diagrams for each of the following words:

a. *reconstruction*   d. *manliness*   g. *misunderstandable*
b. *unaffordable*   e. *impersonal*   h. *irreplaceability*
c. *un-American*   f. *international*

MORPHOLOGY:
WORD FORMATION PROCESSES
IN LANGUAGES

A list of the most common word formation processes in the world's languages is given below:

COMPOUNDING

A *compound* is a word formed by the combination of two independent words. The parts of a compound can be free morphemes, derived words, or other compounds, in nearly any combination:

girlfriend	air conditioner	lifeguard chair
blackbird	looking glass	aircraft carrier
lifeguard	working girl	life insurance salesman
aircraft	watchmaker	
textbook	self-determination	

We can tell that compounding forms *words* and not just syntactic phrases by the difference between the stress patterns in words and phrases. Compounds which have words in the same order as phrases have primary stress on the first word only, while individual words in phrases have independent primary stresses. (Primary stress is indicated below by '.)

Compounds	Phrases
bláckbird	bláck bírd
mákeup	máke úp

Other compounds can have phrasal stress patterns, but only if they can't possibly be phrases. These might also have stress on the first word only, like other compounds. These differences are often, but not always, reflected in writing conventions such as writing the compound as one word or using hyphens to connect the parts.

eásy-góing	eásy-going
mán-máde	mán-made
hómemáde	hómemade

The syntactic category of a word created by compounding depends to some extent on the categories of its parts. In general, two words of identical categories will make a compound of the same category. Also, the second part of a compound seems to dominate when the categories of the parts differ.

Noun-noun	Adjective-Adjective
birdcage	deaf-mute
houseboat	easy-going
playground	highborn

X-noun	X-adjective	X-verb
blackbird	stone-deaf	outrun
backwater	colorblind	spoonfeed
	knee-deep	undergo
	downcast	

The meaning of a compound depends on the meanings of its parts, but almost any kind of meaning connection can be involved between the parts. For example, an *aircraft* is a craft made for use *in* the air, but an *airconditioner* is a conditioner *of* air. Similarly, an *airbrush* is a brush which *uses* air. Can you see the difference in the connections of these compounds?

AFFIXATION

Most of the morphological work in English is performed by *affixes* — that is, bound morphemes (usually shor)that are added to free morphemes. There are basically three kinds of affixes: *prefixes* (added to the beginning of free morphemes or other prefixes), *suffixes* (added to the end of free morphemes or other suffixes) and *infixes* (inserted into a morpheme). English has many *prefixes* —*re-*, *anti-*, *dis-*, and so on — and many suffixes: *-ment*, *-ly*, *-ed*, *-'s*, *-s*, and so on but it has no infixes. (However, the *n* of *stand* is a remnant of a very ancient infix that was used to form certain types of verbs).

Tagalog, one of the major languages of the Philippines, uses infixes quite extensively. For example, the infix *-um-* is used to form many verb forms.

[sulat]	'write	[sumulat]	'to write'
[bili]	'buy'	[bumili]	'to buy'
[kuha]	'take, get'	[kumuha]	'to take, to get'

Tagalog also has an *-in-* infix which is used to form a kind of passive verb. Many other languages of the Philippines have an *-ar-* infix which is used in many words for plants and trees.

Sundanese, a language spoken in Indonesia, has an *-ar-* infix. This infix indicates that the subject of a verb is plural.

REDUPLICATION

In reduplication either all of a morpheme is doubled (total reduplication) or part of it is (partial reduplication). In English, total reduplication occurs only sporadically and it usually indicates intensity:

That's a big, big dog!   (*big* is drawn out)

(Young children will frequently reduplicate words or parts of words.)
Indonesian uses total reduplication to form the plurals of nouns:

[rumah]	'house'	[rumahrumah]	'houses'
[ibu]	'mother'	[ibuibu]	'mothers'
[lalat]	'fly'	[lalatlalat]	'flies'

Tagalog uses partial reduplication to indicate future:

[bili]	'buy'	[bibili]	'will buy'
[kain]	'eat'	[kakain]	'will eat'
[pasok]	'enter'	[papasok]	'will enter'

In conjunction with the prefix maŋ (which often changes the initial consonant of a following morpheme to a nasal), Tagalog uses reduplication to derive words for occupations.

[bili]/	maŋ+bi+bili /	[mamimili]	'a buyer'
[sulat]/	maŋ+su+sulat/	[manunulat]	'a writer'
[ʔisda]/	maŋ+ʔi+ʔisda /	[manʔiʔisda]	'a fisherman'

130

MORPHEME INTERNAL CHANGES

Besides adding an affix to a morpheme (affixation) or copying all or part of the morpheme (reduplication) to make a morphological distinction, it is also possible to make morpheme internal modifications. We have a few examples of this in English.

1) Although the usual pattern of plural formation is to add an inflectional morpheme, some English plurals make an internal modification: *man* but *men*, *woman* but *women*, *goose* but *geese* and so on.
2) The usual pattern of past and past participle formation is to add an affix, but some verbs also show an internal change: *break*, *broke*, *broken*; *bite*, *bit*, *bitten*, and so on. Still others show only the internal changes: *ring*, *rang*, *rung*; *sing*, *sang*, *sung*, and so on.
3) Some word class changes are also indicated only via internal changes: *strife*, *strive*; *teeth*, *teethe*; *breath*, *breathe*; *life*, *live* (V); or *life*, *live* (ADJ), etc.

SUPPLETION

Languages that employ morphological processes to form words will normally have a regular, productive way of doing so according to one or more of the processes discussed above. They might also have some smaller classes of words that are irregular because they mark the same morphological distinction by another of these processes. Sometimes, however, the same distinction can be represented by two different words which don't have any systematic difference in form—they are exceptions to all of the processes. This completely irregular situation is called *suppletion* (or a *suppletive* distinction) and usually only occurs in a few words of a language. This situation arises historically as two different words with similar meanings come to be interpreted as two forms of the "same word."

In English, for example, the regular past tense is formed by the ending realized by the allomorphs /-t/, /-d/, or /-əd/. Most English verbs, and any new made-up words in English such as *scroosh* or *blat* will have this past tense form:

walk	/wak/	walked	/wakt/
scroosh	/skruš/	scrooshed	/skrušt/
blat	/blæt/	blatted	/blætəd/

There are also some smaller classes of very common words in English that form the past tense by an internal vowel change:

sing	/sɪŋ/	sang	/sæŋ/
run	/rʌn/	ran	/ræn/

But a small number of individual verbs in English have *suppletive* past tenses:

I am	/æm/	I was	/wʌz/
I go	/go/	I went	/wɛnt/

There is no similarity at all between the present and past tense forms.

Classical Arabic provides another example. The normal plural form for nouns ending in /-at/ in Arabic involves the lengthening of the vowel of the ending:

/dira:sat/	'(a) study'	/dira:sa:t/	'studies'
/harakat/	'movement'	/haraka:t/	'movements'

There are also some irregular plurals of nouns ending in / -at / that involve other internal changes:

/ǰumlat/   'sentence'   /ǰumal/   'sentences'

/fikrat/   'thought'   /fikar/   'thoughts'

However, the plural of /marʔat/, 'woman' is /nisa:ʔ/, clearly a case of suppletion, since there are no forms like /marʔa:t/ or /maraʔ/ or anything of the sort. The plural is a completely different word.

MORPHOLOGY: ENGLISH WORD FORMATION

In the last file, the most common word formation processes of the world's languages are discussed. As a case study of word formation processes in one language, let us now look at the different ways English employs to put morphemes together and form new words out of existing words. Some of these processes English shares with other languages and they have already been discussed, but there are other ways to form new words in English that have not been mentioned. Let us start with the more common word formation processes.

Derivation: English has a number of derivational morphemes which we use to derive words. There are prefixes (added to the beginning of a stem) or suffixes (added to the end of a stem). Some common prefixes in English are *re-, dis-, un-, anti-, in-, pre-, post-,* and *sub-*. And common suffixes: *-ly, -ness, -y, -er, -ity, -ation, -ful, -able,* and *-al*.

Compounding: Two or more existing words are put together to form a new word: *blackboard, expressway,* and *airconditioner*. Can you think of other examples of English compounds? You may be surprised to find that words like *lord, hussy, women, sheriff* and *stirrup* — which are thought today as being monomorphemic — all originated as compounds themselves. Historical changes have altered the way we view these words.

So far, the processes are familiar: morphemes or words are put together to form words or new words. There are however in English some other ways to form new words, which do not put morphemes together in the familiar way. The parts which are put together are sometimes parts of morphemes or are not morphemes at all.

Acronyms: These words are formed by taking the initial sounds (or letters) of the words of a phrase and uniting them into a combination which is itself pronounceable as a separate word. Thus *NATO* is an acronym for *North Atlantic Treaty Organization, laser* for *light amplification through the stimulated emission of radiation,* and *radar* for *radio detection and ranging*.

Back Formation: Back formation makes use of a process called *analogy* to derive new words, but in a rather backwards manner. For example, we have words like *revision* and *revise* and *supervision* and *supervise*. *Revision* is formed by regular derivation from *revise* and *ion*. When *television* was invented, the verb *televise* was back-formed on the basis of analogy with *revision* and *revise,* that is:

revision : revise :: television : X

To cite another example, the verb *donate* was formed on the basis of pairs like *creation — create*. We borrowed *donation* from French and back-formed *donate*.

creation : create :: donation : X

Blending: A blend is a combination of the parts of two words, usually the beginning of one word and the end of another: *smog* from *smoke* and *fog, brunch* from *breakfast* and *lunch,* and *chortle* from *chuckle* and *snort*. (Lewis Carroll invented this blend and his poem "Jabberwocky" contains several other examples of interesting blends.)

Clipping: Frequently we shorten words without paying attention to the derivational morphology of the word (or related words). *Exam* has been clipped from *examination, dorm* from *dormitory,* and either *taxi* or *cab* from *taxi cab* (itself a clipping from *taximeter cabriolet*).

Coinage: Words may also be created without using any of the methods described above and without employing any other word or word parts already in existence; that is, they may be created out of thin air. Such brand names as *Xerox*, *Kodak*, and *Exxon* were made up without reference to any other word, as were the common words *pooch* and *snob*.

Functional Shift: A new word may be created simply by shifting the part of speech to another one without changing the form of the word. *Laugh*, *run*, *buy*, *steal* are used as nouns as well as verbs, while *position*, *process*, *contrast* are nouns from which verbs have been formed.

Morphological misanalysis (false etymology): Sometimes people hear a word and misanalyze it either because they "hear" a familiar word or morpheme in the word, or for other, unknown reasons. These misanalyses can introduce words or morphemes. For example, the suffix *-burger* results from misanalyzing *hamburger* as *ham* plus *burger*. (*Hamburger* is a clipping from *Hamburger Steak*.) *-Burger* has since been added to other types of foods: *cheeseburger*, *pizzaburger*, *salmonburger*, and *steakburger*. Another example concerns the creation *(a)holic* from a peculiar analysis of *alcoholic*. This suffix can be found in words like *workaholic* and *sugarholic*. It is not clear whether such misanalyses arise from actual misunderstanding or from intentional or creative extension of the morphological possibilities of the language.

Proper names: Many places, inventions, activities, etc., are named for persons somehow connected with them; for instance, Washington, D.C. (for George Washington — and District of Columbia for Christopher Columbus), German *Kaiser* and Russian *tsar* (for Julius Caesar), and *ohm* and *watt* (for Georg Simon Ohm and James Watt)

MORPHOLOGY: HOW TO SOLVE MORPHOLOGY PROBLEMS

57

When a linguist comes in contact with a new language, one of his major tasks is to discover the meaningful units, or *morphemes,* out of which the language is composed. Just as with discovering phonemes and allophones, it is important that the linguist have procedures for discovering these minimal units, since it is impossible to isolate morphemes by intuition.

For example, the Classical Greek word [graphɔː] means 'I write', but the linguist has no way of knowing what sound or sequence of sounds corresponds to what English meaning if he considers the word *in isolation.* It is only by comparing [graphɔː] with another form, for instance, [grapheː] 'he writes' that he is able to determine what the morphemes of these Greek words are.

Comparison, then, is the best way to begin morphological analysis. But of course you will not want to compare just any forms. Comparing a Greek word like [pʰɛːmi] 'to speak' with [graphɔ] will not provide us with much information since the forms are so dissimilar and seem to have no single morpheme in common. What must be compared are *partially similar* forms in which it is possible to recognize recurring units. In this way we can identify the morphemes of which words are composed.

Now let's consider our Classical Greek example once more. If we compare [graphɔː] with [grapheː] 'he writes' we note similarities between the forms. The sequence [graph-] recurs in the forms [grapheː] and [graphɔ]. If we check our English correspondences we find the meaning 'write' recurs also. Here we are justified in assuming [graph-] means 'write', since [graph-] and *write* are constants in both. Further, since the final vowels in both forms contrast—and since this contrast is accompanied by a difference in meaning in our English correspondence—we can safely assume the difference between vowels in Classical Greek corresponds to differences in meaning in our English translation. Therefore we assign the meaning 'I' to [-ɔː] and 'he' to [-eː].

In sum, then, the initial step in doing morphological analysis is:

(1) Comparing and contrasting partially similar forms.

To give yourself practice, identify and translate the morphemes in the made-up data below, from a hypothetical language:

[ǰapi]	'house'
[ǰapit]	'the house'
[aǰapit]	'to the house'
[druta]	'tree'
[drutat]	'the tree'
[adrutat]	'to the tree'

Sometimes just comparing and contrasting partially similar forms is not enough to allow a complete morphological analysis. Consider the following examples:

(1) If we compare the following English words:

work   broad
worker   broader

We notice the morpheme spelled *-er* and pronounced [ɹ̩] for both [bradɹ̩] and [wɹkɹ̩]. However, if we think about it for a minute, it is apparent that *-er* has two different meanings even though phonetically it looks like the same morpheme. The *-er* in *worker* is the same *-er* that shows up in words like *painter, killer, lover,* and *actor.* In each of these cases, *-er* attaches to verbs to form a noun, and means something like 'one who paints', 'one who kills', 'one who loves', etc. The suffix *-er* in these cases is known as the *agentive* morpheme.

The *-er* in *broader*, on the other hand, is the same *-er* that shows up in words like *wider, longer, colder, prettier,* and so on. In each of these cases, *-er* attaches to adjectives to form a new adjective, with the extra meaning 'more'. The suffix *-er* in these cases is known as the *comparative* morpheme.

We will want to argue, then, that [ɾ] represents two separate morphemes—[ɾ] as an agent marker, and [ɾ] as a comparative marker—even though they are the same phonetically, i.e. are *homophonous* morphemes. The [ɾ] which is added to verbs to yield nouns and the [ɾ] which is added to adjectives to yield new adjectives clearly have *distinct* meanings.

(2) If we compare the following set of words in (a), (b), and (c), we notice that each word has a prefix which means 'not'.

      (a) 'imbalance'   [ɪmbæləns]
      (b) 'inability'   [ɪnəbɪləti]
      (c) 'incomplete'   [ɪŋkəmplit]

The problem here is the inverse of the problem in example (1). Whereas in example (1) we had the same phonetic forms representing two different meanings, in example (2) we have three different phonetic forms with the *same* meaning. Since the phonetic forms of the morpheme meaning 'not' here can be predicted on the basis of phonetic environment,

      [ɪm] before labials— [p], [b], [m]
      [ɪŋ] before velars— [k], [g]
      [ɪn] elsewhere (before vowels and other consonants)

we conclude that even though the forms differ phonetically they belong to the *same* morpheme, since they have the same meaning. We call [ɪm], [ɪŋ], and [ɪn] *allomorphs* of the same morpheme. Another example of *allomorphy* in English is the plural morpheme which is realized as either [s], [z] or [əz] depending on the form of the root to which it attaches.

PROCEDURE FOR DOING MORPHOLOGICAL ANALYSIS

Goal:
Given a set of data in phonetic representation, you are asked to perform a constituent morphological analysis of the forms.
Procedure (Keys to Analysis):
1. Isolate and compare forms which are partially similar.
2. If a single phonetic form has two distinctive meanings, it must be analyzed as representing two different morphemes (as in example (1)).
3. If the same meaning is associated with different phonetic forms, these different forms all represent the same morpheme (they are allomorphs of the morpheme), and the choice of form in each case should be predictable on the basis of the phonetic environment (as in example (2)).

Some Cautionary Notes:

People frequently assume that languages are pretty much the same in terms of what each language marks morphologically. For example, English speakers often assume that all languages mark the plurals of nouns with an ending or that the subject and the verb agree in person and number in other languages. This is simply not true. For example, Tagalog does not usually mark the plural of nouns (in most cases, the number is clear from the context). When it is necessary to be specific, a separate word, *mga*, is used to indicate plural.

[aŋ bataʔ] 'the child'

[aŋ mga bataʔ] 'the children'

When a number is specifically mentioned, no plural marker appears in Tagalog, though the plural marker is obligatory in English (*Three dog* is ungrammatical.):

[dalawa] 'two' [dalawaŋ bata] 'two children'

[lima] 'five' [limaŋ bataʔ] 'five children'

[-ŋ] is a "linker" that links numerals and adjectives to the nouns they modify; English does not use this type of device.)

There is also no subject-verb agreement in Tagalog. For example, in English *I eat* but *he eats*. In Tagalog, the same form of the verb would be used, no matter what the person/number of the subject: *kumakain ako* 'eat now I' = 'I eat (now)', *kumakain siya* 'eat now he' = 'he eats (now)'.

Other languages also make distinctions that we don't. While English has only singular versus plural, some languages have a *dual* when just two are involved. Consider Sanskrit *juhomi* 'I sacrifice', *juhavas* 'we (two) sacrifice', and *juhumas* 'we (pl.) sacrifice'.

Some languages also have two kinds of first person plural pronouns — that is, English *we*. Notice that English *we* in *we are going*, for example, may include everyone in the group the hearer is addressing (we, every one of us) or it may include some hearers (me and him, but not you). Many languages distinguish these two *we*'s: Tagalog has *tayo* (inclusive, i.e. *you* and *I*) but *kami* (exclusive, i.e. *he* and *I*).

Comanche makes a number of distinctions that English doesn't. In addition to a *singular/dual/plural* distinction — *inɨ* 'you sg.', *-nikwɨ* 'you (two)', *-mɨɨ* 'you (pl.)' — and an *inclusive/exclusive* distinction *-taa* 'we (incl.)', *nɨnɨ* 'we excl.' — Comanche also makes a distinction between *visible/invisible* and *near/far*. Thus, if you are referring to a thing that is within your view, you use *-ma*ʔ 'it (visible)'. If the thing is invisible to you, 'ʔuʔ 'it (invisible)' is used. A near object is designated with -ʔiʔ 'it (proximate)', but a far object with -ʔoʔ 'it (remote).' (Note: only the subject forms of these pronouns have been given.)

The lesson to be learned here is that you cannot assume that another language will make distinctions in the same way that English does. For example, while every language has some method of indicating number, not all languages do so in the same way or under the same circumstances. As we've seen, English uses an affix, Tagalog uses a separate word, and Indonesian reduplicates the word to show plural. Nor can you assume that the distinctions English makes are the only ones worth making. Languages must be examined carefully on the grounds of their own internal structures.

MORPHOLOGY: MORPHOLOGY PROBLEMS

The following problems are provided to give you practice in doing morphemic analysis problems at the beginning, intermediate, and advanced levels. Be sure to read the directions to each problem carefully. As with the phonology problems, there is enough critical data from each language to enable you to discover the correct generalizations.

I. Beginning
I.1 Turkish

Examine the following data from Turkish and answer the questions that follow.

1. [deniz]	'an ocean'	9. [elim]	'my hand'
2. [denize]	'to an ocean'	10. [eller]	'hands'
3. [denizin]	'of an ocean'	11. [disler]	'teeth'
4. [eve]	'to a house'	12. [disimizin]	'of our tooth'
5. [evden]	'from a house'	13. [dislerimizin]	'of our teeth'
6. [evcikden]	'from a little house'	14. [elcike]	'to a little hand'
7. [denizcikde]	'in a little ocean'	15. [denizlerimizde]	'in our oceans'
8. [elde]	'in a hand'	16. [evciklerimizde]	'in our little houses'

Give the Turkish morpheme which corresponds to each of the following English translations.

_____ ocean	_____ plural	_____ my
_____ house	_____ to	_____ of
_____ hand	_____ from	_____ our
_____ tooth	_____ in	_____ little

What is the order of morphemes in a Turkish word (in terms of noun, preposition, plural marker, determiner, and 'little')?

What would be the Turkish word meaning 'of our little hands'?

I.2 Bontoc
Examine the Bontoc (a Phillipine Island language) data below and answer the questions which follow.

1. [fikas]	'strong'	5. [fumikas]	'he is becoming strong'
2. [kilad]	'red'	6. [kumilad]	'he is becoming red'
3. [bato]	'stone'	7. [bumato]	'he is becoming stone'
4. [fusul]	'enemy'	8. [fumusul]	'he is becoming an enemy'

What morphological process is used to form the verbs?

What type of affix is used to form the verbs? Describe its form and relationship to the rest of the word.

Given [pusi] 'poor', what would be the most likely meaning of /pumusi/?
Given [ŋitad] 'dark', what would be the most likely form meaning 'he is becoming dark'?
Given [pumukaw] 'he is becoming white', what is the most likely form meaning 'white'?

I.3 Luiseño

Examine the following data from Luiseño, a Uto-Aztecan language of Southern California, and answer the questions that follow.

1. [nokaamay]	'my son'		13. [pokaamay]	'his son'
2. [ʔoki]	'your house'		14. [poki]	'his house'
3. [potaana]	'his blanket'		15. [notaana]	'my blanket'
4. [ʔohuukapi]	'your pipe'		16. [pohuukapi]	'his pipe'
5. [ʔotaana]	'your blanket'		17. [nohuukapi]	'my pipe'
6. [noki]	'my house'		18. [ʔokaamay]	'your son'
7. [ʔomkim]	'your (pl.) houses'		19. [pompeewum]	'their wives'
8. [nokaamayum]	'my sons'		20. [pomki]	'their house'
9. [popeew]	'his wife'		21. [čampeewum]	'our wives'
10. [ʔopeew]	'your wife'		22. [čamhuukapi͟ɨm]	'our pipes'
11. [ʔomtaana]	'your (pl.) blanket'		23. [ʔomtaanam]	'your (pl.) blankets'
12. [čamhuukapi]	'our pipe'		24. [pomkaamay]	'their son'

Give the Luiseño morpheme which corresponds to each English translation. Note that the plural marker has two allomorphs; list them both.

_____ son	_____ my	_____ their
_____ house	_____ his	_____ plural marker
_____ blanket	_____ your (sg.)	_____ pipe
_____ wife	_____ your (pl.)	_____ our

Are the allomorphs of the plural marker phonologically conditioned?

If so, what are the conditioning environments?

I.4   Quiché

Some sentences from Quiché, an American Indian language spoken in Guatemala, South America, are given below with their English translation. Analyze the morphemes in these sentences and then fill in the exercises which follow the language data. Note that [x] is a voiceless velar fricative.

Quiché	**English**
1. [kiŋsikíx le líbr]	'I read (present tense) the book.'
2. [kusikíx le líbr]	'He reads the book.'
3. [kiŋwetamáx le kém]	'I learn the (art of) weaving.'
4. [kataxín kiŋwetamáx le kém]	'I continually learn the (art of) weaving.'
5. [kataxín kawetamáx le kém]	'You continually learn the (art of) weaving.'
6. [šiŋwetamáx]	'I learned (it).'
7. [šuwetamáx le kém]	'He learned the (art of) weaving.'
8. [šasikíx le líbr iwír]	'You read the book yesterday.'

Fill in the blanks with the corresponding Quiché morphemes.

A. Pronouns singular subject		**B. Verbs**		**C. Tenses**		**D. Other**	
(I)	_____	learn	_____	present	_____	continually	_____
(He)	_____	read	_____	past	_____	the	_____
(You)	_____					book	_____
						weaving	_____
						yesterday	_____

E. What is the order of Quiché morphemes (in terms of subject, verb, object, and tense)?

I.5 Michoacan Aztec

Examine the following words from Michoacan Aztec, and answer the questions that follow.

[nokali]	'my house'	[mopelo]	'your dog'
[nokalimes]	'my houses'	[mopelomes]	'your dogs'
[mokali]	'your house'	[ipelo]	'his dog'
[ikali]	'his house'	[nokwahmili]	'my cornfield'
[kali]	'house'	[mokwahmili]	'your cornfield'
[kalimes]	'houses'	[ikwahmili]	'his cornfield'
[nopelo]	'my dog'	[ikwahmilimes]	'his cornfields'

Fill in the blanks with the corresponding Michoacan morphemes:

_____	house	_____	my
_____	dog	_____	your
_____	cornfield	_____	his
		_____	plural

What does *ipelo* mean in this language?

How would you say 'his cornfields' in Michoacan?

I.6 Cebuano

The following noun paridigm is from Cebuano, a language of the Philippines. State the rule (in words, precisely) for deriving language names from the names of ethnic groups. What type of affixation is this?

[bisaya]	'a Visayan'	[binisaya]	'the Visayan language'
[inglis]	'an Englishman'	[ininglis]	'the English language'
[tagalog]	'a Tagalog person'	[tinagalog]	'the Tagalog language'
[ilokano]	'an Ilocano'	[inilokano]	'the Ilocano language'
[sibwano]	'a Cebuano'	[sinibwano]	'the Cebuano language'

I.7 Isleta

Consider the following data from Isleta:

[temiban]	'I went'	[mimiay]	'he was going'
[amiban]	'you went'	[tewanban]	'I came'
[temiwe]	'I'm going'	[tewanhi]	'I will come'

List the morphemes corresponding to the following English translations.

_____ I		_____ present progressive	
_____ you		_____ past progressive	
_____ he		_____ past	
_____ go		_____ future	
_____ come			

What sort of affixes are the subject morphemes?

What sort of affixes are the tense morphemes?

What is the order of morphemes in this language?

How would you say the following in Isleta?

'he went'

'I will go'

'you were coming'

I.8 Isthmus Zapotec
Consider the following data from Isthmus Zapotec:

1. [ñee]	'foot'		11. [kazigitu]	'your (pl.) chins'
2. [kañee]	'feet'		12. [kazigidu]	'our chins'
3. [ñeebe]	'his foot'		13. [zike]	'shoulder'
4. [kañeebe]	'his feet'		14. [zikebe]	'his shoulder'
5. [ñeeluʔ]	'your foot'		15. [kazikeluʔ]	'your shoulders'
6. [kañeetu]	'your (pl.) feet'		16. [diaga]	'ear'
7. [kañeedu]	'our feet'		17. [kadiagatu]	'your (pl.) ears'
8. [kazigi]	'chins'		18. [kadiagadu]	'our ears'
9. [zigibe]	'his chin'		19. [bisozedu]	'our father'
10. [zigiluʔ]	'your chin'		20. [bisozetu]	'your (pl.) father'
			21. [kabisozetu]	'your (pl.) fathers'

List the morphemes of Isthmus Zapotec which correspond to each of the following English translations.

foot	your
chin	his
shoulder	our
ear	your (pl.)
father	plural

What is the order of morphemes in Isthmus Zapotec (in terms of noun, possessive, and plural)?

II. Intermediate

II.1 Swahili

Examine the Swahili data which follows and (1) fill in the blanks with the corresponding Swahili morphemes in B and indicate the order in which the Swahili morphemes occur in an utterance (in this case what a speaker of Swahili would call a *word*); (2) translate the English examples in C into Swahili; (3) translate the Swahili examples in D into English.

A.

Transcription	Gloss	Transcription	Gloss
1. [atanipenda]	'he will like me'	15. [atanipiga]	'he will beat me'
2. [atakupenda]	'he will like you'	16. [atakupiga]	'he will beat you'
3. [atampenda]	'he will like him'	17. [atampiga]	'he will beat him'
4. [atatupenda]	'he will like us'	18. [ananipiga]	'he is beating me'
5. [atawapenda]	'he will like them'	19. [anakupiga]	'he is beating you'
6. [nitakupenda]	'I will like you'	20. [anampiga]	'he is beating him'
7. [nitampenda]	'I will like him'	21. [amekupiga]	'he has beaten you'
8. [nitawapenda]	'I will like them'	22. [amenipiga]	'he has beaten me'
9. [utanipenda]	'you will like me'	23. [amempiga]	'he has beaten him'
10. [utampenda]	'you will like him'	24. [alinipiga]	'he beat me'
11. [tutampenda]	'we will like him'	25. [alikupiga]	'he beat you'
12. [watampenda]	'they will like him'	26. [alimpiga]	'he beat him'
13. [atakusumbua]	'he will annoy you'	27. [wametulipa]	'they have paid us'
14. [unamsumbua]	'you are annoying him'	28. [tulikulipa]	'we paid you'

B. Pronouns

	Subject				Object		
	Singular		**Plural**		**Singular**		**Plural**
1. (I) _____		(we) _____		(me) _____		(us) _____	
2. (you) _____		(you) X X X X		(you) _____		(you) X X X X	
3. (he/she) _____		(they) _____		(him/her) _____		(them) _____	

Verbs

like _____	annoy _____	beat _____	pay _____

Tenses

past _____	future _____	present _____ (progressive)	present perfect _____ (in English: with has/have)

Order of Swahili morphemes (in terms of subject, object, verb, and tense):

_____ – _____ – _____ – _____

C. Translation

1. I have beaten them. _____

2. They are beating me. _____

3. They have annoyed me. _____

4. You have beaten us. _____

5. We beat them. _____

6. I am paying him. _____

D. Translation

1. atanilipa _____

2. utawapiga _____

3. walikupenda _____

4. nimemsumbua _____

II.3 Cree

Do a morphological analysis of the Cree data below (Cree is an Algonquian Indian language spoken in Canada) and answer the questions which follow:

1. [či:ma:n]	'canoe'		12. [nitospwa:kan]	'my pipe'
2. [niči:ma:n]	'my canoe'		13. [akimew]	'he counts'
3. [so:niya]	'money'		14. [nitakimen]	'I count'
4. [niso:niya]	'my money'		15. [apiw]	'he sits'
5. [wiyas:š]	'meat'		16. [nɪtapin]	'I sit'
6. [niwiya:š]	'my meat'		17. [ispelohkew]	'he rests'
7. [e:mihkwa:n]	'spoon'		18. [nitispeloken]	'I rest'
8. [nite:mihkwa:n]	'my spoon'		19. [kaakimew]	'he will count'
9. [astotin]	'hat'		20. [nikaakimen]	'I will count'
10. [nitastotin]	'my hat'		21. [kaapiw]	'he will sit'
11. [ospwa:kaɹ]	'pipe'		22. [nikaapin]	'I will sit'

What are the Cree morphemes for:

_____ I _____ my _____ he _____ will (future tense)

What are the allomorphs for 'I' and 'my'? What are the conditioning environments?

How does the morpheme 'I' differ from the morpheme 'my'?

II. 3 Zoque

Examine the following data from Zoque, a language of Mexico, and answer the questions that follow.

1. [kenu]	'he looked'		1a. [kenpa]	'he looks'	
2. [sihku]	'he laughed'		2a. [sikpa]	'he laughs'	
3. [wihtu]	'he walked'		3a. [witpa]	'he walks'	
4. [kaʔu]	'he died'		4a. [kaʔpa]	'he dies'	
5. [cihcu]	'it tore'		5a. [cicpa]	'it tears'	
6. [sohsu]	'it cooked'		6a. [sospa]	'it cooks'	

What is the Zoque morpheme indicating the past tense?

What is the Zoque morpheme meaning 'he' or 'it'?

List the allomorphs of each of the verb stem morphemes, along with their meanings.

What conditions the appearance of these allomorphs? What phonological process is applying?

II.4   Hanunoo

Examine the Hanunoo (a language from the Philippine Islands) data below. Two affixes are illustrated in these data. Identify each of them, state what kind of affix each one is, and tell what information each one provides.

What phonological processes are evidenced in the two morphophonemic changes in the roots?

1. [ʔusa]	'one'	8. [kasʔa]	'once'	15. [ʔusahi]	'make it one'
2. [duwa]	'two'	9. [kadwa]	'twice'	16. [duwahi]	'make it two'
3. [tulu]	'three'	10. [katlu]	'three times'	17. [tuluhi]	'make it three'
4. [ʔupat]	'four'	11. [kapʔat]	'four times'	18. [ʔupati]	'make it four'
5. [lima]	'five'	12. [kalima]	'five times'	19. [limahi]	'make it five'
6. [ʔunum]	'six'	13. [kanʔum]	'six times'	20. [ʔunumi]	'make it six'
7. [pitu]	'seven'	14. [kapitu]	'seven times'	21. [pituhi]	'make it seven'

III. Advanced

III.1 Hungarian

Analyze the Hungarian data below. What are the allomorphs of the Hungarian plural? State the conditioning environments.

Gloss	Singular	Plural
1. 'table'	[astal]	[astalok]
2. 'worker'	[munka:š]	[munka:šok]
3. 'man'	[ember]	[emberek]
4. 'white'	[fehe:r]	[fehe:rek]
5. 'this'	[ez]	[ezek]
6. 'line'	[šor]	[šorok]
7. 'eyeglasses'	[semüveg]	[semüvegek]
8. 'shirt'	[iŋ]	[iŋek]
9. 'head'	[fey]	[feyek]
10. 'box'	[doboz]	[dobozok]
11. 'drum'	[dob]	[dobok]
12. 'age'	[kor]	[korok]
13. 'coat'	[kaba:t]	[kaba:tok]
14. 'flower'	[vira:g]	[vira:gok]

[handwritten notes:]
[ok] after [l], [š], [z],
[b], [r], [
[al], [a:š], [or],
[oz], [ob],
[or], [a:t], [a:g]

[ek] after [er], [e:r], [ez],
[eg], [iŋ], [ey]

III.2 Popoluca

Examine the following data from Popoluca, a language of Mexico.

1. [ʔiŋkuʔtpa] 'you (sg.) eat it'
2. [ʔanhokspa] 'I hoe it'
3. [ʔikuʔt] 'he ate it'
4. [ʔimo·ya] 'his flower'
5. [mo·ya] 'flower'
6. [ʔampetpa] 'I sweep it'
7. [ʔimpet] 'you swept it'
8. [ʔantək] 'my house'
9. [ʔiñhokspa] 'you hoe it'
10. [no·mi] 'boss'
11. [ʔano·mi] 'my boss'
12. [ʔika·ma] 'his cornfield'
13. [ʔiŋka·ma] 'your (sg.) cornfield'
14. [ʔamo·ya] 'my flower'
15. [ʔino·mi] 'your (sg.) boss'

List all of the Popoluca allomorphs corresponding to the following.

cornfield	_____		past tense	_____
flower	_____		present tense	_____
boss	_____		I/my	_____
house	_____		you/your (sg.)	_____
eat	_____		he/his	_____
sweep	_____			
hoe	_____			

State the phonetic environments which condition the occurrence of allomorphs, when one morpheme has more than one allomorph.

III.3 Mongolian

		Stem -	Future Imperative
1.	enter	or-	oro:roy
2.	go	yav-	yava:ray
3.	sit	su:-	su:ga:ray
4.	come	ir-	ire:rey
5.	do	xi:-	xi:ge:rey
6.	come out	gar-	gara:ray
7.	take	av-	ava:ray
8.	study	sur-	sura:ray
9.	finish	büte:-	büte:ge:rey
10.	drink	ü:-	ü:gö:röy
11.	find out	ol-	olo:roy
12.	conquer	yal-	yala:ray
13.	ask	asu:-	asu:ga:ray
14.	finish	tögsg-	tögsgö:röy
15.	beat	dev-	deve:rey
16.	give	ög-	ögo:röy
17.	say	xel-	xele:rey
18.	meet	u:lz-	u:lza:ray
19.	become	bol-	bolo:roy
20.	write	bič-	biče:rey
21.	develop	xögž-	xögžö:röy

List all of the allomorphs of the Mongolian future imperative marker. What environments condition their appearance?

MORPHOLOGY: MORPHOLOGICAL TYPES OF LANGUAGES

Languages are often classified according to the way in which they put morphemes together to form words. The classification is often made on the basis of *morphological* type because the morphological type of a language may reflect both the phonological characteristics and the syntactic characteristics of the language. According to this criterion of classification, there are two basic types (and several subtypes) of language structure that are traditionally designated — that is, there are two basic types of language.

ANALYTIC (ISOLATING) LANGUAGES

Analytic or isolating languages are so called because they are made up of sequences of free morphemes — each word consists of a single morpheme, used by itself with meaning intact. Purely analytic languages do not use prefixes or suffixes to compose words. Semantic concepts which are often expressed in other languages (like English) through the use of suffixes are thus expressed in isolating languages by the use of separate words.

The dialect of Chinese spoken in Peking — called Mandarin or Pekingese — has a highly analytical structure. In the example sentences below, for instance, the concept of plurality and the concept of past tense are shown in Mandarin through the use of free morphemes rather than the use of a change of form (e.g., *I* to *we* to indicate plurality) or the use of a suffix (e.g., *-ed* for past tense).

    a. [wɔ mən tan tɕin]   Literal translation: I-plural play piano
                                          'We are playing the piano.'

    b. [wɔ mən tan tɕin lʌ]   Literal translation: I-plural play piano past
                                            'We played the piano.'

(As the above sentences demonstrate, the basic order of elements in Mandarin is subject — verb — direct object.)

Note that the form of 'we' (I-plural) that is used in the subject position is [wo mən], and that the pronoun has the same form when it is used as the object, placed after the verb.

    c. [ta da wɔ mən]   Literal translation: he hit(s) I-plural
                                            'He hits us.'

The position of a word in a sentence alone shows its function. English is unlike Chinese in this respect, since the personal pronoun *we* is changed in form to *us* when it is used as the object of a verb. But English is like Chinese in that word order is used to show the functions of nouns in a sentence, and in that nouns (unlike pronouns) are not marked (by affixes) to show their functions.

SYNTHETIC LANGUAGES

In synthetic languages, affixes or bound morphemes are attached to other morphemes, so that a word may be made up of several meaningful elements. The bound morphemes may indicate the grammatical function of the stem in a sentence to add another element of meaning to the stem. The term *stem* refers to that part of the word to which affixes are added. It may consist of one or more morphemes: for instance, in *reruns*, *-s* is added to the stem *rerun*, which is itself made up of two morphemes.

Hungarian is a synthetic language. In the examples below, bound morphemes show the grammatical functions of nouns in their sentences:

    a. Az ember lát a kutyát.   Literal translation: the man sees the dog-object
        [ɔz ˈɛmber lɑːt ɔ ˈkutyaːt]   ‘The man sees the dog.’

    b. a kutya lát az embert.   Literal translation: the dog sees the man-object.
        [ɔ ˈkutyɔ lɑːt ɔz ˈɛmbert]   ‘The dog sees the man.’

Note that in English it is the position of the noun phrase *the man* and *the dog* in the sentence that tells one whether the phrase is the subject or object of the verb, but in Hungarian (and other synthetic languages), however, a noun or noun phrase may appear either before or following the verb in a sentence and be recognized as the subject or object in either position due to the fact that it is marked with a bound morpheme (the suffix [t] in Hungarian) as being the Direct Object. So both examples below mean the same thing, even though the position of the noun phrase meaning ‘the man’ is different with respect to the verb meaning ‘sees’.

    c. A kutya lát az embert.   Literal translation: the dog sees the man-object
        [ɔ ˈkutyɔ lɑːt ɔz ˈɛmbert]   ‘The dog sees the man.’

    d. Az embert lát a kutya.   Literal translation: the man-object sees the dog
        [ɔz ˈɛmbert lɑːt ɔ ˈkutyɔ]   ‘The dog sees the man.’

Synthetic languages like Hungarian also use bound morphemes to indicate some concepts which English signals by way of free morphemes. For example, you will note that in the following example sentences, Hungarian indicates personal possession and location by the use of suffixes attached to the stem *ház* ‘house’, whereas, in the English translations, these concepts are expressed by the use of free morphemes.

    e. A házunk zöld.   Literal translation: the house-our green
        [ɔ ˈhaːzuŋk zöld]   ‘Our house is green.’

    f. A házod fehér.   Literal translation: the house-your white
        [ɔ ˈhaːzod ˈfɛheːr]   ‘Your house is white.’

    g. A széked a házunkban van.   Literal translation: the chair-your house-our-in is
        [ɔ ˈseːkɛd ɔ ˈhaːzuŋkbɔn vɔn]   ‘Your chair is in our house.’

Agglutinating Languages

The kind of synthesis (putting together) of morphemes we find in Hungarian is known as agglutination. In agglutinating languages, like Hungarian, the morphemes are relatively ‘loosely’ joined together — that is, it is usually easy to determine where the boundaries between morphemes are, e.g., *haz-unk-ban*: house-our-in ‘in our house’; *haz-od*: house-your ‘your house’; etc.

Swahili is another example of an agglutinating language. Swahili verb stems take prefixes to indicate the person (first, second, or third) of the subject of the verb and also to indicate the tense of the verb, as in the following list of forms for the verb ‘read’.

ni-na-soma	I-present-read	‘I am reading.’
u-na-soma	you-present-read	‘You are reading.’
a-na-soma	he-present-read	‘He is reading.’
ni-li-soma	I-past-read	‘I was reading.’
u-li-soma	you-past-read	‘You were reading.’
a-li-soma	he-past-read	‘He was reading.’
ni-ta-soma	I-future-read	‘I will read.’
u-ta-soma	you-future-read	‘You will read.’
a-ta-soma	he-future-read	‘He will read.’

A second characteristic feature of agglutinating languages is that each bound morpheme carries (ordinarily) only one meaning: *ni-na-soma*: I-present-read ‘I am reading’; *ni-li-soma*: I-past-read ‘I was reading’; etc.

Fusional Languages

In fusional languages, words are formed by adding bound morphemes to stems, just as in agglutinating languages, but in fusional languages the affixes may not be easy to separate from the stem — it is often rather hard to tell where one morpheme ends and the next begins; the affixes are characteristically *fused* with the stem.

Spanish is a fusional language which has suffixes attached to the verb stem to indicate the person (I/you/he) and number (singular/plural) of the subject of the verb. It is often difficult to analyze a verb form into its stem and suffix, however, due to the fact that there is often a fusion of the two morphemes. For example in the forms:

a. hablo
['ablo] 'I am speaking'   [–o] first person singular present tense

b. habla
['abla] 'He (or she) is speaking.'   [–a] third person singular present tense

c. hablé
[ab'le] 'I spoke.'   [– e] first person singular past tense

It is difficult to separate out a stem which means 'speak'. The form *habl-* ['abl‿] never appears in Spanish. In the following forms:

d. hablamos
[ab'lamos] 'We are speaking.'   [–mos] first person plural present tense

e. habla
['ablan] 'They are speaking.'   [–n] third person plural present tense

It seems possible to say that the verb stem is *habla-* ['abla‿], to which the suffixes [–mos] and [–n] are added. But in the case of examples (a), (b), and (c) above, it is apparent that if there is a stem ['abla-], it has been fused together with the suffixes [–o], [–a], and [–e].

Fusional languages often differ from agglutinating languages in another way as well: agglutinating languages usually have only one meaning indicated by each affix, but in fusional languages a single affix may convey several meanings. Russian is a fusional language in which bound morphemes attached to verb stems indicate the person and number of the subject of the verb and the tense of the verb at one and the same time. For example, in the verb form:

f. [či'tayɛt]   'he is reading'

the bound form [–yɛt] signifies third person, singular and present tense, simultaneously. In the form:

g. [či'tal]   'he was reading'

the suffix [– al] means singular, masculine, and past tense, simultaneously. (Compare the Swahili examples, page 54-2, where person and tense are signalled by separate affixes.)

Polysynthetic Languages

In some languages, highly complex words may be formed by combining several stems and affixes; this is usually a matter of making nouns (subjects, objects, etc.) into parts of the verb forms. Sora, a tribal language spoken in India, allows such *incorporation* of objects (subjects, instruments, etc.) into verbs:

a. [anin ɲamyɔten]
anin   ɲam - yɔ - te   –n
he   catch fish non-past do
'He is fish-catching.' — i.e., 'He is catching fish.'

b. [ɲamkɨdtenai]
ɲam - kɨd - te   – n - ai
catch tiger non-past do first person agent
'I will tiger-catch.' — i.e., 'I will catch a tiger.'

Such verbs are roughly comparable to an English construction like *baby-sit*, but the polysynthetic constructions may be more complex, including several nouns as well as a variety of other affixes:

c. [pɔpoŋkontam]

   pɔ – poŋ – kon – t – am

   stab belly knife non-past thee

   '(Someone) will stab you with a knife in (your) belly.'

d. [ɲɛn əɟɟaḏarsiəm]

   ɲɛn əɟ – ja – dar – si – əm

   I not receive cooked rice hand thee

   'I will not receive cooked rice from your hands.'

(The *incorporated* or 'built-in' form of the noun is not necessarily identical to its free form. In Sora, the free form of 'tiger' is [kɨna]; that of 'hand' is [siʔi]; that of 'knife' is [kondi].

SUMMARY

From the language discussion, we can extract the following statements about language types.

1. *Analytic* languages signify the meanings of sentences through the use of isolated morphemes. They do not use affixes (prefixes or suffixes).

2. *Synthetic* languages signify the meanings of sentences by combining free and bound morphemes to make up words:

   a) *Agglutinating* languages are languages in which the affixes can easily be separated from the stems to which they are attached, and in which each affix generally conveys only one meaning.

   b) *Fusional* languages are languages in which the affixes and the base to which they are attached are fused together in pronunciation, as a result of phonological processes or change and therefore not easily separated from one another. In addition, there is generally a fusion of meanings that are represented by the affixes in such languages.

   c) *Polysynthetic* languages are languages in which several stem forms may be combined (along with affixes) into a single word. Such a word is usually a verb with its associated nouns 'built-in' or *incorporated*, so that the verb alone expresses what seems to us to be about the equivalent of a whole sentence.

It is important to note that languages are rarely 'pure' types — they usually combine elements of a variety of types.

INTRODUCTION: SYNTAX

Syntax is the study of the structure of sentences. It attempts to uncover the underlying principles, or *rules,* for constructing well-formed sentences of a particular language. The set of rules constitutes the *grammar* of that language. The rules must produce *only* well-formed sentences and *all* well-formed sentences of a language. By all sentences, we include not only all actual sentences, but all the possible sentences as well, which may never have been uttered but must be accepted by native speakers as well-formed. One such possible sentence could be *Green cheese will fall from the moon tonight.* The state of affairs predicted by the sentence is unlikely to obtain, but the sentence is nonetheless grammatically correct.

Since the ability to construct and recognize well-formed sentences is part of the native speaker's linguistic competence, syntax can also be taken as the description of the native speaker's syntactic competence. The grammar we construct should mirror this competence. In fact, constructing the grammar is the only way to describe competence, since competence is mental and not subject to direct observation.

What are the rules in syntax? First of all, there are two types of rules, *phrase structure rules* and *transformational rules.* The first type involves formal statements of two kinds of facts about the organization of the sentence. Such a rule describes the internal composition of syntactic units, i.e. sentences and phrases, showing what kinds of smaller units they are made up of. It also describes the ordering between these smaller components. For example, a rule of the form S ——→ NP VP can be interpreted as 'a sentence can consist of the component units NP (a noun phrase) and VP (a verb phrase), which are ordered in the way stated'.

It is hardly anything new that sentences have internal composition. We all know they are formed from words. Nor is it particularly shocking that things are ordered in a sentence. We know that words have to be uttered one by one, and it matters in what order we utter them. What is perhaps not so familiar is the idea that there are syntactic units other than words and sentences in our grammar, and that statements about the internal composition and ordering of these units also have to be made. These units are *phrases.* In fact, the rules in our grammar are called *phrase structure rules.* Phrase structure rules are also called *constituent structure rules* because words, phrases, and sentences can all be constituents in larger combinations.

Constituents belong to *syntactic categories* of various types and sizes, such as nouns, verbs, adjectives, noun phrases, verb phrases, sentences and so on. What the phrase (constituent) structure rules actually do is to specify the internal composition and the ordering of different syntactic categories.

What is the second type of rule, then? We know that as native speakers we not only recognize sentences as being well-formed, we also know which sentences are related to each other, such as a declarative sentence like *I like bananas* and its question counterpart *What do I like.* It is the linguist's task to account for such native speaker intuition. To describe the related sentences independently of each other would fail to explain the native speaker's feeling of their relatedness. Some syntacticians have tried to account for this relatedness by proposing that these related sentences have the same structure at a deeper level of the grammar but diverge into different structures at the surface. In technical terms, the related sentences share the same *deep structures,* i.e. are produced with the same set of phrase structure rules, but come to have different *surface structures* due to *transformational rules,* the second type of rule in syntax.

The grammar that results, with the dual components of phrase structure rules and transformational rules, is a *transformational-generative grammar,* schematized as follows:

Phrase structure rules (constituent structure rules)

↓

Deep structure
(meaning given here)

↓

Transformational rules

↓

Surface structure
(pronunciation given here)

To generate a sentence by this grammar, first an appropriate set of phrase structure rules is used to form a deep structure. After undergoing a certain number of transformations, the structure becomes the surface structure to be pronounced. Two sentences like *John gave the book to Mary* and *John gave Mary the book* are generated by using the same set of phrase structure rules. They have the same deep structure and the same meaning. The only difference is that one of them undergoes one more transformation and thus comes to have a different surface structure from the other one.

In this section we explain and justify more carefully this model of grammar. In File 61, word classes are discussed. A contrast is made between the traditional, prescriptive definition of 'parts of speech' and the descriptive definition of word classes as lexical categories. File 62 motivates the concept of constituent. File 63 classifies the different kinds of constituents into syntactic categories of various kinds. File 64 introduces the formal statement and properties of phrase structure rules. File 65 justifies the tranformational component in the grammar. File 66 contrasts different languages from a syntactic point of view.

It should be kept in mind that the grammar we present in this section is only a very incomplete fragment of the grammar of English, due to the limitation of space and pedagogical considerations. Its inadequacies are many. In a real sense, the grammar is a 'toy grammar', to be played with and experimented on. We hope you will learn the principles of syntactic investigation better by pointing out the inadequacies of the grammar and remedying them so that it will better approximate the grammar of English. This kind of activity is essentially what the linguist is engaged in all the time.

SYNTAX: PARTS OF SPEECH AND LEXICAL CATEGORIES

There is a long tradition of morphological and syntactic studies in the western world, beginning with the descriptions written by the ancient Greek and Latin grammarians. A major part of their description involves a terminology for talking about basic sentence units: the parts of speech. To understand sentence structure, we must first learn to recognize these basic units. The first half of this file will address this issue using a traditional approach since this approach introduces terminology in a fairly intuitive, albeit simplistic, way. The second half will address the same issue using a descriptive approach, the approach that linguists prefer since it deals with the formal properties of language.

PARTS OF SPEECH — A TRADITIONAL APPROACH

Traditional grammar, what teachers taught us in grade school English and language arts classes, tells us that there are eight parts of speech:

(1) a. noun(N): a word which names a person, place, or thing. (e.g. Tom, Buffalo, motorcycle)
   b. pronoun(PRO): a word which can replace a noun. (e.g. he, it)
   c. adjective(ADJ): a word which modifies a noun. (e.g. handsome, busy, sleek)
   d. verb(V): a word which names an action or a state of being. (e.g. run, hit, is)
   e. adverb(ADV): a word which modifies a verb, adjective, or adverb. (e.g. quickly, very)
   f. preposition(P): a word which shows some relationship between a noun/pronoun and another word in a sentence. (e.g. in, on, from, by, to)
   g. conjunction(CONJ): a word which connects words or phrases. (e.g. and, but, or)
   h. interjection(INTERJ): a word used as an exclamation. (e.g. oh, ah, well, yeah)

Despite the fact that these definitions are clear-cut and easy to learn, identifying a word based on them can be difficult. Consider the word "painting". Is it a noun referring to an object, or is it a verb referring to an action? The answer we decide upon depends on context:

(2) a. I hung the painting on the wall.
   b. We have been painting the house for days.

In (2a), "painting" is a noun, but in (2b) it is a verb. We cannot attempt to accurately identify a word's part of speech in isolation. Instead, we must consider the word's function in a whole sentence.

Let us try to label all of the words in the following sentence:

(3) The very tall boy ran quickly.

We first begin by trying to identify the verb in the sentence. In this case the verb is "ran", an action word. Having found the verb, we can usually divide the sentence into its subject and predicate.

(4)   The very tall boy/ran quickly
         subject   predicate

The subject consists of a noun phrase which tells who or what is doing the action. To identify the subject, we can ask the question: Who or what V? In our sentence, the answer would be "the very tall boy". Since this subject is a noun phrase, we know that it must contain a noun, "boy", naming a person. The other words must be related to the noun, so we must try to identify their function. "Tall" describes the boy, so since it is modifying a noun, we know that it is an adjective. "Very" tells the degree to which the boy is tall, so since it modifies an adjective, it must be an adverb. "The" denotes that we are referring to a particular boy, but it does not fall into any of the traditional parts of speech. We will refer to it as a determiner (DET). The predicate consists of a verb, which we have identified as "ran" and any other words which directly relate to that verb. In our sentence, we have only one other word in the predicate, "quickly", which tells in what manner the boy ran. Since it modifies the verb, it must be an adverb.

Nouns and verbs can play various roles in a sentence. Sometimes identifying these roles helps to identify these parts of speech. As we have seen, a noun can be the subject of a sentence. It can have other roles as well depending on the verb. In (3), the verb "ran" is more specifically called an intransitive verb because it can stand alone as the whole predicate:

(5)   The very tall boy/ran.

Some verbs, however, cannot stand alone. For example, we cannot say (6):

(6)   *The very tall boy hit.

The sentence sounds incomplete. "Hit", then, is known as a transitive verb, a verb which must be followed by a noun:

(7)   The very tall boy hit the ball.

The noun which receives the action, "ball", is known as the direct object. Sometimes a sentence with a transitive verb will have more than one noun directly related to it in the predicate:

(8)   I sent Mary a letter.

To identify the direct object, we can ask: V what? or in this case *sent* what? The answer, *letter,* is the direct object. This leaves *Mary* which we know is a noun because it names a person. We refer to this noun as the indirect object because it receives the result of the action on the direct object. To identify the indirect object we can ask the question: for/to whom V direct object? Another type of verb is a linking verb or copula. Unlike transitive and intransitive verbs, these verbs do not refer to actions. Instead they refer to states of being. Verbs such as *to-be, seems* and *looks,* often function as linking verbs. When a linking verb is used, it is followed by an adjective or a noun which tell something about the subject.

(9)   He looks tall.
(10)   He is a clown.

The adjective and nouns which follow the linking verb are known as predicate adjectives and predicate nouns. A final type of verb is an auxiliary (AUX) or helping verb. These are verbs which precede the main verb in a sentence.

(11)   I will come home soon.

In (11) *will* is the helping verb and *come* is the main verb.

156

LEXICAL CATEGORIES — A DESCRIPTIVE APPROACH

While understanding traditional grammar does help to identify the parts of speech, structuralist grammar provides a different approach, dividing words into two major classes: open classes and closed classes. The open classes include nouns, verbs, adjectives, and adverbs. Each class can be defined by formal, distributional features which we can classify as morphological and syntactic frames. Morphological frames help identify a lexical class by stating the type of morphemes that can be attached to each word in a class. Syntactic frames state the type of words that can precede or follow each word in a class.

Nouns have two morphological frames: the plural and the possessive. In general, a plural noun will have an -s or an -es ending and a possessive noun will have an -'s ending. Pronouns, a subclass of nouns, have subject and object inflected forms as well as plural and possessive:

(12)

	subject		object	
	sing.	plural	sing.	plural
1st person	I	we	me	us
2nd person	you	you	you	you
3rd person	he, she, it	they	him, her, it	them

	possessive	
	sing	plural
1st person	my	our
2nd person	your	your
3rd person	his, her, its	their

Syntactic frames for nouns include precedence by determiners, possessive pronouns, and adjectives:

(13) the dog   (det N)
(14) my dog   (poss. PRO N)
(15) brown dog   (ADJ N)

We can write sentences with blanks to illustrate a syntactic frame for a noun:

(16)   The_____ is here. These_____ are here.

If a word fits the blank, then we can use it as a noun.

Verbs have two morphological frames; they can be inflected for number and tense. Number agreement only appears in the present tense, an -s ending marking the 3rd person singular form:

(17)   a. I kiss Mary.   *I kisses Mary.
       b. You kiss Mary.   *You kisses Mary.
       c. *John kiss Mary.   John kisses Mary.
       d. We kiss Mary.   *We kisses Mary.
       e. You (pl.) kiss Mary.   *You kisses Mary.
       f. They kiss Mary.   *They kisses Mary.

As for tense, English has three basic tenses: present, past and future.

(18)   Present   Past   Future

a.   I crack   I cracked   I will crack
      He cracks   He cracked   He will crack

b.   I hit   I hit   I will hit
      He hits   He hit   He will hit

The regular method of creating the past tense is to add -ed to the verb, but as (18b) shows, there are irregularities. Future tense is not formed by inflection, but by using the auxiliary verb *will*. Other tense forms, such as the progressive and perfect forms, are formed from both inflectional suffixes and auxiliary verbs. The progressive usually indicates that an action is unfinished at the time referred to. Thus, there is a present progressive, *I am eating (now),* a past progressive, *I was eating (when you arrived),* and a future progressive, *I will be eating.* We form the perfect with the AUX *have,* attaching -ed or -en to the main verb. Syntactically, verbs should follow subject nouns and precede object nouns:

(19) The cat meowed.   (det N V)
(20) She hit the ball   (N V det N)

Again we can write sentences with blanks to illustrate these syntactic frames.

(21) The man_____something.
     The man_____friendly.

Finally, verbs may be the first word in imperative sentences:

(22)   Answer the phone.

For polite requests, rather than orders, the verb may be preceded by *Please.*

Adjectives have morphological frames for the comparative and superlative degrees, -er and -est respectively:

(23) happy, happier, happiest
(24) good, better, best

Sentence (23) illustrates the regular formation of the comparative and superlative whereas (24) illustrates an irregular form. Adjectives have two syntactic frames. They may precede nouns or follow linking verbs.

(25) the young penguin   (det ADJ N)
(26) The penguin is young.   (det N V ADJ)

Again, we can write a sentence illustrating this frame.

(27) The _____ penguin was very _____ .

The most commonly known morphological frame for *adverbs,* which many teachers tell their students about in grade school, is that adverbs are marked by an -ly ending.

(28) quickly, happily, sadly

Unfortunately, a number of adjectives may also have this *-ly* suffix:

(29) manly, queenly, kingly, princely, slovenly

Adverbs themselves may have different endings: *-ward, -wards, -wise* to name a few:

(30) westward, forwards, sexwise

Adverbs may also be difficult to identify using a syntactic frame because they have a tendency to be moveable; that is, they may appear almost anywhere in the sentence.

(31) Anxiously, the bride went to her wedding.
(32) The bride anxiously went to her wedding.
(33) The bride went anxiously to her wedding.
(34) The bride went to her wedding anxiously.

When trying to identify adverbs, sometimes it is simpler to figure out that they are not nouns, verbs, or adjectives.

Closed class words, better known as function words, are those which have little meaning outside of their grammatical purpose, to relate form class words to each other. They include determiners (DET), auxiliary verbs (AUX), prepositions (P), and conjunctions (CONJ). *Determiners* signal that a noun is following:

(35) The sky is falling.

Auxiliary verbs often indicate tense and aspect as we saw in our discussion of verbs. *Prepositions* begin prepositional phrases which act as adjectival or adverbial phrases:

(36) The man with the beard
(37) I ran to the store.

Finally, *conjunctions* join words and phrases.

(38) Bill and Sue went to a movie.
(39) Bill walked to school and to the library.
(40) I like ice cream and Joe likes cake.

Note than *and* is not the only conjunction. *But* and *or* are others:

(41) Sue works hard, but she enjoys her job.
(42) Joyce drives a car or rides her bike to school.

CONCLUSION

Identifying a word's part of speech is the first step in doing a syntactic analysis. For many students, this identification process poses no problem. For others, difficulty on this level may prevent understanding at the phrasal level (noun phrase, verb phrase, adjective phrase, prepositional phrase) or the clausal level (sentence). If recognizing and understanding the parts of speech remain a mystery, consult your instructor for additional help.

EXERCISES

For each of the following sentences, identify the part of speech of the underlined word.

1. My aunt runs a boarding <u>school</u> in Southern Ohio.
2. The Liberty Bell in Philadelphia has a <u>huge</u> crack in it.
3. I <u>would</u> have come to the party if I had had the time.
4. Sue <u>bought</u> a new Mercedes last week.
5. Bill ran <u>down</u> the street as quickly as he could.
6. The cat caught <u>the</u> mouse and ate him up.
7. <u>Give</u> me something unusual.
8. Dave rented a black tux <u>and</u> limousine for the prom.
9. My <u>favorite</u> cake is carrot cake with cream cheese icing.
10. In five years I will <u>gladly</u> retire.
11. <u>Do</u> storks really deliver babies?
12. Mom was <u>frantic</u> when she found out that you had been in an accident.
13. It <u>seems</u> that the natives are going to riot.
14. What are the <u>goals</u> of an astronaut?
15. Einstein was a <u>genius</u>.

SYNTAX: LINEAR ORDER AND HIERARCHICAL STRUCTURE

Though we use sentences all the time, we don't normally think about how they are structured; but a little consideration reveals that the principles by which words are organized into sentences are, in fact, quite complex. In this file, we will consider two basic principles of sentence organization; these are linear order and hierarchical structure.

I. LINEAR ORDER

The most obvious principle of sentence organization is linear order; the words in a sentence must occur in a particular sequence if the sentence is to convey the desired meaning. Consider, for example, the following sentence of English:

(1) John glanced at Mary.

If we rearrange the words in this sentence, we either come up with nonsense, as in (2) —

(2) Mary John at glanced.

or with a sentence whose meaning is distinctly different from that of (1) —

(3) Mary glanced at John.

Clearly, the ordering of the words in (1) is an essential aspect of its organization.

One of the many rules of English is that the grammatical subject of a sentence normally precedes the main verb, which in turn normally precedes its direct object; thus, *she resembles him* is English but *resembles she him* and *she him resembles* are not.

An important fact about rules of word order is that they are language-specific — that is, languages vary in the ways in which they order words. An example will bring this out. Because of its characteristic ordering of subjects (S), main verbs (V), and objects (O), English may be categorized as an 'S-V-O language' (other languages, such as French and Swahili, may be similarly categorized). But there are also S-O-V languages (e.g. Turkish, Navaho), in which main verbs normally follow their direct object; V-S-O languages (e.g. Welsh, Hebrew), in which main verbs normally precede their subject; and a small number of V-O-S, O-V-S, and O-S-V languages as well. In addition, there are languages (such as Dyirbal, an Australian aboriginal language) in which the normal order of subject, verb, and object is remarkably free. Clearly, there is no set of word order rules which is valid for all languages.

II. HIERARCHICAL STRUCTURE

Although linear order is an important principle of sentence organization, sentences are more than just ordered sequences of words: they have internal hierarchical structure as well. That is, the individual words in a sentence are organized into natural, semantically coherent groupings, which are themselves organized into larger groupings, the largest grouping of all being the sentence itself. These groupings within a sentence are called *constituents* of that sentence. The relationships between constituents in a sentence form the *constituent structure* of the sentence.

(4) Business executives eat at really fancy restaurants.

We can easily distinguish a number of meaningful groups of words in this sentence: *business executives* and *eat at really fancy restaurants,* for instance, have clear meanings of their own, and each makes a coherent contribution to the meaning of (4) as a whole. (Specifically, *business executives* is the subject of (4), and *eat at really fancy restaurants* is the predicate). For this reason, they are constituents of this sentence. On the other hand, some groups of words in sentence (4) do not naturally form meaningful units; *executives eat at* and *eat at really,* for example, don't have clear meanings of their own. Thus, these groups of words are *not* constituents of (4).

There are a number of useful ways of distinguishing constituents from groups of words which aren't constituents:

(a) Constituents can often be sensibly used alone, e.g. as exclamations or as answers to questions: —*What do business executives do? —Eat at really fancy restaurants.* This isn't true of nonconstituents: if we were asked "Do fancy restaurants do much business?" we couldn't sensibly answer "Well, executives eat at."

(b) Parenthetical remarks like *of course, as you know, by the way,* etc. naturally appear between constituents: *Business executives, as you know, eat at really fancy restaurants.* But they sound rather unnatural if what precedes or follows is a non-constituent: *Business executives eat at really, as you know, fancy restaurants* (neither *business executives eat at really* nor *fancy restaurants* is a constituent of (4)).

(c) It is often possible to replace a constituent with a single word having the same meaning as that constituent. For example, if someone asked "What do business executives do?" we could answer either with sentence (4) or with sentence (5), in which the constituent *business executives* is replaced with the single word *they* (which, in this context, would mean the same thing as *business executives*).

(5) They eat at really fancy restaurants.

Similarly, if someone asked "Who eats at really fancy restaurants?" we could answer either with (4) or with sentence (6), in which the constituent *eat at really fancy restaurants* is replaced with the single word *do* (which would mean the same thing in this context).

(6) Business executives do.

But there is no word that could possibly replace the nonconstituent *eat at really* in (4) and mean the same thing, no matter what question was asked.

(d) Finally, sentences are always constituents, as are the individual words within a sentence: in sentence (4), for instance, the largest constituent is the sentence itself; the smallest constituents are the individual words *business, executives, eat, at, really, fancy,* and *restaurants.*

Two points must be kept in mind regarding constituents. First, given a group of words, we cannot say once and for all whether or not it is a constituent; rather, we can only say whether or not it is a constituent relative to a particular sentence. To see this, consider sentences (7) and (8).

(7) John and Bill raise weasels.
(8) Mary punched John and Bill kicked Jane.

In (7), *John and Bill* is a constituent: it functions as a coherent, meaningful unit within the sentence—in particular, as its subject. In (8), however, the very same sequence of words is *not* a constituent: because *John* is the direct object of the first clause and *Bill* is the subject of the second clause, the sequence *John and Bill* does not make a coherent contribution to the meaning of this sentence. (Notice that although *John and Bill* can be replaced with *they* in (7), this isn't possible in sentence (8).) Thus, we can properly say that a group of words is a constituent only with respect to a particular sentence.

The second thing that must be kept in mind is that constituent structure is *hierarchical*—that is, one constituent may be part of another. Consider sentence (4) again.

(4) Business executives eat at really fancy restaurants.

Among the constituents in this sentence is the sequence *really fancy*. (To see this, note that *really fancy* can be used by itself:

—How fancy was it?
—Really fancy.

and that it can be replaced with the single word *such*:

—Who eats at really fancy restaurants?
—Business executives eat at such restaurants.)

But *really fancy* is also part of a larger constituent, namely *really fancy restaurants*; this in turn is part of a larger constituent, *at really fancy restaurants*, which is itself part of the still larger constituent *eat at really fancy restaurants* and ultimately of the largest constituent in the sentence, namely the sentence itself. If we underline each of the constituents in (4), the hierarchical nature of its constituent structure becomes obvious:

(9) <u>Business executives eat at really fancy restaurants.</u>

Underlining is, as in (9), one way of representing the hierarchical nature of constituent structure. Another way is with *tree diagrams*: branching structures in which each constituent forms a 'branch'. For example, the tree diagram for sentence (4) is (10):

(10)

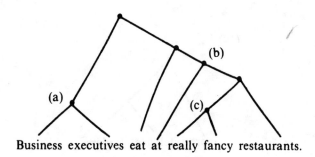

Business executives eat at really fancy restaurants.

In this diagram, each of the constituents of a sentence (4) forms a branch: for example, *business executives* corresponds to the branch labeled (a); *at really fancy restaurants*, to the branch labeled (b); and *really fancy*, to the branch labled (c). Observe, in addition, that groups of words that are not contituents of sentence (4) do *not* form branches in this tree diagram; *executives eat at* and *eat at really,* for instance, clearly aren't constituents according to diagram (10). In principle, underlining is just as good as tree diagrams for representing constituent structure; but because tree diagrams are somewhat easier to read, they are usually preferred.

CONSTITUENT STRUCTURE AND AMBIGUITY

In every human language we can find individual expressions which have two or more distinct meanings. For example, the italicized portions of the following sentences of English can be interpreted in more than one way:

(11) a. Larry raises *miniature badgers and raccoons.*
    b. We need *more intelligent leaders.*

In (11a), *miniature badgers and raccoons* can mean either 'miniature badgers and miniature raccoons' or 'miniature badgers and raccoons (of any size)'; in (11b), *more intelligent leaders* can mean either 'a greater quantity of intelligent leaders' or 'leaders who are more intelligent'. This property of having two or more distinct meanings is called *ambiguity*; an expression with two or more distinct meanings is *ambiguous*.

Often, an expression is ambiguous because it has more than one possible constituent structure. Consider, for example, the expression *miniature badgers and raccoons* in sentence (11a): it can have either of the following constituent structures.

(12)

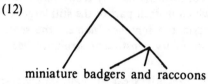

(13)

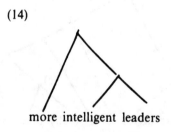

In (12), *badgers and raccoons* forms a constituent; (12) therefore represents the interpretation in which the adjective *miniature* applies to both the badgers and the raccoons. In (13), on the other hand, *miniature badgers* forms a constituent; (13) therefore represents the interpretation in which only the badgers are miniature. An expression which is ambiguous because it has more than one possible constituent structure is said to be *structurally ambiguous*.

The italicized portion of sentence (11b) is also structurally ambiguous: it can have either of the following constituent structures.

(14)

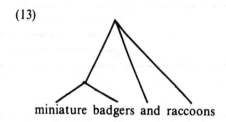

(15)

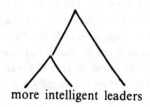

In (14), *intelligent leaders* is a constituent; for this reason, (14) represents the interpretation 'a greater quantity of intelligent leaders'. In (15), however, *more intelligent* forms a constituent; (15) therefore represents the meaning 'leaders who are more intelligent.'

Although structural ambiguity is a very common kind of ambiguity, it is not the only kind. Individual *words* are sometimes ambiguous; for example, *crane* can refer to either a kind of bird or to a large construction device. Because words like *crane* have no internal constituent structure, they clearly can't be structurally ambiguous. (Instead, they are sometimes said to be lexically ambiguous.)

EXERCISES

1. Which of the italicized expressions in the following sentences are constituents? Which are not? Why? (Use the tests (a)-(c) for constituency mentioned above to show this in each case.)

      a. John *ate the stale candy*.
      b. John *ate the stale* candy.
      c. My little *brother snores*.
      d. My *little brother* snores.

2. Discuss the ambiguity of the following sentences. Which is lexically ambiguous? Which is structurally ambiguous?
      a. John sat on Jumbo's trunk.
      b. Marian knows a Chinese art expert.

SYNTAX: SYNTACTIC CATEGORIES

SYNTACTIC CATEGORIES

A very important fact about constituent structure is that there are different types of constituents with very different uses. We refer to these different types of constituents as *syntactic categories*.

One of the most important syntactic categories is the category of *noun phrases*. Examples are the expressions in (1):

(1) John
     mailmen
     most dogs
     many Americans
     a huge, loveable bear
     a student from Brazil
     the table in the corner
     the people that we interviewed
     John and his dog

A noun phrase can be used as the subject of a sentence, as in (2a); as the direct object, as in (2b); as the indirect object, as in (2c); and in many other ways as well:

(2) a. *Most dogs* enjoy hamburger sauce.
     b. Harold likes *most dogs*.
     c. Lilian gave *most dogs* their rabies shots this morning.

In some cases, a single word can count as a noun phrase all by itself; this is true, for instance, of names (e.g. *John*), plural nouns (e.g. *mailmen*), nouns referring to substances (e.g. *water, dirt*), and pronouns (e.g. *I, she, them*). But many noun phrases begin with expressions like the following:

(3) the   most   at least five
     a   all   my
     every   few   Mary's
     many   several
     some   three

These are called *determiners,* and they combine with a single noun or with a noun modified by other sorts of expressions to produce a noun phrase: *the president, many Americans, two new sweaters, a student from Brazil,* etc.

Another extremely important syntactic category is the category of *verb phrases*. Some examples are the expressions in (4):

(4) snore
     like Mary
     give a prize to John
     believe that dogs are smart
     want to leave
     sleep soundly
     can lift 100 pounds
     is wearing sunglasses
     go home and have a beer

A verb phrase can be used as the predicate of a sentence, as in the examples in (5).

> (5)   a.   John and Bill *like Mary*.
>   b.   Henry *wants to leave*.

Certain verbs, such as *snore, swim, talk,* and *die,* can form a verb phrase all by themselves; verbs of this sort are called *intransitive verbs*. Certain other verbs form a verb phrase by combining with a noun phrase. Such verbs are called *transitive verbs;* the noun phrase with which a transitive verb combines is its direct object, as in the following examples:

> (6)   like Mary
>   chase cars
>   annoy three burly sergeants
>   develop every roll of film

Other verbs combine with other sorts of expressions to form a verb phrase: verbs like *give* and *owe* combine with two noun phrases (a direct object and an indirect object), as in *give a prize to John* and *owe Larry's brother several hundred dollars;* verbs like *try* and *manage* combine with a verb phrase marked with *to,* as in *want to leave* and *manage to finish the pizza;* and so on.

Certain verb phrases consist of an *auxiliary or a helping verb* (e.g. *can, should, might, will, be, have*) plus a smaller verb phrase: *can lift 100 pounds, should wear sunglasses, might want to leave*. When the helping verb is *have,* the verb which follows it is in its past participle form: *John has chopped the onions, Henry has found the wallet*. When the helping verb is *be,* the verb which follows it may be in its past participle form or in its present participle form:

> (7) a. The onions were chopped by John.
>   b. The wallet was found by Henry. (passive sentences)
>   c. John is chopping the onions.
>   d. Henry is finding the wallet.

Another important syntactic category is the category of *adjective phrases,* of which the following are examples:

> (8) smart
>   very fat
>   as crazy as John
>   more intelligent than Mary
>   certain to win

Adjective phrases are often used to modify nouns and thus often appear as constituents of noun phrases: *a very fat individual; someone as crazy as John*.

Adverbial phrases, such as those in (9), are often used to modify verbs and adjectives, and thus appear as constituents of verb phrases and adjective phrases, as in (10).

> (9) soundly
>   fiercely
>   as fluently as John
>   almost certainly
>   sleep soundly
> (10) speak French as fluently as John (verb phrases)
>   fiercely loyal
>   almost certainly able to walk (adjective phrases)

Another important syntactic category is that of *prepositional phrases*. Prepositional phrases always consist of a *preposition* (e.g. *to, from, with, for, at, on, under, about, through*) plus a noun phrase:

> (11) from Brazil
>   with John and Bill
>   for nothing

A prepositional phrase can be a constituent of a wide range of expressions:

> (12) go to the movies (verb phrase)
>
> a student from Brazil
>
> angry with John and Bill (adjective phrase)
>
> separately from the others (adverbial phrase)

Perhaps the most important syntactic category of all is the category of *sentences*. Sentences are, of course, often used by themselves:

> (13) a. It is raining.
>
> b. I like hamburger sauce.

But a sentence may also appear as a constituent of another expression; for example, each of the following expressions has a sentence as a constituent.

> (14) the fact that *it is raining*
>
> a student *who met Susan last Thursday* (noun phrases)
>
> discover that *it is raining*
>
> know *who met Susan last Thursday* (verb phrases)
>
> glad that *it is raining* (adjective phrase)

In addition, certain adverbial phrases consist of a sentence preceded by a *subordinating conjuction* (e.g. *if, though, when, after, because*): *if it is raining, though it is raining,* and so on. Any sentence which is a constituent of an expression of another category is an *embedded sentence*.

One other syntactic category that should be mentioned is the category of *coordinating conjuctions:* these are words like *and, or* and *but,* which are used to connect expressions of virtually any category:

> (15) John and his dog (noun phrases)
>
> go home and have a beer (verb phrases)
>
> faster than a speeding bullet and more powerful than a locomotive (adjective phrases)
>
> quickly and very easily (adverbial phrases)
>
> over the river and through the woods (prepositional phrases)
>
> It is raining and it may sleet (sentences)

Note that any expression resulting from the connection of two or more smaller expressions belongs to the same category as they do. That is, because *John* and *his dog* are noun phrases, so is *John and his dog,* because *go home* and *have a beer* are verb phrases, so is *go home and have a beer;* and so on.

LABELED TREE DIAGRAMS

As we saw above, constituent structure can be perspicuously represented by means of tree diagrams such as the following:

(16)

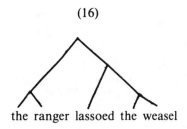

the ranger lassoed the weasel

(16) indicates what group of words are consituents in the sentence *the range lassoed the weasel;* it does not, however, indicate the syntactic categories to which the constituents belong. This limitation can be overcome if we mark each constituent in a tree structure like (16) with the appropriate category label; the result of this procedure is a *labeled tree diagram* such as (17).

(17)

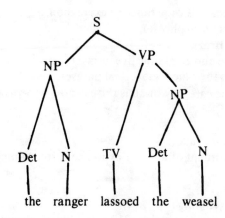

(The following abbreviations are used here: S = Sentence; NP = Noun Phrase; Det = Determiner; N = Noun; VP = Verb Phrase; TV = Transitive Verb.)

EXERCISES

1. Using labeled tree diagrams, give the constituent structure of the following sentences.

    a. Mary snores.
    b. Two elephants noticed the mice.
    c. The train slowly departed.
    d. Ed knows you like cheese.

SYNTAX: PHRASE STRUCTURE RULES

Part of every language user's knowledge of his/her language is the knowledge of how constituents are put together and categorized in that language. This special sort of knowledge can be represented as a set of rules called *phrase structure rules*. In this file, we consider the nature of such rules and discuss several important properties which make them useful for describing the syntactic competence of language users.

PHRASE STRUCTURE RULES

As a speaker of English, you know how to put together constituents of each syntactic category of English. (This knowledge is, of course, largely unconscious: you may not be able to explain how to form complex constituents in English, but your linguistic behavior still shows that you know how to do it.) You know, for example, 1) that a sentence (S) of English can be formed by joining a noun phrase (NP) with a verb phrase (VP), as in (1); 2) that a noun phrase may be formed by joining a determiner (Det) with a noun (N), as in (2); and 3) that a verb phrase may consist of a transitive verb (TV) followed by a direct object noun phrase, as in (3).

(1) S	=	NP	+	VP
		John		snored.
		Everyone		fled the volcano.
		The mayor		smoked a cigar.
		A book		lay on the table.
(2) NP	=	Det	+	N
		the		mayor
		a		book
		every		student
		my		python
(3) VP	=	TV	+	NP
		fled		the volcano
		smoked		a cigar
		imitated		a flamingo
		squeezed		some fresh orange juice

We can represent these three pieces of knowledge in a succinct way with the following three phrase structure rules (or PS rules):

(1′) S → NP VP
(2′) NP → Det N
(3′) VP → TV NP

The arrow in these rules can be read as 'may consist of'. Thus rule (1′) is just a concise way of saying 'a sentence may consist of a noun phrase followed by a verb phrase'; similarly, rule (2′) just says 'a noun phrase may consist of a determiner followed by a noun'. What does rule (3′) say?

Rules (1)-(3) specify three ways in which constituents can be combined to form larger, more complex constituents. Some constituents, however, do not result from the combination of smaller constituents; instead, they consist of a single word. For example, a noun phrase may just consist of a proper name (e.g. *John, Paris),* a plural noun (e.g. *elephants, leaves),* or a noun referring to a substance (e.g. *clay, gasoline);* similarly, a verb phrase may just consist of an intransitive verb, such as *sneeze, die, vanish,* or *elapse.* These sorts of knowledge can also be represented with PS rules:

(4) NP ——→ N
(5) VP ——→ IV

We still need rules which tell us about what word go into the lexical categories like DET, N, TV, IV, etc. They take the form of (6) — (9):

(6) DET ——→ the, a, every, my...
(7) N ——→ major, book, student...
(8) TV ——→ smoke, beat...
(9) IV ——→ sleep, smile...

Thus, there are two different sorts of PS rules: those which, like (1) — (5), specify the structure of complex constituents (constituents which themselves consist of two of more constituents), and those which, like (6) — (9), specify which words may go into a given syntactic category.

GENERATIVITY

Because PS rules represent our knowledge of how constituents are constructed and categorized, we can also regard them as instructions for 'building' labeled tree diagrams (which, after all, indicate the structure and categorization of constituents within a sentence.) To see this, consider the following very simple set of PS rules.

(10) a. S ——→ NP VP
     b. VP ——→ TV NP
     c. NP ——→ N
     d. TV ——→ enjoy, eat, dislike
     e. N ——→ elephants, wolves, apples, Cheerios, Americans, programs

Using these rules, we can build tree diagrams for a number of sentences. Rule (10a) tells how to build the labeled tree in (11):

(11)

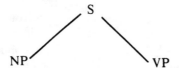

(11) says exactly the same things as (10a) — that a sentence may consist of a noun phrase followed by a verb phrase. Rules (10b) — (10e) allow us to add on to the tree in (11). Rule (10b) says that a verb phrase may consist of a transitive verb followed by a noun phrase; (10b) therefore allows us to convert the tree in (11) into the tree in (12).

(12)

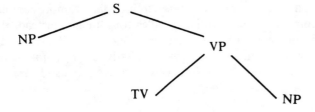

Rule (10c) allows a noun phrase to consist of a noun; (10c) therefore allows us to add Ns under the first NP label and the second one; (10e) allows the first and second N to be 'elephants' and 'Cheerios'. Similarily, rule (10d) entitles us to insert the verb under the TV label in (12). The end result of these additions to (12) is the tree in (13).

(13)

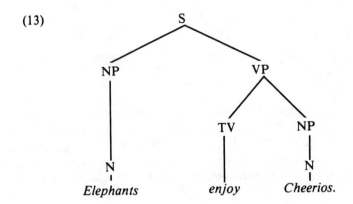

(13) is, of course, the labelled tree diagram corresponding to the sentence *Elephants enjoy Cheerios*. Because rules (10a) — (10e) are by themselves adequate for building the tree in (13), we can say that they *generate* this tree; in a related sense, we can also say that they generate the sentence *Elephants enjoy Cheerios* (i.e. the sentence of which (13) is the diagram). What are some other sentences generated by (10a) — (10e)?

Notice that there are many sentences which rules (10a)-(10c) cannot generate on their own; for example, sentence (14) cannot be generated by these rules.

(14) Most Americans enjoy these programs.

In order to generate this additional sentence, we must add the following three rules to those in (10):

(15) a. NP ⟶ Det N
b. Det ⟶ most, these

Rule (15a) allows us to convert the tree (12) into that in (16):

(16)

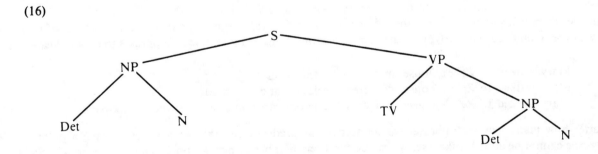

Rule (15b) permits us to insert *most* under the first Det label in (16) and *these* under the second one; rule (10e) lets us put *Americans* under the first N label in (16) and *programs* under the second one; and rule (10d) entitles us to place the verb *enjoy* under the TV label in (16). The result of these additions is (17), the labeled tree diagram for sentence (14).

(17)

Thus, the set of rules in (10) and (15) generates sentence (14).

    Although the set of rules in (10) and (15) generates a fair number of sentences, it is obvious that there are many sentences which it too fails to generate. (What are some of these? Can the rules in (10) and (15) generate the first sentence in this paragraph?) Nevertheless, by adding new PS rules to those in (10) and (15), we will be able to generate more and more English sentences; if we add enough new rules, we will eventually be able to generate every sentence in the English language. A set of PS rules which is capable of generating every sentence of some language is said to be a *generative* set of rules.

INFINITY AND RECURSION

    Suppose we wanted to come up with a generative set of PS rules for English (i.e. a set of PS rules capable of generating every sentence in the English language). How many sentences would this set of rules have to be capable of generating? That is, how many sentences are there in the English language?

    A little consideration reveals that there are in fact *an infinite number* of sentences in English (or in any human language). To see this, consider the following sentence.

(18) Mary walked to Zeke's house.

We can add on to this sentence in a number of ways to form an infinite number of new sentences. One way to add on to sentence (18) is to use a coordinating conjunction like *and* or *or.* For example, we can use *and* to connect one or more new noun phrases to the subject of (18):

        John and Mary walked to Zeke's house.
        Bill, John, and Mary walked to Zeke's house.
        Jane, Bill, John, and Mary walked to Zeke's house.

In principle, there is no limit to the number of new noun phrases that we could connect to the subject of (18) in this way if we were so inclined. Similarly, we can use *and* to connect one or more new verb phrases to the predicate of (18):

        Mary walked to Zeke's house and delivered the letter.
        Mary walked to Zeke's house, delivered the letter, and ran home.
        Mary walked to Zeke's house, delivered the letter, ran home, and downed a six-pack.

No matter how many new verb phrases we connect to the predicate of (18), we will never reach a point at which another one cannot be added. Likewise, we can connect any number of new prepositional phrases to *to Zeke's house* in (18):

        Mary walked to Zeke's house, to the post office, to the bookstore, and to the new Burger Chef.

And we can connect any number of new sentences to (18) itself:

        Mary walked to Zeke's house, John drove to the post office, Bill stopped by the bookstore, and Jane checked out the new Burger Chef.

Thus, one reason why there are an infinite number of English sentences is that it is possible to use conjunctions like *and*

and *or* to connect an indefinitely large number of expressions of a given syntactic category.

Another way to add on to sentence (18) is to join other sentences to it by means of *embedding*. An *embedded sentence* is one which is a constituent of an expression of another category; embedding is thus the use of a sentence as a constituent of an expression of another category. We can embed sentence (18) in a number of ways; we need only consider one of these here. Certain verbs, such as *know, believe, suppose, suspect, imagine, claim* and *deny,* join with a sentence (sometimes preceded by *that*) to form a verb phrase; thus, we can embed sentence (18) by joining it to a verb of this sort. In each of the following sentences, (18) is embedded within the italicized verb phrase:

(19) I *know that Mary walked to Zeke's house.*

(20) The judge *believes that Mary walked to Zeke's house.*

(21) No one *denied that Mary walked to Zeke's house.*

These sentences can, in turn, be embedded in still larger sentences; (19) for example, is itself embedded within the italicized verb phrase of sentence (22).

(22) Jane *suspects that I know that Mary walked to Zeke's house.*

(22) can be embedded in yet a larger sentence; and so on. There is in principle no limit to the number of embeddings that can be used in building up a single sentence. Thus, a second reason why there are an infinite number of sentences in English is that it is possible for a sentence to contain an indefinitely large number of embeddings. (Other reasons for the existence of an infinite number of English sentences can be thought of, but we won't go into these here.)

Given then, that there are an infinite number of sentences in English, consider again the problem of coming up with a *generative* set of PS rules for English. Do we need an infinite number of PS rules in order to generate the infinitely many sentences of English? Or is there a *finite* set of PS rules for English that is generative (i.e. that generates each of the infinitely many English sentences)? As it turns out, it is apparently possible to generate all English sentences with a finite number of PS rules. This is so because of two special properties of PS rules.

First, a PS rule may be written so as to allow an expression to consist of an indefinitely large number of constituents. An example of such a PS rule is rule (23).

(23) NP⟶ NP* *and* NP

Here, 'NP*' is an abbreviation; it stands for one or more instances of 'NP'. Thus, (23) says 'a noun phrase may consist of one or more noun phrases followed by *and* followed by a noun phrase'. For this reason, (23) generates an infinite number of labeled tree diagrams. The three smallest trees that (23) generates are those in (24):

(24)

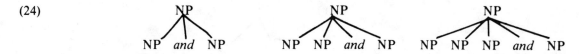

In general, (23) allows an indefinitely large number of NPs to precede *and* in the trees which it generates. In connection with PS rule (25) and (26), (23) generates the noun phrases in (27), as well as an infinite number of longer ones.

(25) N ⟶ Bill, Jane, John, Mary

(26) NP ⟶ N

(27) a. John and Mary

   b. Bill, John and Mary

   c. Jane, Bill, John and Mary

A second property of PS rules which makes it possible for a finite number of such rules to generate an infinite number of sentences is the property of *recursion*. To understand this property, consider the set of PS rules in (28).

(28) a. S ⟶ NP VP

   b. VP ⟶ Vs that S

   c. VP ⟶ IV

   d. NP ⟶ N

   e. N ⟶ Bill, Jane, John, Linda, Mary, Zeke

   f. IV ⟶ snored, sneezed

   g. Vs⟶ knew, believed, supposed, suspected, imagined.

175

(Here, 'Vs' represents the category of verbs which combine with a sentence preceded by *that* to form a verb phrase.) Rule (28a) generates the tree diagram in (29):

(29)

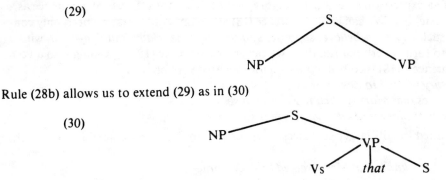

Rule (28b) allows us to extend (29) as in (30)

(30)

Notice that rule (28a) can now be used *again* to extend the lower 'S' of the tree in (30) as in (31):

(31)

And as a consequence of *this* conversion, rule (28b) can be used again, to provide further structure for the lower 'VP' in (31) as in the following tree.

(32)

As you can see, there is nothing to prevent us from using (28a) and (28b) over and over again to extend the tree in (32) to an indefinite length. This ability of certain sets of rules to be used over and over again to generate a tree of indefinite length is called recursion; a set of PS rules with the property of recursion is called a *recursive* set of rules.

Because (28a) and (28b) form a recursive set of rules, rules (28a) and (28b) generate an infinite number of sentences. They generate sentences like that diagrammed in (33), which contains no embedded sentences;

(33)

but they also generate sentences containing one or more embeddings, including the sentence diagrammed in (33), which contains two embedded sentences.

(34)

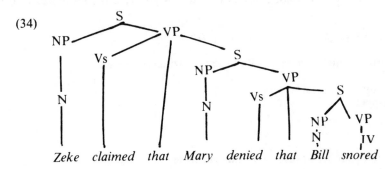

Zeke   claimed   that   Mary   denied   that   Bill   snored

Rules (28a) — (28g) are in principle capable of generating sentences with an indefinitely large number of embeddings, and thus may generate infinitely many sentences.

Because a PS rule may, like (23), generate expressions consisting of an indefinitely large number of constituents, and because some PS rules form recursive sets of rules, it is possible for a finite set of PS rules to generate an infinite number of sentences. In particular, it appears to be entirely feasible to write a finite set of PS rules which generates every sentence in the English language. Of course, the number of PS rules that would be necessary to do this would be quite large — not so large, however, as to prevent a normal child from learning them all.

SUMMARY

In this file, we have discussed *phrase structure rules*, which embody a language user's knowledge of how constituents are put together and categorized in his/her language. We have seen that there are two different sorts of PS rules: those which specify the structure of complex constituents, and those which specify words which may be constituents of a given category. We have seen that a set of PS rules may be regarded as *generating* a certain set of tree diagrams—or, in a related sense, as generating a certain set of sentences; a set of PS rules which generates every sentence in some language is thus a *generative* set of rules. Although there are an infinite number of sentences in English (or in any human language), it appears to be possible to write a finite set of PS rules which generates them all. This is because of two special properties of PS rules: on the one hand, a single PS rule may allow an expression to consist of an indefinitely large number of constituents; and on the other, a finite set of PS rules may be *recursive*—that is, may be used over and over again to generate a tree of indefinite length.

EXERCISES

Answer the first four questions below *based on the following set of rules.*

S ⟶ NP VP   DET ⟶ the, some
NP ⟶ DET N   N ⟶ elephants, raccoons, tigers, bears, grain, peanuts,
VP ⟶ TV NP   mice
VP ⟶ IV   TV ⟶ eat, scare
VP ⟶ VP* and VP   IV ⟶ gallop, swim

1. For each of the following sentences, circle *yes* if these rules generate it; circle *no* if it is not generated by these rules.

a. The elephants and the mice eat peanuts.   yes   no
b. Elephants eat peanuts.   yes   no
c. The tigers scare the grain.   yes   no
d. The raccoons eat the grain, scare the mice, and swim.   yes   no
e. The tigers gallop.   yes   no
f. The tigers eat some grain and scare the mice.   yes   no

2. Draw the trees for *two* of the sentences that you circled *yes* for.

3. What changes can be made for this set of rules so that it will generate the sentences that you circled *no* for? *Be explicit.*

4. How many sentences will be generated by this set of rules? *Why?*

5. Write a set of syntactic rules which generates all of the following sentences.

> John strummed his guitar.
> Janet played the trumpet.
> Marilyn sang.
> Larry danced.

Name a sentence which your set of rules does not generate.

Write a single rule which, when added to your set of rules, allows it to generate both of the following sentences.

> John sang and danced.
> John sang, danced, and played the trumpet.

Give two other sentences which your revised set of rules generates.

6. How many sentences does the set of rules below generate?

> S $\longrightarrow$ NP VP
> VP $\longrightarrow$ TV NP
> NP $\longrightarrow$ Alice, John
> TV $\longrightarrow$ liked, nudged, irritated

If we add the following rules to those above, how many sentences does the resulting set of rules generate?

> VP $\longrightarrow$ Vs that S
> Vs $\longrightarrow$ claimed, denied

SYNTAX:

TRANSFORMATIONS

We have seen in file 64 how syntactic patterns of a language can be described by phrase-structure rules. But not all sentence patterns can be described efficiently by such rules alone. Instead, some sentences are best analyzed as the result of using two kinds of rules — phrase-structure rules, plus a new kind of rule called a transformation. For example, the sentences in (1) illustrate an English transformation called Question Formation:

(1)
(a) What can Mary accomplish?
(b) Who will John introduce to Bill?
(c) What has Sheila tripped over?

The corresponding sentences in which the Question Formation Transformation has *not* been used are (2)(a)—(2)(c), respectively:

(2)
(a) Mary can accomplish what?
(b) John will introduce who to Bill?
(c) Sheila tripped over what?

These sentences are produced by phrase-structure rules. They are simply questioned versions of sentences like:

(3)
(a) Mary can accomplish a great deal.
(b) John will introduce the man to Bill.
(c) Sheila has tripped over the dog.

Notice that *what* in (2)(a) stands in the same position in the sentence as *a great deal* in (3)(a). Likewise, *who* in (2)(b) is in the same position as *the man* in (3)(b). Because of this correspondence, we know that *who* and *what* are noun phrases, just as *the man* and *the dog* are.

In general, transformations change sentences created by phrase-structure rules into sentences with equivalent meanings, but different structures. This is accomplished by adding or deleting words, or rearranging word order. Thus the transformation required for constructing sentences like those in (1) from those in (2) can be described as follows:

Question Formation
(i) Place the first helping verb of the sentence to the left of the subject noun phrase (the first noun phrase in the sentence).
(ii) Find a question word (*what, who, where* — also called *wh*-words) and move this word to the beginning of the sentence.

Part (i) of the Question Formation Transformation tells us that (2)(a), *Mary can accomplish what?* can be converted into *Can Mary accomplish what?* Part (ii) of the transformation further converts this into *What can Mary accomplish?*, which is (1)(a). (Stop at this point to see that this transformation correctly converts (2)(b) into (1)(b), and converts (2)(c) into (1)(c). What is the result of applying this transformation to the sentence *I must put the beer where?*)

In other words, the syntactic structure of a sentence like *What can Mary accomplish?* is described in two steps: the phrase structure rules of English form the basic sentence *Mary can accomplish what?*, then the Question Formation Transformation forms the first sentence from this. Linguists refer to the form of a sentence produced by phrase-structure rules alone as the *Deep Structure* of a sentence, and the form that the sentence has after one of more transformations has applied as the *Surface Structure* of the sentence. For example, the sentence which has the Surface Structure (1a) has the Deep Structure (2a); the same goes for (1b) and (2b), or (1c) and (2c). Of course, the sentence (2a) is also a grammatical English sentence as it stands, and if we are describing (2a) by itself, we might say that its Deep Structure is the same as its Surface Structure, since no transformation was used to form it.

Why do linguists adopt this complicated two-step analysis of the sentences like those in (1)? That is, why couldn't we just as well describe sentences like those directly by phrase structure rules alone, without making use of transformations at all? The answer, essentially, it that it really turns out to be *more* complicated and less systematic to try to use phrase structure rules alone. To see this, it is necessary to reconsider declarative sentences like those introduced in (3) above. Like the questions in (1) and (2), these sentences contain the verbs *accomplish, trip over* and *introduce*. If we compare a sentence, like *What can Mary accomplish?* with the corresponding declarative *Mary can accomplish a great deal,* it becomes evident that *accomplish* is followed by a noun phrase in the declarative, but not in the question. Similarly, *trip over* has a noun phrase following it in *Sheila tripped over the dog,* but not in the question *What has Sheila tripped over?* And the declarative *John can introduce the man to Bill* has two noun phrases following *introduce,* while the question *Who can John introduce to Bill?* has only one.

These 'extra' noun phrases moreover are *required* in grammatical declarative sentences, since the sentences would be ungrammatical if these noun phrases were omitted, as (4) shows:

(4)
*Mary can accomplish.
*John will introduce to Bill.
*Sheila has tripped over.

In fact, *any* declarative sentence formed on the pattern of those in (4) will be ungrammatical unless the 'extra' noun phrase is present. Because this is a general principle about grammatical declarative sentences in English, we will want to be sure that our phrase-structure rules always produce a noun phrase following the verb *accomplish.* Likewise, the phrase-structure rules must guarantee that a noun phrase and a prepositional phrase follow the verb *introduce.*

But the question sentence, like *What can Mary accomplish?,* would be an exception to this general principle if we tried to describe questions by phrase-structure rules alone. In this sentence and the others in (1), the 'extra' noun phrase following the verb is missing, yet the sentences are grammatical. However, the sentences in (1) are not exceptions to this principle *if* we hypothesize that these sentences are formed by the Question-Formation Transformation. In the deep structure produced by the phrase-structure rules (before the Transformation is applied), they obey the principles required for producing grammatical sentences involving *accomplish, trip over* and *introduce,* because *what* is the 'extra' noun phrase placed after the verb by the phrase structure rules. Only after the transformation has applied is there a noun phrase "missing" after the verb.

To summarize this discussion, we have in effect observed that *every question sentence of English beginning with* what, who, *etc. lacks exactly one noun phrase to the right of the verb that would be present in the corresponding declarative sentence* (or question where the WH-word does not begin the sentence, as in (2)). The Question Transformation analysis of such sentences describes the situation exactly correctly, since it stipulates that a noun phrase is *moved* to the beginning of the sentence as the sentence is transformed. This kind of fact about syntax is just what *cannot* easily be described by phrase-structure rules alone.

Having discussed one transformation in detail, we now present two additional examples of transformations in English. We will not explain the reasons for hypothesizing these transformations as we did for Question Formation because, in some cases, these reasons are more complicated to describe.

The Passive:
(5)
a. John ate an apple.   (Deep Structure, before transformation)

b. An apple was eaten by John.   (Surface Structure, after transformation)

Passive Transformation: Move the subject noun phrase (the noun phrase that begins the sentence) to the end of the sentence, insert the preposition *by* just before it, and move the object noun phrase (the noun phrase just after the main verb) to the beginning of the sentence.

Verb-Particle Shift:
(6)
a. The surgeon sewed up the wound.   (Deep Structure, before transformation)
b. The surgeon sewed the wound up.   (Surface Structure, after transformation)

Verb-Particle Shift Transformation: Move the particle (the preposition-like word immediately to the right of the verb) after the first noun phrase following the verb.

EXERCISES

1. Examples (a) and (b) are definitely not grammatical questions in English:

(a) * What has an hour elapsed?
(b) * What will John disappear?

This fact is related to another fact about the verbs *elapse* and *disappear*, namely, that these verbs cannot be followed by a noun phrase in declarative sentences; comparison of (c), (d), with (e), (f) confirms this:

(c) An hour has elapsed.   (e) * An hour has elapsed the clock.
(d) John will disappear.   (f) * John will disappear the rabbit.

Given this second observation, an explanation of why (a) and (b) are ungrammatical is provided by our hypothesis that all questions of English are produced through the Question Transformation. What is that explanation? Why would it be difficult to explain the ungrammaticality of (a) and (b) if we do not use a Question Transformation to form questions?

2. Assume that each set of sentences in *A* and *B* below are related by a transformation. *A* represents the deep structure, and *B* represents the surface structure. Describe the transformation that 'converts' the *A* sentences into the *B* sentences.

A	B
(1)	
a. John gave the apple to Mary.	a. John gave Mary the apple.
b. The pitcher threw the ball to the catcher.	b. The pitcher threw the catcher the ball.
c. The salesman sold a car to the manager.	c. The salesman sold the manager a car.

(2)

a. Jack will marry a German, and Bill will marry a German, too.

a. Jack will marry a German, and Bill will, too.

b. Susan has eaten lobster, and her mother has eaten lobster, too.

b. Susan has eaten lobster, and her mother has, too.

c. Jo is wearing a sweater, and Bob is wearing a sweater, too.

c. Jo is wearing a sweater, and Bob is, too.

(3)

a. Larry ran up the stairs.

a. Up the stairs ran Larry.

b. Three soldiers walked into the room.

b. Into the room walked three soldiers.

c. The boss stormed out the door.

c. Out the door stormed the boss.

3. For each sentence below, determine which transformations mentioned in the text and in Exercise 2 can be applied. In some cases, more than one transformation can be applied to the same sentence.

(1) The boy can eat the beans.

(2) The black cat walked up the street.

(3) The millionaire gave the money to the young woman.

(4) The teacher looked up the word.

(5) Everyone will see the show.

SYNTAX: WORD ORDER TYPOLOGY

The most important fact about word order typology is that languages tend to be consistent about whether modifiers come before heads, or heads come before modifiers. By looking at the ordering between a verb and its direct object, a modifier of the verb, we can in many cases predict what the ordering between other head-modifier combinations are. Languages can then be classified roughly as to whether they are VO languages (with head – modifier order) or OV languages (with modifier – head order). Some examples of the two types of languages are given below, together with the characteristic ordering relations between several head – modifier combinations:

VO LANGUAGES

SVO 35% (Spanish)
VSO 19% (Irish, Arabic, Hebrew)
VOS 2%

  A. verb-object
  B. helping verb-main verb
  C. preposition-noun
  D. noun-relative clauses
  E. noun-possessive
  F. noun-adjective

OV LANGUAGES

SOV 44% (Russian, Turkish)

  A. object-verb
  B. main verb-helping verb
  C. noun-preposition
  D. relative clauses-noun
  E. possessive-noun
  F. adjective-noun

English has mostly VO type of word order, but it also has some OV characteristics:

VO features		OV features
eat apples	A.	
may go	B.	
at home	C.	
man who left	D.	
cover of the book	E.	the book's cover
	F.	good man

Following are some example sentences from Hindi, French and Japanese. To what types of languages do they belong?

Hindi	**French**	**Japanese**
A. Rām-ne seb khāyā	Jean a mangé une pomme	Taroo-ga ringo-o tabeta
Ram apple ate	*Jean ate an apple*	*Taroo apple ate*
B. Rām Angrezī bol	Jean peut parle anglais	Taroo-wa Eigo-ga
Ram English speak	*Jean can speak English*	*Taroo English*
saktā hai		hanas-eru
can		*speak-can*
C. laṛke-ne chaṛī-se	le garçon a frappé	sono otokonoko-wa
boy stick-with	*the boy hit*	*that boy*
kutte-ko mārā	le chien avec un bāton	boo-de inu-o butta
dog hit	*the dog with a stick*	*stick-with dog hit*

D. jis laṛke-ne
   which boy
   mārā, vah merā
   hit   he
   bhāī   hai
   brother is

le garçon qui a frappé
the boy   who hit
le chien est mon frère
the dog is   my brother

inu-o butta otokonoko-wa
dog   hit   boy
watasi-no otooto-da
my   brother-is

E. Rām-kī bahan
   Ram's sister

la soeur de Jean
the sister of Jean

Taroo-no imooto
Taroo's sister

F. safed phūi
   white flower

une fleur blanche
a flower white

sinoi hana
white flower

Based on the sentences given, classify the three languages into the two language types, with respect to each of the ordering relationships of A–F.

VO	OV
A. _____	_____
B. _____	_____
C. _____	_____
D. _____	_____
E. _____	_____
F. _____	_____

184

INTRODUCTION: SEMANTICS

Language is often characterized as a system which links form and meaning: that is, for every form in a language — say, the sequence of letters p-a-p-e-r or the sequence of sounds represented by [pepɹ] — there is some meaning associated with it. In the case of p-a-p-e-r/[pepɹ] the meaning is what enables you to look at the flat sheet in front of you now, and know that someone is talking about the substance it is made of. Forms without meanings are linguistically useless, or to quote the famous linguist Roman Jakobson: ''language without meaning is meaningless.''

The pairing of form with meaning constitutes a linguistic *sign*. The meaning is one side of the coin; it is the thing to be signified. The form is the other side of the coin; it is the thing that does the signifying. In the following diagram, a linguistic sign is represented:

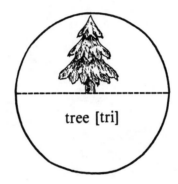

tree [tri]

The previous sections on phonetics, phonology, morphology and syntax all primarily involve the formal aspect of the linguistic sign. *Semantics,* which is the subject of this section, involves the study of the meaning aspect of the sign.

Given that semantics is the study of meaning, what specific questions does semantics address? First, it should be clear that one way in which we use language is to talk about the world, reality, be it the world around us or our own inner experiences and thoughts. Meaning, then, necessarily relates to non-linguistic reality in a certain way. How this relation is to be characterized is an important question to answer, for philosophers, psychologists and linguists alike. File 71 introduces the different conceptions (and misconceptions) of the meaning of 'meaning' and shows just how difficult it is to provide a satisfactory answer to this fundamental question.

Semantics is also concerned with the relationships between meanings. As native speakers of our language, we are all equipped with the ability to recognize that some meanings are similar to each other, to a greater or lesser extent. Some meanings are the opposite of each other. We know that when something is true, some other thing is necessarily true. We want to describe these meaning relationships as they are part of semantic competence. File 72 characterizes these different meaning relationships and a way to explicitly describe these relationships is suggested.

Semantics also deals with the ways meanings of words are combined to give meanings of larger linguistic expressions, such as phrases and sentences. How do we understand and interpret meanings of larger expressions composed of smaller ones? It turns out that the composition of meanings is much more involved than might be supposed at first. File 73 discusses the various factors governing the composition of meaning, ending with a detailed case study of how adjectives and nouns are combined, which shows in sharp relief the complexity involved.

185

SEMANTICS:
WHAT IS MEANING?

Semantics, roughly defined, is the study of *meaning*. In order for meaning to be successfully studied, of course, it must be made clear just what meaning *is*. Although most people do not feel confused about the nature of meaning, very few would find a precise explanation of it easy to give. In fact, meaning is a highly complex, many-faceted phenomenon, and any complete explanation of it must account for a surprisingly wide variety of different facts. In addition, some commonly held ideas about meaning turn out, on careful examination, not to work. The purpose of this file is to point out some of these misconceptions, and to discuss some of the kinds of things an explanation of meaning must address.

DICTIONARY DEFINITIONS

In our culture, where the use of dictionaries is widespread, many people may have the impression that a word's meaning is simply its dictionary definition. A little thought should show, however, that there must be more to meaning than just this.

It is true that when someone wants to find out what a word means, an easy and practical way to do it is to look the word up in a dictionary. Most people in our culture accept dictionaries as providing unquestionably authoritative accounts of the meanings of the words they define.

The role of dictionaries in our society as authorities on meaning leads many people to feel that the dictionary definition of a word more accurately represents the word's meaning than does an individual speaker's understanding of the word. Keep in mind, however, that the people who write dictionaries arrive at their definitions by studying the ways speakers of the language use different words. Some dictionaries are relatively prescriptive, others more descriptive, but all must face the fact that a word means what people use it to mean. There simply is no higher authority than the general community of native speakers of the language. This is obviously the position one must take in descriptive analysis, but even in prescriptive grammar words cannot be given strange definitions that don't correspond to actual uses of those words by the speech community.

A word's meaning is determined by the people who use that word, not, ultimately, by a dictionary.

The idea that a dictionary definition is all there is to a word's meaning runs into even more serious problems if one considers how dictionary definitions interrelate, rather than just looking at individual definitions in isolation.

In order to understand the dictionary definition of a word, one must know the meanings of the words used in that definition. For example, if the word 'ectomere' is defined as 'a blastomere that develops into ectoderm,' one must know the meanings of the words 'blastomere' and 'ectoderm' in order to understand the definition. Not only that, but one must also understand the words 'a,' 'that,' 'develops,' and 'into' (as well as the principles for interpretation of English syntactic constructions). One may take this ability for granted, but it is necessary for understanding definitions nonetheless.

If a word's meaning is its dictionary definition, then understanding this meaning involves understanding the meanings of the words used in the definition. But understanding the meanings of these words must involve understanding the meanings of the words in *their* definitions. And understanding *these* definitions must involve understanding the words they use, which of course would have to involve understanding even more definitions. The process is never-ending and ultimately must form a vicious circle.

Sometimes the circularity of a set of dictionary definitions is apparent by looking up just a few words. For instance, one English dictionary defines 'divine' as 'being or having the nature of a deity,' but defines 'deity' as 'divinity.' Another defines 'pride' as 'the quality or state of being proud,' but defines 'proud' as 'feeling or showing pride.' Examples like this are especially graphic, but essentially the same problem holds for *any* dictionary-style definition. Dictionaries are written to be of practical aid to people who already speak the language, not to make theoretical claims about the nature of meaning. People can and do learn the meanings of some words through dictionary definitions, so it would probably be unfair to say that such definitions are completely unable to characterize the meanings of words, but it should be clear that dictionary definitions can't be all there is to the meanings of all the words in a language. If meanings were just dictionary definitions (or something like dictionary definitons) and nothing else, the meaning system of a language would form a never-ending closed loop.

MENTAL IMAGES

If a word's definition is not all there is to its meaning, what else is there? One possibility is that a word's meaning includes a *mental image*. This is an attractive idea in many ways because words often do seem to conjure up particular mental images. Reading the words 'Mona Lisa,' for example, may well cause an image of the *Mona Lisa* to appear in your mind.

It should be pointed out, however, that a mental image can't be all there is to a word's meaning, any more than a dictionary definition can. One reason for this is that different people's mental images may be very different from each other, without the words really seeming to vary much in meaning from individual to individual. For a student, the word 'lecture' will probably be associated with an image of one person standing in front of a blackboard and talking, and may also include things like the backs of the heads of one's fellow students. The image associated with the word 'lecture' in the mind of a professor, however, is more likely to consist of an audience of students sitting in rows facing forward, and may include things like the feel of chalk in one's hand, and so on. A lecture as seen from a teacher's perspective is actually quite a bit different from a lecture as seen from a student's perspective. Even so, both the student and the professor understand the word 'lecture' as meaning more or less the same thing, despite the difference in mental images. It's hard to see how a word like this could mean essentially the same thing for different people, if meanings were just mental images.

Another problem with the idea that meaning is just a mental image is that the image associated with a word tends to be of a *typical* or *ideal example* of the kind of thing the word represents. Any word, however, can be used to represent a wide range of things, any one of which may or may not be typical of its kind. For example, try forming a mental image of a bird, and make sure it's clear in your mind before reading on.

If you are like most people, your mental image was not one of an ostrich or penguin. Yet ostriches and penguins are birds, and any analysis of the meaning of the word 'bird' must take this into account. It may be that such an analysis should also provide some indication of what the typical bird is like, but clearly some provision must be made for atypical birds.

An even more serious problem with the idea that a word's meaning is just a mental image is that many words, perhaps even most, simply have no clear mental images attached to them. What mental image is associated in your mind, for example, with the word 'forget?' How about the word 'the' or the word 'aspect?' Only certain words seem to have definite images, but no one would want to say that only these words have meanings.

MEANING AND REFERENCE

What else might be involved in a word's meaning, besides a definition and a mental image? One thing worth noting is that language is used to talk about things in the outside world, and many words seem to stand for (or *refer to*) actual objects or relations in the world. It seems reasonable, then, to consider the actual thing a word refers to, that is, its *referent*, as one aspect of the word's meaning.

But once again, it would be a mistake to think of reference as all there is to meaning. To do so would tie meaning too tightly to the real world. If meaning were defined as the actual thing an expression refers to, what would we do about words for things that don't exist? There simply is no actual thing that the words 'Santa Claus' refer to, yet obviously these words are not meaningless. Language can be used to talk about fiction, fantasy or speculation in addition to the real world, and any complete explanation of meaning must take account of this fact.

But even some sentences about the real world appear to present problems for the idea that an expression's meaning is just its referent. If meaning is the same as reference, then if two expressions refer to the same thing, they must mean the same thing. It follows that you should be able to substitute one for the other in a sentence without changing the meaning of the sentence as a whole. For instance, since the name 'Ronald Reagan' and the phrase 'the winner of the 1980 U.S. presidential election' both refer to the same individual, the following two sentences should mean the same thing:

> *Ronald Reagan is married to Nancy Reagan.*
> *The winner of the 1980 U.S. presidential election is married to Nancy Reagan.*

And in fact these two sentences do seem to mean the same thing, at least more or less. Clearly both describe the same fact. But now look at a sentence like the following:

> *Bill wanted to know if Ronald Reagan was the winner of the 1980 U.S. presidential election.*

Try substituting 'Ronald Reagan' for 'the winner of the 1980 U.S. presidential election.' What you get is:

Bill wanted to know if Ronald Reagan was Ronald Reagan.

But these two sentences don't mean the same thing *at all*! They don't even describe the same fact. If the idea of meaning as reference is going to work, it has to provide some explanation for why this sort of substitution doesn't.

MEANING AND TRUTH

No complete explanation of meaning can ignore the phenomenon of reference; yet it is clear that the meaning of an expression is not just its real-world referent. Despite the problems with this idea, however, it is probably not necessary to give up the key insight it provides: that meaning involves a relation between language and the world. To see how the apparent problems with this characterization can be avoided, consider for a moment how a *sentence* relates to the world, rather than just how individual *words* relate to the world.

Sentence meaning, even more than word meaning, may seem like a tricky, difficult-to-define concept; but perhaps it can be understood more clearly if instead of asking simply 'What is sentence meaning?' we take an indirect approach and ask "What do you know when you know what a sentence means?" Stop and think about this a moment, using a particular example (for instance, 'Ronald Reagan is asleep').

Obviously, to know what this sentence means is not the same as to know that Ronald Reagan is asleep, since any English-speaking person knows what the sentence means, but relatively few people know at any given time whether Ronald Reagan is asleep or not. However, anyone who does understand the sentence knows *what the world would have to be like in order for the sentence to be true*. That is, anyone who knows a sentence's meaning knows the conditions under which it would be true; they know its *truth conditions*. You know, for example, that in order for the sentence 'Ronald Reagan is asleep' to be true, the individual designated by the words 'Ronald Reagan' must be in the condition designated by the words 'is asleep.'

Note that the truth conditions of a sentence relate it to the world, but in a somewhat different way than ordinary, real-world reference relates particular words or expressions to the world. Sentences about Santa Claus, for instance, do have truth conditions, even though the words 'Santa Claus' have no real-world referent. Everyone knows what Santa Claus would have to be like *if* he were real, so it is not hard to describe the conditions under which a sentence containing these words would be true. Since the conditions under which something qualifies as Ronald Reagan are different from the conditions under which something qualifies as the winner of the 1980 U.S. presidential election, an explanation of meaning which includes the notion of truth conditions is also able to explain why the phrases 'Ronald Reagan' and 'the winner of the 1980 U.S. presidential election' cannot be freely substituted for one another, despite the fact that they refer to the same individual.

MEANING AND LANGUAGE USE

Specifying truth conditions effectively characterizes many important aspects of literal meaning, especially for ordinary declarative sentences. But how can you determine the conditions under which a *question* is true? Or an *order*, or a *wish*? In fact, many types of sentences do not even seem to be true or false at all. It should be clear, then, that truth conditions are just one aspect of meaning.

In addition to the conditions under which a sentence is *true*, meaning is probably also determined in part by the conditions under which a sentence may be *used*. Questions are used differently from assertions, orders are used differently from wishes, and so on. By specifying the kind of practical situation which must exist in order for a speaker to use a particular type of utterance (or *speech act*), many facts about the meaning associated with that particular speech act type may be made explicit.

By examining general conventions on language use, or *conversational maxims*, it is also possible to explain how utterances can imply things above and beyond their literal meaning.

CONCLUSION

Although there is much more to be said about the nature of meaning than what is discussed in this file, a few things should be clear: 1) Meaning (like any other aspect of language) is provided by a community of native speakers, not by some special authority like a dictionary or grammar-book. 2) The meaning of an expression is not just a definition composed of more words in the same language, since then the meaning system of any language would form a vicious circle. 3) The meaning of an expression is not just a mental image, since mental images seem to vary from person to person more than meaning does, since mental images tend to be only of typical or ideal examples of the things they symbolize, and since not all words have corresponding mental images. 4) The meaning of a word involves more than just the actual thing the word refers to, since not all expressions have real-world referents, and substituting expressions with identical referents for each other in a sentence can change the meaning of the sentence as a whole. 5) Knowing the meaning of a sentence involves knowing the conditions under which it would be true, so explaining the meaning of a sentence can be done in part by explaining its truth conditions. 6) Knowing the meaning of an utterance also involves knowing how to use it, so conditions on language use also form an important aspect of meaning.

Meaning is a complex phenomenon involving relationships between a language and the minds of its speakers, between a language and the world, and between a language and the practical uses to which it is put.

SEMANTICS: MEANING RELATIONSHIPS

Among the most studied types of semantic relationships between words are *synonymy, homonymy, antonymy,* and *entailment.* Native speakers of a language invariably can recognize when some meanings are synonymous, antonymous and anomalous; they can infer when some meaning follows from some other meaning.

Two words are *synonymous* if they have the same meaning, such as *sofa* and *couch,* or *cease* and *stop.* Some people would say that no two words have exactly the same meaning in all cases, but it is clear that pairs of words like the ones above are understood the same way most of the time. We can also entertain the possibility that there are different degrees of synonymy, depending on the degrees of meaning overlap between words. Thus, we can say that the words A and B are synonymous to some extent in the following diagram.

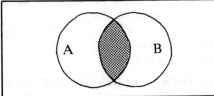

The bigger the overlap, the more similar the meanings are to each other. In the case of complete overlap, we will have complete synonymy.

If synonymy involves two different forms with the same meaning, *homonymy* might be considered its opposite; two different meanings which share the same form. We all know many pairs like this: [nayt] (*knight* and *night*), [flawr] (*flower* and *flour*), [bæŋk] (one for money; one as in river bank), [bɔr] (as in *to be boring,* or *to drill a hole*). *Homonyms* give rise to a kind of ambiguity known as *lexical ambiguity,* where a sentence can be interpreted two different ways depending on which of two homonyms is chosen. For example, in *He looked at the spring,* we could be talking about a source of water or a coiled piece of metal. In *the long drill was boring,* two sets of homonyms are involved, and depending on the context we could understand the sentence as referring to a classroom language drill or to a machine boring a hole in something.

Antonyms are words which are in some sense opposite in meaning. *Complete* and *incomplete, married* and *single* are examples of one type of antonym, where if one adjective isn't applicable, the other one must be — there is no middle ground. This is the familiar relationship of *contradiction,* where something and its negation concur. *Married* and *single* constitute a contradiction, because *single* means *not married.* We can represent the relationship by the use of the following diagram, in which A and B are antonymous in this sense:

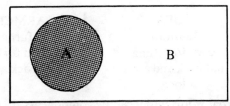

Hot and *cold, big* and *small, tall* and *short* represent another type of antonym, where the two words in a pair stand for opposite ends of a scale of temperature, size height, etc. Unlike cases such as *married/single,* it is possible to be neither hot nor cold, neither big nor small, neither tall nor short. These antonyms do not constitute contradiction but *contrary* relationships. This can also be illustrated by the following diagram:

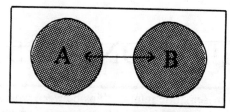

Pairs of words like *over* and *under, doctor* and *patient,* and *stop* and *go* represent still other types of antonyms. They are like *hot/cold, tall/short* in that they are also contrary to each other. It is possible to be neither over nor under something, neither a doctor nor a patient, to be neither stop nor go. They are unlike *hot/cold, tall/short* in that they do not represent extremes on some physical scales.

There is yet another kind of relationship between meanings, *entailment;* when one meaning holds, another meaning necessarily holds. For example, if someone is a man, he must also be human; if something is human, it must necessarily be animate. On the other hand, if someone is not a human, he cannot be a man; if something is not animate, it cannot be human. The definition of entailment is thus:

A entails B just in case:

    (1) If something is an A, it must be a B, too.

    (2) If something is not a B, then it cannot be an A.

This kind of relationship can be demonstrated with the following diagram, where A entails B:

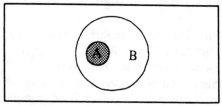

In order to give a correct account of relations like synonymy, antonymy, and entailment, we must look at the internal semantic structure of words. In other words, word-meanings are not monolithic blocks that cannot be analyzed any further. If they were, how could we tell, for example, that *single* and *married* constitute contradiction? We know they do, because 'single' means 'not married', and contrasts directly with 'married'. But understanding 'single' as 'not married' already presupposes analyzing words into meaning components. Similarly, how could we know that *sofa* and *couch* are synonyms, but *sofa* and *armchair* are only similar in meaning? We know this because *sofa* and *couch* share all the same semantic components: say, 'furniture', 'used for sitting', 'has back and arms', 'long', etc. But *sofa* and *armchair* will only share some of these components, but not all. Probably, it is only the first three components listed above that they share:

SOFA	ARMCHAIR
furniture	furniture
used for sitting	used for sitting
has back and arms	has back and arms
long	

In doing this, we have already analyzed words into meaning components. In the case of entailment, how do we know that being a man entails being human? It must be because the properties of being a man includes the property of being human. In the semantic breakdown of *man,* we presumably have the following situation:

MAN
human
male
adult

If we have a man, he must have the property of being human; on the other hand, if some being is not human, it cannot be a man. This is exactly how entailment is defined.

Apart from bringing out clearly the relationships between word meanings, this type of semantic 'breakdown' of the elements of a word's meaning is also crucial for explaining certain inferences that we make. Suppose I say, *The sheriff killed Jesse*. No matter what the circumstances are, without any more information whatsoever, it is possible to infer that Jesse is dead. This is because we know that the verb *kill* includes *die* (kill: cause somebody to die), which can in turn be analyzed as *become dead*. By the same kind of reasoning, we can recognize the contradiction in the sentences *The sheriff killed Jesse, but Jesse is still alive*. We can do this if we analyze *alive* as *not dead*. *Not dead* contradicts *dead* included in the meaning of *kill* (cause somebody to become dead).

The analysis of words into their meaning components is called *semantic decomposition* or *componential analysis*.

SEMANTICS: SEMANTIC COMPOSITION

While many people think of semantics as simply the study of word meanings, much of the work currently being done in linguistic semantics focuses on how meanings are combined to make larger units. Once the meanings of the individual words are determined, we must state rules for combining them as accurately as possible.

Just how do we combine these word meanings to form a sentence meaning? Note first of all that we don't just add up all the word meanings to get the meaning of the whole, as if we were making up a pot of soup. If semantics worked this way, we would expect the two sentences *The cat chased the dog* and *The dog chased the cat* to mean exactly the same thing since they are formed from exactly the same words. By this simplistic principle, we would expect to get the same meaning as well from the string of words *The chased dog cat the;* yet, this has no meaning at all.

Nor is the order of words the only thing that helps determine meaning; if it were, we would be surprised to find that *The dog chased the cat* has the same meaning as *The cat was chased by the dog,* for here the order of words is quite different. We know, though, that the structures of these two sentences are closely related. Similarly, the two sentences *He can't stand beans* and *Beans, he can't stand* have very similar syntactic structures originally and hence have the same meaning. From these examples we see that it is the *syntactic structure* as a whole, not word order alone, that determines the meaning of a sentence together with its word meanings. This relationship between meaning and syntactic structure is often described as the *Principle of Compositionality:* the meaning of a sentence is determined by the meaning of its words *and* by the syntactic structure in which they are combined. (This principle is also called *Frege's Principle,* after the philosopher Frege, who first stated it.)

The role of grammatical structure in semantics can also be seen from a sentence which can be formed by combining words and phrases in two different ways. Such sentences will have two different meanings, depending on which way the sentence is taken to be put together, and this ambiguity is known as *structural ambiguity*. Take the sentence *They are moving sidewalks*. If we assume this is formed by combining *are* with the phrase *moving sidewalks,* then we understand the sentence to refer to sidewalks which move people along, as are found in some airports. But if we assume this is formed by combining *are moving* with *sidewalks,* then it may be describing workmen who are picking up sidewalks and putting them down in another place. The meanings of the words are the same in both cases, but the syntactic structure is different, leading to different meanings. The sentence *They are visiting relatives* paraphrases as *They are relatives who are visiting* and alternatively as *They are going to visit relatives*. Still another example — a favorite one among linguists — is *Flying planes can be dangerous*.

That word meanings normally combine by regular principles dependent on syntactic structure can be seen vividly from the exceptional cases where they *do not*. Such cases are called *idioms*. The sentence *He kicked the bucket* generally means 'He died'. We cannot determine this meaning by combining the meaning of *kick* and the meaning of *the bucket* in the normal way, but rather we must learn the special meaning of the whole phrase *kick the bucket* as if it were a new 'word'. Similarly, in *to pull someone's leg* or *red herring,* we can't just understand the meaning by combining *pull* with *leg,* or *red* with *herring*. Idioms are cases where a sequence of words has a fixed meaning which is not composed of the literal meanings of its words by regular principles.

A Case Study: Adjective + Noun Combinations

We have argued above for the role of syntactic structures in the combination of meanings. This is undoubtedly true, but it is not yet the whole story. When we look closely, we find that grammatically parallel combinations (with the same syntactic structure) can still differ in the way meanings are combined. As a concrete example, let us look at adjective + noun combinations. We will see that adjectives combine with nouns in a number of different ways, depending on the type of adjective involved. (The type of noun also has an effect sometimes, but we will ignore this fact here.)

Most linguists would analyze the phrase *green screen* in terms of sets. Imagine first the set of all things that are screens; then imagine a second set, made up of all the things that are green in color. Anything that belongs to both sets — that is, the intersection of these two sets — is a green screen. This situation is represented visually with the following Venn diagrams:

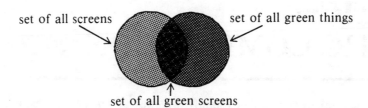

set of all screens   set of all green things

set of all green screens

Other phrases that work the same way are: *Chinese screen, blue suit, married woman, administrative duties*. An important point about these cases of *pure intersection,* as we may call them, is that the two sets can be identified independently. We can decide what is green and what isn't before we even know that we're going to then look for screens, for example.

This pattern of combining adjectives and nouns breaks down when we try to combine the words in *big whale* or *good beer*. In the case of *big whale,* the problem is that it is not possible to identify a set of big things in absolute terms. Size is always relative: what is big for whales is tiny for mountains; what is short for a giraffe is tall for a chicken. While it is possible to find a set of whales independently, the set represented by the adjective can't be just big, but rather must be big-for-a-whale. Similarly, *tall giraffe* will involve a set of things that are tall-for-a-giraffe, and *loud explosion,* a set of things that are loud-for-an-explosion (compare this with, say, *loud whisper,* which would use a completely different norm for loudness). Cases like this we call *relative intersection,* since the members of the set denoted by the adjective are determined relative to the type of thing denoted by the noun.

Good beer is another case of relative intersection. But *good* is even more relative than *tall* or *loud*. *Tall,* for example, always refers to a scale of vertical distance, and loud refers to a scale of volume of sound. We might say that *good* refers to a scale of quality, but what kind of quality? A good beer is probably judged on its taste, but a good ladder on how sturdy and useful it is, and a good record on how pleasurable the music is. *Good beer* could even be a beer that removes dirt well if we said *That's good beer to wash the walls with.* So *good* apparently refers to anything that fits our purposes well, and these purposes vary with the object and with how that object is used in a given case. In order to use and understand good and N correctly, we must have more knowledge about the context than in other cases of relative intersection.

Both types of intersection, pure and relative, have in common that these combinations actually refer to some of the objects denoted by the nouns themselves. For *green screen, tall giraffe,* and *good beer,* we are necessarily talking about screens, giraffes and beer, respectively. But in phrases like *possible solution* and *alleged thief,* this is not the case: a possible solution does not necessarily refer to a real solution, and an alleged thief does not refer necessarily to a thief. These are both examples of *non-intersection.* Logically, we can say that the use of intersection-type adjectives entails the reference to the objects denoted by the nouns, while the use of non-intersection cases does not.

Finally, there is a second non-intersection type that not only does not entail the reference to objects denoted by the nouns, it entails that the use of it does not refer to them. A *fake Picasso* by definition cannot refer to a Picasso. Of course, a fake N must have some characteristics of an N, or the word wouldn't be used at all; in fact, a good fake may be like an N in every respect except actually being a genuine N! Adjectives like *fake* we call *anti-intersection adjectives.*

As if this is not complicated enough, there are many other types of Adjective + Noun combinations besides the four just discussed. Just to give an example, the adjectives in *An occasional sailor walked by* and *I do a daily six-mile run* function very much like adverbs, as seen by the paraphrases *Occasionally, a sailor walked by* and *Every day I do a six-mile run.* These combinations do not follow the same rule of combination as the above four types. Consider yet another case. In *a hot cup of coffee,* what is hot is the coffee and not necessarily the cup. It seems here that what is combined is not the adjective and the N but the adjective and the noun phrase.

Researchers in semantic composition concern themselves with discovering the sorts of differences examined here and with writing precise rules to describe exactly how different types of expressions combine. In this case study of adjectival semantics, we have shown the intricacies in the combination of meaning. The complexity is a far cry from what we normally take the combination of meaning to be.

INTRODUCTION: PRAGMATICS

We have defined semantics as the study of meaning. Given this definition, we may be tempted to think that once we understand the semantics of a language, we completely understand that language. Meaning, however, involves more than just the semantic interpretation of an utterance. To fully understand the meaning of a sentence, we must also understand the context in which it was uttered. Consider the word 'ball'. In a sentence such as, "He kicked the ball into the net," we may visualize a round, black-and-white soccer ball about nine inches in diameter. In a sentence such as "She dribbled the ball down the court and shot a basket", we would visualize a basketball. Given yet another sentence, "She putted the ball in from two feet away," we would visualize another ball, a golf ball. In these examples, the word 'ball' is understood in different ways depending on what type of action is associated with it. Whatever understood meaning is common to ball in all of these contexts will be part of the word's core meaning. If we think of enough types of balls, we can come up with an invariant core meaning of 'ball' that will allow speakers to refer to any ball in any context. Nevertheless, even though we can discover a word's "invariant core", we normally understand more than that. It is the context that fills in the details and allows full understanding — such as the usual color of a soccer ball, the size of a basketball, or the weight of a golf ball. The study of the contribution of context to meaning is often called pragmatics.

We must ask ourselves, then, what is context: Is it simply the reality which fills in meaningful details missed by a theory such as the invariant core theory? No, it is not. Context can be divided into four subparts of which reality is but the first. We call this aspect of context the *physical* context; that is, where the conversation takes place, what objects are present, and what actions are taking place. Second, we have an *epistemic* context, background knowledge shared by the speakers and hearers. Third, we have a *linguistic* context, utterances previous to the utterance under consideration. Finally, we have a *social* context, the social relationship and setting of the speakers and hearers. As stated, this division of context may seem abstract, so let's consider how context helps people interpret a sarcastic remark. Suppose that two people, talking loudly, walk into an individual study section of the library (physical context). They sit down, still talking loudly, but no one says anything to them. After about five minutes, a person across the table from them sarcastically says: "Talk a little louder, won't you? I missed what you just said." The hearers will interpret this utterance as a request for them to be quiet, despite the fact that literally the speaker requests them to talk louder. Certain contextual facts help to signal that this is a request for silence: the utterance interrupts their conversation and breaks the silence between them and others (linguistic context); the request is made in sarcastic tone (linguistic context); people don't usually talk to strangers (epistemic context); libraries are quiet places (epistemic context); and they are in the library (physical context). From these observations, the hearers must conclude that the utterance is a request for silence.

Given this expanded definition of context, we can see that pragmatics does more than just "fill in the details". Pragmatics concerns itself with how people use language within a context and why they use language in particular ways. The files in this section present a selection of the various topics which linguists have included under the topic of pragmatics. File 81 shows how we use language to perform speech acts such as asserting, questioning, and requesting. Given the sentence "It's hot in here," a speaker could be simply stating a fact or requesting that the hearer turn on the air conditioning. Context helps determine which of these meanings the sentence will have. If the sentence were uttered in a museum where the hearer had no control over the environment, then it would have the first meaning. If uttered in the hearer's home, where the hearer can turn on the air conditioning, it might have the second meaning. File 82 shows how our utterances are guided by certain social conventions, the rules of conversation. In conversation we expect people to (1) stick to a topic, (2) be clear about their point, and (3) give just the right amount of information. If a speaker asks "What did you do last night?" and the hearer answers with a thirty minute run-down of the details of dinner, the laundry, TV, etc., a conversational principle about giving the right amount of information has been violated. When conversational principles are violated, the sentences often convey meanings beyond their literal sense. Consider the following conversation:

> Bill: How is Dan doing at his new job?
> Tom: Well, he hasn't been sent to prison yet.

Tom's answer to Bill is not directly relevant to Bill's question, so it must carry some other information, namely that Dan is not a particularly upstanding citizen. This extra information, not overtly stated, we call a conversational implicature. File 83 makes use of the theory presented in Files 81 and 82 to show how advertisers use language to create implicatures about their products. When we hear ''Calgon helps detergents get laundry up to 30% cleaner,'' we infer that Calgon *does* improve the quality of our wash. Yet, we cannot hold advertisers responsible for the truth of this claim. File 83 tells us why. Finally, Files 84 and 85 show how our everyday conversation has structure. The discourse of personal experience stories has a six-part structure: abstract, orientation, complicating action, evaluation, resolution, coda — much like any fictional narrative. But unlike the conversation of fiction, our conversations are marked with such features as hesitation noises, false starts, and speech errors. The most remarkable aspect of these features, however, is that we rarely notice them in our everyday conversations with people.

PRAGMATICS: SPEECH ACTS

FILE
81

We can divide the things that we do in this world into physical acts, mental acts, and speech acts. Hitting a baseball is a physical act. One cannot hit a baseball by imagining hitting a baseball (a mental act) nor by saying "I hit that baseball" (a speech act). Remembering about the one time you hit a baseball is a mental act. You cannot remember simply by swinging a bat (a physical act) nor by stating, "I remember having hit that ball" (a speech act). Finally we perform some acts simply by using language: speech acts.

We use language to do an extraordinarily wide range of activities. We use it to convey information, request information, give orders, make requests, make threats, give warnings, make bets, give advice, etc., as the following sentences suggest:

(1) John Jones has bad breath.
(2) Who ate my porridge?
(3) Shut up, you bubble brain.
(4) Please scratch my nose.
(5) Do that again and I'll punch your lights out.
(6) There is a gremlin in the back seat of your car.
(7) Five bucks says that the Buckeyes will beat the Wolverines this year.
(8) You ought to go to class at least once a quarter.

There can be little doubt that it is our ability to do things with language — to perform speech acts — that makes language useful to us. In fact, with language we can do things that would otherwise be impossible. Consider (4), a request for a hearer to scratch the speaker's nose. If we did not have language, how would this request be made? We could imagine the speaker taking the hearer's hand and rubbing his nose with it, but would this action have the same force as a spoken request? Probably not. How would the hearer know that the speaker meant "scratch", not "rub"? How would the hearer know that this action was a request and not an order? The action itself could not convey the politeness of the word "please", a major difference between requests and orders. In (6), we could warn the speaker that a gremlin is in the back seat of his car by pointing at it, but how could we give the advice in (8) without words? It would certainly be difficult.

Although we use language for all sorts of things, many more than were just listed, four of these uses seem to be of greater linguistic importance than the others because the language makes available special syntactic structures for marking them. We have a declarative sentence type which is dedicated to assertions, an interrogative sentence type which is dedicated to questions, and an imperative sentence type which is dedicated to orders and requests. (Table 1)

SENTENCE TYPE	SPEECH ACT	FUNCTION
declarative e.g. John Jones has bad breath.	assertion	conveys information, is true or false.
interrogative e.g. Can I talk to him? Who is he talking to?	question	elicits information.
imperative e.g. Please leave me alone. Leave me alone.	orders and requests	causes others to behave in certain ways.

Table 1: Four direct speech acts and their corresponding sentence types.

199

PERFORMATIVE VERBS

The special character of speech acts is brought out most clearly by the fact that we have a large number of verbs that we can use expressly to perform speech acts. Compare (9)-(16) with (1)-(8):

(9) I assert that John Jones has bad breath.
(10) I ask who ate my porridge.
(11) I order you to shut up, you bubble brain.
(12) I request that you scratch my nose.
(13) *I threaten you that if you do that again, I'll punch your lights out.
(14) I warn you that there is a gremlin in the back of your car.
(15) I bet you five bucks that the Buckeyes will beat the Wolverines this year.
(16) I advise you to go to class at least once a quarter.

As these sentences illustrate, the speech acts performed by sentences (1)-(8) can also be performed by embedding these sentences as complements of verbs which state the speech act. The usual name for these verbs is performative verbs, which can be defined as verbs that can be used to perform the acts they name. In (11), for example, we have an order, with the performative verb, "order" followed by the specific command, (3) "Shut up, you bubble brain." Interestingly, not every speech act has its own performative verb as is illustrated by (13). We would have to substitute "warn" for "threaten" if we wanted to use a performative verb to make a threat. Though the fact that we do not have a performative verb "threaten" might be an accident, we may not have such a verb because we find no need for a step between a warning and the threatened action.

IDENTIFYING DIRECT SPEECH ACTS

The type of speech acts that we have been considering are called direct speech acts since they perform their functions in a direct and literal manner. In the first set, (1)-(8), the sentences are statements of various actions. In the second set, (9)-(16), the sentences contain performative verbs which actually name the speech act. The only difference between sentences (8) and (16), for example, is the fact that (16) has the performative verb 'advise' which introduces (8). When trying to identify the type of speech act, we should consider its literal meaning by consideration of its form. With the speech acts of question, assertion, request, and order, we have seen that each has a particular form associated with it — interrogative, declarative, imperative, and imperative respectively. With other speech acts, the association with form is not quite so obvious. Let us, then, consider the threat. When we make a threat, we usually say that if something happens, then something negative will happen to the hearer. In this situation, we have uttered a conditional type statement, usually of the "if... then..." variety. Sentence (5) is a threat, yet its form is that of a compound, not a conditional. In English, however, we often express conditionals with compound statements, where the first conjunct can be interpreted as the "if" clause, and the second as the "then" clause. Sentence (5) then could be restated: "If you do that again, then I'll punch your lights out." We should note, however, that not all conditionals or compounds are threats. To fully understand (5) as a threat, we must understand that the "then" clause is something that the hearer will not like.

When identifying direct speech acts containing performative verbs, we may want to conclude that the utterance is the action named by the verb. While our conclusion may be correct, we must look at more than the verb. Consider the following sentences:

(17) I promise to take him to a bar tonight.
(18) John promises to take me to a bar tonight.
(19) I will promise to take him to a bar tonight.

Although all of these sentences use the verb "promise", only (17) uses it as a performative verb. Sentence (18) is a report on a promise, and (19) is a promise to make a promise sometime in the future, without actually using the verb 'promise' performatively. Why? Sentence (18) is not a promise because the subject of the sentence is John. When we use a performative verb, the subject must be "I" since speech acts concern the interaction between speakers and hearers. Sentence (19) is not a performative use of the verb "promise" because it is in the future tense using the helping verb "will". Speech acts, like all actions, take place in the present, so must use the present tense. Note that these grammatical constraints are constraints on direct performative verb speech acts, not all speech acts. Sentence (18) is still a direct speech act, an assertion, though it does not have a first person singular subject, and (19) is a promise though it is not in the present tense.

One test to see whether a verb is used performatively or not is the hereby-test. We take the word 'hereby' and insert it before the alleged performative verb:

> (20) I hereby promise to take him to a bar tonight.
> (21) John hereby promises to take me to a bar tonight.
> (22) I will hereby promise to take him to a bar tonight.

If the sentence sounds fine with 'hereby', then the verb is being used performatively. If the sentence sounds bad, then the verb is not being used performatively. Sometimes, this test is difficult to use because many sentences sound awkward with a performative verb, with or without 'hereby'. This awkwardness may arise because people tend not to utter speech acts using performative verbs.

A further complication arises in identifying speech acts when a performative verb does not match the speech acts. Consider (20):

> (20) I promise to tell Mom if you touch my toys one more time.

Sentence (20), though it has the verb "promise", uses "I" as its subject and is in the present tense, is not a promise. Instead it is a threat. When we make a promise, we offer to do something that we believe is beneficial to the hearer. When we make a threat, we offer to do something that hearers will not like. Since "telling Mom" is something that hearers generally do no appreciate, we must construe (20) as a threat. In identifying speech acts, then, we must consider what it means to perform an action. This consideration leads us to the topic of felicity conditions.

FELICITY CONDITIONS

Sentences can go wrong in a number of ways: words might be mispronounced (e.g., we might say "fog dight" instead of "dog fight"), or we might make an irregular verb regular even though we do not normally do so (e.g., we might say "he doved in" instead of "he dove in"), or we might make an ungrammatical sentence (saying *The boy who that I saw was Bill* instead of *The boy who I saw was Bill*), or a sentence might not make any sense (as in the case of *I know Carter's still President, but I'm wrong.*) Speech acts can go wrong too — by being situationally inappropriate.

Suppose that two drunks in a bar decide to get married and go up to the bartender and ask him to marry them. Suppose that the bartender used to be a court clerk and remembered exactly what must be said and done to marry people. Suppose finally that they go through the whole ceremony in front of witnesses, and that the bartender concludes by saying, "I hereby pronounce you husband and wife." Saying this, in this context, would not effect a marrying of these two people, and not necessarily because they are drunk or they are in a bar, but simply because the bartender does not have the official social status required to marry people. The marriage pronouncement is therefore situationally inappropriate, and we say in such cases that the speech act in question is infelicitous — has gone awry.

Associated with each speech act is a set of felicity conditions that must be satisfied if that speech act is to be correctly (including honestly) performed. Here are some felicity conditions on the acts of questioning and requesting (where "S" stands for the speaker, "H" for the hearer, "P" for some state of affairs, and "A" for some action):

A. S questions H about P:

   1. S does not know the truth about P.

   2. S wants to know the truth about P.

   3. S believes that H may be able to supply the information about P that he or she wants.

B. S requests H to do A:

   1. S believes A has not yet been done.

   2. S believes that H is able to do A.

   3. S believes that H is willing to do A-type things for S.

   4. S wants A to be done.

When we think about what it means to ask a question or make a request, then, what we think about are the felicity conditions associated with each of these speech acts.

Notice that we would regard as peculiar anyone who seriously asks his or her pet dog questions about some upcoming election — indeed one could construct a comedy routine around a dog that somehow answers serious questions. The problem, of course, is that we know that dogs cannot answer serious (or any other) questions (see A.3). And, in normal conversation we do not ask people questions that we already know the answers to. There are, of course, exceptions — people playing trivia or other games, lawyers, teachers giving exams, but we recognize these situations to be socially exceptional in one way or another. Playing trivia violates A.2 for in trivia games people don't seriously want the information they seem to request, interrogating witnesses violates A.1 for a good lawyer tries to avoid any real surprises, and asking exam questions violates A.1 and A.2 for the teacher does know the answer. The fact is that we ask questions for a number of different purposes in different social contexts, and to reflect these differences, we can modify the particular felicity conditions. For trivia players and teachers we could eliminate felicity condition A.2, and for lawyers, we could eliminate condition A.1.

The felicity conditions for requests are less variable in the sense that we make requests for a single purpose: to get something done. Normally, we do not ask people to do things that have already been done. Indeed, doing so would make one extremely unpopular. And asking people to do things they cannot do would normally be regarded as a cruelty or a joke, depending on the nature of the request. If we do not want to get into trouble socially, we will be careful not to ask people who have higher social standing than we do to do things for us unless the circumstances are quite special. Finally, we do not usually request things that we do not want done.

INDIRECT SPEECH ACTS

Perhaps the most interesting single fact about speech acts is that we very commonly, in some cases almost invariably, perform speech acts indirectly. So far, we have discussed direct speech acts which can be performed in two ways: (1) by making a direct, literal utterance, or (2) by using a performative verb that names the speech act. In addition to these direct speech acts, we can use the felicity conditions to make indirect speech acts. Consider the speech acts question and request once again:

C. Questions

   1. Direct

      a. Did John marry Mary?

      b. I ask you whether or not John married Mary.

   2. Indirect

      a. I don't know if John married Mary. (A.1)

      b. I would like to know if John married Mary. (A.2)

      c. Do you know if John married Mary? (A.3)

    D. Requests
        1. Direct
            a. Please take out the garbage.
            b. I request you to take out the garbage.

        2. Indirect
            a. The garbage isn't out yet. (B.1)
            b. Could you take out the garbage? (B.2)
            c. Would you mind taking out the garbage? (B.3)
            d. I would like for you to take out the garbage. (B.4)

There is something up front about the C.1 questions and the D.1 requests. Sentence C.1.a. taken literally is a request for information about John's marrying Mary. The same is true of C.1.b. Notice, however, that C.2.a. taken literally is not a question at all. It is an assertion about the speaker's knowledge. C.2.b. is also an assertion. C.2.c., in contrast, is a question, but a question which literally asks whether the hearer knows something. (We sometimes say things like "It literally scared me to death", but this is not, of course, a literal use of the word literal.)

    As the notes given in connection with the sentences C.2 and D.2 suggest, indirect speech acts enjoy a very close connection with the felicity conditions on speech acts. Indeed, it can be argued that to perform a particular speech act indirectly, one need only formulate a question, assertion, or request or order that evokes a felicity condition on that speech act. In general, if the felicity condition concerns the best interests of the speaker, an assertion or request or order is used. If it concerns the best interests of the hearer, a question is used. So instead of assuming that felicity condition B.3 on requests holds, the speaker might ask if it does, as in "Would you mind taking me to work?", by way of making a polite request. This type of knowledge makes it easy to create indirect speech acts. To identify an indirect speech act, it helps to first consider whether an utterance is a direct speech act since the direct ones are easier to recognize. If it is not direct, then it must be indirect. From there, we can consider the context in which such an utterance would be made and the necessary felicity conditions for that utterance.

SPEECH ACT EXERCISES

I. Identify the speech act in each of the following sentences and state whether it is direct or indirect. Consider the contexts in which these sentences could be uttered. How does context affect their function?

	Speech Act	Direct?
1. Don't smoke.	_____	_____
2. Can you pass the salt?	_____	_____
3. The washing machine is broken, dear.	_____	_____

II. A father tells his child: "I promise to take you to the zoo tomorrow."
      1. What is the speech act?_____
      2. Is it direct or indirect? _____
    Why?

III. Write a direct speech act sentence, once using a performative verb and once without, for the following speech acts. Then write an indirect speech act sentence for each.

      1. question
         direct
            literal _____

            performative verb _____

         indirect _____

      2. request
         direct
            literal _____

            performative verb _____
         indirect _____

      3. promise
         direct
            literal _____

            performative verb _____
         indirect _____

IV. The speech act promise has the following felicity conditions:

    S promises H to do A.
        1. S believes H wants A done.
        2. S is able to do A.
        3. S is willing to do A.
        4. A has not already been done.

In this file we noted that the speech act threat is very similar to promise. Because of this similarity, we can expect their felicity conditions to also be similar. Modify the promise felicity conditions to create the felicity conditions for a threat.

    S threatens H that he will do A.
        1. _____
        2. _____
        3. _____
        4. _____

PRAGMATICS: RULES OF CONVERSATION

The use of language, like most other forms of social behavior, is governed by social rules. Some rules are designed to protect people's feelings by showing respect (e.g. rules governing whether or not you can use a first name in addressing someone or must use a title and last name). Rather more important are rules designed to protect the integrity of our language. It is reasonably clear that if people were to decide to tell lies in some random way, so that listeners would have no way of determining when speakers are lying and when they are telling the truth, language would cease to be of any value to us. In response to this, we have settled on a set of conventions governing language use that preserves its integrity by requiring us, among other things, to be honest in its use, to have evidence for what we say, and to make what we say relevant to the speech context. What is interesting about these conventions is that they were never officially proposed and voted on by anybody, but instead have emerged naturally. And we·learn them in much the same way we learn most social rules—by trial and error.

The primary reason we need rules governing the use of language is that we humans cannot be expected to behave in reasonable ways without them. This is as true of our using language as it is of our driving cars or playing games. The philosopher H.P. Grice formulated a *Cooperative Principle*, which he believed underlies language use, according to which we are enjoined to make sure that what we say in conversation furthers the purposes of these conversations. Obviously, the requirements of different types of conversations will be different. In a business meeting, one is normally expected to keep one's remarks confined to the topic at hand unless it is changed in some approved way. Some close friends having a few beers at a bar would not be governed by tight rules of this sort. Nevertheless, even in a casual conversation, the conversation will normally have one or more purposes and each of the parties to it can be expected by the rest to behave in ways that further these purposes. Thus, even the most casual conversation is unlikely to consist of random sentences like the following:

(1) Kim: How are you today?
     Sandy: Oh, Harrisburg is the capital of Pennsylvania.
     Gail: Really? I thought the weather would be warmer.
     Mickey: Well, in my opinion, the soup could have used a little more salt.

Grice argued that there are a number of conversational rules or *maxims* that regulate conversation by way of enforcing compliance with the cooperative principle. At the heart of the system of maxims are the *Maxims of Quality*:

A. MAXIMS OF QUALITY:
   1. Do not say what you believe to be false.
   2. Do not say that for which you lack adequate evidence.

The first Maxim of Quality is self-evident. Without regular compliance with this maxim, language would quite literally cease to exist because it would be useless to us. The second is more interesting for it is only when we believe we have adequate evidence for some claim that we can have much confidence that we are observing the first Maxim of Quality. Nevertheless, people differ strikingly in what they think is good evidence for their views, especially in the areas of religion and politics (which is why these topics are so often off limits as topics of conversation).

Because we may normally assume that speakers are obeying the Cooperative Principle, we sometimes draw inferences from what people say that are based on this assumption. Consider the following conversation:

(2) Sandy: We need someone to make some sort of fruit salad for the picnic.
     Kim: I can make my family's favorite fruit salad.

Sandy would likely draw the inference that Kim has actually made this fruit salad before, for the very best evidence that Kim can make this salad is that he has actually made it. However, this is not a valid inference. Kim could legitimately say what was said based on the fact that he had watched it being made many times and thought he knew all that needed to be known to make it. People sometimes say that the word *can* in a sentence like this is very weak (because they think it means merely 'is possible') and would say therefore that Sandy's drawing this inference is wrong-headed. However, this literalist view is out of touch with how we use the language. Suppose Kim were to make the salad and it were to come out very badly. Something like the following conversation might take place.

(3)   Sandy: I thought you said you could make this salad!
      Kim: Well, I thought I could.

As Sandy's challenge illustrates, we take claims involving the word *can* quite seriously—because we assume that speakers using it are obeying the second Maxim of Quality.

A second class of maxims consists of the **Maxim of Relation** (often called the **Maxim of Relevance**):

B. MAXIM OF RELATION/RELEVANCE: 1. Be relevant.

This maxim is sometimes called the supermaxim because it is central to the orderliness of conversation—it limits random topic shifts like those of (1) above—but also because it is very important to understanding how we draw *conversational inferences* of the sort we talked about in connection with examples (2) and (3). Consider the following conversation:

(4)   Sandy: Is Gail dating anyone these days?
      Kim: Well, he goes to Cleveland every weekend.

In this case, Sandy will likely draw the inference that Gail is dating someone because she will assume that what Kim has said is relevant to what she had said. In fact, if Kim knew that Gail goes to Cleveland every weekend because he has a job there, what she said would have been very misleading.

The next pair of maxims are the **Maxims of Quantity**:

C. MAXIMS OF QUANTITY:
   1. Make your contribution as informative as is required.
   2. Do not make your contribution more informative than is required.

The first maxim is intended to insure that we make as strong a claim as is warranted (see the second Maxim of Quality) in any given circumstance and the second is meant to insure that we not make a *stronger* claim than is warranted in that circumstance. The following conversation illustrates an inference that might be drawn on the assumption that the speaker is obeying the first Maxim of Quantity.

(5)   Gail: How far can you run without stopping?
      Kim: Twenty-four miles.
      Gail: I guess you can't run a whole marathon without stopping.
      Kim: Nonsense, I've done it a number of times.

Notice that what Kim first says must be true if what she says next is true. Certainly, if someone can run over twenty-six miles without stopping, then they can run twenty-four miles without stopping. However, Gail quite naturally was assuming that Kim was obeying the first Maxim of Quantity.

The final group of maxims we will discuss are the **Maxims of Manner**:

D. MAXIMS OF MANNER:
   1. Avoid obscurity of expression.
   2. Avoid ambiguity.
   3. Be brief.
   4. Be orderly.

These maxims are reasonably self-explanatory. The first enjoins us to avoid use of jargon or other terms our listeners cannot be expected to know. The second maxim requires us to avoid saying things that have two or more meanings (e.g., *He promised to phone at noon.*) unless our listeners can be expected to know which meaning is intended. The third maxim tells us not to expound at length on a topic when a few words will do. The fourth comes down to saying that we should organize what we say in some intelligible way.

In discussing Grice's Conversational Maxims we pointed out that we commonly draw inferences from what people say based on the assumption that they are obeying the Cooperative Principle. This system of inference drawing is a kind of side effect of the maxims, maxims whose primary reason for being is regulate conversation. One major reason for exploiting the maxims in this way is to make conversation easier. (Notice that *How far can you run without stopping?* is shorter than *What is the greatest distance you can run without stopping?*)If we were to be forced in conversation to speak only in logically impeccable ways (e.g., to draw only logical inferences), conversation would proceed at a very slow pace (even assuming counterfactually that most of us actually that most of us have the logical capacities to do this). In conversation (4) above, Kim might have said *I believe that he may be dating someone because he goes to Cleveland every weekend and that's not his hometown and he doesn't have a job there.* Given our set of maxims, Kim can say what she says and rely on the listener to figure out what she means.

There are two other reasons we use these maxims to communicate indirectly: (a) we sometimes need to avoid telling the truth because our frankness may hurt us; and (b) we sometimes need to avoid telling the truth because the truth may hurt someone else. Grice gave an example of a professor who was asked to write a letter of recommendation for a recent Ph.D. who was applying for a teaching position. Suppose that the letter went like this:

Dear Colleague:
    Mr. John J. Jones has asked me to write a letter on his behalf. Let me say that Mr. Jones is unfailingly polite, is neatly dressed at all times, and is always on time for his classes.

                                             Sincerely yours,
                                             Harry H. Homer

Do you think Mr. Jones would get the job? This is an example of a *flouting* of a maxim—in this case, the Maxim of Relation/Relevance. Professor Homer has wanted to convey his negative impression of the candidate without actually saying anything negative about him (perhaps out of a misguided sense of politeness). The receiver of this letter will assume that although Professor Homer has appeared to be violating the Maxim of Relation/Relevance, he is nevertheless not actually intending to be uncooperative, and thus has said all of the relevant positive things he can think of—which is the essence of damning with faint praise.

Conventions of politeness often keep us from insulting people overtly (as well as a desire not to get our lights punched out). By exploiting the maxims, we can insult people and (usually) get away with it. So, if someone does some bragging and another says, "I'm totally awed," the first will probably take this as an insult, but not one that he/she can legitimately take exception to. This conversational inference arises out of the recognition that the insulter is violating the first Maxim of Quality—the recognition that the claim is too strong (see the Maxims of Quantity) to likely be true. Indirect communication like this is very important to us. If a teacher believes that his/her students are cheating on a quiz, he/she might say, "I see a lot of roving eyes!" The students will doubtless take this as an indirect charge that someone appears to be cheating. The Maxim of Relation/Relevance plays a role here because a claim about roving eyes is relevant just in case the eyes are roving to the wrong place. However, this way of trying to stop the cheating, since it falls short of an overt accusation, would probably not poison the atmosphere in the class.

The needs of social harmony and linguistic integrity are not always consistent with each other. It is said that there are societies in which the failure to answer a stranger's question is considered very impolite and therefore people in this society will give a stranger a wrong answer to a question rather than give no answer. Which is to say that Grice's maxims, being conventions, are very different from natural laws.

EXERCISES

1. Grice's actual statement of the third Maxim of Manner was "Be brief (avoid unnecessary prolixity)." What two Maxims of Manner does this statement violate?

2. Suppose you ask a friend what he thought of the new movie in town, and he replies, "Well, the costumes were authentic." Which rule guides you to the inference that your friend probably did not like the movie? Why?

3. Advertisements for over-the-counter drugs often make claims like "contains the most effective ingredient" or "contains the ingredient that doctors recommend most." These claims imply that the drugs are effective. What maxim is involved here? Is the inference a logically sound one? Why?

4. Jokes often rely on the hearer's knowledge of rules of conversation for their humorous effect. In the following joke by Henny Youngman, identify the rule which is being blatantly violated:

> I come home last night, and there's a car in the dining room.
> I said to my wife, "How did you get the car in the dining room?"
> She said, "It was easy. I made a left turn when I came out of the kitchen."

PRAGMATICS: LANGUAGE IN ADVERTISING

FILE
83

Advertising is a business in which language is used to *persuade* people to do things (e.g., buy some product or vote for someone) and/or believe things (believe that some corporation is trustworthy or that some political philosophy is a good one). There are other such businesses: the law (as when a lawyer tries to get a jury to convict or acquit a defendant), politics (as in debates on the floors of the House or Senate), or education (as in introductory linguistics courses where efforts are made to persuade people to abandon various linguistic prejudices).

Language plays a crucial role in advertising. In the case of radio advertising, all there is is language and music. In the case of print advertising, we find both graphic and linguistic messages. Even in the case of television advertising, which people often perceive as being primarily a visual medium, language is often of decisive importance to the conveying of an advertiser's message. One way to get an impression of the importance of language to advertising is to turn off the sound during commercial breaks. What becomes clear from this sort of exercise is that language has at least the function of *interpreting* what we see on screen. Perhaps more important though is the *claim making* role of language in advertising.

Many advertisements have about as much substance as a wisp of smoke, especially some of those that appear on television. The reason for this is, in part, because in many cases there is virtually nothing both substantive and truthful that can be said about a particular product that is not true of some or all other products in its class. In order to convince yourself of this, imagine that you have been asked to write a TV commercial for a new diet cola that costs the same as the two or three most popular brands and which uses the same sweetener and essentially the same flavoring agents they do. Write 50-100 words of truthful, persuasive copy to be read by some star of your choice. (If you succeed, buy an airline ticket for New York City, take your copy to the various firms on Madison Avenue, and you just might get a job.) You might think about why TV might be a haven for members of product groups like soft drinks, deodorants, bars of soap, toilet tissue, etc., in which the various members of each class differ very little from each other.

In the case of advertisements that make or imply substantive claims, the consumer might reasonably require that these claims be true, which brings us to the age-old question of what ought to be the standards of truth in advertising (as if there could or should be different standards of truth for different human activities). Linguists have a great deal to contribute to the answering of this question.

SINCERITY CONDITIONS

We use language to do things: make assertions, ask questions, make requests, give orders, make offers, make bets, give warnings, etc. Each of these different types of *speech acts* is subject to *sincerity conditions* (which are a special case of what are called *felicity conditions*), conditions that must be satisfied before a speech act can be said to be sincerely or honestly performed. Here is a pairing of some speech acts with their corresponding sincerity conditions:

SPEECH ACT	SINCERITY CONDITION
1. Assertion	Speaker believes the assertion to be true.
2. Question	Speaker wants to know the answer to his or her question.
3. Request	Speaker wants the requested action to be performed.
4. Warning	Speaker believes that the danger warned about is real and may require evasive action by the listener.
5. Offer	Speaker believes the offer will satisfy the need that gave rise to it.

So, if a speaker asserts something he knows to be false to you, or idly requests you to find out answers to questions he doesn't care to know the answers to, or offers to do something for you that he knows won't do you any good, he or she has betrayed you by being insincere. (The boy who cried "Wolf!" too often violated the sincerity condition on warnings.)

How can we know whether or not what someone says is true? One attractive approach to this question is to specify the truth conditions of sentences (i.e., spell out the specifics of the sincerity condition associated with assertions) and then see if these truth conditions are satisfied.

A. A truth condition of a sentence S is any condition that must be satisfied for S to be true.

If someone asserts *The snow outside is white*, then, for that to be true, the snow outside must be white. Or if someone says *John left before Bill left*, then it must be the case that John left at some time t1 and Bill left at some time t2 and t1 preceded t2. Or if someone asserts *John has killed his worst enemy*, then John must have had a worst enemy, that enemy must have once been alive, that enemy must no longer be alive, and the latter state of affairs must have resulted from some direct action John took. And so on.

As the examples of the preceding paragraph show, it is often relatively easy to specify the truth conditions of sentences. Let's try our hand, however, at determining the truth conditions of a real (and very complex) and not uncommon type of advertising claim. Examine the following advertisement for the 1978 Chevette automobile and state the truth conditions for the "a lot more car for a lot less money" claim.

> CHEVROLET CHEVETTE (NBC, 2/25/78, prime time) Singers: *See what's new today.* Man: *Chevrolet announces "A lot more Chevette for a lot less money." New Chevette standard equipment includes a radio, reclining bucket seats, white wall tires, console, sports steering wheel, a 1.6 litre engine: 18 new standard features in all. Plus a wide hatch, carpeting, front disc brakes, rack and pinion steering, and more. The '78 Chevy Chevette. A lot more car for a lot less money.*

In order for this "more for less" claim to be true, there must be two cars, C1 and C2, such that C1 is a lot more car than C2 and C1 costs a lot less money than C2. Let's therefore set up the following chart for the truth conditions for this claim:

	A lot more car	for	a lot less money
C1			
vs.			
C2:			

Now, the Standard 1978 Chevette (STD 78) is said to be "a lot more car" than some other car, presumably the Standard 1977 Chevette (STD 77). Let us concede that STD 78 is a lot more car than STD 77 and enter 'true' under this column in the above chart. Now, did STD 78 cost "a lot less money" than STD 77? In fact, it cost more money, not less (See Geis (1982)). So we must enter 'false' in the column under "a lot less money." But that means that the claim as a whole is false.

This Chevette advertisement came with the following five second disclaimer—in very small print at the bottom of the screen during the last part of the oral text: *Comparison of manufacturer's suggested retail prices for a '77 Chevette with features now standard on '78 Chevettes. Except Scooter.* This statement is for all practical purposes unreadable—it takes a reading speed of 228 words per minute; the letters occupy only 3.7% of the vertical height of the screen; and the announcer competes for the attention of the viewer by continuing to talk. Yet it is quite inconsistent with the oral text, which clearly compares STD 78 and STD 77. What it says is that General Motors is comparing STD 78 with a comparable 1977 Chevette (COMP 77), i.e., a 1977 Chevette equipped in the same way as STD 78. Is the more for less claim true of STD 78 and COMP 77? Let us concede that STD 78 costs "a lot less" than COMP 77 since this is rather hopelessly subjective anyway. However, is the STD 78 "a lot more car" than a COMP 77? Of course not, they are *precisely the same car*. So this more for less claim is also false. What we have here is two inconsistent claims—a very attractive offer of a better equipped and cheaper STD 78 over the STD 77 and an inconsistent and much less attractive, but also *false* claim involving STD 78 and COMP 77. We have here a kind of verbal bait and switch offer. Although some more for less claims are genuine, most such claims seem to be of the doubly false variety.

Unfortunately, there are two approaches to the giving of truth conditions: a narrow, legalistic *literalist* approach and a broader, *pragmaticist* approach. Consider what truth conditions you would assign to the following, frequently made type of advertising claim before reading further:

6. X kills the germs that cause infection (or plaque or bad breath or perspiration odor).

A literalist might reason thus:

If X kills (say) 80% of infection-causing germs, then X does kill infection-causing germs. In fact, if it kills 60 or 40 or even 20 or 10 or 5% of such germs, then it must be conceded to kill infection-causing germs. So this claim is a very weak one.

However, a pragmatist might argue:

Generic sentences are normally used to express significant inductive generalizations, as in *Gold is heavier than water, Dogs bark,* or *Mass equals force times accelleration* and thus, by their very nature are strong claims. Claim (6), being a generalization of the same sort, should therefore be considered a strong claim.

Both of these positions are attractive ones. Indeed, they both seem to be true. But how can they both be right? We shall return to this question below.

LINGUISTIC INFERENCES

Advertising messages, like any others, can convey information directly and/or indirectly. If someone says *I hate it that John Jones is President*, he or she makes a direct assertion about his or her feeling hatred about something and, in the process, conveys indirectly the (false) information that John Jones is President. The person saying this, we might say, *asserts* one thing *directly*, and *indirectly implies* something else.

For example, in a commercial for Contac, a man says:

Interesting fact about what he took. Its decongestant lasts only four hours per dose, and it contains aspirin, which can upset your stomach. Contac lasts up to twelve hours per dose and does not contain aspirin.

This commercial conversationally implies that Contac does not upset stomachs. The inference isn't a valid one. The best way to check this is with the *cancellability test: If a sentence S entails a proposition P then the logical conjunction of S and the denial of P should be a contradiction.* Our S is *Contac does not contain aspirin* and P is *Contact does not upset stomachs,* so we need to determine if *Contac does not contain aspirin, but it does upset stomachs* is a contradiction. Clearly it is not, so the inference is not a valid one. It is, instead, a conversationally warranted inference, based on the Maxims of Quantity and Relation. The speaker has been overspecific (i.e., said too much thus violating the Maxim of Quantity) about aspirin in saying that it can cause upset stomachs *unless* this property is peculiar to aspirin, as compared with what is in Contac.

Another example of a conversationally warranted, but invalid inference from over-the-counter drug advertising concerns claims like *P contains the most effective pain reliever* or *the ingredient doctors prescribe most,* etc. Saying that P contains the most effective pain reliever implies that P is effective, but this is not a valid inference. P might not contain enough of the ingredient to do any good. Notice that *P contains the most effective pain reliever, but for some reason, it isn't a bit effective* isn't contradictory. This inference is based on the Maxim of Relation (Relevance): telling the consumer that some product P contains an ingredient which has a property Q is relevant to the consumer only if P also has the property Q.

The question arises as to whether or not in our theory of truth in advertising should we decide to hold advertisers responsible for what they imply as well as what they assert. Should the makers of Contact, for instance, be required to prove that their product does not upset stomachs? In order to deal sensibly with this question it is necessary to make some distinctions among different types of inferences. In regard to the *soundness* of an inference, it is useful to distinguish two types of inferences: *valid inferences* and invalid but conversationally *warranted inferences.*

B. A sentence S *validly implies* (or *entails*) a proposition P if and only if in every circumstance in which S is true, P is also true.

Examples: *John hit Bill again* validly implies that John hit Bill at least once before.

John or Bill will go validly implies that John will go or Bill will go.

C. A sentence S *conversationally implies* a proposition P if and only if P is warranted by the meaning of S, the speech context, sincerity (and other felicity) conditions associated with the speech act being performed in the saying of S, and various rules of conversation

Examples: If John says *I don't have a way home* at the end of a party, he conversationally implies (consider the Felicity Conditions for Requests and the Maxim of Relation) that he wants a ride home and if Mary then says *I've got a car* to him, she conversationally implies that she will take him home (see the Maxim of Relevance and the Sincerity Condition identified earlier in this file on Offers.)

If one weightlifter says to another that she can clean and jerk 435 pounds, she conversationally implies that she cannot clean and jerk more than 435 pounds. The First Maxim of Quantity (saying as much as is required in a given context means not saying less than is required) is involved in this inference. It will normally be taken to imply that she has cleaned and jerked this weight at least once. The reason for this is the speaker will have to be taken following the second Maxim of Quantity and the best evidence that someone *can* do something is that they *have* done this thing. (Satisfy yourself that neither inference is actually a valid one.)

However, if this weightlifter is asked by her husband to lift a 200 pound object for him and she says she can, this would not implicate that she can lift no more than 200 pounds (again she is matching the quantity of her claim to the context). Differences in the speech context evoke the different applications of the Maxims of Quantity in these two weightlifting cases.

Most people seem willing to concede that advertisers should be held responsible for what they assert directly and for valid inferences that consumers might draw from what advertisers say. What about invalid but conversationally warranted inferences?

One crucial consideration in the attempt to answer this last question is whether or not people generally can reliably tell these two types of inferences apart. On the first day of Autumn Quarter of 1983, 272 introductory linguistics students at The Ohio State University were asked to judge, for 50 cases of pairs of sentences like (7) and (8), whether or not the first sentence validly implies the second. (Several ordinary language definitions and examples were given to make clear what sort of judgment was called for.)

7. a. ABC filters remove bacteria from your drinking water.
   b. If you use ABC filters, your drinking water should be free of bacteria.

8. a. I left because I wanted to.
   b. If I hadn't wanted to, I wouldn't have left.

As was predicted by the experimenters, these students had great trouble making the distinction between valid and invalid but conversationally warranted inferences in many cases, including in particular cases involving generic sentences. Some 60% of the students said that (7a) entails (7b), although, as we have seen, a claim like (7a) could be true but (7b) false — at least on the literalist view — if ABC filters were to remove even a small percentage of the bacteria in question. The sentences of (8) are much harder to judge. Suppose that some speaker wanted to leave some place and that the police had also ordered him to leave. In this circumstance, (8a) could be true, but (8b) false. So the inference isn't a valid one. However, 75% of the students said this *was* an entailment. This experiment appears to have confirmed the pragmaticist view that generic sentences are normally taken to be strong claims. It would therefore clearly be a mistake to assume that people are generally able to distinguish valid from invalid advertising claims, for the distinction between valid inferences and conversationally warranted inferences is apparently a distinction which

which makes no difference for most speakers. The question, then, is: Should a theory of truth in advertising be based on the system of inference drawing that we all use in ordinary life or on some other more stringent system drawn from the reasoning practices of logicians or scientists or lawyers—systems that presume the equivalent of a good deal of college-level training?

Let us return to example (6), which had two contradictory but eminently attractive interpretations. Interestingly, it is possible to resolve the conflict by considering the speech act being performed in the saying of a sentence like this. Sentence (6), construed as a bare assertion, i.e., as a speech act which is designed simply to convey information, could occur in some scientist's report even if it were to prove to kill only 5% of the germs that cause infection. It might go into this report at the bottom of a list of germicides, but it could reasonably be placed on such a list. Certainly, it would not go on a list of products that do not kill infection-causing germs. However, if (6) were to occur in a TV commercial, then it is doing much more than simply conveying information, for in this case, it serves as a supporting argument in the attempt by the advertiser to entice the viewer to accept a *commercial offer*. As such, it is subject to the sincerity condition on offers, that the speaker believe that his offer will satisfy the need that gave rise to the offer in the first place—in this case, a need for protection from infection. It would appear therefore that the truth condition for (6) when it occurs in an advertisement is that X must kill enough infection-causing germs to protect the user from infection under normal conditions of use, however much that might be. Thus, it seems that the truth conditions for sentences are sensitive to the speech acts they are used to perform, which should not be surprising since the function of language is to allow us to do speech acts.

It is interesting to speculate about the origins of our modes of inference drawing. The philosopher David Lewis has argued that a condition of truthfulness must exist for assertions in a language community if there is to be a language at all. This would also seem to be true of the sincerity conditions of other kinds of speech acts. Offers would be of no use to a speech community if it could not count on these offers being fulfilled most of the time. And the requirements that we have evidence for what we say, that we say relevant things, and that we not overstate or understate what we believe to be true are necessary for effective, cooperative, social behavior. Language is a social phenomenon and those of us who use it make an implicit commitment to follow the social rules for its use.

EXERCISES

EXERCISE 1: Examine the following advertisement and then informally state the truth conditions for the claim that Duration relieves various conditions for "up to 12 continuous hours" and the claim that Duration relieves these conditions for "12 continuous hours." Are they the same? Comment on the references to "all day" and "all night." What claim(s) do you believe the advertiser should be held responsible for in this case?

DURATION NASAL SPRAY (NBC, 2/25/78, about 9:03 p.m.) Voice over (adult male): *Introduce yourself to a remarkable nasal spray that lasts and lasts up to 12 continuous hours. Duration. Duration Nasal Spray relieves nasal stuffiness and sinus congestion. So just one use lets you work all day. Just one use lets you sleep all night. Duration relieves 12 continuous hours, and that's Duration—with the longest lasting nasal decongestant.*

EXERCISE 2: Comment on the use of the word 'feature' instead of 'option' in the Chevette commercial. How could its use complicate investigation of the question whether or not there were 18 new features? Does this claim entail that 18 1977 *options* were made standard in 1978?

EXERCISE 3: Consider the following commercial for the Reach toothbrush. What particular claims do you think it is trying to convey? Does it convey these claims directly or indirectly?

REACH toothbrush (ABC, 2/24/78, about 9.40 a.m.) Man: *They invented fluoride toothpaste to help fight cavities. Why hasn't somebody invented a better toothbrush? What if you angled it like a dental instrument to reach back teeth and concentrated the bristles to clean each tooth of material that can cause cavities and made rows of higher, softer bristles to clean between teeth? And what if you called it "Reach?" The Reach toothbrush from Johnson and Johnson. To help fight cavities.*

Which of the above inferences (if any) are entailments? Do you think a commercial like this might be successful? -

EXERCISE 4: Advertisements can either occur in "real time" as in television or radio, in which case one cannot review the copy at one's leisure; or not, as in the case of newspaper and magazine advertisements. How does the Duration commercial exploit this property of TV advertising? What do you think the effect might be?

EXERCISE 5: Advertisements can utilize the auditory communications channel (radio), the visual communications channel (print media), or both (TV). How did the Chevette commercial exploit this aspect of TV? What do you think the result was?

EXERCISE 6: Spin a tale about the relative effectiveness of asserting or implying something in a commercial based on your intuitive reaction to the old Texaco claim *We're working to keep your trust* versus *We've got your trust and we're working to keep it*. Does the first of these two sentences validly imply the second?

Examples of TV advertisements as well as aspects of the discussion were taken from: Geis, Michael L., *The Language of Television Advertising*. Academic Press, NY, 1982.

PRAGMATICS: DISCOURSE ANALYSIS: PERSONAL EXPERIENCE STORIES

One of the things we do most frequently with language is to tell stories about ourselves. Children tell about what happened at Uncle Henry's or about what they did at school; adults tell about their day at the office, about what the birth of their child was like, or about what happened when they got stopped by the police. People tell stories around the dinner table, at bars, in dorm rooms: any time they are engaged in informal talk. We tell personal experience stories to instruct, to persuade, or to amuse. Perhaps most importantly, we tell stories in order to re-envision our own experiences so we can evaluate them, reformulate them, and fit them to our images of ourselves and our lives. In the past fifteen or twenty years, linguists have become interested in personal experience stories, for what they can tell us generally about the structure of discourse and about how meaning is created as people talk, and for what they can tell us specifically about things like tense choices and the use of words like *well* and *so*. And while personal experience stories are interesting in their own right, they are also complete, easily observable units of talk that provide examples of many of the things discourse analysts and sociolinguists are interested in.

THE STRUCTURE OF PERSONAL EXPERIENCE STORIES

Before we proceed, we should clarify what we mean by a personal experience story. All stories involve some *narration*, or chronological reporting of events in the past. Narration is characterized by *narrative clauses*: clauses which occur in the temporal order of the events which they describe. Consider, for example, this narrative:

    (1) (a) I went to pick up some groceries
          (b) and the car died
          (c) and I had to wait for the tow truck.

Even though there are no explicit sequence words like *before, after,* or *then*, clauses (a)-(c) are interpreted as being in chronological order. If clause (a) came after (b) and (c), we would interpret the sequence of events differently.

The requirement that stories include some narrative clauses explains why an utterance of a single clause, like

    (2) we ate at the new Chinese restaurant

is not a story. But we would not be likely to call example (1) a story, either. One way to convince yourself of this point is to imagine what would happen if a person were to say, "Listen, I've got a great story," and then give you example (1). Your response would probably be "Well?" or "So what?" or something similar. People often talk about things that happened to them for practical reasons, for example in answer to questions like "Why were you late?" or "Where were you when the theft occurred?" Reports like (1) are appropriate in such contexts, when stories would clearly be inappropriate.

The stories we will be discussing are not traditional. They are stories a teller tells about his or her own experience. While some personal experience stories are told again and again, and may in time become legends, most are only told once, and their telling is so tied to the immediate context that they simply would not work in another context. By studying personal experience stories, as opposed to traditional folklore (myths, legends, fairy tales, etc.), we can be sure that the structure of the stories reflects general linguistic and cultural knowledge about what makes a story, rather than specific conventions associated with particular legends or tales.

All complete, well-developed personal experience stories have been found to include six elements, which are the following.

1. an abstract
2. orientation
3. complicating action
4. evaluation
5. result or resolution
6. coda

In discussing these elements, we will refer to example (3) below.

1   had a hell of a camping trip one weekend
2   been . . . two or three years ago now
3   went out into this woods
4   was a million miles from nowhere
5   and . . . we cleared a campspot . . . campsite . . . John and I
6   and uh . . . set our tents up
7   and gathered up some rocks
8   and made a firepit
9   had a good looking camp when we were done
10 gathered up a bunch of brush
11 and made a big windbreak
12 by late Friday afternoon . . . we were . . . pretty well settled in
13 uh . . . like I said
14 had a good looking camp . . . (breath)
15 the Saturday that followed
16 the Saturday of that weekend
17 we just did a lot of shooting
18 and actually just lounging around camp a lot (laughter)
19 did a little bit of hunting
20 really just . . . took it good and easy that day . . . (cough)
21 but it was Sunday morning
22 when we got up
23 that was the high point of the whole camp
24 we . . . uh . . . got up that morning and
25 wearing our camouflage . . . uh to . . .
26 basically didn't want to be seen by anybody else
27 and preferred to see them before w-
28 them before they saw us
29 we were fixing coffee over the campfire
30 and I happen to look up
31 out across this field
32 at the edge of the woods
33 about three hundred yards out
34 this . . . six buck deer
35 beautiful
36 just majestic as hell
37 they stood out there for about a half hour
38 noses in the wind
39 trying to catch our scent (breath)
40 never really did
41 we finally decided to show them what we were
42 and so we both stood up
43 and (small laugh) . . . all you saw was six white tails
44 headed the opposite direction
45 but it was a truly fantastic sight
46 we closed up camp that day
47 and came back to civilization
48 never really been able to forget that day
49 or that campout
50 as a result of it (long pause)
51 its th-
52 that's the sort of thing I guess that makes life worth living

ABSTRACT

The teller of a story often begins with one or more clauses which summarize the story. In (3), the abstract is in lines 1-2. Examples of abstracts from other stories are these:

    (4)   You want to know how I met this guy?

    (5)   Well, this is the story of how I found my first cat, named Tom.

Sometimes, another participant in a conversation may provide a story's abstract, by saying something like:

    (6)   Tell the one about when your nephew almost drowned.

In other cases, the abstract function may be served by the conversational context as a whole. If a group of people are telling stories about high-school pranks, for example, the third or fourth teller may not need to announce that that is what he or she is going to do too.

ORIENTATION

After the abstract, and before the narrative part of a story, there are usually a number of free (non-narrative) clauses in which the teller sets the stage for the action. In these orientation clauses, we find relevant details about the background of the story: the time, the place, who was involved and what they were doing. Lines 3-23 in example (3) provide orientation. Orientation clauses can also appear in other parts of a story, to provide descriptive information which becomes relevant as the story emerges, as the teller, reacting with his or her listeners, creates it. One example in (3) is line 29. In addition to giving background details, orientation clauses can also serve as evaluations, as we will see. Orientation clauses are often in the past progressive (*was V-ing*) tense.

COMPLICATING ACTION: RESULT OR RESOLUTION

The complicating action and the result or resolution form the narrative core of the story. The complicating action part of a story answers the quesion "Then what happened?" and the result or resolution tells "What finally happened?" In (3), the complicating action begins in line 24 and the result or resolution ends at line 44. Read through this part of the story to get a feel for how the dramatic tension rises (up to line 39) and then falls. You will note that while many of the clauses are narrative clauses in the simple past or historical present tense, some are not; they would not have to be in the position they are in. We will examine the function of clauses like these shortly; see if you can form a hypothesis.

CODA

At the end of a story, the teller often summarizes it, or provides a kind of moral, relating the story to the surrounding conversation and bringing the hearers back out of the world of the story and into the present. There is a clear coda in (3), in lines 45-52. Here are examples of codas from other personal experience stories:

    (7)   and that's the honest-to-God truth
    all that happened
    he's still alive and well
    and believe it or not he's in Paris
    becoming a gourmet chef.

    (8)   and that's how Tom found a home.

EVALUATION

In normal conversation, the alternation of speakers (or *turn-taking*) proceeds fairly regularly. While some speakers may talk more than others, all are following linguistic and cultural rules about when it is permissible to take over the conversational floor (for example, when the current speaker pauses or reaches a syntactic break), and about what sorts of simultaneous back-channeling (*uh-huh*'s, *right*'s, *oh yeah*'s, and non-verbal cues) are required to show that a listener is attending to a speaker. When one speaker is telling a story, however, some of these rules are suspended. The story-teller takes an unusually long turn in the conversation and is generally not interrupted, except for brief requests for clarification and for back-channeling, until he or she announces, by means of a coda, that the story is over. Clearly, a person who wants others to allow him or her to take up a large block of conversational time with a story had better have something worthwhile to say. The story had better have a *point*. Pointless stories are unacceptable in conversation, and a person who tells a story without a point will be greeted with an unpleasant response like "So what?"

What makes a story worth telling? What sorts of things can count as the point of a story? The answer depends on the context, both general (what is unusual enough, funny enough, or scary enough to tell a story about in one culture may not be in another) and specific (a person's best story may fall flat if it's told to the wrong person, or in the wrong situation). In very broad terms, a story has to be about something unusual: a situation which resulted in something different than one would expect, a dangerous situation, or a situation in which the teller demonstrated special courage, intelligence, civic responsibility, or humor. The point of a story may in fact change as the story is being told, as a result of listeners' questions and comments; if it becomes clear that the teller's original claim about what makes the story tellable will not satisfy the audience, the teller may try to recast the story with a new point.

There is a wide variety of linguistic strategies a storyteller can use to underscore the fact that his or her story has a point. These strategies are referred to as *evaluation*. Evaluation occurs throughout a story—an effective storyteller constantly reminds the audience that the story is worth telling—but tends to be especially prominent immediately before the result or resolution part of the story, when the tension needs to be especially high.

Evaluative devices fall into two main categories: *external* and *internal*. External evaluation is provided by phrases and clauses which interrupt the narrative, thereby creating suspense. In story (3), the teller stops for an evaluative comment in line 23 ("that was the high point of the whole camp"). External evaluative commentary can also be placed in the mouth of another character besides the teller, as in the following example:

(9)   oh, man, he felt bad as hell about that for a long time.

Internal evaluative devices are special features of clauses which do serve other functions in the story. Internal evaluation is provided by *intensifiers, comparators,* and *modifiers. Intensifiers* are verbal or nonverbal elements, or structural choices, which highlight a phrase or clause. These include gestures, expressive phonology (loudness or drawn-out syllables), repetition (as in the description of the "good looking camp" in (3), or the series of prepositional phrases in lines 31-33), and phrases like "by God" or "you know."

Since stories are about events in the past, one might ask why there should be any clauses in a story which are not in the past tense. One answer is that clauses that are not simple, positive, past-tense narrative clauses provide internal evaluation by comparing what did happen with what could have, should have, will, or didn't happen. Such clauses are called *comparators*.

Modifiers of various kinds also serve as evaluation devices. The teller can slow down the action with extra descriptions of what people are doing. Appositive (i.e., parenthetical) nouns, adjectives, and adverbial clauses can also create suspense. In (3), for example, the teller creates interest in the physical setting and in the deer by providing details about them.

If (3) had been a simple narrative report, of the kind one might be required to deliver in court, for example, it would only have been necessary for the teller to say something like, "I saw six deer in the woods one weekend." The fact that he has instead evaluated his narrative is what gives the report a point and makes it a story. Evaluation, then, is the key to what makes a group of chronologically-ordered clauses into a story.

BROADER PERSPECTIVES

Most of us are aware that groups of written sentences (paragraphs, term papers, novels) are highly structured, because we have undergone the often agonizing conscious process of learning how to structure them, in freshman composition, creative writing, and introductory literature classes. We tend to be much less aware that groups of spoken utterances are structured, and are often surprised to find that something as casual and spontaneous as a personal-experience story has the kind of elaborate organization that we have seen. The functional, content-based approach to discourse structure that we have examined here is not the only model linguists have used. Some discourse analysts use models of the internal structure of discourse which are analogous to models of the structure of sentences, talking about story- or text-grammars. Others look at discourse cohesion, or what makes a group of sentences function as a single unit of discourse at all. Still others start from the assumption that the meaning of a story, or any other kind of text, is more than the sum total of the meanings of its words or sentences; they examine the cognitive schemas, cultural models, or previous knowledge that hearers use to construct the meaning of a text as they hear it.

One thing that becomes clear through any of these approaches, though, is that lexical and grammatical choices are as much the result of discourse-level requirements as they are the result of sentence-level syntactic or semantic requirements. Think, for example, about the alternation in personal-experience stories between simple past and historical present tenses. In isolated sentences, the present tense ("I get out of the car") and the simple past tense ("I got out of the car") do not refer to the same time (if the simple present tense can really be said to refer to any time at all). In a story, these two sentences *could* be used to refer to the same time. But they cannot always be used interchangeably. At the beginning of a story, the teller must use the past tense to establish that he or she is talking about the past. Later in the story, the teller can switch tenses, but will only do so if it is relevant for purposes of evaluation. A complete explanation of these two tenses in English (and none exists yet) would have to make reference to their functions and contexts in discourse.

A topic that we have barely touched on in this File is the relationship of stories to the conversations they are part of. We have alluded to the requirements imposed on a storyteller by the rules of conversation. (If you want to take up a large chunk of conversation you need to have something worthwhile to say, and you need to use evaluative devices to show that it's worth saying.) There are many other questions we could have asked: What do listeners contribute to the telling of a story? What kinds of conversations can include stories? How is conversation structured, in general; what are the rules? Sociologists and linguists have provided partial answers to some of these questions, particularly the last. Another interesting topic, which we have not touched on at all, is how oral stories differ from written ones, or oral language use from written language use in general. Linguists are beginning to explore this topic, too.

Perhaps the most interesting question that is raised in the study of personal experience narrative concerns the ways in which speakers and hearers cooperate in the reconstruction, re-evaluation, and re-creation of the past through the process of talking about it. Nobody ever talks about everything; we select things to tell stories about, and we choose ways to give them a point and create ways to make them memorable and pleasing to the ear. In doing this, we create language as we talk, and we create the world as we talk about it.

FOR FURTHER READING

Labov, William. 1972. The transformation of experience in narrative syntax. *Language in the inner city* (Philadelphia: University of Pennsylvania Press), 354-96.

(Uses Labov and Waletzky's framework in analyzing fight stories told by inner-city black adolescents.)

Labov, William & Joshua Waletzky. 1967. Narrative analysis: Oral versions of personal experience. *in* June Helm, ed., *Essays on the verbal and visual arts* (Seattle: University of Washington Press), 12-44.

(This study describes, in more detail, the kind of analysis that has been examined in this File.)

Linde, Charlotte. 1984. *The Creation of Coherence in Life Stories.* (Norwood, NJ: Ablex)

(The creation of self in personal-experience stories.)

Polanyi, Livia. 1983. *The American Story: From the Structure of Linguistics Texts to the Grammar of a Culture.* (Norwood, NJ: Ablex)

(What can count as the point of a story?)

Sachs, H., E. Schegloff, and G. Jefferson. 1974. "A simplest systematics for the organization of turn-taking for conversation." *Language* 50: 696-735.

(An analysis of how conversations are structured.)

Tannen, Deborah, ed. 1981. *Spoken and Written Language: Exploring Literacy and Orality.* Norwood, NJ: Ablex.

(A collection of essays comparing speaking and writing, many having to do with narrative.)

Wolfson, Nessa. 1982. *CHP: The Conversational Historical Present in American English Narrative.* Dordrecht: Foris.

(A detailed study of tense choices in personal experience stories.)

PRAGMATICS: CONVERSATION

The Language of Conversation

It is easy when studying the basic units of language—sounds, morphemes, words, sentences, and so on—to lose sight of the fact that the parts must function together smoothly when we put our linguistic ability to actual use. Virtually the entire linguistic system is called into play when, for example, we write a letter, sing a song, or read a magazine, but by far the most common use of human language is in *conversation*, a highly skilled activity in which two or more people take turns at speaking, each turn adding or reacting to what has been said, and done, during previous turns.

Ordinary conversation is quite different from written language, not only because more than one person is involved, but also because conversation is constructed 'on the spot' and is therefore full of hesitations and other discontinuities. Despite these 'dysfluencies' and the complex requirements of turn taking, however, the participants in a conversation are in general able to understand each other without great difficulty.

Some of the particular features of conversation that differentiate it from careful prose are listed below. It is important not to regard these as kinds of errors (except #10), but simply as terms descriptive of features of conversational structure. Many of these features occur because conversation is largely an unplanned, collaborative activity in which the speakers are performing constant 'on line' adjustments to make sure that what they say is understandable and appropriate.

1. *Hesitation noises.* So-called hesitation noises (sometimes called 'filled pauses') like *uh* and *um* are used frequently by most people in spontaneous conversation, even many teachers and broadcasters who try to speak as fluently as possible. These sounds have many uses in conversation, but most often they indicate that the speaker is pausing to consider what to say next and doesn't wish to give up his or her turn at speaking.

2. *Interjections.* Words like *well, oh, say,* and expressions like *y'know* are also sometimes used at points where the speaker has paused to think. *Y'know,* which is not only found at points of pause, seems to be used by speakers to check to see if those listening to them have understood what has been said. *Well* can indicate that the speaker is considering something, without saying exactly what is being considered (though sometimes this is obvious from the context). There are dozens of interjections in English, each with its own use and meaning. These items were once regarded as useless bits of 'verbal garbage', but many of them are now understood to be syntactically and semantically complex.

3. *False starts.* Speakers frequently break off a sentence before completing it and begin a new one: 'She was— There were people all around her.' Often these restarts are accompanied by part of the sentence that was broken off: 'I was— I was going to let him clip it.' In the latter case, the false start is said to be 'retraced.'

4. *Repair.* Sometimes when a speech error or something that is problematical or unclear is said, the speaker will notice the problem and make a correction: 'So are we all set then? . . . I mean for Tuesday'; at other times another participant in the conversation may ask for a correction or clarification, for example by asking a question like 'John who?', or 'It was *what*?'.

5. *Overlapping talk.* Although in general speakers talk one at a time, sometimes the speech of one person will overlap that of another. These overlaps rarely last for more than a second or two—after that one speaker or the other almost always stops talking and lets the other continue. Multiple overlaps in which several speakers talk at once also occur.

6. *Casual pronunciation.* In relaxed speaking situations, pronunciation is often less distinct than, for example, in carefully reading aloud a written passage. Casual forms such as *gotta, kinda, wanna,* and pronunciations like *wudju* instead of *would you,* and *sump'm* for *something,* cannot be regarded as speech errors due to sloppiness. The kinds of phonological alterations that are found in casual speech occur under specifiable conditions and can be described quite precisely; that is, they are rule governed.

7. *Paralinguistic features*. Conversation usually contains many sound features that are not strictly linguistic, such as laughter, throat clearing, audible inhalations, and the like. Such sounds can be used communicatively, although the meanings they convey are often not very specific.

8. *Historical present*. Use of the 'historical present' is quite common in spoken narratives (for example, in telling a joke). Speakers using the historical present use the present tense of verbs to talk about past events: 'I look over and he's asleep' instead of 'I looked over and he was asleep.' The historical present probably functions to make what is being talked about seem more vivid.

9. *Narrative 'go'*. The verb *go*, with a meaning roughly equivalent to *say* ("So Mary goes, 'But that's three weeks off'.") is often used, particularly by speakers under about thirty, to introduce quotations. This use of *go* is rarely found in writing.

10. *Speech errors*. Conversation often contains phonological and lexical errors of various kinds.

Conversation Transcription

Below is a transcript of a few moments of casual conversation between two young women. One woman is recounting an incident that occurred in her parents' home. As you read through the transcript, notice how different unedited, spontaneous talk is from the carefully composed written language found, say, in a newspaper article. You should be able to find in this transcript examples of most of the features listed in 1-10 above.

SUE: And so we had um - her dog Shane - for like two years. - A-nd h-e g-ot th-e b-i-r-r-d.
EVA: In (h)is mouth like?
SUE: In (h)is mouth. But (h)e ditn' (h)ave a *chance* ta bite *down* on (h)im. Because my Mo:m - y'know had *seen* (h)im.
                                                                                    [
EVA: Oh my gosh!
SUE: An(d) man! She just—
          [
EVA: Oh:::::wuh!
SUE: (A)n(d) yihknow and they're so— they're so fragile.
EVA: Oh I kno:::::::::::w
            [
SUE: They can smash easy.
EVA: They sure could. My gosh an(d) a dog's - jaw (h)as got so much force in it too. Specially a *black lab*, My gosh!
                                                                [[
SUE: m hm
SUE: ⌐ m hm
SUE: ((Laughs.)) I was watch- I was downstairs watchin(g) t.v. when it happened.
EVA: Oh I woulda *died*.
SUE: An(d) she w-as j-ust ((inhalations)) I thought she was gonna have a heart attack ((Laughs.))
EVA: W(e)ll how'd she make (h)im spit (h)im ou:t?
SUE: As soon as she- She would- She *saw* the bird flyin(g) around y'know?
EVA: m hm.
SUE: An(d) sne saw Shane - the dog watchin(g) (h)im. Usually he would just sit there an(d) watch the
     bird. He woutn' touch the bird or anything.
          [
EVA: Yea:h
SUE: An(d) (h)e just outa the blue just- jumped towards it- towards the bird an(d) my mom just - y'know was right
     there an(d) just s:snapped (h)im
               [
EVA: Yah.
SUE: m hm

EVA: Huhuh I could see me. I'd be - sw- hittin(g) the back outa . . .
                                                              [
SUE: ((Laughs . . . .
EVA: that dog so hard an(d) he wouldn'(t) let that bird g-o ((Laughs.))
                                       ]
SUE: . . . .))

EVA: Dogs are funny, y'know when they- - My dog, a lotta times when we're playing an(d) stuff y'know mbuh my hand'll get into (h)is mouth er like just one finger or sump'm like that. And the minute - he senses that that's me he hyihknow he won't bite- He's *ne*ver accident(al)ly- bit down on me - at all - or an- my little sister, Nobody.
                                                                                                    [
SUE: m hm
EVA: (A)n(d) (th)at's- (Th)at goes ta show how they can- sense that they've got sump'm in their mouth they don't wanna have in there or sup'm but
SUE: m hm
EVA: if he had sump'm like *that* in (h)is mouth
SUE: eheh eheh Yeah.
                   [
EVA: I don't think he'd let it go.

Symbols used: The meaning of some of the symbols will be obvious when you listen to the tape. A few should be explained, however.

   [indicates the point where talk by one speaker begins to overlap that of another
   - when between two words and surrounded by spaces, indicates a brief pause
  ( ) indicates that the segments enclosed were not pronounced
(( )) indicates something which was not transcribed, for example, complex laughter
   : indicates extra length of a sound or syllable

INTRODUCTION: PSYCHOLINGUISTICS

Psycholinguistics is the study of the relationship between language and the mind. As such, psycholinguists search for answers to three basic questions:

1.   How is language represented in the mind?
2.   What are the mental processes involved in the production and comprehension of speech?
3.   How does a person acquire language?

These questions are difficult to answer, partially because of our limited knowledge about the brain, the repository of our linguistic knowledge. Yet, if we want to make claims about the psychological reality of our linguistic theory (e.g., a claim that certain linguistic rules like flapping have some physical manifestation in the brain), then we must find answers to these questions.

One area in which psycholinguists look for these answers is in the study of child language acquisition. As early as 1887, ethnologist Horatio Hale claimed that language was instinctive. If his claim were correct, then language would simply be another biological function like breathing. While no linguist would want to accept this claim in its strongest form, we must accept a certain degree of innateness, because of the fact that children acquire language in an imperfect environment. Total innateness would imply one of two consequences. Either all children would acquire the same language, or children from different nationalities, say Chinese and American, would have different biological make-ups to account for the fact that they speak different languages. We know that the first one is false because children do acquire different languages. We know that the second one is false because children of, say, Mexican parents grow up in the United States speaking perfect native English. Thus, they have a Mexican biology but the English language. It is not people's biological heritage which determines the language that they will acquire. We also know, however, that language cannot be acquired simply on the basis of experience since the linguistic environment is imperfect. The language that a child hears everyday contains ill-formed sentences, with pauses and slips of the tongue, yet the child acquires a correct grammar. The language stimulus that a child receives is finite, yet he is able to construct a grammar that can produce a countless number of novel grammatical sentences. These 'poverty of stimulus' facts argue for the innateness of grammar. Thus, we must view language as arising from an interaction between innateness and experience.

A number of theories have been posited regarding the role of experience in language acquisition. One of the more prominent theories, the reinforcement theory, suggests that children learn language by having selected utterances reinforced by their parents. When we first consider the relationship between parent and child, this theory may seem correct. Imagine a father coming home from work and hearing his baby babbling in the crib. Out of the numerous noises the child makes, he picks out the sequence 'd-a-d-a', at which point he might say: "That's right, Dada. Dada's home." Then he would rush off to tell the child's mother that the baby said his first word, before returning to the child and practicing this great accomplishment. However, the reinforcement theory suffers from several serious flaws. First, the theory cannot account for a child's initial utterances. The child must say something before it can be reinforced. Second, adults do not necessarily reinforce on the basis of grammaticality. Some ill-formed utterances are reinforced because they are true:

Child: Mama isn't boy, he a girl.
Parent: That's right.

Other utterances, though grammatically correct, are not reinforced because they are untrue:

Child: There's the farmhouse.
Parent: No that's a lighthouse.

Another prominent theory, the imitative theory, suggests that children learn language through imitation. While children do imitate, one study finding that imitated utterances ranged from 6% to 27% of a child's total utterances, they also produce new and unique utterances:

Parent: Did you like the doctor?
Child: No, he took a needle and shotted my arm.

No child will hear an adult say 'shotted'; therefore, the child must have some creative, linguistic capacity, which allows for the creation of words like 'shotted' and which imitation cannot account for.

Though psycholinguists do not support either the reinforcement or the imitative theories of language acquisition, they do realize the importance of studying children and their utterances. By studying the way that children acquire language, psycholinguists try to determine the nature of the grammatical rules children develop as they acquire their phonology, morphology, syntax, and semantics. In this way, linguists can find answers not only to question 3, but also to question 1. Other areas of psycholinguistics include the study of adult production and comprehension, and neurolinguistics, the study of the relationship between language and the physical structure of the brain. Here we can find answers to numbers 1 and 2, discovering the relationship between proposed linguistic structures, the physical composition of the brain, and comprehension and production patterns. While the majority of our files deals with language acquisition in all of its forms, Files 92-95, File 96 considers the way in which adults talk to children, Files 97 and 98 talk about adult processing and speech errors, File 99 discusses learning a foreign language, and File 91 describes the structure of the brain and its role in language.

PSYCHOLINGUISTICS: LANGUAGE AND THE BRAIN

To fully appreciate the amazing human ability for language it is necessary to know something about the way the brain controls language. Because the human brain is complex and our knowledge of its inner workings is somewhat limited, there are many aspects of brain function which are simply not understood at this time. In this file we will discuss some of the more clearly understood aspects of the way our brains store and use language.

PHYSICAL FEATURES OF THE BRAIN

A summary of some of the anatomy of the brain will help you follow the discussions later in this file. One of the first noticeable physical features of the brain is the fact that it is divided into two halves. These two halves are called the *right* and *left hemispheres.* The two hemispheres are connected by a bundle of nerve fibers called the *corpus callosum.* This bundle of nerve fibers (plus a few other interhemispheric connections) make it possible for the two hemispheres to communicate with each other. The hemispheres are covered by a 1/4 inch membrane called the *cortex.* As you can see from the drawing on the following page, the surface of the hemispheres is not flat; rather, there are bumps and depressions on it. The bumps in the hemispheres are called *gyri* and the depressions are called *fissures.* The fissures in particular serve as physical boundaries for the identification of sections of the brain.

Another feature of the nervous system which will be referred to in this file is the fact that the connections between the brain and the body are contralateral. What this means is that the right side of the body is controlled by the left hemisphere, while the left side of the body is controlled by the right hemisphere. It is also important to realize that contralateral connection also means that sensory information from the right side of the body is received by the left hemisphere, while sensory information from the left side of the body is received by the right hemisphere.

LATERALIZATION

Not surprisingly, neither of the hemispheres in adults duplicates the functions carried out by the other; rather, each side of the brain performs specific functions. Lateralization refers to this specialization of each of the hemispheres of the brain for different cognitive functions. Paul Broca, in the 1860s, was one of the first physicians to observe that damage to the left side of the brain resulted in impaired language ability while damage to the right side of the brain did not influence language ability. Since that time researchers have observed that approximately 70% of the people with damage to the left hemisphere experience *aphasia,* an inability to perceive, process or produce language because of physical damage to the brain. *Hemispherectomies,* operations in which one hemisphere or part of one hemisphere is removed from the brain, also provide evidence for lateralization. Performed on people who experience severe seizures, this operation affects the patient's behavior and ability to think. It has been found that hemispherectomies involving the left hemisphere result in aphasia much more frequently than those involving the right hemisphere. This indicates in most people the left side of the brain is used to process language while the right side has much less to do with language processing.

Further evidence for lateralization comes from *split-brain patients.* Normally, the two hemispheres are connected by the corpus callosum. In certain kinds of severe epilepsy, the corpus callosum is cut, preventing the two hemispheres from transmitting information to each other. Also, since the connections from the brain to the rest of the body are contralateral, various experiments can be performed on these split-brain patients which help to identify the cognitive characteristics of the two hemispheres. For example, in one experiment a patient is blind-folded and an object is placed in his/her right hand. The patient can say the name of the object. If an object is placed in the *left* hand, the patient usually cannot identify the object verbally. The results of this kind of experiment indicate that language is lateralized; that the left hemisphere is the location of those abilities which are used in producing language while the right hemisphere is essentially devoid of such cognitive abilities. When the object is in the subject's right hand the left hemisphere is experiencing the heightened sensory activity associated with holding the object. When the

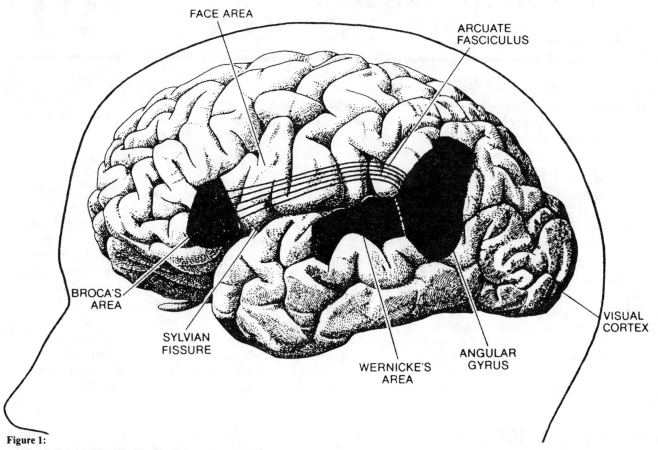

Figure 1:

PRIMARY LANGUAGE AREAS of the human brain are thought to be located in the left hemisphere, because only rarely does damage to the right hemisphere cause language disorders. Broca's area, which is adjacent to the region of the motor cortex that controls the movement of the muscles of the lips, the jaw, the tongue, the soft palate and the vocal cords, apparently incorporates programs for the coordination of these muscles in speech. Damage to Broca's area results in slow and labored speech, but comprehension of language remains intact.

Wernicke's area lies between Heschl's gyrus, which is the primary receiver of auditory stimuli, and the angular gyrus, which acts as a way station between the auditory and the visual regions. When Wernicke's area is damaged, speech is fluent but has little content and comprehension is usually lost. Wernicke and Broca areas are joined by a nerve bundle called the arcuate fasciculus. When it is damaged, speech is fluent but abnormal, and patients can comprehend words but cannot repeat them.

object is placed in the subject's left hand only the right hemisphere experiences the sensory feedback associated with holding the object. Because the subject in this situation is unable to state the name of the object, we infer that the cognitive abilities and memory store needed to name the object are not available to the right hemisphere.

Dichotic listening experiments have also provided evidence about the cognitive properties of the two hemispheres of the brain. In these experiments, two sounds are presented at the same time to a normal person. The sounds might be two different words or one word and one environmental sound (for example, a dog barking). Responses to the right ear stimuli are more accurate when the stimuli are linguistic, responses to the left ear stimuli are more accurate when the stimuli are non-verbal, as in music. This right ear advantage for language stimuli indicates that the left hemisphere is engaged in processing language. In order for a linguistic signal presented to the left ear to reach the left hemisphere it must go first to the right hemisphere and then across the corpus callosum to the left hemisphere. On the other hand, a linguistic signal presented to the right ear has a more direct connection with the left hemisphere. Thus, dichotic listening experiments support the notion of left hemispheric dominance in language processing because the ear with a more direct link to the left hemisphere shows an advantage in processing linguistic stimuli.

228

THE CRITICAL PERIOD

The period of time from birth to puberty is sometimes called the critical period. A child must learn a language during this period to gain normal, native competence in the language. Some of the properties of the brain which we have discussed up to this point may provide an explanation of the critical period. We have seen that the left hemisphere is normally the location of the abilities needed for the use of language in adults. Language lateralization indicates that there is something about the left hemisphere which *predisposes* it for use in language production. Just exactly what it is about the left hemisphere that causes this predisposition is not known, but the fact that there is a predisposition is important for an understanding of the critical period. The predisposition of the left hemisphere for language is an indication that in children the left hemisphere is open to language learning. As the child's brain matures and the patterns of neural activity become set, the readiness for language learning which was once present becomes less and less available. This loss of flexibility can have two results. The first and most common result is that it becomes much more difficult to learn a second language after the critical period than it was as a child. Most American college students who take up a second language feel the effects of this loss of flexibility. On the other hand, children who learn two or more languages during the critical period usually can speak the languages without an accent. The second result is that if a child is not exposed to language during childhood it may become impossible to later learn language. Genie, a child who was discovered at the age of 13 in 1970, is an example of this second, tragic result. She received virtually no linguistic stimulation from ages 1 to 13. Even after 11 years of intense instruction her linguistic ability was not normal.

APHASIA

The evidence for language lateralization comes from a variety of sources. One of these sources of information which was only briefly mentioned above deserves more detailed attention.

It was stated above that aphasia is an impairment of language abilities because of physical damage to the brain. One type of aphasia is called *Broca's aphasia*. Broca's aphasics suffer from an inability to plan the motor sequences used in speech. When they attempt to speak, they speak haltingly and have a hard time getting the words out. There is also a tendency for telegraphic speech (i.e., they leave out small function words and inflections) although the basic word order used is correct.

EXAMPLE 1: Broca's Aphasia
Examiner: Tell me, what did you do before you retired?
Aphasic: Uh, uh, uh, pub, par, partender, no.
Examiner: Carpenter?
Aphasic: (shaking head yes) Carpenter, tuh, tuh, tenty year.

Broca's aphasia seems to result in primary *expressive* disorders. Comprehension of the speech of others doesn't seem to be a problem for Broca's aphasics. Damage to the area in figure 1 labeled Broca's area will result in Broca's aphasia.

While Broca's aphasia results in primarily expressive difficulties, *Wernicke's aphasia* results in primarily *receptive* disorders. A patient with Wernicke's aphasia does not find it hard to speak, but there is a tendency for Wernicke's aphasics to produce semantically incoherent speech, as you can see in example 2.

EXAMPLE 2: Wernicke's Aphasia
Examiner: Do you like it here in Kansas City?
Aphasic: Yes, I am.
Examiner: I'd like to have you tell me something about your problem.
Aphasic: Yes, I ugh can't hill all of my way. I can't talk all of the things I do, and part of the part I can go alright, but I can't tell from the other people. I usually most of my things. I know what can I talk and know what they are, but I can't always come back even though I know they should be in, and I know should something eely I should know what I'm doing . . .

Often these patients speak nonsense or in circumlocutions. Circumlocutions are expressions which people use when they are unable to name the word they want. The patient may say 'what you drink' for 'water' and 'what we smell with' for 'nose'. The syntactic order of words is also altered. 'I know I can say' may become 'I know can I say.' That patients with Wernicke's aphasia are unable to comprehend the speech of others is demonstrated by the fact that they often cannot follow simple instructions, such as *stand up, turn to your right,* and so on. Damage to Wernicke's area results in Wernicke's aphasia (see Figure 1.)

The last type of aphasia which will be discussed in this file is called *conduction aphasia.* A patient suffering from conduction aphasia sounds something like a Wernicke's aphasic (fluent but meaningless speech) but shows signs of being able to comprehend the speech of others. The patient will be able to understand utterances but will not be able to repeat them. Conduction aphasia results from damage to the Arcuate Fasciculus. The pattern of symptoms which results from this type of damage may indicate that these fiber tracts transmit meanings formed in Wernicke's area to Broca's area where they are translated into motor commands for the vocal organs.

CONCLUSION

Although a detailed understanding of how the brain stores and uses language is not possible at this time, there are some aspects of the brain's involvement in language which are understood. We have seen that language is a left hemisphere phenomenon. Evidence for this comes from patterns of aphasia, the effects of hemispherectomies, the language abilities of split-brain patients, and the results of dichotic listening experiments. We have discussed the critical period for language learning and seen the connection between it and the lateralization of language. And finally, we have seen that through the study of aphasia the location of specific types of linguistic abilities in the brain is possible.

SOURCES AND FURTHER READING
Bayles, Kathryn. 1981. "Language and the Brain." In *Language: Introductory Readings*. Clark, Eschholz, and Rosa, eds. New York: St. Martin's Press.

Fromkin, Victoria; Steven Krashen & others. 1981. "The Development of Language in Genie: A Case of Language Acquisition Beyond the 'Critical Period'." In *Language: Introductory Readings*. Clark, Eschholz and Rosa.

Springer, Sally and George Deutsch. 1981. *Left Brain, Right Brain*. San Francisco: W.H. Freeman & Co.

PSYCHOLINGUISTICS: MILESTONES IN MOTOR AND LANGUAGE DEVELOPMENT

At the Completion of:	Motor Development	Vocalization and Language
12 weeks	Supports head when in prone position; weight is on elbows; hands mostly open; no grasp reflex.	Markedly less crying than at 8 weeks; when talked to and nodded at, smiles, followed by squealing-gurgling sounds usually called *cooing*, which is vowel-like in character and pitch-modulated; sustains cooing for 15 to 20 seconds.
16 weeks	Plays with rattle placed in hands (by shaking it and staring at it); head self-supported; tonic neck reflex subsiding.	Responds to human sounds more definitely; turns head; eyes seem to search for speaker; occasionally some chuckling sounds.
20 weeks	Sits with props.	The vowel-like cooing sounds begin to be interspersed with more consonantal sounds.
6 months	Sitting: bends forward and uses hands for support; can bear weight when put into a standing position, but cannot yet stand without holding on. Reaching: unilateral. Grasp: no thumb apposition yet; releases cube when given another.	Cooing changing into babbling resembling one-syllable utterances; neither vowels nor consonants have very fixed recurrences; most common utterances sound somewhat like *ma, mu, da,* or *di.*
8 months	Stands holding on; grasps with thumb apposition; picks up pellet with thumb and finger tips.	Reduplication (or more continuous repetitions) becomes frequent; intonation patterns become distinct; utterances can signal emphasis and emotions.
10 months	Creeps efficiently; takes side-steps, holding on; pulls to standing position.	Vocalizations are mixed with sound-play such as gurgling or bubble-blowing; appears to wish to imitate sounds, but the imitations are never quite successful; beginning to differentiate between sounds heard by making differential adjustment.
12 months	Walks when held by one hand; walks on	Identical sound sequences are repli-

At the Completion of	Motor Development	Vocalization and Language
	feet and hands — knees in air; mouthing of objects almost stopped; seats self on floor.	cated with higher relative frequency of occurrence, and words (*mamma* or *dadda*) are emerging; definite signs of understanding some words and simple commands (*Show me your eyes*).
18 months	Grasp, prehension, and release fully developed; gait stiff, propulsive and precipitated; sits on child's chair with only fair aim; creeps downstairs backward; has difficulty building tower of three cubes.	Has a definite repertoire of words — more than three, but less than fifty; still much babbling but now of several syllables, with intricate intonation pattern; no attempt at communicating information and no frustration at not being understood; words may include items such as *thank you* or *come here*, but there is little ability to join any of the lexical items into spontaneous two-item phrases; understanding progressing rapidly.
24 months	Runs, but fails in sudden turns; can quickly alternate between sitting and stance; walks stairs up or down, one foot forward only.	Vocabulary of more than fifty items (some children seem to be able to name everything in environment); begins spontaneously to join vocabulary items into two-word phrases; all phrases appear to be own creations; definite increase in communicative behavior and interest in language.
30 months	Jumps up into air with both feet; stands on one foot for about two seconds; takes a few steps on tiptoe; jumps from chair; good hand and finger coordination;can move digits independently; manipulation of objects much improved; builds tower of six cubes.	Fastest increase in vocabulary, with many new additions every day; no babbling at all; frustrated if not understood by adults; utterances consist of at least two words — many have three or even five words; sentences and phrases have characteristic child grammar — that is, are rarely verbatim repetitions of an adult utterance; intelligibility not yet very good, though there is great variation among children; seems to understand everything within hearing and directed to self.
3 years	Tiptoes three yards; runs smoothly with acceleration and deceleration; negotiates sharp and fast curves without difficulty; walks stairs by alternating feet; jumps 12 inches; can operate tricycle.	Vocabulary of some one thousand words; about 80 percent of utterances intelligible even to strangers; grammatical complexity of utterances roughly that of colloquial adult language although mistakes still occur.
4 years	Jumps over rope; hops on right foot; catches ball in arms; walks line.	Language well established; deviations from the adult norm tend to be more in style than in grammar.

PSYCHOLINGUISTICS: THE ACQUISITION OF PHONOLOGY

When an eighteen-month-old child attempts to pronounce the word *water*, he might say [wawa], falling considerably short of the adult pronunciation; or his pronunciation of *that* may sound like[dɛt] . Errors like these may persist for some time, despite constant drilling by the child's parents, and despite the child's own realization that his pronunciation is less than perfect. All children make mistakes like these before they have mastered the phonological system of their native language. Yet such errors reveal that they have already learned a great deal, and in another two-and-a-half years or so, their speech will resemble that of their parents in all important respects.

Linguists interested in the acquisition of phonology attempt to trace its development from 'baby talk' to mature adult pronunciation. In doing so, they try to answer two central questions in child-language research:

    1. Why does children's speech differ from that of adults?

    and,

    2. How does the evidence from the acquisition of phonology bear on the claim that the capacity for human language is innate?

What follows is a sketch of the milestones of phonological development, which provides a glimpse of the answers to these questions.

BABBLING

At the age of six months or so, normal children in all cultures begin to babble, producing long sequences of vowels and consonants. Though babbling is far from being a true language, it resembles adult language in a number of important respects. For one thing, babbled sequences are not linked to immediate biological needs like food or physical comfort, and are thus frequently uttered in isolation for sheer pleasure. Moreover, babbled sequences have many physical characteristics of adult speech. In a sequence like[gɔŋgɔg], syllables can be identified, and in longer sequences, intonation patterns which might be interpreted as questions in some languages can be discerned. However, the resemblance to adult speech stops here, since there is no evidence for the existence of more abstract structures like sentences, or even single words. Only later does the child come to associate word meanings with vocal noises.

Just how babbling relates to later speech is not clearly understood. Yet psychologists and linguists have concluded that babbling has at least two functions.

Babbling serves primarily as practice for later speech. This is intuitively plausible because the fine motor movements necessary for accurate articulation are exercised extensively during babbling. Indeed, babbling children produce a greater variety of sounds than actually occur in their native language. For example, American children, like children all over the world, are often heard to utter clicks and trilled r's when they babble, even though English does not use these sounds to make distinctions in meaning. On the basis of observations like this, some psychologists have claimed that during the babbling period, children practice sounds found in all languages of the world.

Children babble for social reward. When children talk, parents encourage them to continue talking, giving them important experience with the social rewards of speech. According to some psychologists, babbling is the child's first experience with the social character of language. Evidence for the importance of the social factor in babbling comes from the study of severely neglected children. Though they may begin to babble at approximately the same age as children reared in normal settings, they will stop if not encouraged by their parents.

Yet it remains to be explained why babbling occurs at more or less the same time in all children, since children must certainly practice for later speech at different rates, or receive encouragement for their efforts in unequal doses. According to one hypothesis, children babble because language development involves a process of biological maturation. Thus babbling occurs automatically when the relevant structures in the brain reach a critical level of development. If all children have brains which develop at comparable rates, the universality of babbling is no longer surprising.

Dramatic evidence for this hypothesis comes from some children studied by the psychologist Eric Lenneberg. These children had vocal passages that had become so narrow, because of swelling caused by various diseases, that they were in danger of choking to death. Breathing could be restored only by constructing an alternative route which bypassed the mouth; this was accomplished by inserting tubing in the trachea through an opening in the neck. Under such conditions, babbling and any other vocalizations are prevented, since air never reaches the vocal cords. Yet Lenneberg observed that when children of babbling age underwent this operation they produced the babbling sounds typical of their age as soon as the tubing was removed. The behavior of these children demonstrates that babbling is possible when the brain is ready—even if physical limitations prevent any real practice.

FIRST WORDS

The next major task in the acquisition of phonology involves understanding the word as a link between sound and meaning. When children first acquire the concept of a word at the approximate age of 12-16 months, they attempt to learn the fifty or so most common words in their everyday environment.

These first words show tremendous variability in pronunciation. Some may be perfect adult productions; others may be so distorted that they are comprehensible only to the child's closest companions. Still others vary considerably in their pronunciations from one occasion to the next. Because of this instability, psychologists have come to believe that children do not show an understanding of phonemes in their first words. Consider the one-year-old child who pronounces *bottle* as [ba] and *daddy* as [da]. We might conclude that [b] and [d] belong to separate phonemes because [ba] and [da] constitute a minimal pair—just as they would be if these words existed in adult English. But [b] and [d] are *not* members of separate phonemes in the speech of one-year-old children, because they are not used consistently to distinguish among words. Thus the same child may pronounce *bottle* either as [ba] or [da] on different occasions, and do the same with *daddy*. What seems to be going on is that children first learn entire words as single units, and pay little attention to the meaning distinctions induced by changes in single sounds.

PHONEMES AND PHONOLOGICAL PROCESSES

Once the minimum vocabulary is acquired, another change occurs. Because it is difficult to communicate successfully with variable pronunciations of *all* words, children adopt the strategy used in mature adult phonological systems: they represent words in terms of *phonemes*, whose pronunciation is systematic and predictable. How children accomplish this task is unknown. But it is a major achievement, and marks the beginning of the last stage of phonological development before adult pronunciation is mastered.

Despite the use of a mature strategy for pronouncing words, children's speech at this stage is still different from that of adults. Children must still acquire the complete set of phonemes, as well as the set of phonological processes found in the language of the adults in their surroundings. These tasks are to some extent independent of one another.

When children learn the phonemes of their native language, they first master sounds which differ maximally from one another. Thus it is no accident that the first meaningful word learned in many languages is often [ma] or [pa]. When a bilabial stop or nasal is pronounced, the passage of air in the mouth is completely blocked; but the vocal tract is wide open in the low back vowel [a]. Moreover, bilabials are made in the front of the mouth, while [a] is formed in the back. Consonants like *l*'s and *r*'s, which share many properties of vowels, are mastered last. Children as old as three and four years old often pronounce words like *train* as [twen] and *drown* as [dwæn].

Children's speech at this stage is also distinguished from that of adults because phonological processes are used in different ways. For one thing, the speech of a two-year-old child exhibits *more* processes than does adult speech. As we have seen, adult speech is full of assimilations, deletions, metatheses, and so on. Child speech simply has more of these. In the speech sample below, at least one syllable has been deleted from every word — which would certainly seem excessive if said by an adult:

banana næne   bicycle baikəɬ   granola owʌ   potato dedo

Secondly, children's speech exhibits a greater variety of processes than does the speech of the adults in their home environments. For example, the phonological systems of German and Russian, but not English, contain a process which devoices consonants at the ends of words. Yet children learning English as their native language devoice final consonants as well, as the examples below indicate:

pig bɪk   bib bɪp   bird bɪt   egg ɛk

Though children's speech exhibits more processes than is found in that of the adults around them, these 'extra' processes *are* found in the phonological systems of other adult languages. In general, children's speech exhibits the phonological processes below, most of which occur in one adult language or another.

1. *Substitutions*
   A. fronting—*goat* doʈ ; *goose* dus
   B. gliding—*drip* dwɪp
   C. stopping—*sea* ʈi ; *say* ʈeɪ
2. *Assimilations*
   A. voicing assimilation—*paper* beːbə
   B. consonant harmony—*taxi* gɛgi ; tickle gigu
3. *Syllable-structure processes*
   A. consonant cluster reduction—*play* pe
   B. deletion of final consonant—*bike* bai ; *bib* bɪ
   C. deletion of unaccented syllables—*banana* nænə ; *potato* dedo
   D. reduplication—*T.V.* didi ; *water* wawa

It is largely the presence of these phonological processes which makes two-year-old speech sound vastly different from that of adults.

Because processes in children's speech are very predictable, the following generalizations can be made:

1. *Processes are universal.* Roughly the same processes are found in all child speech, regardless of the adult language the child is learning. This means that however phonological development is eventually explained, it must be attributed to learning strategies which are more complex than imitation. Indeed, children must sometimes *un*learn certain processes. For example, the American child who voices all consonants appearing between vowels must eventually realize that English does not make consistent use of this process.

2. *Children start with a large number of processes, eliminating them as adult pronunciation is achieved.* Of the processes mentioned above, assimilations are more widespread in child speech than in adult speech. As children grow older, their number must gradually be reduced. But the substitutions like those mentioned above must be eliminated entirely, since they don't exist in normal adult speech at all.

It may seem counterintuitive that children begin their last major phase of phonological development with *more* processes than are found in adult speech, but keep in mind what processes accomplish: they make pronunciation easier. Accordingly, children's speech exhibits many assimilations because they have the effect of reducing the number of articulatory gestures necessary for producing words. Syllable-structure processes like cluster reduction and reduplication also result in sequences of sounds that are easier to pronounce than those found in the corresponding adult words. And the sounds eliminated in substitutions are often precisely those which are the most difficult for children to pronounce.

TOWARDS ADULT PRONUNCIATION

From this point until adult pronunciation is achieved at the approximate age of 4 or 5, children's phonological systems are constantly changing, as they bring their use of processes in line with that of the adults around them. But if a child's pronunciations are changing during this period, what evidence do we have that a system exists at all?

One compelling observation is that children can recognize their own mispronunciations. If an English-speaking child says [mæws] for *mouth* and his mother repeats it, he may get upset. It is as though he realizes that he systematically substitutes [s] for the [θ] he hears in adult speech. Secondly, children know more than they can say. Many children have identical pronunciations for different words, like [bik] for *big* and *beak*, yet are able to recognize them as different words when adults say them. Finally, many 'difficult' sounds appear in unexpected places in children's speech. For example, suppose that a child said [brt] for *bird*, a common enough substitution. From this we might conclude that the child is simply unable to pronounce [d]. But he may also say *dog* as [dak], where the difficult 'd' sound appears. What seems to be happening is that the child is not simply learning sounds in any order of articulatory difficulty, but is developing a *system* for pronouncing the phonemes of his language; at this stage, the child's phonological system contains a process which devoices stops at the ends of words. But since this process is not part of the adult system, he will eventually abandon it.

SUMMARY

We have shown that when children acquire the phonological system of their native language, they must master the fine muscle coordination necessary for producing a rich variety of sounds, learn that combinations of sounds are associated with particular meanings, and eventually realize that their pronunciations of words must consistently match that of adults. Since this is certainly a complex series of lessons, psychologists have wondered why children approach them in just this order.

One speculation is that this progression does not result from a conscious learning strategy spontaneously invented by children, or from a teaching method devised by their adult models — but is instead a consequence of the human brain's innate capacity for learning language. Children of all backgrounds master the phonological system of their native language in stages, each involving a successively more complex task, and each giving rise to speech which deviates from adult productions in systematic ways. Thus the acquisition of phonology appears to involve a process of biological maturation — and is in many respects like motor development, which also occurs in an invariant series of stages. Nevertheless, the adult phonological system is achieved only when children are given models to imitate, and are provided with constant encouragement to continue in their linguistic development.

EXERCISES

The data below are from Paul, two years old; they were collected by his father, Timothy Shopen. Consider the examples section by section, and answer the questions at the end of each section.

I.

	Adult word	Paul		Adult word	Paul
1.	"sun"	[sʌn]	4.	"snake"	[nek]
2.	"see"	[si]	5.	"sky"	[kay]
3.	"spoon"	[pun]	6.	"stop"	[tap]

a. State a principle that describes Paul's pronunciation of these words.

II.

	Adult word	Paul		Adult word	Paul
7.	"bed"	[bɛt]	13.	"bus"	[bʌs]
8.	"wet"	[wɛt]	14.	"buzz"	[bʌs]
9.	"egg"	[ɛk]	15.	"man"	[mæn]
10.	"rake"	[rek]	16.	"door"	[dɔr]
11.	"tub"	[tʌp]	17.	"some"	[sʌm]
12.	"soap"	[sop]	18.	"boy"	[bɔy]

b. State another principle describing Paul's pronunciations here. Be sure to word your statement so that 15-18 are not affected.

III.

	Adult word	Paul
19.	"laugh"	[læp]
20.	"off"	[ɔp]
21.	"coffee"	[kɔpi]

c. State a third principle describing Paul's pronunciation in this section.

d. Based on the principles you have seen so far, suggest how Paul would pronounce "love".

IV.

	Adult word	Paul		Adult word	Paul
22.	"truck"	[tʌk]	27.	"clay"	[ke]
23.	"Brownie"	[bawni]	28.	"cute"	[kut]
24.	"plane"	[pen]	29.	"beautiful"	[butəpəl]
25.	"broken"	[bokən]	30.	"twig"	[tɪk]
26.	"crack"	[kæk]			

e. State a fourth principle describing the new aspects of Paul's pronunciations in these examples.

V.

	Adult word	Paul
31.	"quick"	[kwɪk]
32.	"quack"	[kwæk]

f. Do these two words illustrate an exception to the fourth principle? If so, how?

PSYCHOLINGUISTICS: THE ACQUISITION OF MORPHOLOGY AND SYNTAX

Children's first vocalizations are present at the very beginning of life. (Everyone knows how adept babies are at crying!) In a few weeks a child begins to coo, producing sequences of vowel-like sounds. The child uses these cooing and gurgling noises to indicate contentment and pleasure. Later the child's vocal repertoire expands to include babbling, which consists of long strings of vowel and consonant-like sounds. It may sound remarkably like speech, yet contain no recognizable words. Not until about the age of 12 months will a child begin to consistently produce words of the language he or she is learning. It is at this stage that we can begin to examine the development of syntax and morphology in children's speech.

Before beginning a discussion of the stages of language acquisition, however, it is important to note that although children tend to go through those steps at about the same ages, this is only a *tendency*. Just because a child is slower or faster than average, that child is not necessarily more or less intelligent or well-developed than average. It is normal for there to be quite a lot of variation between children. The ages associated with the different stages of language acquisition discussed below are only averages, then. They're not specific to children learning English, however, because all children tend to go through the same stages no matter what language they're acquiring.

THE ONE-WORD STAGE

The first words uttered by a year-old child typically name people, objects, pets, and other familiar and important parts of his or her environment. The child's vocabulary soon comes to include verbs and other useful words as well as nouns (including *no, gimme,* and *mine*). Often a phrase used by adults will become a single word in the speech of a child, such as *allgone* and *whasat*? The single words produced at this stage are used as more than just labels for objects or events; they may be used for naming, commenting, requesting, inquiring, and so on. In fact, this level of development has been called the *holophrastic* stage — a holophrase being a one-word sentence. Children at this stage are limited to a word at a time in their production, but they understand and probably intend the meaning of more than a single word. Certainly children can understand the utterances of other people even when they consist of much more than one word. The intonation children use on their one-word utterances may be that of a question, an ordinary or emphatic statement, or an imperative. If children do consistently use these adult-like intonation patterns (and researchers disagree about whether they do or not), it would seem even more likely that "holophrastic" is an appropriate name for this stage.

THE TWO-WORD STAGE

Between approximately 18 and 24 months of age, children begin to use two-word utterances. At first they may seem to be simply two one-word sentences produced one right after the other. There may be a pause between them, and each word may bear a separate intonation contour. Before long, however, the two words are produced without pausing and with a single intonational pattern.

Children at this stage do not just produce any two words in any order; rather, they adopt a consistent set of word orders which convey an important part of the meaning of their utterances. At this level of development, the structure of utterances is determined by semantic relationships, rather than syntactic ones. Word order is used to express these semantic relations; only later are syntactic devices added to the basic word order rules. Most of the utterances produced by a child at this stage will express a semantic relation like one of the following:

agent + action	*baby sleep*
action + object	*kick ball*
action + locative	*sit chair*
entity + locative	*teddy bed*
possessor + possession	*Mommy book*
entity + attribute	*block red*
demonstrative + entity	*this shoe*

Words such as *more* and *'nother* may be used as modifiers of nouns *(more juice, 'nother cup)* to indicate or request recurrence. *Here* and *there* may be used as demonstratives or locatives. Some children at this stage of development also use pronouns. For the most part, however, their speech is lacking function morphemes and words. These function morphemes include prepositions, auxiliary verbs, articles, and inflectional affixes. All of these (as well as pronouns, *more, 'nother, here* and *there)* belong to closed sets of morphemes or words — speakers rarely produce new pronouns or prepositions, but new nouns, verbs, and adjectives are invented regularly.

These little function morphemes are omitted during this stage and even after the child begins to produce more than two words at a time. Because of this omission, the speech of young children is often called *telegraphic*. When you send a telegram or run a classified ad, every word you include costs you money. Therefore, you only put in the words you really need, and not the ones that carry no new information. Children follow the same principle of economy. The words they use and the order in which they use them convey the relevant information; function morphemes would be redundant. Of course, pronouns, *more, 'nother,* and the other words mentioned earlier carry independent meanings and can fill one of the positions in the semantic relations listed above. Eventually, of course, children do acquire the full set of function morphemes of their language — the "syntactic devices" mentioned above that supplement the expression of semantic relations through word order rules.

LATER STAGES OF DEVELOPMENT

Three-word utterances are originally formed by combining or expanding two-word utterances. Two two-word strings with a common element may be combined; for example, *Daddy cookie* and *cookie eat* may be combined to form *Daddy eat cookie.* A two-word utterance may also be expanded from within, when (for example) *throw ball* becomes *throw red ball.* That is, one of the elements of a two-term relation itself becomes a two-term relation.

There is no strictly three-word stage of language acquisition, however. Once children are capable of combining more than two words into an utterance, they may use three, four, five or even more words at a time. These longer utterances soon are syntactically organized — that is, they possess hierarchical syntactic structure rather than being flat sequences of words like those produced in the two-word stage.

Children's speech at this stage is still telegraphic, including only morphemes and words that carry important semantic content. Gradually a child will begin to include function morphemes in his or her utterances, but these function morphemes are not acquired randomly. Instead, children acquire them in a remarkably consistent order. For example, the present progressive verbal suffix *-ing (she walking)* appears in children's speech before the third person present marker *-s (she walks),* which in turn is acquired well before the past tense marker *-ed (she walked).* Around the time *-ing* appears, so do the prepositions *in* and *on.* Three homophonous morphemes, all phonologically /s/, are acquired at different times. First children use the plural morpheme *-s* (for example, *shoes);* later they acquire the possessive *-'s (Mommy's);* then the present tense morpheme mentioned above is added to verbs. Articles *(a* and *the)* are acquired fairly early, but forms of the (highly irregular) verb *be* only appear at a relatively late stage.

PLURALS

Recall that the plural morpheme *-s* is acquired quite early by children — in fact, it is usually one of the very first function morphemes to appear, along with *in, on,* and *-ing.* That does not mean, however, that very young children have complete mastery over the plural system of English.

At first, no plural marker is used at all. Nouns only appear in their singular forms (for example, *man).* Next, irregular plural forms may appear for a while — that is, a child may say *men* instead of *man,* using the same form adults do. Then the child discovers the morpheme *-s,* and suddenly applies it to plural nouns. In some cases this involves *overgeneralization* of the rule of plural formation; for example, the plural of *man* becomes *mans.* During this stage the child leaves nouns ending in sibilants *(nose, house, church,* for example) in their singular forms. Once the child discovers the generalization about how the plural of these nouns are formed, however, he or she may go through a brief period during which [əz] is added to *all* nouns. This soon passes, however, and the child produces all plurals correctly, except for irregular ones. These are learned gradually, and may not be fully acquired when the child is five years old. Once they are learned, however, they are exceptions to the child's regular process of plural formation. When they first appear in a young child's speech, they are simply isolated forms that fit into no pattern.

NEGATIVES

Children also go through a series of stages in learning to produce negative sentences. At first they simply put the word *no* in front of a sentence to negate it: *no baby sleep* or *no I drink milk*. Next, they insert a negative word, especially *no, not, can't* or *don't,* between the subject and the verb of a sentence, resulting in *baby no sleep* or *no I drink milk.* It is interesting to note than at this stage, *can't, won't* and *don't* are unanalyzable negative words. The auxiliaries *can, will,* and *do* are not acquired until later; three-year-olds tend to still have trouble with them. Furthermore, children often omit forms of the verb *be* in their negated sentences, producing sentences such as *I not break car* and *I not thirsty*. Recall that *be* is a difficult verb. The full set of its forms takes children quite a while to acquire.

The child's system of negation continues to become more adult-like, but for a while he or she will use words such as *something* and *somebody* in negated sentences, producing results such as *I don't see something*. Later these are replaced by *nothing* and *nobody* in "double negative" sentences such as *I don't see nothing*. Finally the child replaces these words with the adult-like *anything* and *anybody*.

INTERROGATIVES

Very young children can produce questions using only a rising intonation, rather than a particular syntactic structure. The meaning of *Mommy cup?* or *More ride?* would be quite clear when produced with the same question intonation that adults use. Later, at around three years, children begin to use *can, will* and other auxiliary verbs in yes-no questions, using the appropriate word order. That is, the auxiliary precedes the subject in these questions; for example, *are you sad?* At this point, however, children still fail to use adult word order in *wh*-questions. They follow a question word with a sentence in normal declarative order: *Why you are sad?* In time, of course, they learn to consistently produce questions in the same ways that adult speakers around them do.

The fact that children produce words and sentences like *foots* or *I don't want something* or *Where he is going?* provides clear evidence that they are not merely imitating the adult speakers around them. Children gradually construct grammars for themselves, as they learn and gain control over the elements and the rules of their language. Their mistakes are not random, but reflect the system they are in the process of constructing for themselves. In fact, the linguistic sophistication of children is quite amazing — within the space of a few short years, a crying, speechless infant transforms itself into a fully competent speaker of some language.

PSYCHOLINGUISTICS: THE ACQUISITION OF WORD MEANING

FILE 95

When children hear a word for the first time, they have no way of knowing what makes the use of the word appropriate. Consider the plight of the nursery-school pupil who played softball in school one day. The teacher chose teams by dividing the class in half, asking each team to sit on a blanket until the game started. At home later that day, one of the students got annoyed because her younger brother kept crawling onto her blanket while she was watching television. "He won't stay away from my team," she complained. With a single exposure to the word *team*, this child formed a definition something like 'a group of people on a blanket'—a reasonable, but wrong guess.

Though this trial-and-error process may seem laborious from an adult perspective, consider what every normal child is able to accomplish: children produce their first words at age one, and by age six, they have a vocabulary approaching 14,000 words. Simple arithmetic will reveal that children master almost ten words a day starting from their first birthday. This feat might suggest that children learn the vocabulary of their native language in a more systematic fashion than is apparent from a single example. While it is not possible to speak of stages like those identified in the acquisition of phonology and syntax, psychologists have determined that the acquisition of word meaning is made systematic in two familiar ways. For one thing, children's first definitions do not deviate randomly from those of adults, but exhibit their own structure. Secondly, the order in which words are learned reflects the intrinsic complexity of the concepts involved. We will explore these sources of regularity in turn below.

CHILDREN'S DEFINITIONS

Initial definitions of words adopted by children fall into three major categories. To some extent, they are present in a child's speech at the same time, though they probably result from different psychological processes.

COMPLEXIVE CONCEPTS

Many nouns are used to single out classes of objects with something in common. For example, the adult word *chair* is used appropriately with desk chairs, rocking chairs, easy chairs, and so on—because all of these things can be sat on. But this apparently elementary fact about our semantic knowledge must be learned by children. Many early definitions of words shift unpredictably from one occasion to the next, with the result that the word fails to identify a class of objects with a single common property. A word with such a definition is said to represent a *complexive concept*.

For example, a child might learn that the word *doggie* refers to dogs, and then use it to name other furry things like soft slippers; on later occasions, he may use *doggie* to refer to things that move by themselves, like birds, toads and small toy cars. The linguist William Labov reports a more exaggerated complexive concept. His 1 year-old son used the word *oo* to refer to the music produced by his brother's rock and roll band; and on later occasions, the same word was applied to the group's jackets, their musical instruments, their cigarettes, and other people's cigarettes. Note that in both examples, any two successive uses of the word pick out objects with similar properties, but that the class of objects as a whole has little in common. Complexive concepts serve to form a loose bond between items associated in the child's experience, and are thought to represent the most primitive conception of word meaning.

OVERGENERALIZATIONS

Overgeneralizations result when the range of a word is extended beyond that of normal adults. For example, one American-English-speaking child called specks of dirt, dust, small insects and bread crumbs *fly*; another gave *moon* as the name for cakes, round marks, postmarks and the letter *O*. A third child overgeneralized the word *ticktock*, using it to refer to clocks, watches, parking meters and a dial on a set of scales.

At first glance, the set of objects named in overgeneralizations may look as varied and random as those in complexive concepts. In fact, children of age two or so frequently have overextensions and complexive concepts in their speech at the same time. But closer inspection reveals that the concept defined in an overextension does not shift from one occasion to the next. In the above examples, the child's definition of *moon* is applied consistently to pick out any round thing. Likewise, *fly* refers to any small, possibly mobile object. The concept underlying the use of *ticktock* is perhaps more complex, but all of the objects in the child's list contain a dial with small marks.

241

In general, the common properties of objects included in the overgeneralization of a word are perceptual features like shape, size, color and taste. And in this respect, the child's strategy for defining a word resembles that of adults, since adults also define words in terms of perceptual features. For example, most English-speaking people insist that only sweet things can be fruits; thus tomatoes are excluded from the definition of *fruit*, though they *do* possess all of the necessary botanical properties. But if the child's definitions of words now resemble those of adults, what misunderstanding is responsible for the overgeneralizations?

The psychologist Eve Clark offers one plausible explanation. In her view, the child who uses overgeneralizations has only an incomplete definition of the adult word. The child who calls dogs, cats, slippers, fur coats and rugs *doggie* has recognized the significance of being furry, but the adult definition mentions more properties; for example, dogs are four-legged. Once the child grasps this property as part of the definition of *dog*, he will no longer overextend the word *doggie* to slippers, rugs and fur coats. Eventually the child becomes aware of *all* properties in a definition, which enables him to narrow down the class of objects named by *doggie* to just those observed in adult usage.

UNDEREXTENSIONS

An underextension is the application of a word to a *smaller* set of objects than is appropriate for mature adult speech. Though less commonly observed than overextensions, careful study reveals that underextensions are at least equally frequent in the language of children.

The psychologist Katherine Nelson observed that children before the age of two years form underextensions because they have trouble distinguishing the essential from the accidental features of common objects. For example a child may call a ball *ball* only when it happens to be under the sofa. The child who underextends the word *ball* in this fashion must eventually realize that the word can be used with the appropriate object, regardless of its location. Underextensions also occur among older, school age children when they encounter category names like *fruit* or *mammal*. Since most people are unsure of the properties which constitute the definitions of these words, they prefer to think of them in terms of their most ordinary members; thus dogs are the most ordinary mammals for many Americans, and apples are the most ordinary fruits. But children are surprised to learn that whales are mammals, or that olives are fruits—because they deviate so profoundly from the ordinary members of these categories. As a result, children underextend the words *mammal* and *fruit*, failing to apply these labels to the unusual members.

Why do children's first definitions fall into the three classes we have discussed? It might be possible to limit the answer to this question somewhat, since complexive concepts are clearly more primitive than overgeneralizations and underextensions, and are present in a child's speech for a shorter period of time. Psychologists have determined that a child who overgeneralizes a word tries to make the most out of a limited vocabulary. Accordingly, overgeneralizations decrease dramatically after age two, when children experience a rapid vocabulary expansion. The opposite strategy underlies the formation of underextensions: children attempt to be as conservative as possible in their use of language, with the result that they perceive restrictions on the use of words not observed by adults. By systematically over- and underextending the range of a concept, the child eventually arrives at the adult definition.

THE INTRINSIC COMPLEXITY OF CONCEPTS

The words discussed so far have been limited to one type: those whose meaning identifies the members of a class. For example, the word *chair* is used correctly when it is applied to the class which includes objects as different as straight chairs, folding chairs and rocking chairs. The same skill in identifying instances of the same class is required for understanding some types of verbs. For example, all people walk differently, but native speakers of English use the word *walk* correctly when they realize that these minor differences are irrelevant.

But not all words in a language involve the identification of classes. In fact, the mastery of a working vocabulary in any human language appeals to a wide range of intellectual skills, some easier and some more difficult than those required for grasping the meaning of common nouns and verbs. As an example of a relatively easy concept, consider what is required for understanding proper nouns: one must simply point out a single individual and attach a label, like *John* or *Daddy*. Because it is easier to associate a label with a single individual than to name a class with common properties, children master proper nouns first, sometimes when they are as young as six to nine months old.

In contrast, a relational term like *large* or *small* constitutes a relatively complex concept. The correct use of words like these requires that two things be kept in mind: the absolute size of the object in question, and its position on a scale of similar objects. For example, an elephant which is six feet tall at the shoulders may be small as far as elephants go, but a dog of the same height would be huge. Five- and six-year-old children are unable to make the shift in perspective necessary for using relational words appropriately. In one well-known experiment which documents this conclusion, children were engaged in a pretend tea party with dolls and an adult observer. The adult gave the child an ordinary juice glass and asked the child if it was large or small. Though all of the children in the study agreed that the glass was small from their own perspective, it appeared ridiculously large when placed on the toy table around which the dolls were seated. Nevertheless, the youngest children were still inclined to say that the glass was small, when asked about its size with respect to its new context.

Another complex concept underlies deictic expressions, which are words used to point to objects and indicate their distance from the speaker. For example, the speaker may use *here* or *this* to point out objects which may be close to him, while *there* and *that* are appropriate only when the objects are relatively far away. (These are one kind of *indexical expression.*) But since there are no absolute distances involved in the correct use of a deictic expression, children have difficulty determining when the 'close' terms are to be preferred over the 'far' terms. As with relational terms, it is necessary to take into account the size of the object pointed to. Thus a thirty-story building six feet in front of us is close enough to be called *this building,* but an ant removed from us by the same distance is far enough away to be called *that ant.*

Common and proper nouns, relational terms and deictic expressions do not exhaust the range of concepts mastered by children, but they do illustrate the variety of tasks involved in acquiring the vocabulary of a first language. Linguists can examine the evidence from the acquisition of word meaning and find support for two fundamental hypotheses: that some concepts are more complex than others, and that the acquisition of language requires a considerable exercise of intelligence.

PSYCHOLINGUISTICS: HOW ADULTS TALK TO YOUNG CHILDREN

When people talk to one another, their general goal is to get listeners to understand what they are saying. This applies just as much when listeners are young children as when they are adults. The problem is that young children know very little about the structure and function of the language adults use to communicate with each other. As a result, adult speakers often have to modify their speech to make sure that children understand them.

How adults talk to children is influenced by three things. First, adults have to make sure that children realize an utterance is being addressed to them, and not to someone else. To do this, they can use a name, a special tone of voice, or even get their attention by touching them. Second, once they have a child's attention, they must choose the right words and the right sentences so the child is likely to understand what is said. For example, they are unlikely to discuss philosophy, but very likely to talk about what the child is doing, looking at, or playing with at that moment. Third, they can say what they have to say in many different ways. They can talk quickly or slowly, use short sentences or long ones, and so on. How adults talk also has certain incidental consequences: children are presented with a specially tailored model of language use, adjusted to fit, as far as possible, what they appear to understand.

How Adults Get Children to Attend

Speakers depend on their listeners being cooperative and listening when they are spoken to. But when the listeners are children, adult speakers normally have to work a bit harder. They use *attention-getters* to tell children which utterances are addressed to them rather than to someone else, and hence which utterances they ought to be listening to. And they use *attention-holders* whenever they have more than one thing to say—for example, when telling a story.

Attention-getters and attention-holders fall into two broad classes. The first consists of names and exclamations. For example, adults often use the child's name at the beginning of an utterance, as in **Ned, there's a car**, and even four-year-olds know that this is an effective way to make two-year-olds attend. Or, instead of the child's name, adults use exclamations like **Look!** or **Hey!** as a preface to each utterance.

The second class of attention-getters consists of modulations that adults use to distinguish utterances addressed to young children from utterances addressed to other listeners. One of the most noticeable is the high-pitched voice adults use for talking to small children. When the linguist O. Garnica compared recordings of adults talking to two-year-olds, five-year-olds, and adults in the same setting, she found that the pitch of the adult's voices was highest to the youngest children, next highest to the five-year-olds, and lowest to other adults.

Another modulation adults use is whispering. If children are sitting on their laps or standing right next to them, adults will speak directly into their ears so it is clear they are intended to listen. Garnica observed that all the mothers in her study on occasion whispered to two-year-olds, a few whispered to five-year-olds, but none whispered to adults.

Not all attention-getters and attention-holders are linguistic. Speakers often rely on gestures as well, and may touch a child's shoulder or cheek, for example, as they begin talking. They also use gestures to hold a child's attention and frequently look at and point to objects they name or describe.

What Adults Say to Young Children

Adults both observe and impose the cooperative principle when they talk to young children. They make what they say relevant, talking about the "here and now" of the child's world. They encourage children to take their turns and make their contributions to the conversation. And they make sure that children make their contributions truthful by correcting them.

The "Here and Now"

Adults talk to young children mainly about the "here and now." They make running commentaries on what children do, either anticipating their actions—for example, **Build me a tower now**, said just as a child picks up a box of building blocks—or describing what has just happened—**That's right, pick up the blocks**, said just after a child has done so. Adults talk about the objects children show interest in: they name them (**That's a puppy**), describe their properties (**He's very soft and furry**), and talk about relations between objects (**The puppy's in the basket**). In talking about the "here and now"—usually whatever is directly under the child's eyes—adults are usually very selective about the words they use. They seem to be guided by the following assumptions:

> (1) Some words are easier for children to pronounce than others.
> (2) Some words are more useful for children than others.
> (3) Some words are hard to understand and best avoided.

Most languages contain "baby talk" words that are considered appropriate in talking to very young children. For example, adult speakers of English often replace the words for animals by words for their sounds—**miaow, woof-woof**—or by a diminutive form of the adult word—**kitty, doggie**. As one would expect, the domains in which baby talk words are found overlap considerably with the domains young children first talk about. They include kinship terms and nicknames, such as **mommy, daddy**; the child's bodily functions and routines, **wee-wee, night-night**; names of animals; games and the occasional toy, **peek-a-boo, choo-choo**; and a few general qualities, **uh-oh!** (disapproval), **teenie**. Adults appear to use baby talk words because they seem to be easier for children to pronounce. This assumption may well have some basis in fact since in many languages baby talk words seem to be modeled on the sounds and combinations of sounds that young children tend to produce when trying their first words. At the same time, baby talk words provide yet another signal that a particular utterance is addressed to a child rather than anyone else.

R. Brown argued that the words parents use in speaking to young children anticipate the nature of the child's world. This seems to be true not only of baby talk words but also of the other words used in speaking to young children. Adults select the words that seem to have the most immediate relevance to what their children might want to talk about. For instance, they would not point to an Irish Wolfhound and say to a one- or two-year-old, **That's an Irish Wolfhound**. They would be much more likely to say **That's a dog**. They supply words for different kinds of fruit the child might eat, such as **apple** or **orange** but not the word **fruit**. They likewise supply the names of animals, but not the word **animal**. In other domains, though, they provide more general words—like **tree**—and do not use the more specific words for different kinds of tree—like **oak, ash**, or **birch**. Some of the words adults select are very frequent in adult-to-adult speech, others are not. The criterion adults seem to use can be characterized by what Brown called "level of utility": the judgment that one word is more likely to be useful than another in the child's own utterances.

Adults are selective in another way too: they omit some words and word endings and avoid other words. Adults tend to use fewer word endings (e.g., plural -s or possessive -'s) and articles (**the, a**) when speaking to two-year-olds than to ten-year-olds, and fewer to ten-year-olds than to adults. Adults seem to leave out function words and word endings because they think this simplifies what they are saying. In fact, they do the same thing when talking to foreigners. Adults also try to avoid certain words. Instead of using pronouns like **he, she**, or **they**, they often repeat the antecedent noun phrase instead, as in **The boy was running, the boy climbed the tree**, where the second instance of **the boy** would normally be changed to **he**. Where **I** and **you** would be used in adult-to-adult speech, adults often use names instead, as in **Mommy's going to lift Tommy up** for **I'm going to lift you up**, or **Daddy wants to brush Julie's hair** for **I want to brush your hair**. Adults often use names in questions addressed to children too, for example, **Does Jennie want to play in the sand today?** addressed to Jennie herself. Adults seem to realize that pronouns are complicated for young children and so they try to avoid them.

Taking Turns

From very early on, adults encourage children to take their turns as speaker and listener in conversation. Even when adults talk to very small infants, they thrust "conversational turns" upon them. During the first months of life, adults respond to small infants *as if* their burps, yawns and blinks count as turns in conversations. This is illustrated in the following proto-dialogue:

> *Mother:* Hello. Give me a smile then [gently pokes infant in the ribs].
> *Infant:* [yawns]
> *Mother:* Sleepy, are you? You woke up too early today.
> *Infant:* [opens fist]
> *Mother:* [touching infant's hand] What are you looking at? Can you see something?

> *Infant:* [grasps mother's finger]
> *Mother:* Oh, that's what you wanted. In a friendly mood, then. Come on, give us a smile.

Whatever the infant does is treated as a conversational turn, even though, at this stage, the adult carries the entire conversation alone. As infants develop, adults become more demanding about what "counts" as a turn. Yawning or stretching may be enough at three months, but by eight months babbling is what really counts. And by the age of one year or so, only words will do.

Once children begin to use one- and two-word utterances, adults begin to provide both implicit and explicit information about conversational turns. For example, they may provide model dialogues in which the same speaker asks a question and then supplies a possible answer to it.

> *Adult:* Where's the ball?
> [picks up ball] THERE'S the ball.

> *Adult:* [looking at picture book with child]
> What's the little boy doing?
> He's CLIMBING up the TREE.

These model dialogues also give the adult speaker the opportunity to show how new information can be combined with given information in the answers to questions. On other occasions, adults expatiate on whatever topic the child introduces:

> *Child:* Dere rabbit.
> *Adult:* The rabbit likes eating lettuce.
> Do you want to give him some?

By ending with a question, the adult offers the child another turn, and in this way deliberately prolongs the conversation. In fact, when necessary they also use "prompt" questions to get the child to make a contribution and so take his turn as speaker:

> *Adult:* What did you see?
> *Child:* [silence]
> *Adult:* You saw WHAT?

Prompt questions like **You saw what?** or **He went where?** are often more sucessful in eliciting speech from a child than questions with normal word order.

Making Corrections

Adults seldom correct what children have to say, but when they do, they only seem to do it to make sure the child's contribution is true. They may correct children explicitly, as in 1 and 2 below, or implicitly, as in 3:

> 1. *Child:* [points] Doggie.
>   *Adult:* No, that's a HORSIE.
> 2. *Child:* That's the animal farmhouse.
>   *Adult:* No, that's the LIGHTHOUSE.
> 3. *Child:* [pointing to a picture of bird on nest]
>   Bird house.
>   *Adult:* Yes, the bird's sitting on a NEST.

In each instance, the adult speakers are concerned with the truth of what the children have said, with whether they have used the right words for their listeners to be able to work out what they are talking about. The other corrections adults make are of how children pronounce certain words. If a child's version of a word sounds quite different from the adult version, a listener may have a hard time understanding what the child is trying to say. Getting children to pronounce recognizable words is a prerequisite for carrying on conversations. What is striking, though, is that adults do not correct any other "mistakes" that children make when they talk. Even blatant grammatical errors go uncorrected as long as what the child says is true. As a result, utterances like **He a girl**, said by a child of her mother, are received with approval. In correcting children's language, adults seem to be primarily concerned with the ability to communicate with a listener.

How Adults Talk to Children

Just as adults select what they say to young children by restricting it to the "here and now," so they alter the way they say what they say when talking to children. They do this in three ways: they slow down, they use short, simple sentences, and they repeat themselves frequently. Each of these modifications seems to be geared to making sure young children understand what adults say.

Speech addressed to two-year-olds is only half the speed of speech addressed to other adults. When adults talk to children aged four to six, they go a little faster but still speak more slowly than they do to adults. To achieve a slower rate, adults put in pauses rather than stretch out each word.

Adults also use very short sentences when talking to young children. The psychologist J. Phillips found that adult utterances to two-year-olds averaged less than four words each, while adult utterances to other adults averaged over eight words. These short sentences are generally very simple ones.

There is a great deal of repetition in adult speech to children. One reason for this is the adults' use of "sentence frames" like those in the left-hand column.

$$
\left\{
\begin{array}{l}
\text{Where's} \\
\text{Let's play with} \\
\text{Look at} \\
\text{Here's} \\
\text{That's a} \\
\text{Here comes}
\end{array}
\right\}
\quad + \quad
\left\{
\begin{array}{l}
\text{Mommy} \\
\text{Daddy} \\
\text{[the] birdie} \\
\ldots \\
\ldots \\
\text{etc.}
\end{array}
\right\}
$$

These frames mark off the beginnings of new words by placing them in familiar slots, and one of their main uses besides attention-getting seems to be to introduce new vocabulary.

Adults also repeat themselves when giving instructions. Repetitions like those below are three times more frequent in speech to two-year-olds than in speech to ten-year-olds:

> *Adult:* Pick up *the red one.* Find *the red one.* Not the green one. I want *the red one.* Can you
> find *the red one?*

These repetitions provide structural information about the kinds of frame the repeated unit (here *the red one*) can be used in. Repetitions also allow children more time to interpret adult utterances because they don't have to try to remember the whole sentence.

When all these modifications are put together, it is clear that adults adjust what they say to make themselves better understood. They first get children to attend, then select the appropriate words and the way to say them. This suggests that young children are able to understand only short sentences and need to have the beginnings and ends of sentences identified. In addition, the sentences used are about the "here and now" since children rely heavily on the context to guess whenever they don't understand. But as children show signs of understanding more, adults modify the way they talk less and less. The shortest sentences and the slowest rate are reserved for the youngest children: both sentence length and rate of speech increase when adults talk to older children.

How Necessary Is Adult Speech?

The fact that adults systematically modify the speech they address to very young children forces us to ask two questions. First, are the modifications adults make *necessary* for acquisition? Second, even if they are not necessary, are they at least helpful? Some exposure to language is obviously necessary before children can start to acquire it. But it is quite possible that any kind of language might do. Unfortunately, there have been virtually no studies of this aspect of acquisition. We need to know, for example, whether children could learn language if their only information came from speech they overheard between adults, or from what they heard on the radio or television. If they could, it would be clear that adult modifications are not necessary, even though they might be helpful. On the other hand, if children could not, it would be clear that some adult modifications are not only helpful but necessary.

Experiments on these topics are difficult if not impossible to devise, but occasionally a naturalistic situation presents itself in a way that provides a glimpse of the answers to these questions. For example, the hearing children of deaf parents who only use sign language sometimes have little spoken language addressed to them by adults until they enter nursery school. The parents' solution for teaching their children to speak rather than use sign language is to turn on the radio or television as much as possible. The psychologists J. Sachs and M. Johnson reported on one such child. When Jim was approximately three and a half years old, he had only a small vocabulary that he had probably picked up from playmates plus a few words from television jingles. His language was far behind that of other children his age. Although he had *overheard* a great deal of adult-to-adult speech on television, no adults had spoken to him directly on any regular basis. Once Jim was exposed to an adult who talked to him, his language improved rapidly. Sachs and Johnson concluded that exposure to adult speech intended for other adults does not necessarily help children acquire language.

Exposure to a second language on television constitutes another naturalistic situation in which children regularly hear adults talking to each other. However, the psychologist C. Snow and her colleagues reported that young Dutch children who watched German television every day did not acquire any German. There are probably at least two reasons why children seem not to acquire language from radio or television. First, none of the speech on the radio can be matched to a situation visible to the child, and even on television, people rarely talk about things immediately accessible to view for the audience. Children therefore receive no clues about how to map their own ideas onto words and sentences. Second, the stream of speech must be very hard to segment: they hear rapid speech that cannot easily be linked to familiar situations. All this suggests that one ingredient that might prove necessary for acquisition is the "here and now" nature of adult speech to children.

PSYCHOLINGUISTICS: ADULT LANGUAGE PROCESSING

A child of six can "hear" her own first cry through her mother's remembrance of her birth. A child can laugh at the jokes of a grandfather whose life ended before his own began. Even in commonplace happenings like these, each of us can use language to step across the limits of a single life to touch times and places far beyond the reach of our own senses. These are extraordinary abilities, which we seem to share with no other animal.

One part of psycholinguistics tries to understand the psychological processes that underlie this ability in normal adults. How do we share information through language? How does talk allow us to know what we have not experienced ourselves?

At present, very little is known about the processes that allow us to achieve these remarkable mental feats. Nevertheless, many investigators feel that a better understanding of these processes is worth pursuing in the hope that it will lead to a deeper understanding of human nature in general and of the mind in particular. It may also be that a better understanding of these processes will contribute to more effective treatments for language disorders ranging from aphasia to dyslexia. It might be possible to teach reading more effectively if the fundamental process of speech comprehension were better understood.

Much of the research on adult normal processes of the last 20 or 30 years has focused on three areas: word recognition, syntactic analysis and interpretation. This brief article will introduce only these aspects of comprehension, though many parallel issues arise in the study of language production.

Word Recognition

Most people can recognize and appropriately interpret tens of thousands of words by early adulthood, which requires that information about all of those words be stored in the brain somehow. Since this vast store of word information is essential to understanding every sentence we hear, we are apparently able to quickly and reliably "look up" hundreds of words per minute in the "dictionary in the head".

Two very general ideas about this look-up process have shaped much research in this area. One suggestion is that the mind works internally in somewhat the same way as a computer search for some item in a large memory. There is an executive element that somehow acquires a description of a stretch of incoming speech that seems likely to be a word. By examining this bit of speech, the executive estimates where in its memory it will find words like this, much as a person will flip to the *T* section of the dictionary to begin searching for the definition of *tort*. Then the executive retrieves from memory the first word entry in the section it has decided to search first. The phonetic description of this word is compared to the bit of speech the process began with. If the match is good, the executive may decide the word retrieved is the one the speaker meant. In this case, the word has been recognized. Often, however, the match will be poor; the entry is discarded and the next word is retrieved. This continues until there is a match.

Kenneth Forster, a psycholinguist, has proposed a model of this process in which the words in each subsection of the word memory are organized according to how frequently each is used, with the most common words listed first. This leads to a very straightforward account of the most frequently discussed feature of word recognition: commonly used words are recognized more quickly than less common words.

There are, however, other features of word recognition that this sort of model accommodates less easily. Some of these are more readily understood in terms of the other major conception of the word recognition process. The psychologist John Morton has advocated a model that assigns a unique recognition device to each word. This device he terms a logogen. The logogen is conceived as a simple counting device that can respond whenever one of the features of the word it stores is found in the incoming utterance. So, for example, if the visual system detects odd angles at the beginning of a capitalized word, logogens for words beginning with *R* and *K* might count this feature. When a logogen has counted a relatively large number of the features of its words in the input, it is said to "fire", meaning that it releases information about the word to the rest of the cognitive system. The word is recognized.

One common observation about word recognition is that it is generally easier to recognize a word when it follows one or more related words or a phrase that somehow suggests or implies the word. These are called context effects. One of the attractions of the logogen model is that it accommodates context effects; it allows the features each logogen counts to be not only physical properties of the stimulus, but also more abstract properties of the context. Such a property might be "About Medical People". Properties of this sort would be detected by the cognitive system and somehow announced to all the logogens at once. The appearance of this property would be counted by the logogens for words such as *doctor, nurse, interns, patient,* etc. In this way these words could be made easier to recognize when they appear after a context related to medical people in some way. A logogen would have to count up fewer features of the stimulus to fire because some context features would already have raised the count closer to the "threshold" at which the logogen fires.

Unfortunately, as sharp as the differences between these two models seem on this sketchy introduction, in the actual course of research it has become very difficult to find a significant difference between them. As the proponents of each model have attempted to adjust it so that it can account for a wider range of phenomena, the cases where the models make distinct predictions have become fewer. Meantime, new phenomena have emerged which do not seem especially compatible with either model. It is just this sort of difficulty in understanding a function that seems so basic to language that excites the interest and enthusiasm of many current investigators.

Syntactic Processing

In every natural language there is an infinite variety of possible sentences. It has been estimated that even if we consider only the sentences of English that are up to 20 words long, there would not have been time to say them all if one had been uttered every second since the beginning of the universe. The same could be said of any natural language. Of course, not every sequence of words is a sentence, e.g., *John saw what the monkey put the banana, but didn't tell anybody.* Yet people are able to apply the intricate system of syntactic principles that determine, in part, what is and is not an acceptable sentence so rapidly and effortlessly that most are never aware of the process itself, just the results.

Perhaps just because syntactic analysis is so rapid and effortless, it has proven very difficult to study. To date practically nothing is known about how strings of words are assembled into phrases, or how choices are made among the many alternative analyses that are often available.

One early series of experiments, conducted by the psycholinguist George Miller and his colleagues, established that syntactic processing can contribute to the perception of words. Various scrambled word strings were constructed from normal sentences. In some cases the scrambled strings were syntactically well-formed but made no sense: *Accidents carry honey between the house.* In others they were "anagram strings" like *Deter drives accident fatal careful.* These were syntactically scrambled but still interpretable if the words were rearranged. Other test strings were syntactically scrambled and senseless no matter how they were rearranged: *On trains hive elephants the simplify.* Recordings of strings of these kinds, together with some fully normal sentences, were played against a noisy background and subjects were asked to report as many words as possible. With both the syntactically well-formed scrambled strings, and the anagram strings, subjects were able to correctly report more words than they could when the strings were syntactically scrambled and senseless. This shows that both syntactic well-formedness and interpretability contributed to the subject's ability to hear words correctly against the noise.

The issue in syntactic processing theory that has perhaps received the most attention in recent years concerns the relation between syntactic processing and semantic or interpretive processing. In brief, the question is whether syntactic processing is somehow influenced by semantic and interpretive processing, or whether it is even a separate system. The question is important because it relates to a very general issue in the study of the mind. The philosopher Jerry Fodor, among others, has argued recently that the mind includes various "input systems" that provide our conscious intelligence with a fast, automatic preliminary analysis of our sense experience. For example, in vision there might be an input system that provides an analysis of the kinds of objects we see in a scene; it would identify cats, trees, people, etc. in a scene and retrieve basic information about each. When we spot a bear in forest, this visual input system both identifies the kind of animal and retrieves the information that it is dangerous. What's most interesting about this view is Fodor's suggestion that input systems, while they may be capable of very sophisticated analysis, are only able to take advantage of a limited range of knowledge. So a person walking through a carnival horror house will first "recognize" the object leaping out of the darkness as a wolf and be appropriately frightened, even though they know perfectly well that everything in the horror house is fake and harmless. Somehow the input system that first notices the wolf is not able to use this knowledge.

This proposal suggests that in part the mind consists of a collection of "modules"; a kind of committee of specialists, each very expert in dealing with one particular area of experience but having access only to a limited body of information relevant to the kind of analysis it performs.

On Fodor's account, syntactic analysis is performed by an input system; it runs rapidly and automatically and provides an analysis of a sentence whether it is sensible or not, so long as it is syntactically more or less well-formed. The psycholinguists William Marslen-Wilson and Lorraine Tyler, and others, have argued that this is not the case. They have performed various experiments that seem to show that semantic and interpretive analyses can guide and constrain syntactic processing. If this is true, Fodor's account is wrong; either there are no input systems or syntactic processing is one of them. Recently, however, Keith Rayner, Marcia Carlson and Lyn Frazier reported an interesting experiement that seems to show that syntactic processing is independent in the way Fodor's theory would predict.

These investigators constructed sentences that contained a temporary syntactic ambiguity. For example, in *The florist sent the flowers was very pleased* it is possible to take the first five words of this structure as a simple sentence with *sent the flowers* as its verb phrase. However, the sub-string *sent the flowers* could also be taken as a relative clause, as in *who was sent the flowers*. As a reader scans *sent the flowers* there is no way to tell which of these alternatives is most appropriate. However, when the reader gets to *was very pleased* it becomes clear that *sent the flowers* must be analyzed as a relative clause.

All other things being equal, there is reason to believe that readers prefer to treat structures like *sent the flowers* as the verb phrase of a simple sentence until forced to do otherwise. This tendency appears to some to be based on the structure of the sentence alone.

The work of Marslen-Wilson and Tyler and others suggests, however, that structure will not be considered alone. As the reader or listener is computing the structure of the sentence, they suggest, the plausibility or likelihood of the alternatives will be considered as well. According to this view, people will also be more likely to take *sent the flowers* as the conclusion of a simple sentence because it is more plausible to speak of florists sending flowers, as in the simple sentence analysis, than to speak of florists receiving flowers, as in the relative clause analysis.

The Rayner, Carlson and Frazier experiment was designed to test the role of the plausibility of the alternative analyses. They used sentence pairs such as those in (1).

(1) (a) *The florist sent the flowers was very pleased.*

(b) *The performer sent the flowers was very pleased.*

If syntactic analysis considers only structure, there should be a tendency to treat *sent the flowers* as the end of a simple sentence in both these cases. But if plausibility is also considered, the sentences will be different. Florists are more likely to send flowers, as in the simple sentence analysis, but performers are more likely to receive flowers, as in the relative clause analysis.

Rayner, Carlson and Frazier used a special computer system to precisely track and record the eye movements of subjects reading sentences such as those in (1). They found that as subjects read sentences like (1a) they spent more time reading each word (adjusting for length) in the disambiguating region *(was very pleased)* than they did on words preceding this section. This suggests that readers analyzed the first five words as a simple sentence, then had to revise their analysis when it was shown to be wrong. If the plausibility of the sentence is considered, this difficulty in the disambiguating section ought not to appear with sentences like (1b). Plausibility considerations should lead readers to analyze the first five words of (1b) as *The performer (who) was sent the flowers...* and the last three words should be easy to fit in with this analysis. However, the results showed that the same difficulty in the disambiguating region appeared with sentences like (1b) as with those like (1a). Thus, plausibility seems not to have been considered. This supports the suggestion that the syntactic processing system is organized along the lines of one of Fodor's input systems and that it does not have access to some of the knowledge people have that is potentially relevant to syntactic processing.

Rayner, Carlson and Frazier's finding is only one of several results suggesting that there is in fact an independent syntactic processor. It is likely, however, that much further research will be required to resolve the controversy provoked by Fodor's proposals. For this and other reasons, syntactic processing is likely to be an active research area for a long time to come.

Interpretive Processing

Finding an appropriate interpretation for each sentence we hear involves an extraordinarily complex system of principles and knowledge. It appears that almost anything we know or believe can influence the way we will interpret some sentence in some context. Nevertheless, this immense body of knowledge is brought to bear so easily that we often apply these comprehension processes to ten or fifteen sentences per minute in casual conversation without the least sense of strain or difficulty.

One early indication of the power and significance of these processes came from a study by the psychologists John Bransford, J.R. Barclay and Jeffrey Franks. They presented each subject with a list of sentences. Subjects were told that they would later have answer some questions about the sentences. The critical sentences were pairs like (2) and the lists were organized so that each subject saw one of the members of each pair.

(2) (a) Three turtles rested *beside* a floating log, and a fish swam beneath *them*.
(b) Three turtles rested *on* a floating log, and a fish swam beneath *them*.

Later subjects were presented with a new list of sentences and asked, among other things, which of them matched sentences that appeared on the earlier list. In the critical cases the new sentences were similar to those in (3).

(3) (a) Three turtles rested *beside* a floating log, and a fish swam beneath *it*.
(b) Three turtles rested *on* a floating log, and a fish swam beneath *it*.

The difference between the two (a) sentences is exactly the same as the difference between the two (b) sentences, but the differences were not always equally noticeable. The subjects who saw (2a) were very good at detecting the change from *them* to *it* and they rejected (3a) as a match. However, those who saw (2b) were very often deceived by (3b); they thought it matched the sentence they had seen before. This difference appears to arise because those who first saw (2b) drew the conclusion (made the inference) that if the fish swam beneath the turtles it also swam beneath the log. This sort of inference is warranted for (2b) but not for (2a).

It appears that people do not merely interpret sentences, they examine them more generally for what they may imply. The results of this analysis seem to be stored in memory in such a way that things a person infers from what they read cannot be distinguished from what was directly asserted in the text.

People interpret individual sentences and integrate information from multiple sentences into a coherent understanding of a conversation, a lecture or a text. Along the way listeners must select interpretations for ambiguous words, identify antecedents for pronouns, and consider new information against the background of their prior knowledge. Exploring the mechanisms by which these feats are achieved constitutes one of the major active research areas in psycholinguistics.

PSYCHOLINGUISTICS: ERRORS IN SPEECH PRODUCTION AND PERCEPTION

When we investigate the nature of language carefully, we sometimes make some surprising discoveries. For example, acoustic analysis of the speech signal reveals that it is for the most part continuous — i.e., in most cases, it is not possible to divide words, or even a series of words, into a sequence of discrete sounds, or phonetic segments. This fact is at odds with our common sense; we feel that words and sentences *are* composed of discrete parts. It could well be that our common sense is simply wrong here (for after all, common sense also tells us that the earth is flat and stationary), but in fact there is good evidence that, although the speech signal *is* physically continuous, it is also, from the perspective of how our brains process this signal, composed of discrete units. Mental (or psychological) aspects of language such as this are clearly of great interest, and a number of different areas have provided evidence to support or refute what common sense tells us about these aspects of language. One such area, which has been particularly helpful in this respect, is the study of errors in speech production and perception (also known as *performance errors)*.

SLIPS OF THE TONGUE (PRODUCTION ERRORS)

By "slips of the tongue" we mean any inadvertent flaws in a speaker's use of his or her language. These mistakes can provide evidence for many of the linguistic constructs we will be discussing throughout this course. First and foremost, of course, is the evidence they supply for the psychological reality of discrete units in the speech wave. These units can be of various sizes—some, surprisingly, even *smaller* than a single sound! Evidence to support these claims is provided by the fact that the units can be moved, added or omitted during a speech error. For example, in the errors illustrated below, individual sounds are being manipulated in various ways. This is only possible if the speaker does indeed organize the speech wave in terms of these units.

ANTICIPATIONS

This type of error involves the substitution for one sound or addition of another sound which is coming later in the phrase being said.

INTENDED UTTERANCE (IU)	ACTUAL UTTERANCE (AU)
spl*i*cing from one t*a*pe	spl*a*cing from one t*a*pe
M.*U*. values	M. *v*iew *v*alues

PERSEVERATIONS

These involve the substitution or addition of a sound which has occurred earlier in the phrase being uttered.

IU	AU
p*a*le sk*y*	p*a*le sk*ay*
John *g*ave the *b*oy	John *g*ave the *g*oy

METATHESES (TRANSPOSITIONS)

Metathesis is the switching of two sounds, each taking the place of the other. When a metathesis involves the first sounds of two separate words, the error is called a *spoonerism*, named after the Reverend Spooner, a chronic sufferer of this type of slip of the tongue.

IU	AU
*d*ear old *q*ueen	*q*ueer old *d*ean
f*i*ll the p*oo*l	f*oo*l the p*i*ll
a h*eap* of j*unk*	a h*unk* of j*eep*

ADDITIONS AND OMISSIONS

These errors involve the addition of extra sounds (out of the blue, so to speak) and the omission of sounds, respectively.

IU	AU
spic and span	spic and splan
chrysanthemum plants	chrysanthemum pants

In these examples the speaker is *imposing* a structure on the speech signal in his/her mind; this structure does not exist physically. This is why we say that the sound unit is psychologically real.

As we mentioned above, the same is true for units of speech smaller than the sound as well. For example, in the following speech errors aspects of pronunciation (called *phonetic features)* are being moved from one sound to another.

IU	AU
clear blue sky	glear plue sky
Cedars of Lebanon	Cedars of Lemadon

In the first case vibration of the vocal folds is moving from the *b* in *blue* to the *c* in *clear* resulting in the phrase *glear plue* instead of *clear blue*. In the second example, air is allowed to resonate in the nasal cavity during the *b* rather than during the *n*, resulting in *Lemadon* rather than *Lebanon*. The fact that individual articulatory movements can move from one sound to another shows that they too are psychologically real units to the speaker; i.e., that speakers do mentally organize sounds according to articulatory movement.

Units of speech larger than the single sound can be identified as well. In the following examples, meaningful *groups* of sounds (called *morphemes)* are being metathesized. Thus these too must be part of our mental organization of the speech wave:

IU	AU
a *floor* full of *hole*s	a *hole* full of *floor*s
a language *learn*er *need*s	a language *need*er *learn*s
I *turn*ed in a *change* of address	I *change*d in a *turn* of address

Language, of course, involves more than just units of speech. In particular, linguists maintain that there is a complex set of rules which the language user follows when making use of these units. The existence of these rules is much less compatible with our common sense than, say, the existence of phonetic segments—especially when we find that we cannot, without fairly extensive study, say what these rules are. Nevertheless, there is considerable evidence for their existence, including much that can be obtained by examining speech errors.

One type of rule whose psychological reality can be confirmed by studying speech errors are *phonotactic constraints.* These rules tell us which sequences of sounds are possible in a given language. For example, the sequence of sounds *sr* cannot occur at the beginning of a word in English. That speakers of English follow this rule is clear from the following slip:

IU	AU
Freudian slip	Fleudian shrip

Notice that this looks almost like the metatheses illustrated in the first section, in that the *l* and *r* were interchanged. But the *s* of *slip* has also been converted to *sh*. If we recall that *sr*, which would have resulted from a simple metathesis, cannot occur word-initially, then we can see *why* this further change was made—to avoid violating this phonotactic rule. Thus, speakers unconsciously follow these rules, even when making mistakes.

The rules that tell us how morphemes are to be pronounced are also obeyed when making speech errors. For example, the morpheme that is the most often used to indicate past tense has three different pronunciations, -*d* ([d]), -*t* ([t]), and -*ed* ([əd]), depending on the nature of the preceding sound. The reality of the rule governing the distribution of these pronunciations is indicated by the fact that it is followed even when the past tense morpheme is attached to a word as the result of a slip.

IU

going to get them *cleaned* ([d])

*cook*ed a *roast* ([kʊk+t])

likes to have his *team rest*ed

([rɛst+əd])

AU

. . . get them *teethed* ([t])

*roast*ed a *cook* ([rost+əd])

. . . have his *rest team*ed ([tim+d])

Since these rules are always followed, they must be part of our mental organization of the language.

These examples also demonstrate the reality of the rules for combining morphemes, since even during a speech error we only find past tense morphemes combined with verbs, plural morphemes combined with nouns, etc. Since we never get nonsensical combinations like "noun + past tense," the rules which tell us how words are built must also be part of our mental organization of language.

Finally, speech errors can also give us insights into the organization of words in the brain (i.e., the *lexicon*, or mental dictionary). For example, many errors in the production of speech involve the substitution of one word for another because of some semantic relationship between the words. The errors which follow, and many more like them, reveal that the intended word and the substituted word share some common semantic property, and that the retrieval process spoken of earlier mistakes one word for another. Thus, these semantic similarities must be recognized and the lexical entries in the brain organized accordingly.

Intended	*Spoken*
My thesis is too long.	My thesis is too short.
There's a small Japanese restaurant near here.	. . . small Chinese . . .
. . . before the place opens	. . . before the place closes
He got hot under the collar.	He got hot under the belt.
. . . when my gums bleed	. . . when my tongue bleeds

A similar type of speech error involves a substitution of one word for another based on phonological, rather than semantic, similarities. What happens in these cases is that the speaker's retrieval process inadvertently pulls out a word that sounds like the one they intended to use, but is semantically distinct. Examples include:

IU	AU
spreading like wildfire	spreading like wildflowers
equivalent	equivocal

This type of error, called a *malapropism*, must be distinguished from cases where the word the speaker used is the one they *intended* to use though it is semantically incorrect. This latter type of mistake, called a *classical malapropism*, does not involve a *performance* error, per se, since the speakers are saying what they meant to say, rather it is a *competence* error since the speakers have incorrect beliefs about the meaning of a particular word. Mrs. Malaprop, a character from Richard B. Sheridan's 18th century play *The Rivals* (and after whom this kind of error is named) was particularly prone to this kind of error, as is the television character Archie Bunker. Such errors reveal more about how words are learned than how they are organized, since the retrieval process is functioning perfectly in these cases. Some examples:

IU	AU
deputize	jeopardize
obscure	obtuse
express appreciation	. . . depreciation (Archie Bunker)

SLIPS OF THE EAR

Slips of the ear provide evidence for many of the same things as slips of the tongue. They do this, however, from the point of view of the *listener* rather than the speaker. For example, since many slips of the ear involve the misperception of a single segment or phonetic feature, or a metathesis of a pair of these, this shows that the speech stream is divided into units as it is *perceived*, not just when spoken. In addition, since such slips always result in possible (though not always actual) words, this kind of slip indicates that listeners know what to expect in the way of sequences of sounds. That is, they have unconscious knowledge of phonotactic rules; if they did not, we would expect to find slips in which impossible words were perceived as having been said. Also, since many slips of the ear involve the misperception of word boundaries, we have evidence that the listener also divides the speech stream into morphemes, just as the speaker does.

The simplest slips of the ear involve only the misperception of the one or more sounds, or the mishearing of a word boundary as in the following examples:

Said	*Heard as*
death in Venice	deaf in Venice
'ron yon virgin	round young virgin
What are those sticks?	What are those ticks?
Maybe we could give them an ice bucket.	Maybe we could give them a nice bucket.
Of thee I sing.	Of the icing

Other perception errors are more drastic in nature; the phrase that is heard is significantly different from the intended phrase. This occurs because the listener is trying to edit what is heard into a meaningful utterance, as we do whenever we listen to speech, and if part of the speech signal is not heard then the listener unconsciously reconstructs what was said, often filling in the gaps with sounds or words that were never there in the first place and changing other words to make sense out of the whole phrase. Examples of this type include:

Said	*Heard as*
kill germs where they grow	kill germs with eggroll
a Coke and a Danish	a coconut Danish
Do you own a grey Cortina?	Do you know a Grey Cortina?

CONCLUSION

Performance errors such as slips of the tongue and slips of the ear provide us with a great deal of valuable information concerning language and how it is processed and produced. We have seen that the speech wave, despite its physical continuity, is mentally organized into discrete units and that these units follow specific rules and patterns of formation. Moreover, these constraints are the same for both speaker and listener. The fact that they are never violated, not even by mistake, shows that the constraints are an intrinsic part of language itself; that is, they *define* for us what the language is like. Thus, by studying cases in which an individual's linguistic *performance* is less than perfect we can gain more insight into the nature of linguistic *competence*, the unconscious knowledge that speakers of a language possess, and make hypotheses about the mental constructs that represent this knowledge.

PSYCHOLINGUISTICS: LEARNING A FOREIGN LANGUAGE

The apparent ease with which children learn their native language contrasts sharply with the experiences of high school and college students in foreign-language courses. Psychologists and teachers have long been aware that foreign languages pose special difficulties for older students, but have been unable to identify the source of the problem. One attractive speculation is that normal children under age six have the advantage of learning their native language before the brain's hemispheres have acquired their adult functions—when there is a critical period during which the brain is especially sensitive to linguistic inputs. But after the critical period, the brain loses its ability to achieve native mastery of a human language.

Evidence for a critical period comes from observations made on isolated children like Genie, who learned their native language after puberty. Through unfortunate and very unusual circumstances, this child was prevented from speaking or even hearing speech during the first thirteen years of her life. Though she has been given intensive language training since she was rescued from this situation ten years ago, to this day she still has halting speech, her sentences are short and formulaic, and she demonstrates little control of the fine muscles necessary for articulation. Significantly, neurolinguistic tests have revealed an abnormal right hemisphere dominance (whereas the left hemisphere is usually dominant in normal persons), indicating to some psychologists that Genie's language centers simply failed to develop when they were not stimulated during the critical period. But evidence that a *second* language cannot be learned after the critical period is less compelling, since it is difficult to measure the extent to which people with a normal upbringing lose their language-learning abilities. Nevertheless, some psychologists believe that phonological systems are difficult to master after the critical period. Thus it is not surprising that many otherwise fluent speakers of a second language often have traces of a foreign accent.

Of course, a positive conclusion can be drawn from an observation like this because it shows that some degree of proficiency in a foreign language *can* be achieved after the critical period. Teachers and psychologists are encouraged by this conclusion, and are confident that the trauma of foreign-language instruction can be reduced considerably when teaching methodologies are introduced which make best use of the adult's language-learning strategies. But there is widespread disagreement concerning the nature of these strategies. Is a foreign language best treated as yet another academic subject—or does it involve a qualitatively different set of skills, whose mastery requires more from students and instructors than the usual kinds of efforts? By attempting to answer this question, we acquire a grasp of the theory behind the foreign-language curricula followed by American high schools and universities, and gain considerable insight into the psychological complexities of human language.

THE GRAMMAR-TRANSLATION METHOD

The grammar-translation or 'traditional' method has been known to students of classical languages for several centuries. Courses taught by the traditional method attempt to instill a mastery of the literary language, and proceed from the assumption that this goal is best achieved by treating a foreign language like a rigorous academic discipline. Students in these courses must memorize long lists of words, some of which appear only in the most elevated styles. And they receive extensive practice in translation to and from their native language, since a complex subject like syntax is presumably learned best if it is related to familiar knowledge.

Despite its unpopularity with legions of schoolchildren, the grammar-translation method persisted in American foreign-language curricula throughout the 1940s. But during World War II, US government officials recognized a need for bilinguals in all levels of government. Linguists and psychologists were recruited to develop more painless ways to learn foreign languages. As part of their efforts, they characterized the problems with the grammar-translation method:

1. *The grammar-translation method emphasizes writing rather than speaking.* As we have seen, writing is different from speaking, and mastery of one skill does not lead automatically to mastery of the other. The main difference is that

with writing (but not with speech) one can take as much time as one pleases to produce a sentence. For example, the French novelist Gustav Flaubert, who was a master of French style, would sometimes spend an entire day composing a single sentence. But speaking must always be done 'on the spot,' which leaves little time for editing and the consultation of grammars and dictionaries.

2. *The major learning strategy in a grammar-translation course is memorization.* Students in traditional courses are forced to memorize vocabulary lists, tables of adjective and verb conjugations—and even entire texts, since the glib recitation of memorized material can give the appearance of fluency. But psychologists now believe that memorization is unsuitable for complex subjects.

The major problem is that most memorized knowledge cannot be very deep, since we are able to memorize verbal material without understanding it at all. To some extent, the ability to memorize meaningless material is useful, and we exercise it in a variety of tasks. For example, we can memorize material with no intrinsic meaning, like telephone nimbers, or sequences of nonsense words like *blip-flong-spork-glarf*. Essentially the same skill is involved in memorizing lists of words with their tranlations, such as the Russian/English pairs *dom/house, chellovek/man, sadit'/tosit,* and *okno/window*. But knowledge gained in this fashion disappears without constant practice. Thus it is not surprising that we can no longer remember our telephone numbers from five years ago, and we are not always able to retrieve an entry in a list of memorized Russian verb conjugations when the need arises for it in a conversation.

3. *The emphasis on translation in grammar-translation courses is misplaced.* Contrary to popular belief, it is difficult for fluent bilinguals to translate from one language to the other. They must receive college-level training to become proficient translators, and even then the skill is highly specialized. For example, students in translation institutes may learn to translate from their native language into their second language, but not in the opposite direction. Or they may learn to translate oral rather than written material.

The behavior of fluent bilinguals supports the conclusion that translation is not a primary linguistic skill like speaking or listening comprehension and may even be independent of them to some degree. Results from comprehension tests given on simultaneously translated passages suggest that *oral* translators, at least, simply do not have enough time to gain a deep understanding of their material. Evidence for the marginal status of translation can also be found among those aphasics whose language skills are all intact, except for their ability to translate. In view of observations like these, critics claim that an emphasis on translation need not lead to a mastery of the primary linguistic skills—and that speaking, reading, writing and listening comprehension should be taught directly instead.

THE DIRECT METHOD AND THE AUDIOLINGUAL METHODS

How can an adult in a foreign-language course learn the major skills of linguistic competence directly? A satisfactory solution to this problem might be formulated by observing how children perform the same task when acquiring their native language, and adopting their learning strategies for classroom use. This general approach to foreign-language instruction characterizes the direct method, which was a significant alternative to the grammar-translation method in the first half of the twentieth-century—and the audiolingual method, which resulted from the collaboration of linguists, psychologists and the U.S. government in the 1940s and 1950s.

The *direct method* represents a literal attempt to duplicate the conditions under which children learn their native language, since the entire class is conducted in the target language. High-school and college students in direct-method courses first learn the names of common objects in their environment—as do children; but the students' first words are most likely to be *chalk* or *teacher* or *French class*, since the most probable setting is a classroom. After this stage, the instructor involves the students in ordinary situations like ordering food in a restaurant or going to the movies with a friend, in which they are expected to participate actively in dialogs. And like children in similar situations, they have no access to the written language. But how are grammatical constructions learned under such conditions? They are simply 'picked up' automatically without instruction—presumably the same method by which children learn the syntax of their native language.

The first practitioners of the direct method were confronted with a surprise. Though children can learn syntax with little conscious instruction, teenagers and adults find the same task extrodinarily difficult. To appreciate the exercise of intelligence required to master the syntax of a foreign language, consider a problem from a foreign-language aptitude test, and reflect on the thought processes involved in solving it:

Below are two sentences from Kabardian. Answer the question which follows.

Shi gader le—The horse sees Father
Shi gader la—The horse saw Father
be—carries

How would you say *The horse carried Father*?

Now think about how much more challenging this task would have been if you were not provided with translations, you were not systematically presented with all of the relevant pieces to the puzzle, and you were not permitted to read the question and solve it on paper. Thus it is not difficult to understand why the direct method was never widely adopted in foreign-language programs.

The audiolingual method represents an attempt to remedy the problems introduced by the direct method. To make the learning task more manageable, grammatical constructions are presented systematically. For example, a foreign student learning English may be required to master the word order of a sentence like *I saw a book*, substituting noun phrases to get variations like *I saw a hat* and *I saw a boy*; more advanced exercises might contain noun phrases with adjectives, as in *I saw a red book*. This step-by-step procedure continues throughout the course, until all sentence patterns are mastered.

The second innovation introduced by the audiolingual method has a more theoretical source. Linguists and psychologists of the 1950s determined that fluent speech is possible because language is a complex set of habits, much like those which guide an accomplished tennis player to a flawless performance. And just as the tennis player acquires habits through extensive practice, so does the native speaker of a language. Accordingly, audiolingual courses attempt to facilitate the formation of habits, primarily through extensive use of drills like the pattern substitutions mentioned above. Intensive audiolingual courses may devote as much as three to six hours a day to oral drills.

ASSESSMENT

All of the foreign-language teaching methodologies discussed in the previous section were developed before the 1960s. Yet versions of the audiolingual or the grammar-translation methods are still used in virtually all foreign-language courses currently taught in the United States. Their continued use reflects an unresolved theoretical debate.

Proponents of the updated grammar-translation method emphasize the fact that adults approach language-learning as an intellectual activity, and make use of the educational experiences that children lack. They criticize the audiolingual method because it fails to engage an adult's analytical skills. Thus students find sentence drills meaningless if they are not accompanied by thorough explanations of the syntax involved. Supporters of 'analytical' methods also defend the decision to involve the student's native language because adults need not 'start from scratch' when learning a second language. A foreign-language course which takes full advantage of a student's knowledge might assume an adult's deep understanding of how languages are structured, and emphasize the points of divergence between his native and foreign languages.

But proponents of the audiolingual and other 'naturalistic' methods insist that advances in foreign-language teaching will be made only by incorporating even more language-learning strategies used by children, since native fluency appears to require more than consciously applied analytical skills. In one recently developed naturalistic program, students become fluent with giving and receiving commands before mastering other sentence types, and learn concrete words like 'chair' before abstract words like 'freedom'—both reflections of the order preferred by children.

The existence of divergent theoretical positions underlying 'analytic' and 'naturalistic' foreign-language teaching methods makes it reasonable to ask how the programs compare in effectiveness. Results from a recent large-scale study designed to answer this question showed that after one year of instruction, students in audiolingual courses had a superior performance in the skills required to carry on simple conversations while students in grammar-translation courses excelled in writing; listening and reading comprehension were the same for both groups. But by the end of the second year of study, all students performed at comparable levels of proficiency in all four skills.

261

If the 'naturalistic' and 'analytical' methods can be regarded as roughly equivalent in some respects, they also have some common shortcomings. A major problem is that students in both types of programs fail to achieve an active grasp of productivity; they may learn to understand novel utterances, but are unable to participate in spontaneous conversation. In the analytical courses, it is easy enough to identify the source of the problem: conversation is simply not emphasized, and students always remain too conscious of the complex set of rules needed to construct even a single sentence. But in the naturalistic courses, another problem is responsible for the students' failure. The linguist Sol Saporta once noted that memorization skills are taxed to an even greater extent in some naturalistic courses because students must memorize sentences and entire dialogs, as well as single words. But memorization is precisely the wrong strategy if the goal is a fluent production of novel utterances, since it is impossible to memorize *all* sentences in a human language.

One conclusion to be drawn from this discussion is that we are far from understanding how foreign languages should be taught to adults. But by examining past failures, it is at least possible to isolate problems for future investigation. What kind of skill *does* a fluent bilingual possess, if adults cannot acquire it using their analytical abilities? And what kind of effort, then, *is* required for learning a foreign language after puberty?

INTRODUCTION: HISTORICAL LINGUISTICS

When linguists describe the current phonological processes of a particular language, isolate that language's morphemes, or discover that language's syntactic rules, they analyze that language *synchronically;* that is, they analyze that language at a particular point in time. Languages, however, are not static, but just like other human institutions they are constantly changing entities. Linguists can then study language development through time, providing *diachronic* analyses.

Historical linguistics is the subfield of linguistics which tries to describe and explain the changes that occur in a language during its history. The field as we know it began in the late 18th century when Western European scholars began to notice that modern European languages shared similar linguistic characteristics with ancient languages such as Sanskrit, Latin, and Greek. These similarities led linguists to believe that today's European languages and those ancient languages must have evolved from a single ancestor — or "mother" — language. They called that language Proto-Indo-European.

If these languages did in fact share a common ancestor, a reasonable question to ask is what caused them to change into the different languages that they are today? One of the causes for language change is geographical division. As groups of people spread out through Europe, they lost communication with each other, so that the language of each group went its own way, underwent its own changes, and thus came to differ from the others. Another cause for language change is language contact, with the effect that languages become more alike. English, for example, has borrowed many Spanish words from contact with Mexican and Cuban immigrants. Language contact does not, of course, explain why Proto-Indo-European subdivided as it did, but it does help to explain a number of shared characteristics — especially lexical items — among the world's languages. Language contact, like any other explanation for language change, does not provide a complete explanation, only a partial one. At times, linguists cannot find any particular cause which would motivate a language to change in a particular direction. Language change, then, may simply just happen.

Often people view such change as a bad thing, so they try to resist it. Jonathan Swift, the late 17th-early 18th century satirist who wrote *Gulliver's Travels,* felt that if the language changed, people would no longer be able to read his essays. Having this belief, he supported the movement among English grammarians to stipulate prescriptive rules which would have the effect of regulating current language usage as well as change. These grammarians based their rules on Classical Latin from the first century BC, viewing it as the perfect, model language since it did not change. Even today when we don't look to a language such as Latin as a model, some people consciously resist linguistic change. Consider the word *comprise.* Traditionally, the whole comprises its parts as in *A chess set comprises thirty-two pieces.* Increasingly, however, people say *Thirty-two pieces comprise a chess set* in which the parts now comprise the whole. Strict prescriptive grammarians regard this second utterance as ungrammatical. Despite these social views towards change, linguists regard change as neither good nor bad; it is simply a fact of life and a fact of language.

In what ways and how, then, do languages change? They change in all aspects of the grammar, the phonology, morphology, syntax, and semantics. These changes are discussed and documented in the files in this section as are some of the methods used by linguists to recognize, describe, and analyze change. The files, then, survey different aspects of historical linguistics beginning with the comparative method. The goal of this method is to reconstruct proto-languages, i.e. languages considered to be the ancestors of modern languages, through the comparison of related languages. File 101 presents the theory of the genetic relatedness of languages. Without such a theory, reconstruction would be impossible. File 102 presents some data illustrating some of the similarities between languages which give rise to comparative analysis. File 103 presents the method and problems of comparative reconstruction. File 104-108 turn away from the comparative method, showing how language can change with respect to its phonology, morphology, syntax, and semantics. Finally, File 109 presents problems concerned with these different areas of change.

HISTORICAL LINGUISTICS: THE FAMILY TREE AND WAVE MODELS OF LANGUAGE CHANGE

Historical linguistics is concerned with language change. That is, what kinds of changes occur (and why) — and equally important, what kinds of changes don't occur (and why not) — how we might discover the changes that have occurred in a language's history, and the relationship of languages historically. The notion that similar languages are related and descended from an earlier, common language (a *proto-language*) goes back to the late 18th century when Sir William Jones suggested that the linguistic similarites of Sanskrit to ancient Greek and Latin could best be accounted for by assuming that all three were descended from a common ancestral language.

Jones' suggestion was developed in the 19th century, and gradually came under the influence of Darwin's theory of the evolution of the species. Scholars at the time considered language and linguistic development to be analogous in many ways to biological phenomena. Thus, it was suggested that languages, like other living organisms, had "family trees" and "ancestors". The next page gives a sample "genealogical tree" for the Indo-European (I-E) family of languages.

The *Family Tree Theory* as formulated by August Schleicher in 1871 assumes that languages change in regular, recognizable ways (the *Regularity Hypothesis*) and that because of this, similarities between languages are due to a "genetic" relationship between those languages (the *Relatedness Hypothesis*). In order to fill in the particulars of such a relationship it is necessary to *reconstruct* the hypothetical parent from which the related languages are derived. The principle technique for reconstructing the common ancestor (the proto-language) of related languages is known as the *comparative method*.

In keeping with the analogy of language relationships to human families, the theory makes use of the terms mother (or parent) *daughter,* and *sister* languages. In the family tree of I-E on the next page, French and Spanish are sisters, both are daughters of Latin; Germanic is the mother of English, and so on. The model shows the direction of change and the relations among languages clearly, the older stages of the languages being located higher in the tree and direct descendants being linked to their ancestors through the straight lines or "branches".

However, a disadvantage exists in that the structure of the family tree may lead people to develop faulty views of two aspects of language change: 1) that each language forms a uniform speech community without internal variation and without contact with its neighbor languages, so that all speakers of Latin, for example, are assumed to have spoken exactly the same way at the time French and Spanish split off; and 2) that the split of a parent language into its daughter languages is a sudden or abrupt occurrence, happening without intermediate stages.

These two views are not supported by the linguistic evidence we have from modern languages. No language is uniform or isolated from others, but is always made up of dialects which are still recognized as belonging to the same language, and always shares similarities with other languages in its family, even those belonging to a different subgroup. And as studies of modern language change show, languages do not split apart abruptly but rather drift apart indiscernibly, starting as dialects and only ending up as separate languages after years of gradual change. In fact, the dividing point between two "dialects" and two "languages" is often impossible to locate exactly and is often obscured by non-linguistic (e.g., political) factors.

To supplement the Family Tree Model and overcome these difficulties, Johannes Schmidt proposed the *Wave Theory* in 1872. This theory recognizes the gradual spread of change throughout a dialect, language or a group of languages, much as a wave expands on the surface of a pond from the point where a pebble (i.e., the source of the change) has been tossed in. Dialects are formed by the spread of different changes from different starting points and

I. INDO-EUROPEAN FAMILY TREE DIAGRAM

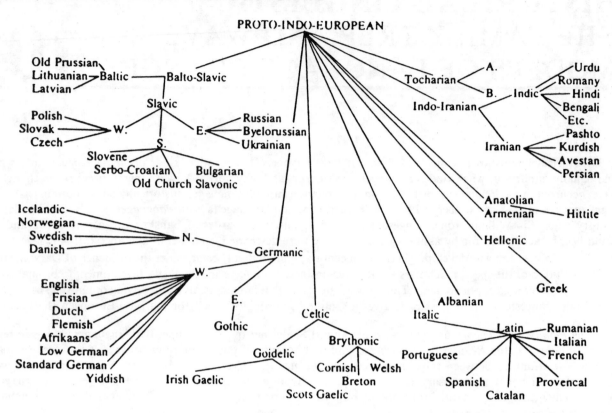

II. INDO-EUROPEAN WAVE DIAGRAM

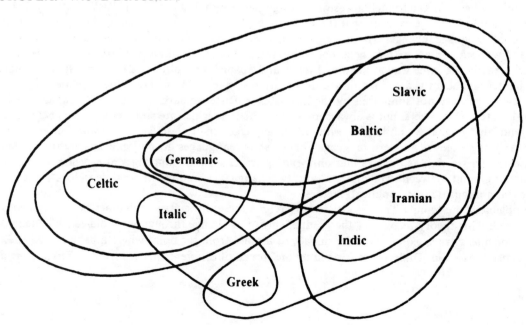

at different rates; some changes reinforce each other while others only partially overlap or affect only a certain area, much as the waves formed by a scattering of pebbles thrown into a pond may partially overlap. In the wave diagram for I-E above, the same basic subgroups shown in the family tree are indicated; in addition, however, similarities *between* various subgroups are also indicated by circles enclosing those languages which share some linguistic feature or set of features, thus cutting across the traditional categories of the family tree. By looking at ever smaller linguistic changes one can also show the languages within each group and the dialects within each language, indicating clearly how variable languages can be, even though distinct from others. In this way the wave diagram avoids the two faults of the family tree model, though it in turn suffers from disadvantages relating to problems in analyzing the genetic history of the languages displayed in such a diagram.

In fact, neither the family tree model nor the wave model presents entirely adequate or accurate accounts of language change or the relatedness of languages. For example, it is now known that languages can exhibit linguistic similarities without necessarily being related. The similarities may be the result of borrowing from *language contact, drift* (that is, independent but identical changes in distinct dialects or languages), similarities in *types of morphological structures, syntactic similarities,* or other reasons. Nonetheless, the family tree model and wave model do provide useful frameworks for the discussion of language change.

HISTORICAL LINGUISTICS: SOME COGNATES IN INDO-EUROPEAN LANGUAGES

The following lists of words contain cognate sets from six Indo-European languages: English, Greek, Latin, Old Church Slavic, Old Irish, and Sanskrit. The transcription is phonetic.

	1. *father*	2. *mother*	3. *brother*
Indo-European	pətɛ:r	ma:tɛ:r	bʰra:tɛ:r
English	faðr̩	mʌðr̩	brʌðr̩
Greek	patɛ:r	mɛ:tɛ:r	pʰra:tɛ:r
Latin	patɛr	ma:tɛr	fra:tɛr
Old Church Slavic	——	mati	bratrə
Old Irish	aθɪr	ma:θɪr	bra:θɪr
Sanskrit	pɪtər-	ma:tər-	bʰra:tər-

	4. *mead*	5. *is*	6. *bear*
Indo-European	mɛdʰu	ɛsti	bʰɛr-
English	mid	ɪz	bɛr
Greek	mɛtʰu	ɛsti	pʰɛrɔ:
Latin	——	ɛst	fɛro:
Old Church Slavic	mɪd	yɛstə	bɛrõ
Old Irish	mič	——	bɛrɪð 'bears'
Sanskrit	mədʰu	əstɪ	bʰəra:mɪ

HISTORICAL LINGUISTICS: THE COMPARATIVE METHOD

One of the major reasons for the systematic comparison of languages is the desire to establish language relationships, i.e., we want to determine what languages have descended from a common parent language, and we want to determine how closely these languages are related.

Two tendencies make it possible to determine language relationships. First, the relationship between the form of a word and the meaning of a word is *arbitrary*. This means that it is reasonable to assume that two (or more) languages which share words of similar form and meaning are *related*, that is, descended from a common parent language. Notice how important the fact is that this relationship is an arbitrary one. If the relationship were a *natural* one then we would expect languages which were unrelated to share many words with similar form and meaning. In fact it would be impossible to determine which languages were related and which were not. Second, sounds do not change in random ways, rather sounds change *regularly*.

When a language undergoes a certain sound change, that change will (eventually) be reflected systematically throughout the vocabulary of that language. For example, a language might undergo a change of [p] to [f] in which every [p] in every word is replaced by [f]. Or, for example, a language might undergo a change of [b] to [v] between vowels, in which case every word with a [b] between two vowels would acquire a [v] in this position. A sound change may be either unconditioned (as in the [p] to [f] example) or conditioned by phonetic environment (e.g., occurs only when the sound in question is between two vowels, or before a certain other sound, or after a certain sound, or at the beginning of a word, or at the end of a word, etc.), but nothing *other* than the phonetic environment ever limits a sound change. A sound change never randomly affects some words but not other phonetically similar words, never occurs just in words with a certain kind of meaning, etc. That is what is meant by the *regularity* of sound change.

These then are the two tendencies which make it possible for linguists to establish language relationships. The arbitrary relationship between a word's form and meaning is important because it makes it highly unlikely that unrelated languages will share large numbers of words of similar form and meaning. The regularity of sound change is important because it means that two (or more) languages which are related will show regular sound correspondences. Let us consider an example to illustrate what we mean. Consider the following forms:

English		German		Dutch		Swedish	
	[mæn]		[man]		[man]		[man]
	[hænd]		[hant]		[hant]		[hand]

If we compare the vowel sounds in all four languages for the word *man* we can establish the following sound correspondence: [æ] in English corresponds to [a] in German, Swedish, and Dutch. In order for this sound correspondence to be regular, it must occur in other words which have similar form and meaning. And of course it does, as a comparison of the words for *hand* confirms. Note that since this correspondence (æ — a — a — a) occurs regularly (is not unique) we have eliminated the possibility of being misled by chance similarity between words with similar form and meaning in *unrelated* languages.

The task of the comparative linguist does not end with the discussion of similarities between languages, or with the assumption that these similarities indicate that the languages in question are related. The linguist is also interested in discovering how languages which are related developed from the parent language into their present forms; in other words, the linguist is interested in linguistic history.

In order to discover how languages have developed from a parent language, the parent language itself must be *recoverable*. And in some cases it is. For the Romance languages (French, Spanish, Portuguese, Rumanian, etc.) the parent language (Vulgar Latin) is attested by numerous written records, for example, manuscripts, public inscriptions, funeral inscriptions, graffiti, etc. As a result it is possible to trace the development of the various Romance languages from their parent with considerable accuracy. In other cases, however, written records for the parent language do not exist. But this does not mean that we cannot gather any information about the parent language; in these cases it is possible to infer what the parent language looked like by comparing the forms and grammar of the related languages. Since inferences are made by comparing words of similar form and meaning in the languages we assume to be related, the method is called the *comparative method*. Please note that the comparative method is itself possible because of the regularity of sound change. If two or more languages show regular correspondences between themselves in words where the meanings are the same or similar it means that these words have descended from a common source.

As a small preliminary example of how the comparative method works let us return to our English-German-Dutch-Swedish example. We note that the first consonant in the word in question is an [m] and that the final consonant is an [n] in all four languages. Thus we can safely assume that the parent language had an initial [m] and a final [n] in the word for *man*, so that at this point we can reconstruct *m_n in our Proto-language. With respect to the vowel sound there is some uncertainty because there is variation in the sound: English has [æ] while German, Dutch, and Swedish have [ɑ]. However, since there is numerical superiority on the side of *a* it is best to assume that this is the sound the parent language possessed, and that English alone has changed [ɑ] to [æ]. Thus we reconstruct the Proto-word for *man* as *man, and the sound change ɑ > æ (" ɑ changes to æ ") in English.

COMPARATIVE METHOD PROCEDURE

The goal of the comparative method is to reconstruct the proto-forms of the parent language from cognates of languages which are assumed to be related. Once the parent language forms have been reconstructed, it is possible to determine the changes by which the daughter languages have become distinct by comparing the reconstructed forms with the forms present in the daughter languages.

1. The first step is to gather and organize data from the languages in question, forming *cognate sets*. A cognate of a word is another word which has descended from the same source as the original one; they are very similar in form and usually are identical or similar in meaning. For example, the word meaning 'female friend' is *amiga* in Modern Provençal, *amiga* in Spanish, *amica* in Italian, and *amica* in Rumanian. These words form a *cognate set* since they are quite similar in form and identical in meaning.

2. While gathering cognates you should make sure that "suspicious-looking" forms are eliminated; that is, words may be borrowed into one of the languages which have the same meanings as the words in the other languages but are not cognate with them, and most likely they will have distinctly different forms from the other *true* cognates. Whenever you are comparing data to check for language relationships, you should beware of such forms.

3. Next determine the *sound correspondences* which exist between sounds in the same positions of each set of cognate words in the languages. For instance, the first (or initial) sound correspondence in our cognate set cited above (in number one) will be:

> a — Provençal
> a — Spanish
> a — Italian
> a — Rumanian

The sound correspondences for the rest of this cognate set are equally straightforward:

position	Provençal	Spanish	Italian	Rumanian
2	m	m	m	m
3	i	i	i	i
4	g	g	k	k
5	a	a	a	a

4. Given the sound correspondences determined in step 3, you must try to determine the earlier form of the word from which the cognates have descended, using two rules of thumb:

a) *Majority Rule.*   Often a majority of the cognates will have the same sound; if this is the case, and if no other factors are known that would favor one of the other sounds, then assume that the most common sound was the one present in the older stage of the word.

b) *Most Natural Development.* Years of study in phonetics and historical linguistics have shown that certain types of sound changes are very common, while others almost never happen. For instance, the change of a stop to a fricative of approximately the same point of articulation is a very common change, while the reverse change is much less common. Thus, if one cognate contains a stop where the other contains a fricative, a safe bet is to assume the stop is the older sound and changed to a fricative in the other cognate word.

a. Common sound changes affecting consonants:
—voiceless sounds become voiced between vowels, before voiced consonants
—stops become fricatives between vowels, generally around continuants
—consonants become palatalized before front vowels
—consonants become voiceless at the end of words
—difficult consonant clusters are simplified
—difficult consonants are made easier

5. Now determine for each set of cognates the older stage of the word in the parent languages and the sound changes which have affected the sounds in each daughter language. On the basis of majority rule we can reconstruct all but the last consonant sound of the word 'female friend': *ami_a. Here there are two voiced consonants attested, and two voiceless consonants. Obviously majority rule is of no use: we must appeal instead to the most natural development. Since it is more common for a sound to become voiced between two voiced sounds than to become voiceless, it is best to assume that the sound in the proto-language was voiceless and that Modern Provençal and Spanish have undergone a development whereby * k > g between vowels.

COMPARATIVE RECONSTRUCTION PROBLEMS

We have tried to order the reconstruction problems according to degree of difficulty, but the first few problems are no doubt of comparable difficulty. The following directions pertain to all of the reconstruction problems contained in this file:

(A) set up the sound correspondences for each cognate set and reconstruct the earlier form for the word from which the cognates have descended;

(B) establish the sound changes that have affected each language.

1. Proto-peninsular Spanish.

	Castilian	Andalusian	English gloss
1.	[mayo]	[mayo]	'May'
2.	[kaλe]	[kaye]	'street'
3.	[poλo]	[poyo]	'chicken'
4.	[poyo]	[poyo]	'stone bench'
5.	[dos]	[dosⱼ]	'two'
6.	[dieθ]	[dies]	'ten'
7.	[θiŋko]	[siŋko]	'five'
8.	[si]	[si]	'yes'
9.	[kasa]	[kasa]	'house'
10.	[kaθa]	[kasa]	'a hunt'
11.	[θiƀiliθaθion]	[siƀilisasion]	'civilization'

[λ] represents a palatal liquid.

2. Proto-Numic.

	Yerington Paviotso	Northfork Monachi	English gloss
1.	[mupi]	[mupi]	'nose'
2.	[tama]	[tawa]	'tooth'
3.	[piwɨ]	[piwɨ]	'heart'
4.	[soŋo]	[soŋo]	'lungs'
5.	[sawaʔpono]	[sawaʔpono]	Proper Name (female)
6.	[nɨwɨ]	[nɨwɨ]	'liver'
7.	[tamano]	[tawano]	'springtime'
8.	[pahwa]	[pahwa]	'aunt'
9.	[kuma]	[kuwa]	'husband'
10.	[wowaʔa]	[wowaʔa]	'Indians living to the West'
11.	[mɨhɨ]	[mɨhɨ]	'porcupine'
12.	[noto]	[noto]	'throat'
13.	[tapa]	[tape]	'sun'
14.	[ʔatapɨ]	[ʔatapɨ]	'jaw'
15.	[papiʔi]	[papiʔi]	'older brother'
16.	[patɨ]	[petɨ]	'daughter'
17.	[nana]	[nana]	'man'
18.	[ʔati]	[ʔeti]	'bow, gun'

3. Proto-Numic.

Shoshone	Ute	Northern Paiute	English gloss
1. [tuhu]	[tuu]	[tuhu]	'black'
2. [nika]	[ni̥ka]	[nika]	'dance'
3. [kasa]	[kḁsi]	[kasa]	'feather'
4. [tuku]	[tu̥ku]	[tuku]	'flesh'
5. [yuhu]	[yuu]	[yuhu]	'grease'
6. [pida]	[pida]	[pita]	'arm'
7. [kadi]	[kadi]	[kati]	'sit'
8. [kwasi]	[kwḁsi]	[kwasi]	'tail'
9. [kwida]		[kwita]	'excrement'

4. Proto-Romance.

Spanish	Sardinian	Rumanian	English gloss
1. [hilo]	[filu]	[fir]	'thread'
2. [viða]	[bita]	[vita]	'life'
3. [vino]	[binu]	[vin]	'wine'
4. [riva]	[riba]	[ripa]	'bank'
5. [rio]	[riu]	[riu]	'river'
6. [riso]	[rizu]	[ris]	'laugh'
7. [muða]	[muta]	[muta]	'change'

5. Proto-Tupi-Guarani

Guarani	Tupinamba	Siriono	Guarayo	English gloss
1. [kičȋ]	[kitȋ]	[kišȋ]	[kičȋ]	'cut'
2. [čȋ]	[tiŋ]	[šȋ]	[čȋ]	'white'
3. [meʔẽ]	[meʔeŋ]	[meẽ]	[meẽ]	'give'
4. [kwa]	[pwar]	[kwa]	[kwa]	'tie'
5. [ki]	[kib]	[ki]	[ki]	'louse'
6. [kiʔa]	[kiʔa]	[kiaˌ]	[kɪa]	'dirty'
7. [abačí]	[abati]	[ibaši]	[abačí]	'corn'

6. Proto-Middle-Indic

Magadhi Prakrit	Pali	Maharastri Prakrit	English gloss
1. [abaḷa]	[apara]	[avara]	'other'
2. [dȋba]	[dȋpa]	[dȋva]	'lamp'
3. [hasta]	[hattʰa]	[hattʰa]	'hand'
4. [ḷoga]	[ḷoka]	[ḷoa]	'world'
5. [ṇaḷa]	[ṇara]	[ṇara]	'man'
6. [ṇispʰaḷa]	[ṇippʰaḷa]	[ṇippʰaḷa]	'fruitless'
7. [paskʰaḷadi]	[pakkʰaḷati]	[pakkʰaḷai]	'(he) stumbles'
8. [pidā]	[pitā]	[piā]	'father'
9. [puspa]	[puppʰa]	[puppʰa]	'flower'
10. [šuska]	[sukkʰa]	[sukkʰa]	'dry'

[ṇ] is a retroflex nasal stop.

7. Proto-Central Pacific

Maori	Hawaiian	Samoan	Fijian	English gloss
1. [pou]	[pou]	[pou]	[bou]	'post'
2. [tapu]	[kapu]	[tapu]	[tabu]	'forbidden'
3. [taŋi]	[kani]	[taŋi]	[taŋi]	'cry'
4. [takere]	[kaʔele]	[taʔele]	[takele]	'keel'
5. [noho]	[noho]	[nofo]	[novo]	'sit'
6. [marama]	[malama]	[malama]	[malama]	'moon'
7. [kaho]	[ʔaho]	[ʔaso]	[kaso]	'thatch'

8. Proto-Western Turkic

Turkish	Azerbaijani	Crimean Tartar	Kazan Tartar	English gloss
1. [burun]	[burun]	[burun]	[bɨrɨn]	'nose'
2. [kabuk]	[gabɨx]	[ǰoŋga]	[kabɨk]	'bark'
3. [boyun]	[boyun]	[moyun]	[muyɨn]	'neck'
4. [toprak]	[torpax]	[toprak]	[tufrak]	'earth'
5. [kuyruk]	[guyruk]	[kuyruk]	[kɨyrɨk]	'tail'
6. [yaprak]	[yarpak]	[ǰaprak]	[yafrak]	'leaf'

HISTORICAL LINGUISTICS: SOUND CHANGE

Sound change is the most widely studied aspect of language change. There are a number of reasons why this is so. First, the study of how the sounds of languages change has a long tradition behind it, more so than any other area of linguistics. As a result we are more informed about this particular area of language change than others. Second, it is often impossible to understand changes in other areas of the language system without studying sound change, for sound change does not just affect the system of sounds of a language but may also affect a language's morphology, syntax, and semantics. Third, the study of sound change provides the basis for the study of language relationships and the reconstruction of parent (proto-) languages. Finally, sound change provides a very good introduction to the basic aims and goals of those who study language change: to describe the types of changes possible in language systems and to determine the causes of those changes.

WHAT IS SOUND CHANGE?

Sound change is an alteration in the phonetic shape of a sound as a result of a phonological process. If a phonological process is introduced into a language where it did not formerly occur it may result in a sound change. For example, at early period in the history of English the voiceless velar stop [k] occurred before the front vowel [i:] in words like 'chide' *cidan* [ki:dan]. Later in the Old English period the velar consonant [k] was palatalized to a [č] before the front vowel [i:]. The introduction of the phonological process of palatalization resulted in the sound change k > c before [i:] in Old English. The phonetic shape of [k] (the voiceless velar stop) was altered to [c] (a voiceless palatal affricate) as a result of the phonological process of palatalization.

At this point, it is necessary to make the distinction between the introduction of a phonological process and sound change clearly understood. The introduction of a phonological process into a language alone cannot be considered sound change. While it is a necessary first step in the process of sound change, the introduction of a phonological process at first changes the structure of a word in certain specific speech contexts. For example, the basic pronunciation of the word *interesting* is [ɪntərɛstɪŋ], and this pronunciation occurs most often in formal speech situations, e.g. when talking with business associates. When, however, we speak with close friends in a casual situation, we may allow the phonological process which deletes schwa [ə] before liquids [r, l] to apply and pronounce the word [ɪntrɛstɪŋ]. We cannot assume that there has been a sound change of ə > ∅ before liquids on the basis that a phonological process has applied in casual speech. For sound change to occur the basic form of a word must be permanently altered in all contexts. In the example above, speakers would have to choose the variant pronunciation of *interesting* [ɪntrɛstɪŋ] in *all* speech situations, and abandon the pronunciation [ɪntərɛstɪŋ] altogether. Obviously this has not happened (yet!) in the case of *interesting*, though it did happen in the Old English example discussed above. Recall that the introduction of palatalization resulted in alternate pronunciations for the word 'chide' *cidan* [ki:dan] and [či:dan]. When the pronunciation [či:dan] was first introduced into Old English it was no doubt tied to certain speech situations much as the pronunciation [ɪntrɛstɪŋ] is in Modern English. Gradually, however, over a considerable period of time, the pronunciation [či:dan] was adopted by Old English speakers and the pronunciation [ki:dan] was abandoned. In this way the basic form of the word was permanently altered in Old English to [či:dan]. Thus the introduction of the palatalization process resulted ultimately in the sound change k > č before [i:].

THE REGULARITY OF SOUND CHANGES

One of the most fascinating aspects of sound change is that if a particular sound change is studied over a long enough period of time it will be completely regular, i.e., every instance of the sound in question will undergo the change. Thus, in our Old English example we would say that the sound change k > č before [i:] is regular because every Old English word which contained [k] before [i:] changed to [č]; the change was not isolated to the word 'chide'. Sound change does not affect all possible words instantaneously, nor does every speaker in a community pick up a sound change overnight. Sound change is a very gradual process, spreading from one word to the next, and from one speaker to the next until all possible words and speakers are affected.

Though sound change takes place gradually, the ultimate regularity of sound change can be verified quite easily. In Old English, for example, the ancestor of our Modern English word *house* was spelled *hus* and pronounced [hu:s]. If we compare these two words, we observe a change in the quality of the vowel. In Old English, the vowel was the high back rounded vowel [u:] while in Modern English the vowel is a dipthong, [aw]. What is important is that this is not the only example of the sound change u: ˃ aw in the history of English. In fact we can find any number of Old English words with [u:] which are pronounced with the dipthong [aw] in Modern English, e.g., Old English *mus* [mu:s]: Modern English *mouse* [maws]; Old English *louse* [lu:s]: Modern English *louse* [laws]; Old English *out* [u:t]: Modern English *out* [awt], etc.

TYPES OF SOUND CHANGE

The development of Old English [u:] is what is known as *unconditioned sound change*. That is, every instance of [u:], no matter where it occurred in a word, or what sounds were next to it, became [aw]. More often than not, it is the case that sounds are influenced by the sounds which occur around them. When a sound changes due to the influence of a neighboring sound the change is called a *conditioned sound change*. We have already considered a good example of a conditioned sound change from the history of English, namely the palatalization of [k] before the front vowel [i:]. Notice that only the voiceless velar stops which were palatalized were those occuring before the vowel [i:]; all other velar stops remain non-palatal. Evidence of this is Old English *ku* [ku:] corresponding to Modern English *cow* [kaw].

Conditioned and unconditioned sound changes are often subcategorized as follows: conditioned sound changes according to what type of conditioning is involved; unconditional sound changes according to changes in articulation, e.g. according to changes in tongue position, lip rounding, etc. We will only list some of the more common types of sound changes, followed by an example or two.

CONDITIONED SOUND CHANGES

1. *Assimilation.* Assimilation refers to a situation in which one sound becomes more like another sound. In Old English voiceless fricatives became voiced when they occurred between voiced sounds, e.g., Old English *wolves* [wulfas] became [wulvas].

2. *Dissimilation.* Dissimilation refers to a situation in which two similar sounds become less like one another. In some varieties of English the word *fifth* [fɪfθ] has undergone a sound change whereby the final fricative has dissimilated to a stop [fɪft].

3. *Metathesis.* Metathesis refers to a change in the order of sounds. Some English dialects have reversed the order of the velar stop and the alveolar fricative in the word *ask* so that the word is pronounced [æks] instead of Standard English [æsk].

4. *Deletion/Insertion.* At the end of the Middle English period unstressed word-final [ə] was deleted, e.g., Middle English *nose* [nɔ:zə] Modern English *nose* [noz]. In a considerable number of Modern English varieties the basic form of the word *athlete* is pronounced [æθəlit]. In this word a sound change has taken place inserting [ə] between consonants of a cluster which was perceived to be difficult to pronounce. The older, basic form of the word is [æθlit].

UNCONDITIONED SOUND CHANGES

1. *Monophthongization.* Monophtongization refers to a change from a dipthong (a complex vowel sound consisting of a vowel followed by a glide) to a simple vowel sound, a monophthong. A good example of monophthongization occurred at the beginning of the Modern English period. In Middle English the dipthong [w] occurred in words such as *rude* [rɪwdə], *rule* [rɪwłə], *new* [nɪwə], *due* [dɪwə], and so forth. In Modern English this dipthong became a simp)le vowel [u]; witness the modern pronunciations for these words: *rude* [rud], *rule* [rułł], *new* [nu], *due* [du], etc.

2. *Diphthongization.* Diphthongization refers to the change of a simple vowel sound to a complex one. The history of English once again provides us with a very good example. In the Middle English period the high back rounded vowel [u] became a diphthong [aw], e.g., Middle English *house* [hu:s] became Modern English *house* [haws].

3. *Raising/Lowering.* Raising and Lowering refer to changes in the height of the tongue in the production of sounds. At the beginning of the Middle English period the word *noon* was pronounced [nɔ:n], with a mid-back round vowel. By the end of the Middle English period, however, the word was pronounced [nu:n], the tongue height being raised from mid to high. Thus the sound change u:˃o: is called raising.

280

4. *Backing/Fronting*. The terms backing and fronting refer to alterations in the frontness or backness of the tongue in the production of sounds. At the beginning of Modern English period there was a sound change whereby the back vowel [ɑ] became the front vowel [æ], for example in words like *calf, path, glass, past, ask*, etc.

PHONETIC AND PHONEMIC CHANGE

When we speak of sound change it is possible to make a distinction between *phonetic* and *phonemic* change. Phonectic change refers to a change in pronunciation of allophones which has no effect on the phonemic system of the language. For example, over the course of time the English phoneme /r/ has underdone several changes. Early in the history of English the unrestricted allophone of the phoneme /r/ was pronounced as a trill (and still is in Scottish English). Presently, however, the unrestricted allophone of /r/ is pronounced as a retroflex liquid.

Similarly, in the Middle English period voiceless stops were not aspirated in initial position. There was only one allophone for the three stop phonemes: /p/-[p], /t/-[t], /k/-[k]. Then these sounds underwent a sound change whereby stop consonants became aspirated initially before an accented vowel. This sound change altered the pronunciation of the stop phonemes by adding one allophone to each phoneme: /p/-[p] and [pʰ], /t/-[t] and [tʰ], /k/-[k] and [kʰ]. Still, the phonemic system of English has remained unaffected. This, then, was a phonemic change. Phonetic changes do not affect the phonemic system at all, but rather add or delete an allophone of a phoneme, or substitute one allophone for another.

Phonemic change, on the other hand, refers to sound change which changes the phonemic system of a language in some way, usually by the addition or loss of a phoneme. In Old English the phoneme /f/ had one allophone, [ɸ], until about 700 A.D. At this time a change occurred whereby [ɸ] was voiced when it occurred between voiced sounds, e.g. Old English *wives* [wīvas]. At this period the sound change had no effect on the phonemic system; it merely created an additional allophone for the phoneme /f/, namely [v]. Later borrowings from French into English, however, created situations in which the two sounds came into contrast with one another, e.g., *safe* [seɸ] and *save* [sev]. As a result, we must now consider these two sounds members of *separate* phonemes—/f/-[ɸ] and /v/-[v] respectively. Thus, the sound change ɸ > v ultimately led to a phonemic change since it resulted in the creation of a new phoneme, /v/.

EXERCISES

1. For each word specify the sound change(s) beween Proto-Quechua and Tena. Then say whether each sound change is conditioned or unconditioned, and further what type of conditioned or unconditioned change each sound change is.

P-Q	Tena	gloss
čumpi	čumbi	'belt'
timpu	timbu	'boil'
nutku	nuktu	'brains'
akla	agla	'choose'
wakli	wagli	'damage'
utka	ukta	'fast'
kunka	kunga	'neck'
lyantu	lyandu	'shade'
mutki	mukti	'smell'
pukyu	pugyu	'spring'
inti	indi	'sun'
sanku	sangu	'thick'
hampatu	hambatu	'toad'

2. Specify the changes between Proto-Slavic and Bulgarian. Classify the changes as conditioned or unconditioned. Then say what type of conditioned or unconditioned change each sound change is. Finally, note that these changes have to occur in a particular chronological order. What is the order of the changes? Why do they have to be in this particular order?

P-S	Bulgarian	gloss
gladuka	glatkə	'smooth'
kratuka	kratkə	'short'
blizuka	bliskə	'near'
žežika	žeškə	'scorching'
lovuka	lofkə	'adroit'

3. Determine the sound changes that took place in the development of the Maharastri Prakrit from Old Indic. Classify the sound changes as conditioned or unconditioned. Then specify what type of conditioned or unconditioned change each sound change is.

Old Indic	Maharastri Prakrit	gloss
agni	aggi	'fire'
anta	anta	'end'
aŋka	aŋka	'hook'
arka	akka	'sun'
bʰakti	bʰatti	'devotion'
catwāri	cattāri	'four'
kalpa	kappa	'rule'
kardama	kaddama	'mud'
kaṭaka	kaḍaa	'bracelet'
kā̇ka	kāa	'crow'
mudgara	muggara	'mallet'
pitā	piā	'father'
rudra	rudda	'terrible'
sapatnī	savattī	'co-wife'
supta	sutta	'asleep'
šabda	sadda	'sound'
šata	saa	'hundred'
utkaṇṭʰā	ukkaṇṭʰā	'desire'
vikrama	vikkama	'strength'
viṭapa	viḍava	'branch'

[₆bʰ represents a murmured bilabial stop; ṭ , ḍ , ṭʰ, ṇ represent retroflex stops]

4. Determine the changes which have taken place between Middle English and Modern English. What sound changes are conditioned? What sound changes are unconditioned? Further classify the unconditioned sound changes. Finally, is it possible to find a pattern to the vowel changes in these words? If so, what is it?

Middle English	*Modern English*	*spelling*
hu:s	haws	'house'
wi:f	wayf	'wife'
stɔ:n	ston	'stone'
he:	hi	'he'
hro:f	ruf	'roof'
so:n	sun	'soon'
hwi:t	wayt	'white'
kwe:n	kwin	'queen'
na:m	nem	'name'
bɔ:n	bon	'bone'
ba:k	bek	'bake'
hlu:d	lawd	'loud'

HISTORICAL LINGUISTICS: THE GERMANIC CONSONANT SHIFTS

Proto-Indo-European had three series of stop consonants: a voiceless series, *p, *t, *k, a voiced series, *b, *d, *g, and a series of (so-called) voiced aspirates written *bh, *dh, *gh. In the transition from Proto-Indo-European to Proto-Germanic, these series of consonants underwent an organized set of changes, or *shifts*, as follows:

Indo-European:	*p	*t	*k	*b	*d	*g	*bh	*dh	*gh
	v	v	v	v	v	v	v	v	v
Germanic:	f	θ	x	p	t	k	b	d	g

This change is known as *Grimm's Law* and is one of the changes that distinguishes the languages of the German subgroup from all other Indo-European language groups. That is to say, every Germanic language will show a different set of developments in the Proto-Indo-European (PIE) sounds. Examples of words affected by Grimm's Law are listed below.

PIE	Non-Germanic	Germanic (English)
*pəter	Lat. pater	father
*trei-	Lat. tres	three
*kerd	Gk. kardia	heart
*leb-	Lat. labium	lip
*dekm	Lat. decem	ten
*gᵂenā	Gk. gyne	queen
*bhrater	Sanskrit bhrāter	brother
*dhē	Lat. facere	do
*ghos-ti	Lat. hostis	guest

Modern High German has undergone a second consonant shift similar to the first in nature; this *Second Germanic Consonant Shift* differentiates the High German dialects from other Germanic dialects and languages. Thus, only High German will exhibit evidence of the shift.

The second consonant shift was a rather complicated change. The table below captures the major changes but omits certain details.

Proto-German		High German	
		After Vowels	Elsewhere
*p	>	f	pf
*t	>	s	ts
*k	>	x	k (but *kx* in some dialects)
*d	>	t	t

Consider the following examples of the correspondence between Modern English, which did not undergo the second shift, and Modern German, which, of course, did undergo the shift.

English	German
o*p*en	o*ff*en
*p*ath	*pf*ad
bi*t*e	bei*ss*en
*t*o	*z*u (z = [ʦ])
*b*ook	*B*u*ch* (ch = [x])
*c*ome	*k*ommen
ri*d*e	rei*t*en
*d*oor	*T*ur

Based on the statement of the changes and the examples cited above, what sound in Modern German would correspond to the underlined English sounds?

English	Modern German
floo*d*	Flu_____
shi*p*	Schi_____
boo*t*	Bu_____e
re*ck*on	rei_____en
ha*t*e	Ha_____

Now, given the underlined German sounds, what would the corresponding sound be in English?

Gri*ff*	gri_____
Her*z*	hear_____
Fu*ss*	foo_____
ma*ch*en (ch = [x])	ma_____e
wa*ff*enlos	wea_____onless
*Pf*lug	_____low

HISTORICAL LINGUISTICS: MORPHOLOGICAL CHANGE

106

We have now seen that change in the sounds of language can occur over periods of time. Language change, however, is not restricted to just changes in aspects in phonology; all components of a language — phonology, morphology, syntax, and semantics — can and do change. In what follows, we examine change in the morphological subsystem of a language.

PROPORTIONAL ANALOGY AND PARADIGM LEVELING

As a first example of morphological change which will serve to introduce the topic, let us consider the early Modern English past tense of the verb *climb*. As recently as several hundred years ago, the usual past tense of this verb was *clomb* (phonetically [kʰlom]). In Modern English, on the other hand, the past tense is *climbed* ([kʰlaymd]). Thus, over the course of the past few centuries *climbed* has replaced *clomb* as tne past tense of *climb*.

It should not have escaped your notice that in this example, the new form of the past tense of *climb* is exactly what would be expected as the regular past tense of an English verb, i.e. [-d] after a voiced consonant (compare *rhyme* [raym]/*rhymed* [raym-d]). In terms of the formation of the past tense, *clomb* is an irregularity because past tense in English is not generally formed by altering the vowel of the base. Thus, it appears that the irregular past tense form (*clomb*) has given way to a past tense form made with the productive, regular past tense morpheme —*ed*. In a sense, then, we can talk of the change as being one that brought *climb* more in line with a majority of verbs of English, and that these verbs and in particular the productive pattern of forming the past tense with these verbs exerted some influence on *climb*, leading to the replacement of *clomb* by the more expected and usual (by the rules of English past tense formation) *climbed*.

This account also provides us with some insight into the nature of morphological change: it often involves the influence of one form or group of forms over another. In the case of *clomb* ⟶ *climbed*, the influence of the regular past tense forms led to the change; this type of morphological change can often be schematized as a four-part proportion, as in:

rhyme : rhymed :: climb : X

and you don't have to be a mathematician to solve for X and get climbed. *Rhyme* was chosen here only as an example; it is perhaps more accurate to state the proportion in terms of a general pattern which is extended to another verb, i.e.:

VERB : VERB + *ed* :: climb : X, X ⟶ climbed.

[present] [past]   [present]   [past]

Since this type of morphological change can be schematized as a four-part proportion, it is generally known as *proportional analogy*.

In general, morphological change involving the influence of a form or set of forms over another is called *analogy* (or *analogical change*). As with *clomb* ⟶ *climbed*, analogical change generally introduces regularity into a system. For example, in early stages of Latin, the paradigm (a set of closely, inflectionally related forms) for the word 'honor' was as follows:

NOMINATIVE honos
GENITIVE honos-is
ACCUSATIVE honos-em (etc.)

This paradigm was perfectly regular, in that there was just a single form of the stem (*honos*-) to which the inflectional endings were added. Somewhat later in the development of Latin, a sound change took place by which intervocalic *s* became *r*; this was quite general and affected all instances of intervocalic *s* in that language. The effect on the paradigm of 'honor' was to create two different forms of the stem, *honos-* in the nominative and *honor-* in the other cases (because the *s* was intervocalic in them but final in the nominative):

NOMINATIVE honos
GENITIVE honor-is
ACCUSATIVE honor-em

The resulting paradigm was thus irregular in having two stem shapes. Later on in Latin, a further change took place creating a regular paradigm once more: the nominative took the form *honor*, giving:

NOMINATIVE honor
GENITIVE honor-is
ACCUSATIVE honor-em

This last change was not a widespread one and there are many instances of final *s* in Latin which did not change to *r* (e.g., *genus* 'kind', *navis* 'ship', etc.).

Note that this morphological change has a result similar to that in the first example, namely introducing regularity. This change introduced regularity into a paradigm that had been disturbed by the workings of sound change. This type of analogical change that takes place within a paradigm is often called *paradigm leveling*; the motivation though is the same as with the form-class type of analogy (proportional analogy) seen with *clomb* ———→ *climbed*.

The two analogical changes discussed above involve the elimination of irregularities in the morphological subsystem of a language. While the striving toward regularity is perhaps the most notable result of analogical change, it is not, however, the only outcome. There are other analogical changes which have little if anything to do with regularization. We turn now to a brief discussion of these changes.

BACK FORMATION AND FOLK ETYMOLOGY

The process of *back formation* can be illustrated by the following schema:

worker   :   work   ::   burglar   :   X, X   burgle

[agent noun]   [verb]   [agent noun]   [verb]

As you may have noticed, the process of back formation appears to be similar to the process of proportional analogy. However, the fundamental difference becomes apparent upon closer inspection. Back formation involves the creation of a new *base form*, in the example above the verb *burgle*, whereas proportional analogy involves the creation of a new *derived form*.

One of the more important differences between back formation and proportional analogy has to do with the fact that back formation is often preceded by *misanalysis*. The example of back formation cited above is a case in point. English speakers borrowed *burglar* from Norman French speakers as a monomorphemic word. This word was misanalyzed by English speakers as consisting of a verb *burgle* plus an affix *-er* because its phonological structure and its meaning resembled other formations of this type, e.g. *worker*, *runner*, etc. As a result, the identification of *burglar* with this pattern of word formation, or better, the misanalysis of *burglar* according to this pattern of word formation, namely *verb + -er* ———→ *agent noun*, has resulted in the creation of a new verb *burgle*.

As we saw from the preceding discussion, the primary motivation for the back formation of *burgle* from *burglar* was the common derivational process *verb + -er* ———→ *agent noun*. Interestingly, the influence of productive inflectional processes can also result in back formations. Consider the case of Modern English *cherry—cherries*. This word was borrowed from Norman French *cherise*. Note, however, that this word was a singular, not a plural, noun for French speakers. But to English speakers this noun sounded like a plural because it ended in a sibilant, i.e., this word appeared to follow the regular pattern for the formation of plural nouns: *singular + -(e)s* [-s, -z, -əz] (compare *boy* [bɔy] — *boys* ['bɔy+z]. As a result, the word *cherise* was misanalyzed as a plural and a new singular noun was back-formed, namely *cherry*.

As a final example of analogical change we consider the process known as *folk* or *popular etymology*. As we saw from the example of back formation discussed above, misanalysis played an important role as a motivating factor for the creation of the verb *burgle*. Similarly, the driving force behind the process of folk etymology is misanalysis. In the case of folk etymology, however, obscure morphemes are misanalyzed in terms of more familiar morphemes. As an example of folk etymology consider the following case taken from an article in the OSU student newspaper (*The Lantern,* May 1984). In this article the author referred to a variety of snake known as the 'garter' snake as a 'garden' snake. In this example the morpheme *garden* has been substituted for the morpheme *garter.* There were probably a number of reasons for the misanalysis of *garter* as *garden.* Foremost among them was undoubtably the fact that the two morphemes are very similar phonologically, differing only in the point and matter of articulation of the final consonant. Morever, from the point of view of sematics it is not very clear to most English speakers why the morpheme *garter* should be used to describe the longitudinal stripes which are found on most varieties of garter snakes, particularly since the noun *garter* refers most commonly to an elasticized band worn around the leg to support hose. The final factor contributing to this misanalysis was undoubtably the fact that, at least in urban areas, garter snakes are commonly found in and around gardens.

The case of folk etymology just discussed illustrates an important point about this analogical process: it occurs most often in cases where the morphological make-up of a word is obscure to speakers. There are a variety of reasons for morphological obscurity. One variety is illustrated by the Old English *samblind* 'half blind' to Modern English *sandblind.* The morphological make-up of this word was obscured by the fact that *sam* 'half' ceased to exist as an independent word in English. In order to make this word more accesible in terms of its structure English speakers substituted the word *sand.* Note again that, as was the case with the substitution of *garden* for *garter,* the substitution of *sand* is motivated by phonological similarity (*sam* and *sand* sound a lot alike) and a semantic relationship (blowing sand can cause temporary blindness).

SUMMARY

Proportional analogy and paradigm leveling are characterized by the elimination of irregularities from the morphological subsystem of a language. Back formation and folk etymology do not involve the elimination of irregularities *per se.* Rather, they involve the misanalysis of unfamiliar morphemes in ways that make them more accessible to speakers. Nevertheless, the four varieties of analogical change which we have discussed are characterized by the fact that they involve the influence of one particular form or set of forms over another.

As with sound change, the new forms introduced by morphological changes do not necessarily take hold instantaneously. Most often, there is a period of competition between the old form and the new form. This helps to explain some of the fluctuation that is evident in Modern English past tense formations, for instance, in which some people say *fit* and others say *fitted,* some say *lit* and others say *lighted,* some say *hung* and others say *hanged,* etc. Thus the process of morphological change are often at the heart of synchronic variation evident in all languages. Similarly, children often analogize in much the same way as adult speakers do, creating regularized forms like *bringed, eated,* and the like.

EXERCISES

1. Historically, the past tense of the verb *dive* is formed by the regular pattern of past tense word formation, i.e. *verb + -ed ⟶ past tense* (*dived*). However, in a number of American English dialects *dived* has been replaced by *dove.* It is normally assumed that *dove* replaced *dived* as the result of the pattern *drive* [present tense] :: *drove* [past tense]. Would you consider the replacement of *dived* by *dove* as an example of *proportional analogy?* What does this tell us about the notion of *productivity/regularity* and analogical change?

2. We have seen that the regularity of sound change provides one of the bases for the *comparative method.* How might the workings of analogical change pose problems for the comparative method?

3. Try to come up with other aspects of English morphology that currently show some degree of fluctuation and variation (e.g. *saw* vs. *seen* as the past tense of *see*). To what extent are analogical processes at work in causing these fluctuations?

4. We have seen that natural phonological processes were at the heart of most sound changes. As a result, when an unnatural change is encountered, e.g. the addition of final [-d] as part of the change of *clomb* to *climbed,* we should suspect that morphological change is at work. What is the unnatural aspect of the change of final *s* to *r* that we saw in the Latin example of *paradigm leveling?* We have a good indication from the lack of regularity of this change that it is the result of morphological change, but is there any phonetic reason for being suspicious of this as a sound change?

HISTORICAL LINGUISTICS: SYNTACTIC CHANGE

As we have noted in the introduction to this section, linguistic change is not restricted to one particular component of a language. Thus in the same way that the sounds and words and meanings of a language are subject to change, so, too, are the patterns into which meaningful elements — words and morphemes — fit in order to form sentences. That is to say, change can be found in the *syntactic* component of a language, that domain of a grammar concerned with the organization of words and morphemes into phrases and sentences.

In syntactic change, therefore, the primary data that historical linguists deal with are changes in the variety of elements that go into the syntactic structuring of a sentence. These include (but are not restricted to) changes in word order, changes in the use of morphemes that indicate relations among words in a sentence (e.g. agreement markings on a verb caused by the occurrence of a particular noun or on an adjective caused by the noun it modifies), and changes in the type of elements that one word "selects" as being able to occur with it (e.g. the adjective *worthy* requires the preposition *of*, as in *worthy of consideration;* the verb *believe* can occur with a *that*-clause following it; etc.). All of these aspects of sentence structure are subject to change through time *(diachronically)*.

For example, in earlier stages of English, it was quite usual (though not obligatory) for a possessive pronoun to follow the noun it modified, in the opposite order from what is the rule today. Thus, where currently we say *our father,* in Old English the phrase was *fæder u:re.* One way of describing this change is to say that the generalization about the placement of words in such a noun phrase has changed. Thus whereas one of the expansions for a noun phrase in Old English was NP ⟶ N + POSS.PRO, that expansion is not a part of the grammar of Modern English; instead, the phrase structure rule for a noun phrase has NP ⟶ POSS.PRO + N as one of its possibilities. Similarly, in earlier stages of English, in an imperative (command) sentence, the pronoun *you,* if expressed at all, could appear either before or after the verb, while today, such a pronoun regularly precedes the verb (so that *you go!* is acceptable while **go you!* is not).

The change of *fæder u:re* to *our father* shows another type of syntactic change as well. In Modern English, a noun phrase such as *our father* has the same form regardless of whether it is a subject (as in *Our father drinks a lot of coffee*) or an object (as in *We love our father*). In Old English, however, such a difference in grammatical function of a noun phrase was signalled by changes in the form of a noun phrase, with *u:re faeder* being the subject form and *u:rne faeder* being the object form. Thus the passage from Old English to Modern English has seen a change in the way that grammatical function — a matter of sentence structure — is marked (from a "case-marking" system to a system based on word order). Similarly, adjectives in Old English regularly agreed with the noun they modified in gender (masculine, feminine, neuter), number (singular/plural), and case (e.g. subject case versus object case); in Modern English, only remnants of number agreement can be found, and only with the demonstrative adjectives *this/that* (only with singular nouns) and *these/those* (only with plural nouns).

Finally, as an example of a syntactic change involving selectional facts, we can consider the adjective *worthy.* In earlier stages of English, this adjective regularly occurred with a *that*-clause following it, as in:

> ic ne   eom wyrðe þæt ic þin   sunu beo genemned
> I not   am worthy that I your son be called

which literally is "I am not worthy that I be called your son"; the Modern English equivalent of this sentence, though, is *I am not worthy to be called your son,* indicating that the selection properties of *worthy* have changed from permitting a following *that*-clause to allowing not *that*-clauses but instead infinitival clauses (with *to* plus a verb).

The examples given here have been drawn from the history of English, but they can be taken as illustrative of change in the syntactic component of any language. Moreover, they are representative of the nature of syntactic change in general, and show ways in which syntactic change differs from sound change (discussed in an earlier file), for example. Perhaps the most striking characteristic of sound change is that it is regular, in that it affects all possible candidates for a particular change; for example, all instances of Old English (u:) became Modern (American) English (aw), and no examples of the older pronunciation remain . With syntactic change, on the other hand, while new patterns are produced that the language generally adheres to, nonetheless exceptions can occur; for example, even though word order in commands changed, the interjectional commands *mind you* and *believe you me* retain the older order with the pronoun after the verb, and so does the (consciously) archaic expression *hear ye, hear ye.* Also, as noted above, number agreement is found still but only with the demonstrative adjectives. Moreover, unlike sound change and more like morphological change, syntactic changes are often specific to the syntactic properties of particular words; thus the change in the syntax of a clause following *worthy* mentioned above is one that is specific to that word, and not, for instance, generally true for all adjectives that occur in such a construction (e.g. *hopeful* can still occur with a *that*-clause).

To close, a few words on the causes of syntactic change are in order. As with all other language change, there is both a language-internal and a language-external dimension to the causation of change. Thus, word-order changes in specific constructions, e.g. the noun + possessive pronoun construction, are often linked (correlated) with other changes in word order (e.g. involving the placement of an object with respect to the verb, a relative clause with respect to the noun it modifies, a noun with respect to a prepositional element, etc.). That is, there is often a system-wide change in the ordering of elements that is realized in different ways in different constructions. At the same time, though, such system-internal factors are only one side of the story. Innovative syntactic patterns often compete with older patterns for some time, and external, i.e. social factors, often play a role in deciding the competition. An example is the case-marking distinction involving *who* versus *whom* in Modern English, where the use of one as opposed to the other in a sentence such as *I like the man who/whom I met yesterday* is tied to such socially relevant factors as speakers' education level, their attitudes towards education, the impression they wish to convey, and the like. On the matter of causation, then, syntactic change follows much the same pattern as other types of change.

HISTORICAL LINGUISTICS:
SEMANTIC CHANGE

The semantic system of a language, like all other aspects of its grammar, is subject to change through time. As a result, the meanings of words do not always remain constant from one period of the language to the next. If we think of the meaning of a word as being determined by the set of contexts in which the word can be used, we can characterize semantic change as a shift in the set of appropriate contexts for that word. Alternatively, we could view semantic change as a change in the set of *referents* for a word, i.e., as a change in the set of objects the word refers to. Since context of utterance and reference are simply two aspects of what we call meaning, these two characterizations of semantic change are more or less equivalent.

The motivating factors behind semantic change are not well understood. Such changes sometimes result from language contact or accompany technological innovations or migrations to new geographic regions. In each of these cases the introduction of a new object or concept into the culture may initiate a change in the meaning of a word for a related object or concept, though this does not always occur. Semantic changes can also result from changes in the relative status of the group referred to by the word; that is, the word will take on new aspects of meaning to reflect this difference in social status. Sometimes changes result from a change in the status of the word *itself*, as is often the case with *taboo* words. It is, however, frequently the case that the sources of particular changes are not at all obvious; they appear to be spontaneous and unmotivated (though this may simply be due to our own lack of understanding).

Whatever the underlying source, only certain types of changes seem to occur with any frequency. Some of the most common types include:

1. extensions
2. reductions
3. elevations
4. degradations

SEMANTIC EXTENSIONS

Extensions in meaning occur when the set of appropriate contexts or referents for a word increases. These are frequently the result of generalizing from the specific case to the class of which the specific case is a member. An example of this type would be the change in meaning undergone by the Old English (OE) word *docga*, modern day *dog*. In OE *docga* referred to a particular *breed* of dog, while in modern usage it refers to the class of dogs as a whole. Thus the set of contexts in which the word may be used has been *extended* from the specific case (a particular breed of dog) to the general class (all dogs, dogs in general). A similar type of change has affected modern English *bird*. Though it once referred to a particular species of bird, it now is used for the general class.

A more timely example of this type of change would be the shift in meaning undergone by the recently formed verb *nuke*. This verb was based on the noun *nuke*, a shortening of *nuclear weapon* (as in "no nukes"), and originally meant to drop a nuclear bomb on something. In the speech of some this verb has been extended to mean simply *to damage* or *to destroy* as in "Buffy nuked her Porsche last night." Thus the meaning of *nuke*, for these speakers at least, has gone from referring to a particular *type* of damage or destruction to damage or destruction in general. Notice that this particular change shows us quite a lot about the times in which we live.

Semantic extensions are particularly common with proper names and brand names. Thus the name *Benedict Arnold* has come to be synonymous with the word *traitor*. Similarly, the name of the fictional character *Scrooge* can be used to refer to anyone with miserly traits. Examples of the semantic extension of brand names are equally easy to find: *Jell-O* is often used to refer to any flavored gelatin, regardless of brand. *Kleenex* is used for facial tissues and *Xerox* for photocopies. In some parts of the United States *Coke* can be usd for any carbonated beverage, not just one particular brand. In each of these cases the meaning of the word has been generalized to include related items in its set of referents.

In the examples discussed thus far the relationship between the original meaning of the word and the extended meaning of the word has been quite straightforward: the name of a particular traitor has been generalized to any traitor, the name of a particular type of photocopy has been generalized to any photocopy, and so on. This needn't always be the case, however. The meanings of words often become less narrow as a result of what is referred to as *metaphorical extension*. Thus, the meaning of a word is extended to include an object or concept that is like the original referent in some *metaphorical* sense rather than a literal sense. A classic example of this type is the word *broadcast*, which originally meant to scatter seed over a field. In its most common present-day usage, however, *broadcast* refers to the diffusion of radio waves through space—a metaphorical extension of its original sense. Another classic example of metaphorical extension is the application of pre-existing nautical terms (such as *ship, navigate, dock, hull, hatch, crew,* etc.) to the relatively new (and unrelated) realm of space exploration. Again, notice that space exploration is not like ocean navigation in a *literal* sense, since very different actions and physical properties are involved. Rather, the comparison between the two realms is a *metaphorical* one.

We can also find cases of metaphorical extension *in progress* in the language around us, particularly if we consider creative uses of slang terms. For example, the dictionary definition of the noun *load* is something like 'unit or quantity that can be carried' or 'burden of responsibility.' In some circles the meaning of this word has been extended to refer to people who are lazy or unproductive, presumably because these people do not do their fair share and, therefore, place a burden on others. Literally speaking, however, it is not people *themselves* who are the burden, rather it is the result of their actions that is the burden. Thus this use of the word is an abstraction from its original sense, i.e. a metaphorical extension. Another example of this type of change in progress is the use of the verb *nuke*, discussed above, to refer to microwave cooking. In this case, the metaphor hinges on the idea that microwave radiation is released during nuclear explosions. Thus, a parallel is being drawn between cooking in a microwave and bombing your food, though literally the two actions are quite different. Notice that these uses of *load* and *nuke* are not accepted by all speakers. However, if enough people adopt these meanings we may eventually have a full-fledged semantic change in the language.

SEMANTIC REDUCTIONS

Reductions occur when the set of appropriate contexts or referents for a word decreases. Historically speaking this is relatively less common than extensions of meaning, though it still occurs fairly frequently. An example of a semantic reduction would be the OE word *hund*, modern day *hound*. While this word originally referred to dogs in general, its meaning has now been restricted, for the most part, to one particular breed of dog. Thus its usage has become less general over time. Similarly, the word *worm* once was used for any crawling creature, but is now restricted to a particular type of crawling creature.

Additional examples of this type of change include the modern English words *skyline* and *girl*. *Skyline* originally referred to the horizon in general. It has since been restricted to particular types of horizons—ones in which the outlines of hills, buildings or other structures appear. In Middle English the word corresponding to modern day *girl* referred to young people of either sex. A semantic reduction has resulted in its current, less general, meaning.

SEMANTIC ELEVATIONS

Semantic elevations occur when a word takes on somewhat grander connotations over time. For example, the word *knight* (OE *cniht* or *cneoht*) originally meant 'youth' or 'military follower,' relatively powerless and unimportant people. The meaning of *knight* has since been elevated to refer to people of a somewhat more romantic and impressive status. Similarly, the word *chivalrous* was at one time synonymous with *warlike*; it now refers to more refined properties like fairness, generosity and honor. A particularly good example of this type is the shift in meaning undergone by the word *squire*. The Middle English (ME) equivalent of this word (*squier*) was used to refer to a knight's attendant, the person who held his shield and armor for him. In Modern English, however, a *squire* is a country gentleman or large landowner. Thus the meaning of *squire* has changed rather drastically over time, acquiring a socially more positive meaning.

SEMANTIC DEGRADATIONS

Semantic degradations are the opposite of semantic elevations; they occur when a word acquires a more pejorative meaning over time. Examples of words whose meanings have been degraded include *lust, wench* and *silly*. In OE *lust* simply meant 'pleasure,' making its current association with sinfulness a degradation of the original meaning. Similarly, the ME word *wenche(l)* meant 'female child' and later 'female servant.' It then came to mean 'lewd female' or 'woman of a low social class.' The word *silly* is a particularly interesting example of semantic degradation because the social force of the word has almost completely reversed. Whereas in ME *silly* meant something akin to 'happy, blessed, innocent' it now is more on a par with 'foolish, inane, absurd.' Thus the connotations of *silly* have gone from strongly positive to strongly negative in a matter of a few centuries.

DISCUSSION

In conclusion, it is interesting to note that semantic changes in one word of a language are often accompanied by (or result in) semantic changes in another word. Note, for instance, the parallel changes undergone by OE *hund* and *docga*, discussed above. As *hund* became more specific in meaning *docga* became more general. Thus, the semantic system as a whole remains in balance despite changes to individual elements within the system.

A somewhat more elaborate example of the same principle involves the OE words *mete, flǣsc*, and *foda*. In OE, *mete*, modern day *meat*, referred to food in general while *flǣsc*, now *flesh*, referred to any type of animal tissue. Since then the meaning of *meat* has been restricted to the flesh of animals and the meaning of *flesh* to human tissue. *Foda*, which was the OE word for animal fodder, became modern day *food* and its meaning was generalized to include all forms of nourishment. Thus the semantic hole left by the change in referent for *meat* has been filled by the word *food* and the system remains in balance.

EXERCISES

1. Particularly interesting cases of semantic change are ones in which the meaning of a word appears to have been reversed through time. For example, the English word *black* is closely related to Slavic words meaning 'white.' *Black* is actually derived from a Germanic past participle meaning 'to have blazed' or 'to have burned.' Given these facts, can you think of a plausible explanation for the present-day meaning of *black*? Using a good etymological dictionary (such as the *Oxford English Dictionary*) for reference, list some Modern English words that are related to *black*. Try to determine the types of semantic change these words must have undergone to arrive at their present day meanings.

2. The following paragraph is logically incoherent if all the words are understood in their current meanings. But, if we take each of the italicized words in a sense it once had at an earlier stage of English, the paragraph has no inconsistencies at all. Your job is to determine an earlier meaning for each of the italicized words which will remove the logical contradictions created by the current meaning. The earlier meanings need not be contemporary with one another. They can be found in the OED or in a comparably complete dictionary.

> He was a happy and *sad girl* who lived in a *town* 40 miles from the closest neighbor. His unmarried sister, a *wife* who was a vegetarian member of the Women's Christian Temperance Union (WCTU), ate *meat* and drank *liquor* three times a day. She was so fond of oatmeal bread made from *corn* her brother grew that one night, when it was dark and *wan* out, she *starved* from overeating. He fed nuts to the *deer* who lived in the branches of an *apple* tree which bore pears. He was a *silly* and wise *boor*, a *knave* and a *villain*, and everyone liked him. Moreover, he was a *lewd* man whom the general *censure* held to be a model of chastity.

What types of semantic change are illustrated here?

HISTORICAL LINGUISTICS LANGUAGE CHANGE EXERCISES

One of the major topics of interest to historical linguists is why languages change—what are the reasons for language change? Unfortunately, this topic is not very easy to discuss coherently because there are so many different and seemingly independent reasons. Speaking very broadly however, we may recognize three large categories of causation: (1) *Social* reasons (e.g. change via imitation of forms which are considered prestigious); (2) *Psychological* reasons (e.g. misanalysis of unfamiliar morphemes in terms of familiar ones; replacement of forms which have become taboo); (3) *Physiological* reasons (e.g., the assimilation of one sound to another for ease of articulation; the elimination of consonant clusters which are difficult to pronounce). Note that each large category may cover a great number of different reasons for change, and that each large category is not entirely independent of the other.

The following problems are designed to get you to think about some of the reasons for language change (as well as some of the ways language can change). Do not consider this file exhaustive because it is not. Nevertheless, it does provide a reasonable introduction to possible sources of language change.

Read each problem carefully and then answer the question(s) which follow the problem.

1. In careful speech the first word of the phrase "Redman chewing tobacco" is pronounced [rɛdmæn]. In casual speech the pronunciation is [rɛbmæn]. Why?

2. English has borrowed the word *memorandum* from Latin. The plural is *memoranda*. Some English speakers have replaced *memoranda* with *memorandums*. Suggest a reason for this change.

3. Middle English borrowed the word *penne* 'feather, quill' from Old French. The modern word *pen* 'writing instrument using ink' is a descendent of this word. Suggest a reason for this change.

4. Until the nineteenth century, the male chicken was referred to (on both sides of the Atlantic) by the word *cock*. In America, *rooster* has gradually replaced this word; it is now the only term used by many Americans. Why has the word *cock* been replaced by the word *rooster*?

5. English speaking tourists in Finland are often introduced to an after-dinner drink called *jaloviina*. This drink is not yellow and it is not wine, but most of the tourists call it 'yellow wine'. Why?

6. In Trinidad English the suffixes indicating present and past tense have been lost. Present tense is indicated by use of the auxiliary *do*, so that Trinidad English *He does give* equals Standard English *He gives*, and Trinidad English *He roll* equals Standard English *He rolled*. Why is the use of the auxiliary *do* to indicate present tense understandable?

7. Middle English borrowed the word *femelle* 'woman' from Old French. The expected modern development is [fɛməl̄]; instead we have [fimel]. Why?

8. Beginning in the 17th Century, *kine* as plural of *cow* was gradually replaced by *cows*. Suggest a reason for the replacement of *kine* by *cows*.

9. During World War I in the United States, *sauerkraut* 'fermented cabbage used for food' was abandoned in favor of *liberty cabbage*. Why?

10. In Old English the word *bead* meant 'prayer'. In the religious practice of the time it was very important to keep track of the number of prayers. The instrument which was used to do this was the rosary with its small balls. When one prayed and used this device to count the prayers it was called 'counting one's beads', that is, 'prayers'. Now the word *bead* means 'small ball'. Suggest a reason for this meaning change.

11. In Finnish the word *kutsua* means 'to invite', but it may also mean 'to call' in some contexts. In a Finnish dialect spoken in Sweden *kuhtua* retains the meaning 'to invite' but the Finnish speaking Swedes have borrowed the Swedish word *kalloa* meaning 'to call'. Why do you think this Finnish dialect borrowed a different word for the second meaning?

12. In the fifteenth and sixteenth centuries most central and southern British English dialects lost the consonant / r / when it occurred at the end of a word before a pause or when it occurred before a consonant. As a result a word like *better* was pronounced /bɛtə/ before words beginning with a consonant but /bɛtər/ before words beginning with a vowel. What is interesting is that at the present time British speakers pronounce phrases such as *the idea of it* and *America and England* as / ði aydiər əv ɪt / and /əmɛrɪkər n ɪŋglənd /. How might you account for such pronunciations?

13. A particular sound change cannot be fully understood without studying it in its social context. The reason that a sound might change is usually due to a complex series of causes—social, physiological, psychological, etc. The linguist William Labov, interested in language variation and how it may affect language change, conducted a study of the diphthongs / əy / and / əw / in Martha's Vineyard. The phonetic characteristic which varied between speakers was the degree of *centralization* of the first element of the diphthong. That is, while some speakers maintained the usual pronunciation of / ay / and / aw /, others *centralized* the / a / to / ə /, with a schwa as the first element; they pronounced *sky* as [skəy] and *cow* as [kəw].

Labov's findings indicate that there was a clear parallel between people who centralized their diphthongs more and people who were more closely 'rooted' to the island. The social connotation attached to centralization seemed to be "Vineyarder", and people who did not centralize their / a / were considered outsiders—not true native Vineyarders.

One interesting statistic involved 15-year-old high school students, some of whom lived on what is called down-island and who were planning on leaving the island after school, and up-island students who were planning on staying on the island. There was much more of a tendency to centralize the diphthongs by this latter group of students. Why do you suppose the up-island students were adopting the centralized pronunciation and the down-island students were not?

14. Between Proto-Slavic and Old Church Slavonic (a language related to but not identical with Old Russian) a number of interesting sound changes took place. (1) There was a metathesis of vowel-liquid sequences, so that a Proto-Slavic structure CVLCV became CLVCV in Old Church Slavic. (2) Proto-Slavic diphthongs became monophthongs, e.g., CeyCV became CiCV. (3) Consonant clusters were simplified. (4) Word-final consonants were lost. So for example Proto-Slavic *supnos* became Old Church Slavic *sŭnŭ* 'sleep' Note that though all of these changes are quite different from one another they are all responsible for creating the same type of syllable structure in Old Church Slavic. What do you think this syllable structure is and how did these changes work together to create it? Moreover, what is significant about this type of syllable structure in the first place?

300

15. Middle English borrowed the word *naperon* from Old French. The modern descendant of this word is *apron*. What reason can you give for the disappearance of the initial *n*?

16. The fourteenth century compound *ekename* (from *eke* 'to increase' and *name* 'name') was, by the sixteenth century, replaced by *nekename*, modern *nickname*. What reason can you give for the appearance of the *n* initially?

INTRODUCTION: THE HISTORY OF ENGLISH

During the 5th century, the Jute, Saxon, and Angle tribes invaded England. Their Low German evolved into Old English. From the language of the Jutes arose the Kentish dialect of Old English; from the Saxons, the West Saxon dialect; and from the Angles, the Anglian dialect which subdivided into Mercian and Northumbrian. Kentish and West Saxon converged to form the Southern dialect of Middle English; Mercian became the Midland dialect, and Northumbrian evolved into the Northern dialect. It was not until the end of the 14th century that East Midland, a further subdivision of Midland, became the favored English dialect. It is from this dialect that Standard Modern English developed.

Though we can trace the history of our language back to its 5th century origins, much of the language itself remains unaccessible to the modern speaker of English due to the changes that have so radically altered our language. Anyone who has read Shakespeare is aware that our language has changed a lot in only 300 years, if only because his English is so much more difficult for us to read than our Modern English.

> *Macduff: I believe drink gave thee the lie last night.*
> *Porter: That it did, sir, i' the very throat on me; but*
> *I requited him for his lie, and, I think, being too strong*
> *for him, though he took up my legs sometime, yet I*
> *made a shift to cast him.*

(*Macbeth*, II, iii, 37-41)

Despite the differences in language, historical linguists consider this English to be part of Modern English! While it is possible to struggle through Shakespeare without too much recourse to notes, Chaucer's 14th century Middle English cannot be read without extensive reference to a glossary:

> *When that Aprill with his shoures soote*
> *The drought of March hath perced to the roote,*
> *And bathed every veyne in swich licour*
> *Of which vertu engendered is the flour.;*

(General Prologue to the *Canterbury Tales*, 1-4)

Furthermore, Old English may seem like a totally different language:

> Ongyrede hine þā geong Hadeð—þæt wæ God ælmihtig—,
> strang and stīðmōd; gestāh hē on gealgan hēanne,
> mōdig on manigra gesyhðe, þā hē wolde mancyn lȳsan.
> Bifode ic þā mē Beorn ymbclypte; ne dorste ic hwæðre būgan
>   to eorðan,
> feallan tō foldan scēatum, ac ic, sceolde fæste standan.
>   Rōd wæs ic á ræred; āhōf ic rīcne Cyning,
>   heofona Hlāford; hyldan mē ne dorste.

(*The Dream of the Rood*, 39-45)

Some have even claimed that a knowledge of German may be more beneficial to reading Old English than our knowledge of English.

These files begin with an essay on the Indo-European origin of English, File 111, followed by samples of the Lord's Prayer at different stages of English in File 112. File 113 presents a chronology of English history since we can often draw correlations between historical and language change. This historical influence we divide into external and internal history, external referring to the influence of other languages and cultures, and internal referring to changes occurring without such influences. File 114 presents an example of internal change by illustrating English phonology from Old English to the present. File 115 presents an example of external change by illustrating lexical borrowings throughout the history of our language.

HISTORY OF ENGLISH: THE INDO-EUROPEAN ORIGIN OF ENGLISH

Speaking to the Asiatick Society in Calcutta on February 2, 1786, the English orientalist and jurist Sir William Jones uttered his famous pronouncement:

> .... The Sanskrit language, whatever be its antiquity, is of a wonderful structure; more perfect than the Greek, more copious than the Latin, and more exquisitely refined than either, yet bearing to both of them a strong affinity, both in the roots of verbs and in the forms of grammar, than could possibly have been produced by accident; so strong, indeed, that no philologer could examine them all three, without believing them to have sprung from some common source, which, perhaps, no longer exists.

Jones was content with the assertion of a common original language, without exploring the details. Others took up the cause, notably the German philosopher Friedrich von Schlegel, to whom is principally due the popular diffusion of the long-lived misconception that the European languages were in some sense derived from Sanskrit. But it remained for another German, Franz Bopp, to found the new science of comparative grammar, with the publication in 1816 of his work *On the conjugational system of the Sanskrit language, in comparison with that of the Greek, Latin, Persian, and Germanic languages*. He was twenty-five when it appeared.

It had been rightly said that the comparatist has one fact and one hypothesis. His one fact is that certain languages present similarities among themselves which are so numerous and so precise that they cannot be attributed to chance, and which are such that they cannot be explained as borrowings or as universal features. His one hypothesis is that these languages must then be the result of descent from a common original. Certain similarities may be accidental: the Greek verb "to breathe," "blow" has a root *pneu-*, and in the language of the Klamath Indians of Oregon the verb "to blow" is *pniw-*. In the languages of most countries where the bird is known, the *cuckoo* has a name derived from the noise it makes. A vast number of languages around the globe have "baby-talk" words like *mama* and *papa*. Finally, languages commonly borrow words and other features from each other, in a whole gamut of ways ranging from casual or chance contact to learned coinage of the kind that English systematically makes from Latin and Greek.

But where all of these possibilities must be excluded, the comparatist assumes genetic filiation: descent from a common ancestor, which, in the case of Indo-European, as Sir William Jones surmised almost two centuries ago, no longer exists.

In the early part of the 19th century, scholars set about exploring systematically the similarities observable among the principal languages spoken now or formerly in the regions of Iceland and Ireland in the west to India in the east, and from Scandinavia in the north to Italy and Greece in the south. They were able to group these languages into a *family* which they called *Indo-European* (the term first occurs in English in 1813, though in a sense slightly different from today's). The similarities among the different Indo-European languages require us to assume that they are the continuation of a single prehistoric language (called *Indo-European* or *Proto-Indo-European*). In the words of the greatest Indo-Europeanist, the French scholar Antoine Meillet, "we will term *Indo-European language* every language which at any time whatever, in any place whatever, and however altered, is a form taken by this ancestor language, and which thus continues by an uninterrupted tradition the usage of Indo-European."

Those dialects or branches of Indo-European still represented today by one or more languages are: Indic and

Iranian, Greek, Armenian, Slavic, Baltic, Albanian, Celtic, Italic, and Germanic. The present century has seen the addition of two branches to the family, neither of which has left any living trace: Hittite and other Anatolian languages, the earliest attested in the Indo-European family, spoken in what is now Turkey in the second millenium B.C.; and the two Tocharian languages, the easternmost of Indo-European dialects, spoken in Chinese Turkestan in the first millenium A.D.

It should be pointed out that the Indo-European family is only one of many language families that have been identified around the world, comprising several thousand different languages. We have good reason, however to be especially interested in the history of the Indo-European family. Our own language, English, is the most prevalent member of that family, being spoken as a native language by nearly 300 million people, and being the most important second language in the world. The total number of speakers of all Indo-European languages amounts to approximately half the population of the earth.

English is thus one of many direct descendants of Indo-European: one of the dialects of the parent language became prehistoric Common Germanic, which subdivided into dialects of which one was West Germanic. This in turn broke up into further dialects, one of which emerged into documentary attestation as Old English. From Old English we can follow the development of the language directly, in texts, down to the present day. This history is our linguistic heritage: our ancestors, in a real cultural sense, are our linguistic ancestors. Only a small proportion of people in the United States can trace their biological ancestry back more than a century or two; and certainly large segments of the population had languages other than English in their backgrounds only a few generations ago. But every individual is part of a culture, with language its external expression. That language, our language, has an ancestry, a history; indeed, languages have perhaps the longest uninterrupted histories of all the cultural phenomena that we can study.

But it must be stressed that linguistic heritage, while it may well tend to correspond with cultural continuity, does not imply genetic or biological descent. That is, there is no more reason to suppose that we, as speakers of an Indo-European language, are descended biologically from the speakers of Proto-Indo-European, than that the English-speaking population of Nigeria is Anglo-Saxon. The transmission of language by conquest, assimilation, migration, or any other ethnic movement is a complex and enigmatic process which this discussion does not propose to examine — beyond the general proposition that in the case of Indo-European no genetic conclusions can or should be drawn.

The comparative method remains today the most powerful device for elucidating linguistic history. When it is carried to a successful conclusion, the comparative method leads not merely to the assumption of the previous existence of an antecedent common language, but to a reconstruction of all the salient features of that language. In the best circumstances, as with Indo-European, we can reconstruct the sounds, forms, words, and even the structures of sentences — in short, both grammar and lexicon — of a language spoken before the human race had invented the art of writing. It is worth reflecting on this accomplishment. A reconstructed grammar and dictionary cannot claim any sort of completeness, to be sure, and the reconstruction may be changed because of new data or better analysis. But it remains true, as one distinguished scholar put it, that a reconstructed protolanguage is "a glorious artifact, one which is far more precious than anything an archeologist can ever hope to unearth."

English, genetically a member of the Germanic branch of Indo-European, and retaining much of the basic structure of its origin, has an exceptionally mixed lexicon. During the millenium of its documented history, it has borrowed extensively from its Germanic and Romance neighbors and from Latin and Greek. At the same time it has lost the great bulk of its Old English vocabulary. However, the inherited vocabulary, though numerically a small proportion of the total, remains the genuine core of the language; all of the 100 words shown to be the most frequent in the Brown University *Standard Corpus of Present-Day Edited English* are native, inherited words; and of the second 100, 83 are native. Precisely because of its propensity to borrow from ancient and modern Indo-European languages, especially those mentioned above but including nearly every other member of the family, English has in a way replaced much of the Indo-European lexicon it lost. Thus, while the distinction between native and borrowed vocabulary remains fundamentally important, more than 50 per cent of the basic roots of Indo-European, as represented in Julius Pokorny's *Indogermanisches Etymologisches Wörterbuch* (Bern, 1959), are represented in modern English by one means or the other. Indo-European therefore looms doubly large in the background of our language.

HISTORY OF ENGLISH: THE LORD'S PRAYER

Below are three versions of the Lord's Prayer from the three major periods in the history of English. A contemporary version is included for comparison.

Note: the symbol þ, called *thorn*, is an Old English symbol for the voiceless interdental fricative [θ], as in *th*ree; ð, called *edh*, or *eth*, is the symbol for the voiced inter-dental fricative [ð], as in *th*en.

Old English (c. 1000 A.D.)

Fæder ure þu þe eart on heofonum,si þin nama gehalgod. Tobecume þin rice. Gewurþe þin willa on eorðan swa swa on heofonum. Urne gedæghwamlican hlaf syle us to dæg. And forgyf us ure gyltas, swa swa we forgyfað urum gyltedum. And ne gelæd þu us on costnungen ac alys us of yfele. Soðlice.

Middle English (c. 1400 A.D.)

Oure fadir that art in heuenes halowid be thi name, thi kyngdom come to, be thi wille don in erthe es in heuene, yeue to us this day oure bread ouir other substance, & foryeue to us oure dettis, as we forgeuen to oure dettouris, & lede us not in to temptacion: but delyuer us from yuel, amen.

Early Modern English

Our father which art in heaven, hallowed be thy Name. Thy kingdome come. Thy will be done, in earth, as it is in heaven. Giue vs this day our dayly bread. And forgiue vs our debts, as we forgiue our debters. And leade vs not into temptation, but deliuer vs from euill: For thine is the kingdome, and the power, and the glory, for euer, Amen.

Contemporary English

Our Father, who is in heaven, may your name be kept holy. May your kingdom come into being. May your will be followed on earth, just as it is in heaven. Give us this day our food for the day. And forgive us our offenses, just as we forgive those who have offended us. And do not bring us to the test. But free us from evil. For the kingdom, the power, and the glory are yours forever. Amen.

HISTORY OF ENGLISH: A CHRONOLOGICAL TABLE OF THE HISTORY OF ENGLISH

The following table presents some of the major influences and developments in the history of English. The first section presents major landmarks in the *external history* of English — that is, factors such as conquest of English speakers by speakers of other languages; intellectual attitudes towards languages; social, religious, and political changes, and so on, which affect how a language changes. English has been influenced by other languages throughout its development and has borrowed a great many vocabulary items, samples of which are listed in parentheses following the events which started the new wave of borrowing. The second section mentions some of the major landmarks in the *internal history* of English — that is, the actual changes in the language itself which have been influenced by outside events.

EXTERNAL HISTORY

Dates	Events	Language Influence	Stages
	Settlement of British Isles by Celts	*Celtic* — in London, Dover, Avon, Cornwall	
55 B.C.	Beginning of Roman raids		Pre-English
43 A.D.	Roman occupation of 'Brittania'	*Latin*	
Early 5th C.	Romans leave British Isles		
449	Germanic tribes defeat the Celts	*Germanic*	
about 600	England is converted to Christianity (borrowings: abbot, altar, cap, chalice, hymn, relic, sock, beet, pear, oyster, cook, lily, rue, school, verse, meter)	*Latin* borrowings	
about 750	*Beowulf* composed writings (only extant manuscript written about 1000)		Old English (450-1100)
9th-11th C.	Invasions by Scandinavians (borrowings: birth, sky, trust, take, skirt, disk, dike; simplified pronoun system	*Scandinavian* borrowings	
1066	Battle of Hastings — Norman Conquest (borrowings: court, battle, nation, enemy, crime, justice, beef, pork, veal, mutton, charity, miracle)	large *French* influence	
about 1200	Normandy and England are separated		Middle English (1100-1450)
13th-14th C.	Growing sense of English-ness		
1340-1400	Chaucer		

Dates	Events	Language Influence	Stages
1337-1453	Hundred Years' War		
1476	First English book is published; spelling is eventually standardized		**Early Modern English** (1450-1700)
1564-1616	Shakespeare Borrowings: anachronism, allusion, atmosphere, capsule, dexterity, halo, agile, external, insane, adapt, erupt, exist, extinguish	*Latin* and *Greek* borrowings and neologisms	
16th-19th C.	Imperialism	borrowings from various languages	**Modern English** (1700-present)
	Development of American English		
19th-20th C.	Scientific and Industrial Revolution	technical vocabularies	

INTERNAL HISTORY

Proto-European to Germanic	Grimm's Law
OE to ME	Loss of /x/ Adoption of /ž/ Allophonic variants [f]/[v], [θ]/[ð], [s]/[z], [ŋ]/[n] become phonemic. Vowel reduction and subsequent loss of final [ə] in unstressed syllables lead to loss of case endings, more rigid word order, greater use of prepositions.
ME to EModE (1300-1600)	The Great Vowel Shift Simplification of some initial consonant sequences: [kn] > knee, [hl] > [l] *(hlaf > loaf)*; [hr] > [r] *(hring > ring)*; [wr] > [r] *(wrong).*

HISTORY OF ENGLISH: EPISODES IN THE HISTORY OF ENGLISH PHONOLOGY

This file describes some of the major sound changes which have occurred in English between the Old English period and Modern English. The history of the English language is usually divided into three periods of development. *Old English* covers the period from the alleged invasion of Britain by the Angles and Saxons in 449 A.D. to 1050 A.D. Written records are not attested for Old English however until around 700. The *Middle English* period extends from 1050 to 1450, approximately 50 years after the death of the poet Chaucer. The period from 1450 to the present is usually considered the *Modern English* period, though there are some scholars who prefer to divide this period into two sections and recognize an *Early Modern English* period, roughly 1450 to 1700, as well as a *Modern English* period, from 1700 to the present.

In order to give you a rough idea of the chronology of the major sound changes, we have arranged them according to the three periods of historical development: Old, Middle, and Modern. The Old and Middle English words are in broad transcription. The Modern English forms are in current orthography.

1. Old English

A. One of the most important changes to occur in the Old English period was *i-umlaut*. Umlaut is a type of assimilation whereby one vowel sound becomes more like some other vowel sound which follows it. In Old English the back vowels [a, ā, ɔ, ō, ʊ, ū] became [ɛ, æ, ɛ, ē, ɪ, ī] when an [ɪ] or [i], that is, a high front vowel, occurred in the following syllable. Later, [ɪ] was lost if the preceding syllable ended with a consonant or contained a long vowel:

Change in Old English	Modern English
fōtɪ > fēt	feet
lūsɪ > līs	lice
mannɪ > mɛnn	men
dālɪ > dæl	deal
fullɪan > fɪllan	fill
brūdɪ > brīd	bride

B. The velar consonants [g] and [k] were palatalized when they occurred before the front vowel sounds [æ, ā̆, ɛ, e, ɪ, ī] or before the dipthongs beginning with a front vowel.

Old English	Modern English
kɪnn	chin
gɪə̯ldan	yield
kɪə̯l	chill
gæə̯r	year

C. The consonant cluster [sk] was palatalized to [š] before front vowels:

Old English	Modern English
skēēp	sheep
skīr	shire
skıẹld	shield
skɛẹkan	shake

D. Fricative consonants became voiced when they stood between voiced sounds:

Old English	Modern English
nɔsu	nose
wulfas	wolves
baθɪan	bathe
knafa	knave

2. Middle English

A. Two changes occurred early in the development of Middle English which affected the quantity of vowels.

(i) Long vowels were shortened when they were followed by two or more consonants:

Old English	Middle English	Modern English
sōftɛ	sɔftə	soft
fīfta	fıftə	fifth
kēptɛ	kɛptə	kept
wīzdɔm	wızdəm	wisdom

(ii) The short vowels [a e ɔ] became long when they occurred in open syllables (i.e., in syllables that don't end in a consonant):

Old English	Middle English	Modern English
nama	nāmə	name
stɔlɛn	stōlən	stolen
	mētɛ	meat
nɔsu	nōzə	nose
knafa	knāvə	knave

B. Between the beginning and end of the Middle English period, two important changes occurred in the final syllables of words.

(i) When the vowels [a, ɛ , ɔ , ʊ] occurred in the final syllable of a word and were unaccented, they became schwa [ə]. (Note however that the vowel [ɪ] did *not* become schwa but remained as [ɪ].) Word final schwa was lost by the end of the Middle English period. (For the development of syllable-final schwa followed by a consonant, see Modern English D.)

Old English	Middle English	Modern English
krabba	krabə	crab
hɛlpan	hɛlpən	help
sunu	sunə	son
klǣnɛ	klǣnə	clean
nakɔd	nākəd	naked

(ii) Word-final [m] and [n] were lost very frequently in unstressed syllables:

Old English	Middle English	Modern English
sɪŋgan	sɪŋgə	sing
ɛndum	ɛndə	end

C. The sound [h] was lost when it began a word and occurred before the sounds [l, r, n, w]:

Old English	Middle English	Modern English
hrɪŋg	rɪŋg	ring
hnɛkka	nɛkkə	neck
hlāf	lɔ̄f	loaf
hwætɛ	wǣtə	wheat

3. Modern English

A. In the first two periods of the development of the English language the vowel sounds underwent very few changes. But the development of the Middle English vowels into Modern English is quite a different story indeed. Between 1400 and 1600 almost all of the English vowels (and diphthongs) underwent some sort of change. In fact only two vowels [ɪ] and [ɛ] were unaffected. So great was the alteration of the English vowel system that these changes are often collectively referred to as the *Great Vowel Shift*.

If we focus on the development of the back vowels, the appropriateness of the term vowel shift can easily be illustrated. The Middle English long vowel [ɔ̄] was raised to [ō]; but [ō] in turn was raised to [ū]. The high back rounded vowel was diphthongized, becoming [aw]. Notice that the first element is a *low* back vowel. Finally, to complete the shift the Middle English diphthong [aw] was monophthongized to [ɔ]. Diagrammatically, the shift can be characterized as follows:

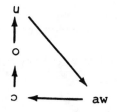

	Middle English	Modern English
High long vowels become diphthongs		
a. ī > ay	līk	like
	wīd	wide
b. ū > aw	ūrə	our
	θūsənd	thousand
Nonhigh long vowels are raised		
c. ē > i	bēə	bee
	bētə	beet
d. ō > u	mōnə	moon
	dō	do
e. ǣ > i *via* ē	dǣd	deed
	tǣčən	teach
f. ɔ̄ > ō	hɔ̄l	whole
	ɔ̄k	oak
g. ā > ē *via* ǣ	nāmə	name
	mādə	made
Short vowels become unrounded and centralized		
h. ʊ > ʌ	sʊnə	son
i. ɔ > a	ɔks	ox
Diphthongs become monophthongs		
j. aw > ɔ/a	fawxt	fought
k. æy > e	sæyd	said
l. ɪw > u	rɪwdə	rude
m. ɔ̄w > o	sɔ̄wlə	soul
n. ɔw > a	θɔwxt	thought

B. The velar fricative [x] was lost when it occurred before a word-final [t]:

Middle English	Modern English
fawxt	fought
nīxt	night
θɔwxt	thought
brīxt	bright

C. Word-initial and word-final consonant clusters have undergone considerable simplification between the Middle English and Modern English period.

(i) Word initial velar stop consonants [k g] were lost when they occurred before the nasal [n]:

Middle English	Modern English
gnawən	gnaw
knɪxt	knight

(ii)   Initial [w] was lost when it occurred before [r]:

Middle English	*Modern English*
wrі̄tən	write
wrɛkkən	wreck

(iii)   Word final [mb] was reduced to [m]:

Middle English	*Modern English*
dʊmb	dumb

(iv)   Word final [ŋg] was reduced to [ŋ]:

Middle English	*Modern English*
θɪŋg	thing

D. As we mentioned earlier (Middle English B.) the Old English vowels [a̋ ɛ ɔ ʊ] became [ə] in Middle English when they occurred in an unaccented final syllable. Subsequently [ə] was lost when it occurred word-finally, e.g. [nɔsu > nɔ̄zə > nɔ̄z]. But [ə] remained in the final syllable of a word throughout the Middle English period *if it was followed by a consonant,* e.g., in the Middle English plural ending [əz], *things* [θɪŋgəz] and in the Middle English past tense ending [əd] *loved* [ˈl ʊvəd]. At the beginning of the Modern English period this [ə] was lost in the plural inflectional ending *except* after [s z š č ǰ], e.g., Middle English *fishes* [fɪšəz] Modern English *fishes* [fɪšəz], and in the past ending except after [t d.], e.g., Middle English *hunted* [hʊntəd] Modern English *hunted* [hʌntəd]. After the loss of [ə] in these inflectional endings the final consonant of the ending was assimilated to the voicing of the final sound of the stem, e.g., *books* [bō̄kəz > bʊkz > bʊks].

Middle English	*Modern English*
θɪŋgəz	things
fɪšəz	fishes
wі̄vəz	wives
trē̄əz	trees
sʊnəz	sons
čɪrčəz	churches
mū̄ðəz	mouths
lō̄kəd	looked
hʊntəd	hunted
stɪrəd	stirred
lʊvəd	loved

4. MORPHOLOGICAL ALTERNATIONS

As we have seen from our survey of sound changes which have occurred in the history of English, one of the effects of conditioned sound change is the creation of alternate pronunciations for the same morpheme, what is usually called *morphological alternation.* For example, early in the history of English fricatives became voiced intervocalically. As a result the plural form of the word 'wife' changed from [wifas] to [wı̄vas]. In the singular form [wı̄f] however, the fricative [f] did not become voiced because it did not occur before vowels. The net result of this sound change that was to create alternate pronunciations for the morpheme 'wife': [wı̄f] in the singular but [wı̄v] in the plural. The alteration is still evident in Modern English today, as the form *wife/wives* bear witness.

When morphological alternations are created by sound change, we can often examine the phonetic context of the alternate pronunciations and infer what sound change(s) caused the alternations in the first place.This type of analysis, whereby the linguist examines data available from one language and one language only and makes hypotheses about that language's history, is known as *internal reconstruction*. It is distinct from *comparative reconstruction* which compares related languages in order to hypothesize about sound changes. Using the internal reconstruction method, a linguist may learn much about a language's history, even if for some reason there are no known related languages to compare it with.

English can provide us with a very straightforward example of the recovery of an earlier sound change via morphological alternation. In English the voiced velar stop [g] is not pronounced when it precedes a word-final nasal. e.g., *sign* [sɑyn], but it is pronounced if this nasal is not word-final, e.g., *signal* [sɪgnəɫ]. As a result, morphological alternations occur between morphemes with and without the voiced velar stop, e.g., *dignity* [dɪgnəti]*deign* [dayn]; *paradigmatic* [pɛrədɪgmætɪk]*paradigm* [pɛrədaym]. On the basis of these alternations we can make some inferences about the history of English. Specifically, we can assume that at an earlier period the morphological alternation did not exist—that there was only *one* pronunciation for morphemes which had the sound sequence [gn], and that at some point there was a sound change whereby voiced velar stops were lost when they occurred before a word-final nasal.

Sometimes however it is impossible to detect the sound change(s) which have created the morphological alternations which exist in a language. This is usually the case when later sound changes take place which obscure the original cause of the alternate pronunciations. Consider the following example for the history of English. Presently in English the past tense of the verb *sleep* is [slɛpt] and not [slipt] as we might expect. It is only natural to wonder why the morpheme 'sleep' has alternate pronunciations [slɛp] and [slip]. Unfortunately we can arrive at no satisfactory answer just by considering the evidence which exists in Modern English. We cannot say that the alternation is due to the fact that the vowel is followed by two consonants in the past tense form because other verbs which form the past tense in a similar manner do not have alternate pronunciations, e.g. *freak* [frik] *freaked* [frikt] and *peak* [pik] *peaked* [pikt]. Since we have morphemes which form the past tense regularly and form which have an alternate pronunciation in the past tense and we can determine nothing from the phonetic contexts, it is impossible to attempt internal reconstruction in the way we did with *sign* and *signal*. In cases such as this we must consider evidence from the Middle English period in the form of written records to find out how the alternate pronunciation came into existence.

EXERCISES

1. Refer to the episodes discussed above and indicate how the following Old English words are pronounced today.

Old English	*Modern English*
dǣl	
nōn	
līf	
mūs	
knīf	
stān	
swētɛ	
lūd	
alu	
kēsɪ	

tōθɪ

kɪnn

knafa

gnæt

2. Indicate the changes which have taken place between the following Old English words and Modern English.

mūθas

hūs

skɪp

kēp

rād

skɛll

latɛ

knēɔ

rīxt

wīnan

3. Is it possible to reconstruct the sound change which caused the morphological alternation [na] in *knowledge* and [kna] in *acknowledge*? If so, state the sound change. Can you find any other pairs of words which exhibit this particular type of alternation?

4. The Modern English words *goose* [guˢ] and *gosling* [gaslɪŋ] both have, historically, the same root morpheme: [gōs] (note Old English [gōs]). What is the source of this morphological alternation?

5. In Modern English the plural of *house* is *houses* [hawzəz]. The morpheme *house* thus has two pronunciations: [haws] and [hawz]. Let's assume that you had no written records for the history of English. Could you suggest a plausible sound change to account for this alternation? Is it possible to suggest more than one plausible sound change to account for this alternation?

THE HISTORY OF ENGLISH:
ENGLISH BORROWINGS

In a survey of the 1000 most frequently used words in English, it was found that only 61.7% had Old English origins. The other 38.3% were borrowed from a variety of other languages: 30.9% French, 2.9% Latin, 1.7% Scandinavian, 1.3% mixed, and .3% Low German and Dutch. The following list provides a sample set of words that we have incorporated into English. While some of these words will sound foreign, those that were borrowed early in the history of our language will sound amazingly English.

FRENCH: aisle, apparel, arch, art, assault, assets, bail, bailiff, barber, barricade, beauty, bisque, boil, brassiere, broil, butcher, campaign, captain, carpenter, cartoon, catch, cattle, cell, chancellor, chaplain, charity, chase, chattel, chemise, chivalry, color, column, commandant, company, corps, corpse, county, court, design, dinner, dragoon, dress, embezzle, enemy, evangelist, exchequer, fork, format, garment, govern, grace, grocer, hors d'oeuvres, jail, judge, jury, lance, lease, lieutenant, lingerie, mason, mercy, minister, miracle, napkin, nativity, navy, painter, paradise, passion, perjury, pillar, plaintiff, plate, plead, porch, power, reign, sacrament, saint, sergeant, soldier, suit, supper, table, tailor, tapestry, transept, troops

LATIN: abbot, affidavit, agenda, alibi, alms, animal, bonus, clerk, coaxial, deficit, diet, exit, extra, fiat, fission, geography, interstellar, item, logic, maximum, memento, memorandum, monk, neutron, omnibus, penicillin, physic, pope, posse, priest, propaganda, quorum, radium, rhetoric, spectrum, sponsor, sulfur, surgeon, synod, terminus, theology, verbatim, veto, via

SCANDINAVIAN LANGUAGES: batten, billow, blight, by-law, clumsy, doze, fiord, floe, geyser, law, maelstrom, nag, outlaw, riding, saga, scamp, ski, them, their, they

ARABIC: bedouin, emir, fakir, gazelle, giraffe, harem, hashish, lute, minaret, mosque, myrrh, salaam, sirocco, sultan, vizier

CHINESE: mandarin, pongee, serge, tea

GREEK: adenoids, bacteriology, botany, catastrophy, climax, comedy, dialog, drama, dynatron, epilog, episode, histology, kenatron, melodrama, osteopathy, pediatrics, physics, physiology, prolog, psychiatry, psychoanalysis, scene, telegraph, theater, tragedy, zoology

INDIAN LANGUAGES: bandanna, brahmin, bungalow, calico, chutney, curry, indigo, juggernaut, jungle, loot, pajama, pundit, rajah, sandal

ITALIAN: alto, attitude, balcony, fiasco, fresco, isolate, motto, opera, piano, soprano, stanza, studio, tempo, torso, umbrella

JAPANESE: hara-kiri, jujitsu, kimono, tycoon

RUSSIAN: icon, tsar, vodka

SPANISH: armada, cargo, castanet, cigar, desperado, grande, guerilla, matador, mosquito, Negro, punctilio, quadroon, renegade, vanilla

YIDDISH: chullah, chutzpah, gefilte fish, goy, klutz, knish, latke, matzah (ball), mazeltov, nebbish, oy vey, schlemiel, schlep, schmuck, schnook

DUTCH: avast, bow, bowsprit, buoy, commodore, cruise, curl, dock, freight, hops, keel, keelhaul, leak, lighter, pump, scour, scum, spool, stripe, yaught, yawl

GERMAN: bockbeer, blutwurst, bub, delicatessen, dunk, frankfurter, hausfrau, hex, hum, kindergarten, lager, liverwurst, loafer, noodle, ouch, pinochle, poke, pretzel, pumpernickel, rathskeller, sauerbraten, sauerkraut, schnitzel, spiel, spieler, stein, wunderlund, zwieback

INTRODUCTION: LANGUAGE CONTACT

Language contact occurs when speakers of different languages interact with one another for various reasons. The specific contact situations and the effects of these situations on languages can take a variety of forms.

Consider a situation in which one speech community is invaded and conquered by another speech community, a phenomenon which has occurred repeatedly throughout history. One such case of this was the Norman Conquest of Britain in the 11th century — an invasion which has left an indelible imprint on the English language in the form of a vast number of French borrowings (e.g. *court, battle* and *nation*). What happens to languages in a situation like this? To what extent do these languages influence each other? Are both languages maintained or is there a shift in favor of one over another? These questions and others are addressed in File 121 which discusses language contact situations and effects.

Another type of language contact situation can be observed in the United States, a country that many may consider to be monolingual. In cities like San Diego, Tucson, Houston and Miami, which contain large Hispanic populations, English and Spanish speech communities interact and mingle. The large flow of Southeast Asian refugees to the U.S. in recent years has produced similar situations in cities such as Minneapolis and Seattle, where English and Hmong (a Southeast Asian language) have come into contact. Industrial cities of the Northeast (e.g. Pittsburgh, Cleveland, and New York), as a result of the waves of European immigrants during the late 19th and 20th centuries, have long been areas of divergent speech communities. Thus, one would find an Italian speech community alongside a German community alongside a Slovenian community, and so on.

After a while, in situations like the above, some speakers will begin to alternate between languages; they will become bilingual. It is this result of language contact, i.e. bilingualism, which is the subject of File 122, a file which discusses the notions of *fluency* as well as various types of bilingualism.

Sometimes two or more distinct speech communities are thrown into contact and select a *common* language for communication. Thus it is that within the international scientific community, English has been selected as the *lingua franca* or common mode of communication. However, historically there has often been another response to the type of situation in which speakers of diverse speech communities find themselves in contact. That response, probably the most radical result of languages in contact, is the development of simplified forms of language known as *pidgins*. Files 123-125 deal with this linguistic phenomenon and with a subsequent language form known as a *creole*.

LANGUAGE CONTACT: LANGUAGE CONTACT

The gradual divergence of a parent language into its daughter languages constitutes one widely studied type of linguistic change. A second type of change, however, may result when one language acquires features from another. This development, known as *borrowing*, can occur whenever two or more languages are *in contact*—that is, when they are used alternately by the same persons.

The effects of borrowing are most apparent in the lexicon. Frequently, a word is borrowed in order to describe some previously unnamed concept, thereby filling a "semantic slot" in the borrowing language. The Russian word *czar* was borrowed into English and refers to an autocratic, all-powerful ruler. Sometimes, however, a foreign word may be incorporated into a language in which an equivalent term already exists. In such cases, the native word may gradually fall into disuse, or the native and borrowed words may both continue to exist in the language, with each developing a distinct meaning. After the French borrowed *guerre* 'war' from the Franks, its native *Bellum* 'war' was no longer used. Yet when Estonian borrowed the Baltic word *hummas* 'tooth', the native Estonian word *pii* tooth was not lost, but came to be used to refer only to the tooth of a comb or rake.

As a prime cause of linguistic change, it is useful to explore the sources and effects of prolonged language contact. To consider an extreme example, suppose a speech community which spoke language X was invaded and conquered by a people who spoke language Y. After a period of time, members of each group may come to understand the language of the other. From this language contact, several developments are possible. Native speakers of Y, perhaps due to a sense of cultural inferiority, or being few in number, may gradually abandon their language altogether in favor of the language of the indigenous population. Nevertheless, this period of language contact results in a number of borrowings from Y into X: this "trace" of Y in X is said to constitute a *superstratum* of X. French retains a Germanic superstratum resulting from the invasion of the Franks into the region now known as France in the Sixth Century A.D. While the invaders gradually adopted the French of those they conquered, the French did incorporate some of their words into French, most notably terms referring to warfare and weaponry.

Conversely, language Y may ultimately replace X as the primary language of the region. The introduction of English to the Celtic-speaking British Isles in the fifth century A.D. resulted in a shift to English by the inhabitants. Yet the learning of this new language by the Celts and its subsequent transmission to later generations resulted in a variety of English in Wales and Scotland which displays the effects of a "Celtic accent." Because these effects persist to the present day, Celtic is said to constitute a *substratum* of English in this region.

Of course, the presence of more than one linguistic community within a geographical region does not necessarily mean that one community will abandon its language in favor of the other. Linguistic communities, such as the French and English in Canada, may retain their native languages while in contact with other languages. In such cases, each language is said to constitute an *adstratum* of the other. Canadian English has borrowed from French words such as *aboiteau* ('dam'), *seigniory* ('Lordship') and *caribou*, while Canadian French speakers have borrowed from English words such as *boghei* ('buggy'), *mache-malo* ('marshmallow'), *papermane* ('peppermint') and *litousse* ('lighthouse').

In such multilingual communities, language can serve as a symbol of group solidarity. For example, in a region of northeast Italy, German, Italian and Friulian are widely spoken. German is the native language of most of these people, and is spoken in the home. Italian is the official language of the church and school. Children acquire Italian early, either at home or in their first years in school. Friulian is the dominant language of the neighboring area. Individuals typically learn it after having attended secondary school outside of the community, and may use it when speaking to one another despite the fact that their native language is German. Their use of Friulian in such cases identifies them as members of a group which has had extensive contact with people from outside of their community.

Because language in a multilingual society can come to have this symbolic power, it has frequently been the source of political conflict: if one of several languages spoken in a community is regarded as socially prestigious, those who do not command it have limited opportunities for political or economic advancement. For example, the majority of the population of Belgium are native speakers of Flemish, yet French is the language of prestige and hence power. Thus those who did not master French are handicapped in their efforts to increase their social status. "Language riots" in Belgium have centered on the Flemings' demands for equal status for their language.

In some societies which are not, strictly speaking, multi-lingual, two varieties of the same language may be used with each variety having a clearly-defined function. Such a phenomenon is known as *diglossia*. In a diglossic situation, one variety of a language is more prestigious; that is, it is used in "high" functions such as education, politics and literature; the other form, the colloquial variety, is less prestigious and used in "low" functions such as everyday conversation.

One case of diglossia occurs in Greece, where the literary form, Katharevousa, serves as the "high" form while the speech of the people, the low form, is Dhimotiki. Swiss German diglossia involves the use of standard German for "high" functions and a less prestigious form for everyday communication. In Haiti, Standard French occupies the high position with Haitian Creole (derived from a pidgin French) serving as the low form. In these diglossic situations, the high variety is acquired primarily through formal education and carries greater prestige than the low form. Nonetheless, each form plays an important role in the speech community, roles which are sharply defined and largely mutually exclusive. Thus, the high form is generally not used when speaking to one's family members or close friends and, by the same token, the low variety would be avoided by educators in classrooms.

LANGUAGE CONTACT: BILINGUALISM

What does it mean to be fluent in a foreign language? Many people respond to this question by saying that someone who knows a language fluently can speak it like a native. But the problem with this definition of fluency is that complete native mastery of more than one language is very uncommon. In fact, it would exclude the vast majority of the bilinguals who can function effectively in their second language. If someone is to achieve native mastery of a second language, he must have occasion to use it in daily affairs for prolonged periods of his life. Yet few societies provide the opportunity for extensive exposure to more than one language. If two languages are spoken in a single society at all, it frequently happens that one language is spoken in the home and among close friends, while the other is used for specialized functions, such as communication in business or government.

The psychological consequence of a situation like this is that one of a bilingual's languages is almost always less dominant than the other. To some extent, it is possible to support this conclusion from ordinary observations. For example, think about the linguistic performance of government officials like Henry Kissinger or Menachem Begin, whose positions as international leaders force them to function in English, in addition to their native languages. As far as we can determine from our limited exposure to them, their command of English is certainly sufficient to allow them to participate in spontaneous interviews, perform sensitive acts of diplomacy, tell jokes, get angry, propose to women— and perhaps conduct themselves successfully in all of the situations in which native English speakers might find themselves.

But no native English speaker would have trouble identifying someone like Henry Kissinger as a non-native speaker of English. Like most people who speak English as a second language, he sometimes has difficulty finding the words that characterize his thoughts precisely. And like many foreigners who find themselves in this situation, he substitutes a phrase or a definition for the word he is unable to locate. A more striking sign that English is not Kissinger's native language is his 'foreign accent.' Foreign accents result when a bilingual attempts to pronounce his second language using the phonological system of his first language. Though the presence of an accent need not interfere with a bilingual's ability to speak spontaneously in his less dominant language, it still indicates that his knowledge is less complete than that of a native. An accent is evidence that a bilingual has not mastered the phonological system of his second language.

Another observable difference between native speakers and non-native but reasonably fluent speakers involves their treatment of taboo words. Words like *shit, piss* and *fuck* elicit strong reactions from native speakers of English, reflecting years of experience with people in their culture who were shocked and offended by the use of these words on inappropriate occasions. But non-native speakers, lacking extensive firsthand experience with the culture whose language they command to some extent, often do not have the same strong reaction to foreign taboo words. Thus they may feel considerably less inhibited in using them. Kermit Schafer, the collector of television and radio 'bloopers,' once saw an interview with a foreign baseball player on national television. When asked what he did in his spare time, he replied instantly, *I fock gorls!* Of course, he only made a 'blooper' from the point of view of the American television audience.

In addition to commonplace observations, it is possible to identify the bilingual's less dominant language on the basis of psychological tests. One simple test involves asking the bilingual to name the first word that leaps to mind when he hears a word like *house*. This task is carried out separately for each language. The results reveal something about the sociological conditions under which the language is learned, since word associations differ from culture to culture. For example, an American English speaker might give *garden* as a response to *house* because American houses frequently have gardens. But a native speaker of Swedish is just as likely to respond with *red*, since Sweden has many red houses. Now suppose that a Swedish-English bilingual is given this test. If he responds with *red* to the English word *house*, it is safe to presume that he learned English in his Swedish culture—perhaps at a local school. Moreover, Swedish is probably his dominant language, since the associations appropriate for Swedish are carried over when he uses English.

Results from commonplace observations and psychological tests reveal the subtlety of linguistic competence, and show how extraordinarily difficult it is to achieve complete native mastery of a foreign language. This conclusion has led some psychologists to believe that languages of bilinguals are measurably different because they are represented differently in the brain. The most direct evidence for this hypothesis comes from bilingual victims of aphasia. In many cases, a single lesion (injury) results in a greater degree of language loss in the bilingual's less dominant language. Likewise, bilinguals who recover from aphasia tend to regain complete mastery of their dominant language first. But the rare bilingual aphasics who are truly native speakers of two languages do not exhibit these uneven injury and recovery patterns.

The upshot of this discussion is that bilinguals rarely have equal mastery of both languages, though they may still be considered 'fluent' in their less dominant language. This means that fluency is perhaps best defined as a continuum, with native mastery at one extreme and the knowledge of a single word in a foreign language at the other. Of course, most people who strike us as fluent in a foreign language fall somewhere near the upper end of this scale.

Yet it still makes sense to recognize intermediate levels of fluency because it is often possible to be proficient in a limited domain of language. For example, the United States government employs people who must master enough of a language like Russian to study Russian military technology. A person in such a job may be fluent in Russian to the extent that he can read, write and translate passages that deal with his specialized subject matter, but may be at a loss when trying to tell a joke or buy food in a Russian market. Similarly, many college language majors have mastered skills which require years of schooling, even for natives—like reading epic poetry and writing term papers and in-class essay exams—but they can't understand the language of a cabbie or an illiterate farmer. However, partial fluency need not always involve specialized vocabulary or complex literacy skills. Some people who learned a second language as children but later had no opportunity to use it lose their ability to speak it as adults, though their passive understanding remains excellent.

The performance of partial bilinguals suggests that speaking, reading, writing and listening are to some degree independent linguistic skills. Thus it is possible to comprehend, but not speak; speak but not write—and in general, be relatively fluent in one skill but not another. The performance of partial bilinguals also suggests that 'thinking' in a foreign language requires a mastery of 'information-processing' skills, as well as an adequate knowledge of vocabulary and grammatical rules. Fluent, but not partial bilinguals can read quickly with great comprehension, think of words without undue hesitation when speaking or writing, and learn easily when presented with a subject like history or biology in their second language. These observations are of paramount importance to those interested in creating foreign-language programs that produce 'balanced' bilinguals and to those concerned with the special problems of educating bilingual children.

LANGUAGE CONTACT: PIDGIN AND CREOLE LANGUAGES

INTRODUCTION

What happens when people need to communicate but have no common language? You may have taken part in conversations such as this, or perhaps you've witnessed one from a more comfortable distance. They point, they grimace, they gesture, they talk with their hands and feet, and—somewhat surprisingly—they speak, as well. That is surprising because they really cannot hope that anyone will understand much more than their mood, if he can't understand the language. But they go ahead and speak anyway, and we can understand bits and pieces of what they say by paying close attention to the rest of the communication.

Usually, travellers go their separate ways and soon forget whatever scraps of other languages they briefly understood. But there are other situations involving speakers of several languages that may last much longer. Industry may attract foreign workers; war may throw the unlikeliest peoples into alliance; or marketplaces may last lifetimes, providing for the exchange of goods between people of different tongues. In these cases new systems of communication spring up to fill the obvious needs.

A *pidgin* is a simplified form of language developed by speakers who otherwise share no common language. This means of course that pidgins begin in multilingual situations—where at least two, and more likely several, languages co-exist. Typically, pidgins spring up in trading centers or in areas under industrialization (including agricultural industrialization, i.e. plantations). They develop here because the opportunities for trade and work attract large numbers of people with different native tongues.

Two well-known pidgins are Cameroonian Pidgin, used in Cameroon (in West Africa, near the bend in the coast), and Korean Bamboo English, which developed among Koreans and Americans during the Korean war.

Pidgins develop from several languages simultaneously. Usually, however, the pidgin takes most of its vocabulary from one socially and economically dominant language, and we say that the pidgin is based on that language. There are or have been pidgins based on English (Cameroonian), Portuguese (Angolar in Angola), Spanish (Palenquero in Columbia), French (Haitian), Dutch (Guyana in Surinam), Arabic (Ki-Nubi in East Africa) and Chinese (Makista in Macao). Note that most of these are found in colonies, and are based on the language of the colonial power. Colonial markets, plantations and wars provided excellent conditions for pidginization.

The term 'pidgin' developed from a pidgin pronunciation of 'business': 'business English' became 'pidgin English.' Let's take care to understand the technical term 'pidgin' as it is used in linguistics (as it is defined above). The term is also used nontechnically outside of linguistics to speak (insultingly) of any sort of broken or incorrect language. But a pidgin in the technical sense is a sort of language serving the needs of a community. Thus a pidgin is *not* simply the broken English of a waiter in a foreign restaurant (who speaks his native language with his co-workers), *nor* is pidgin an idiot's version of a language, or a kind of inevitable deterioration in the hands of barbarians. In fact, it is probably the more intelligent and ambitious people in a culture who muster the energy and courage needed for the move to an industrial or market area.

Another warning: Movies and television have provided us with a characterization of one likely pidgin, 'Indian English,' but not accurately. The "Tonto-ride-fast-get-help-Kemosabe" sort of English common to television Indians isn't exactly like pidgins (e.g., pidgin speakers, unlike Tonto, have no difficulty with pronouns).

The scriptwriters weren't completely off the mark, however. Pidgins do have simpler structures than other languages, mostly because they're used in situations with specific and limited communicative needs. In these situations, there is no need for elaborate communication and no time to master a complex system.

Some people feel that pidgins are wrong because of the fast and loose way they play with the structural patterns of their base language. As we'll see below, the charge is correct: pidgins have *no* respect for the grammars of their base languages. But this doesn't make pidgins wrong since the radical simplification we find in pidgins serves a worthwhile goal: communication. Because of its simple structure a pidgin is easier to learn than other languages. By providing a means of communication in a community, it facilitates the integration of newcomers, who would have a much more difficult time learning a standard European language. The linguist Robert Hall argued in World War II that a native of Polynesia or the East Indies might learn pidgin English in just a few months, and so become an collaborator of the Allies. The same native would need over a year to learn Standard American English.

Moreover, pidgin speakers are often in no position to learn the foreign language on which the pidgin is based. Learning a new language requires time, energy, and a model to imitate. A laborer or sharecropper in a plantation system simply doesn't have the extended contact with foreigners he would need to learn their language serviceably. Native speakers of the base language are often a small and exclusive minority in societies where pidgins arise, so that they have little direct influence on language habits. Even market vendors, those who might have the best chance to learn the base language thoroughly, probably have little leisure for conjugation drill, pronunciation exercise, and pattern practice.

Finally, let's not forget that pidgins are a reality whose existence is not subject to debate. There are dozens of pidgins, many of which show no signs of dying out. Since they arise spontaneously wherever people need to talk, pidgins probably represent the primitive communication system out of which our more respected modern languages developed. This fact alone makes them well worth our attention.

SOME CAMEROONIAN

The following is from Loreto Todd's *Some Day Been Dey*, with a free translation into English. (As we join the tortoise and the hawk, the hawk is going on a hunting trip when she meets the tortoise, explains that she needs food for her children, and invites the tortoise to visit them after the tortoise says that he would like to. The tortoise accepts.)

1. "a, datwan go gud pas mak, trɔki. yu go kam, e?

    "Oh, that would be great, tortoise. You will come, won't you?

2. a go glad dat dey we yu go kam fɔ ma haws."

    "I'll be glad the day when you come to my house."

3. i tɔk so, i tɔn i bak, i go,

    She said this, turned her back, and left.

4. i di laf fɔ i bele. i tɔk sey:

    She was laughing inside and said:

5. "ha! so trɔki tink sey i tu fit go flay ɔp stik. i go si."

    "Ha! So Tortoise thinks he too can fly up trees. We'll see."

[The tortoise notices the hawk's disdain and tricks her into carrying him to her nest where he eats the hawk's young. She tries to kill him by dropping him from the sky.]

6. bɔt trɔki gɛt trɔŋ nkanda. nɔtiŋ no fit du i.

    But the tortoise has strong skin. Nothing could hurt him.

7. i wikɔp. i šek i skin, muf ɔl dɔs fɔ i skin.

    He got up, shook himself, removed all the dust from his body,

8. i go, i sey: "a! a dɔn du yu wɛl!

    and left, saying: "Oh! I have taught you a good lesson!

9. ɔl dis pipul we dem di prawd!

    All these people who are proud!

10. dem tink sey fɔseka sey

They think that because

11. a no gɛt wiŋ a no fit du as dem tu di du

I don't have wings I can't do as they do.

12. a no fit flay, bɔt mi a dɔn šo yu sey sens pas ɔl."

I can't fly, but I've shown you that intelligence beats everything."

PIDGIN FEATURES

We find pidgin structures simplified in many ways. The following list isn't true of all pidgins, but represents the sorts of simplifications we usually find in going from a true language to a pidgin (e.g. in going from English to Cameroonian Pidgin or Korean Bamboo English). Exceptions exist, but the tendencies are strong.

PHONOLOGY

Pidgins usually use a simple phonemic inventory. This means that the unusual sounds like [θ, ð] are replaced by more common ones like [t, d]. Notice the pronunciation of *these* and *think* (lines 9 and 10). Unusual *places* of articulation (like uvular, pharyngeal, and palatal) and unusual *manners* of articulation (like clicks, implosives, ejectives) are not used in pidgins.

Pidgins also usually have simple 5-vowel [i , e , a , o , u] or 7-vowel [i , e , ɛ , a , ɔ , o , u] systems, possibly including the diphthongs [ay] and [aw]. Notice that 'that' in line 1 is pronounced [dat] rather than [dæt]. It is also usually the case that consonant clusters are reduced in pidgins (see *strong* (6) and *dust* (7)). Consonant cluster reduction is an indication that pidgins have a preference for syllable types closer to the ideal type (CV).

MORPHOLOGY

Pidgins simplify morphology by using no affixes, using no case or gender marking, allowing little irregularity, and by using reduplication. Notice from the Cameroonian example that 'wings' is wiŋ (11), that 'thinks' is *tink* (5), and 'passes' is *pas* (12), and that 'Hawk's' is hɔk . In all of these examples Cameroonian does not use affixes while English does.

It is also interesting to notice that *i* is the only third person pronoun in Cameroonian, replacing *he, she, him, her* (objective), and *his* and *her* (possessive). This simplification avoids the use of case and gender marking. Finally, it should be noted that reduplication is often used in pidgins as a simple word formation process (a) to avoid homonymy as in *san* 'sun' and *sansan* 'sand' (this example is taken from Korean Bamboo English), or (b) for emphasis as in *talkytalky* 'very talkative' (again from Korean Bamboo English).

VOCABULARY

Pidgins usually have very small vocabularies. To compensate for lack of variety meanings are extended, thus *stik* means not only 'stick' but also 'tree' (5), and wikɔp means not only 'wake up' but also 'get up' (7). Extensions are also used with modifications as in the Korean Bamboo English uses of *gras* 'grass' in *gras bilong head* for 'hair' and *gras bilong mouth* for 'mustache.' Because there aren't many words in the vocabulary of the typical pidgin, compounds are more frequent. This, just like extensions, makes it possible to extend the range of things that can be talked about without increasing the number of vocabulary items used in the language. As examples of compounding notice that 'dog baby' and 'cow baby' can be used for 'puppy' and 'calf.' One other way that a small number of words can be extended is by letting one word be used as two parts of speech. The adjective *fit* in the Cameroonian passage is an example of this type of extension. It occurs both as an adjective and as a verb (see lines 6 & 11, and 5 & 12).

SYNTAX

The basic word order for pidgins tends to be SVO and, like other SVO languages, pidgins generally use prepositions rather than postpositions, order auxiliaries before main verbs and nouns before relative clauses. These features of pidgin sentence structure can be found in the Cameroonian example above. Pidgins also show a preference for compound sentences (sentences connected by *and, or,* etc.) over subordinate clauses, though subordinate structures do sometimes exist (see if you can find the relative clauses in our Cameroonian example). Articles are generally not used (cf. (7) ɔl dɔs 'all the dust,' no 'a' or 'the' represented). Double negatives and double comparatives are also common.

SEMANTICS

Pidgins do not usually mark tense, though aspect is sometimes allowed. Cameroonian, for example, classifies actions as to whether they are *ongoing, completed* or *repeated*, as shown below:

ongoing   *di* [di laf] 'was laughing' (4)

completed <u>dɔn</u>   [dɔn du] 'have done' (8)

repeated   *di* [di du] 'do (always)' (11)

Pidgins also allow for a subjunctive (or conditional) mood, usually marked by an auxiliary verb. Cameroonian can mark something as strongly expected via the verb *go* as in (1), (2), and (5). Finally, pidgins often permit indefinite number reference, allowing a single noun phrase to refer to one or more things without distinction. Note that this is impossible in English. We must say either 'fly up to the tops of the trees' or 'fly up to the top of a tree.' But Cameroonian [flay ɔp stik] (5) can mean either.

A METHODOLOGICAL PROBLEM

Pidgins are languages in the making. Their grammatical patterns often haven't had the time to solidify. They are also learned later in life when all language learning tends to be imperfect. Moreover, they always exist side by side with several other languages—not just in a given community, but in the minds of their speakers, too. This is so because there are *no native speakers* of pidgin languages. Each speaker of a pidgin language also commands a native, nonpidgin language, which typically has contributed some elements into the pidgin. This leads to some insecurity about what is pidgin, and what isn't. Finally, as we noted above, pidgin speakers come to the language under some duress.

These factors lead to a great deal of variability in the language. The structures used by one speaker overlap only roughly with those employed by another. Often a pidgin speaker uses the vocabulary of the pidgin, but uses the structural patterns of her native language with the result that the generalizations above would describe her speech very poorly.

The problem of variability is a methodological problem for the linguist, a problem concerning the methods needed to determine the vocabulary and grammar of the pidgin. Obviously, it would be foolish to rely on just a few speakers in studying pidgins, so the linguist tries to observe a large community.

It turns out that pidgins tend to develop toward a standard form, however, which eases this problem considerably.

THE LIFE-CYCLE OF A PIDGIN: CREOLIZATION

If a pidgin becomes well established in a community, families may begin to bring their children up speaking the pidgin, rather than any of the other languages available in this sort of situation. Once a language acquires native speakers, it is no longer a pidgin; it passes into the family of *creoles.* Some well-known creoles are Hawaiian 'pidgin,' Jamaican Creole, both based on English, Haitian Creole, based on French, Indonesian and Swahili. Tok Pisin is a very recent creole and is now the official language in Papua, New Guinea.

According to Derek Bickerton, who has investigated the Hawaiian Creole in depth (and who first discovered many of the properties of pidgins listed above), the grammar of creole languages is much less variable than that of pidgins. At first blush this is not too surprising, since creoles are learned early in life, when language learning is most effective, and since creoles are, in general, better established socially (we know this since otherwise parents would not bring their children up speaking it). As we shall see below, however, Bickerton has shown that some surprising insights about human language ability follow from this superficially unsurprising fact.

The properties of recent creoles are exactly the properties we listed as features of pidgins, with the difference that we can verify the properties of creoles more reliably.

Once creolization has taken place, the language may later add potentially any of the structures and grammatical devices we find in other languages. Plural markings and additional vocabulary tend to be added soon, but little is known about the general order in which other features might be added. The process in which a creole loses its distinctively creole features (by acquiring different or additional grammatical devices) is known as decreolization.

DECREOLIZATION: SPECULATION ABOUT THE HISTORY OF BLACK ENGLISH

Some linguists have hypothesized that Black English originated in a creole language that in turn originated in a pidgin based on West African languages, English, French, and perhaps Portuguese. Since these linguists recognize that contemporary Black English no longer has all the usual properties expected of a creole, they describe the recent linguistic history of Black English as *decreolization*—the process in which a creole loses its distinctively creole features. In this case we suppose that the creole gradually assumed more of the features of the dominant standard language. It is difficult to say whether this hypothesis is true, but it is intriguing first because some evidence suggests that it is correct, and second because it is a stunning rebuttal of those who view Black English as a collection of standard English errors. (According to the creole hypothesis, contemporary Black English did not arise as a collection of deviations from standard English, but rather from the massive change of pidginization involving several languages.) We now summarize the evidence for the Creole Hypothesis.

First, the social conditions were correct for pidginization. Slaves were brought from many different language areas to work on the plantations of the south, and they were forced to communicate with one another as best they could.

Slave traders were explicit about using Africans of different languages. William Smith, in *A Voyage to New Guinea* (1744), spoke of the dangers of having many aboard who spoke the same language, who might organize and overpower the crew.

> But the safest way is to trade with the different Nations, on either side of the river, and having some of every sort
> on board, there will be no more chance of their succeeding than of finishing the Tower of Babel.

Second, there are pidgin and creole languages throughout the Caribbean that originated in slavery, making the area the world's richest in pidgins and creoles. Jamaican English (currently heard in reggae music) is the creole language that most closely resembles American Black English.

Third, there is one creole still in use among one group of American blacks—Gullah, the variety spoken by blacks on the Carolina Sea Islands.

Fourth, Dillard, the best-known proponent of the creole hypothesis, tries to show that the speech of black slaves on southern plantations was a creole intermediate between Gullah and contemporary Black English, and that, in general, Black English has been growing more similar to standard American English over the course of the last two centuries. Dillard's evidence is hard to evaluate, however, because it consists largely of naive reports which portray blacks humorously or stereotypically.

Fifth, Black English resembles true creole in several suggestive points. Its phonology lacks interdental consonants and tends to reduce consonant clusters; the present tense singular *-s* has been eliminated (in keeping with the general elimination of affixes); double negatives are common; and it uses aspectual markers, *be* for repeated activity and *been/done* for completed action, just as creoles do.

These points confirm the Creole hypothesis, but not conclusively. It is virtually certain that the slaves were taken from various language areas, and that language groups weren't respected in distributing slaves to plantations, so that we can confidently postulate a plantation pidgin. The difficulty comes in showing that this postulated structure developed into contemporary Black English. The fact that creoles developed elsewhere doesn't show this (even where they are as close as Gullah) unless it can be shown that they are related. But, as mentioned above, the historical record is too fragmentary to allow anything very conclusive to be said. The creole-like features of contemporary Black English are suggestive, but here we must keep in mind that many nonstandard dialects (i) have similarly dropped interdentals and reduced consonant clusters, (ii) treat affixes differently from standard English, (iii) use double negatives, and (iv) use *been/done* to mark a completed aspect. The only creole feature unique to Black English seems to be the repeated aspect marked by *be*.

LANGUAGE ACQUISITION AND CREOLIZATION

Many researchers have noted similarities in the structures of various pidgins and creoles, but how are these to be explained, especially where they extend beyond pidgins based on the same language? Why, for example, is English-based Cameroonian similar to Chinese-based Makista?

Bickerton has further noticed that pidgins and creoles are very similar in structure to the language that children use before they master their native language. This too tends to be simpler than its base language, and child language and pidgins and creoles tend to be simpler in the same ways. Both tend to use only labial, alveolar, and velar consonants; they both have 5- or 7-element vowel charts; and neither is fond of consonant clusters. Children, like pidgin and creole speakers, avoid affixes, ignore morphological irregularity, and are known to use reduplication spontaneously. SVO word order is used even by children learning SOV languages, and children everywhere are late in learning the use of articles.

There might be two sorts of explanations for this convergence in structure. We might postulate either that the common properties are naturally simpler, or that language learners are psychologically predisposed toward languages with these properties. In the first case, pidgins and creoles represent a kind of easiest symbol system that any learning animal (or machine) would be likely to arrive at if it wanted to communicate. In the second case, the properties may not be the simplest imaginable, but human beings arrive at them because they are hardwired for communication systems with these properties. In this case the properties give us a window into the human mind.

If we restricted our attention only to the above properties common to child language and pidgins and creoles, there would be no way to decide which of these explanations is correct. But Bickerton argues further and even more strikingly that pidgins and creoles resemble child language in respects that are not immediately attributable to simplicity.

For example, it is not clear why aspect should be simpler to deal with than tense, why double negatives should be easier, why indefinite number would be fundamental, or even why conditional/subjunctive mood would be a necessary linguistic building block. It is clear that one can speculate about these questions, but if the parallels between child language and pidgins and creoles rest on their both using the naturally simplest devices, it should be clear why the common devices are simplest—else we would expect to find a range of equally simple grammatical devices in use. Since we don't find this range we would have to admit to an unlikely coincidence.

The debate on these matters continues today, and it is likely to occupy theorists for some time to come.

SOURCES AND SUGGESTIONS FOR FURTHER READING

Bickerton, Derek "Creole Languages" in *Scientific American* 249.1, July, 1983, pp. 116-122.

This is a very readable introduction to Bickerton's ideas on the analysis of pidgins and creoles, and it contains references to his more technical work (at the end of the issue, not at the end of the article).

Todd, Loreto *Pidgins and Creoles* (Boston & London: Routledge and Kegan Paul), 1974.

An earlier but still useful work which includes maps.

This conversation was recorded in the Ohio State University Department of Linguistics' phonetic laboratory in April 1975. The language is Krio, a creole spoken in Sierra Leone on the west coast of Africa.

Both informants are in their late 20's and are natives of Sierra Leone. The first speaker is from Bo and is a native speaker of Mende; Krio is a second language. The second speaker is from Kambia and speaks Temne, Soso Malinke, Bullon, and French, in addition to Krio. Both are fluent in English.

There are three lines in the transcription:

    (A) is phonetic

    (B) is fairly literal translation

    (C) is translation into Colloquial American English.

First Speaker:	(A)	[bo a si mi frɛn kʰam ba]
	(B)	Hey! I say, my friend, come by.
	(C)	Hi! Say, there, come over here.

First:	(A)	[ɛ̃ na sa lu i kʰɔmɔt]
	(B)	Eh! It's Sierra Leone you have come from?
	(C)	Oh! You're from Sierra Leone?

Second:	(A)	[yɛ bwa a kʰɔma sa lɔ̃]
	(B)	Yes, friend, I come from Sierra Leone.
	(C)	Yes, I'm from Sierra Leone.

First:	(A)	[ɛ̃ bo kʰuš ow a glædi fɔr si yu]
	(B)	Oh? Greetings! I glad for see you.
	(C)	Oh yeah? Great! I'm glad to see you.

Second:	(A)	[o]
	(B)	Oh!
	(C)	Oh!

First:	(A)	[wʌčə nɔr i nem]
	(B)	What is your name?
	(C)	What's your name?

Second:	(A)	[a nem sori pʰa a nem sori]
	(B)	I name Sorie, old man, I name Sorie.
	(C)	My name is Sorie, my name is Sorie.

First:	(A)	[soriwičɪn]
	(B)	Sorie what?
	(C)	Sorie what?

Second:	(A)	[sori yilá pʰa]
	(B)	Sorie Yillah, old man.
	(C)	Sorie Yillah.

First: (A) [o: æn mĩ neŋ ʝoko seŋgova ya]
            (B) I see,   and my name Joko Sengova.
            (C) I see, and my name's Joko Sengova.

First: (A) [e bwa ar glædi fɔr si yu a glædi fɔr si yu]
            (B) Well are   glad   for see you; glad   for see you.
            (C) Well, I'm glad to see you; I'm really glad to see you.

Second: (A) [yɛ tʰɛŋki]
            (B) Yes, thank you.
            (C) I'm glad to see you, too.

First: (A) [yu no frʌ̃ wa a kʰã a nɔ]
            (B) You know since I came, I have not
            (C) You know since I came, I haven't

                 [sɪ no:bədi wɛ kɔmɔ   stər lyon kʰušɛ]
                 seen nobody who has come from Sierra Leone? Greetings!
                 seen anybody who's from Sierra Leone? That's great!

Second: (A) [ɛ̃]
            (B) Oh?
            (C) Oh?

First: (A) [no kʰušo]
            (B) No! Greetings!
            (C) No! It's great to see you!

Second: (A) [yɛ bo]
            (B) Yes, friend.
            (C) Yes, it sure is.

First: (A) [wuse u kʰã]
            (B) Which time you came?
            (C) When did you come?

Second: (A) [wɛl a dɔn tʰye na ya lili bit a kʰʌm buɔt]
            (B) Well, I done stayed at here little bit. I came about
            (C) Well, I've been here quite a while. I came

                 [nayntʰin sɛvɛntʰi sɛvɛntʰi wɛn]
                 nineteen seventy . . . . seventy one.
                 sometime around 1970 . . . . 1971.

First: (A) [ɛ̃]
            (B) Oh, yeah?
            (C) Oh, really?

Second: (A) [yɛ]
            (B) Yup.
            (C) Yup.

First: (A) [mi ʝɛs kʰã: a dɔn di ya nɔ mɔ sɛvi mɔnt]
            (B) Me just came, I have been here no more seven months!
            (C) I have just come, I have only been here seven months!

Second: (A) [yɛ]
            (B) Yup.
            (C) I see.

First: (A)   [kušo]
           (B)   Greetings!
           (C)   It's really great to see you!

First: (A)   [wu...wusay diw wʌč i di stʌdi]
           (B)   Where are you?   What do you   study?
           (C)   Where do you live? What are you studying?

Second: (A)   [a di na nu yɔk ə...na di stʌdi liŋwɪstɪks]
           (B)   I   do at New York and I   do study   linguistics
           (C)   ·I'm in New York and I'm studying linguistics

                 [na kʰwinz kɔlɛǰ   na nu yɔk]
                 at   Queen's College   at New York.
                 at Queen's College in New York.

First: (A)   [o liŋwɪstɪks]
           (B)   Oh, linguistics?
           (C)   Oh, linguistics?

Second: (A)   [yɛ̃]
           (B)   Yes!
           (C)   Yes!

First: (A)   [næ   mi sɛf di du]
           (B)   That's what myself   do do.
           (C)   That's what I'm doing, too.

Second: (A)   [ɛ̃]
           (B)   Oh!
           (C)   Oh!

First: (A)   [yɛ̃ næ   mi sɛf di stʌdi hə? mi na wɪskʰansɪn mi du]
           (B)   Yes, that's what   myself do study; but   me at Wisconsin   me do.
           (C)   That's what I'm studying too, but I'm at Wisconsin.

Second: (A)   [e bra]
           (B)   Oh, I see.
           (C)   Oh, I see.

First: (A)   [ã̃ də nə   fayn tʰiŋ]
           (B)   Oh! That is a   fine   thing.
           (C)   Oh! That's good.

First: **(A)** [ɑr glædi fɔr si yu]
                 (B) Are glad   for see you.
                 (C) I'm glad to see you.

Second: **(A)** [yɛ mi tʰu mi sɛf]
                 (B) Yes, me too, myself.
                 (C) Yes, me too! I am too.

LANGUAGE CONTACT:
GULLAH: THE TAR BABY

The following story in the Creole language Gullah provides a number of examples of the characteristic features of Creole languages.

One big dry drought bin puntop (on) de lan, en all de watuh hole en cow track dem dry up en de creeter ain hads no watuh fur dem drink.

Buh Rabbit en Buh Fox lib kine uh close turgedder en Buh Rabbit tell Buh Fox say, "Les we dig one well turgedder twix we house, den all two uh we kin nuse (use) um bidout haffuh walk too fur."

Buh Fox gree tuh dit, en Buh Rabbit tell um say, "Buh Fox, e's berry hot middle day now, les we meet dey fus day 5 (daybreak) een de mawnin, en time day clean we kin sta-a-t wuk, en mebby puhaps we kin git um done befo e git too hot." En Buh Fox gree tuh dat, too.

Fo day een de mawnin Buh Fox bin tuh de place. E ain see Buh Rabbit. Time e could uh see fuh wuk e sta-a-t fuh dig. Sun done up, e yet ain see Buh Rabbit.

Buh Fox git tuh good watuh, en e come out de well duh lebble (to level) de groun roun de well, yuh comes Buh Rabbit. 10

"Oh, Buh Fox, us so sorry yo didn' wait fuh me fo yo sta-a-t. Muh ole ooman bin ha de feeber en de head ache all de Gawd sen night. Fo day uh baig um fuh do lemme run out yuh tell yo say don't does dig de well, but e keep duh tell me e duh gwine dead, en do fuh don' le'm stay fuh dead by e self. E did now drop sleep, en uh run hope yo bin uh wait for me."

Buh Rabbit den ax Buh Fox is e got watuh. Buh Fox tell um say yeh e gots good watuh.

Buh Rabbit den say, "Buh Fox, us so sorry yo had uh dig de well by yo self, but at uh diddy (since I'm here) en yo gots 15 watuh, uh'l tek some back een dis yuh can tuh muh ole ooman fuh cool um een e feeber.

Buh Fox tell Buh Rabbit say, "Buh Rabbit, yo wouldn' hep me dig dis yuh well, yo ain fuh tek no watuh out um. Ef yo wa' watuh, go dig yo own well."

Buh Rabbit say, "Do, Buh Fox, yo ain duh gwine hinduh me fuh tek leetle uh dis yuh watuh tuh muh ole ooman wuh bin ha de feeber all inight."   20

Buh Fox tell um gen say e ain fuh tetch de watuh een de well. En e tell um mo'ober gen, ef e ketch um duh teef (thief) de watuh e duh gwine kill um.

Ebby mawnin fo day Buh Rabbit does go tuh Buh Fox well en e tek all de watuh, en when Buh Fox come dey soon duh mawnin fuh git watuh e ain meet no watuh een de well. But e see Buh Rabbit track dey roun bout de well.

Buh Fox git some ta (tar), en e mek uh gal out de p'yo (pure) ta en set um up tuh de well.   25

Buh Rabbit come dey fo day een de mawnin fuh teef watuh en e see de gal duh set by de well. E tell um say, "Good mawnin, gal." De gal ain gie um no ansuh. Buh Rabbit ax de gal mek (why) e (she) don' talk tuh people when dey tell um good mawnin. De gal ain yet gie um no ansuh.

Buh Rabbit say, "Gal, ef yo don' tell me good mawnin uh duh gwine slap yo head off." De gal ain yet say nuttin. Buh Rabbit haul off en slap um, POW. E han fasen. E say, "Gal, yo bes tun me loose fo uh slap yo wid de yedder han." De gal 30 ain tun um loose en e slap um wid de — POW. De yedder han fasen.

Buh Rabbit say, "Gal, uh done play wid yo now fuh de las, ef uh ebber butt yo uh'l bus yo brains wide open." E haul back e head en butt um, BIM. E head fasen.

E dey (is) dey (there) now all fasen up to de gal. When Buh Fox come tuh de well, time Buh Rabbit shum (see him) duh e

35 holler say, "Buh Fox, uhyyeddy (heard) say yo had cuse (accused) me fuh come yuh teef yo watuh, en uh come yuh fo day een de mawnin en meet dis yuh gal duh teef yo watuh. See de bucket wuh e bring fuh teef de watuh een, en uh run yuh ketch um en duh hole um tell (until) yo come."

Buh Fox come dey en loose Buh Rabbit en tek um duh gwine (along). Buh Rabbit say, "Buh Fox, fuh whuffuh yo duh hole me, mek yo don' tun me loose so we kin walk turgedder?"

40 Buh Fox tell Buh Rabbit say, e had uh tell um say ef e teef e watuh e duh gwine kill um, en e say e duh gwine kill um.

Den duh gwine on en Buh Rabbit say, "Buh Fox?" Buh Fox anser um e say, "Eh?" Buh Rabbit say, "Buh Fox, how yo duh gwine kill me, yo gwine hang me wid rope?" Buh Fox tell um say e dunno how e duh gwine kill um, nummer (except, only) e duh gwine kill um.

Buh Rabbit ax Buh Fox is e duh gwine cut um wid knife? Buh Fox tell um e ain know wuh e duh gwine do.

45 Buh Rabbit say, "Buh Fox, yo gone tide (tie) me wid chain en bun (burn) me duh fiah?" Buh Fox tell um say, "Fuh Gawd sake, Buh Rabbit, uh done tell yo say uh dunno how uh duh gwine kill yo, uh dis duh gwine kill yo."

Den duh gwine on en turrecly dem come tuh one ole briar patch. Time Buh Rabbit see de briar patch e holler, "Oh Lardy, Buh Fox, duh dat yo duh gwine do wid me? Do Buh Fox, do don' trow me een da briar patch fuh dem sperrit fuh tarrify (terrify) me tuh dat. Tek me home, Buh Fox, en hang me wid rope, eeder cut me wid knife, eeder tide me wid chain en bun 50 me by fiah. But do, Buh Fox, do don' trow me een da briar patch fuh dem sperrit fuh tarrify me tuh dat."

When Buh Fox yeddy Buh Rabbit duh baig so ha-a-d fuh e don' trowed um een de briar patch e say da's de berry ting e duh gwine do tur um.

E tek Buh Rabbit en e swing um, en e swing um. E turn um loose. Buh Rabbit gone way yonder out een de briar patch.

E light, BIM. E jump up on e foots en run off. Quing, quing, quing, quing. "Dis de berry place uh bawn, Buh Fox. Dis de 55 berry place uh bawn."

NOTES ON GULLAH

The notes which follow illustrate the properties of Creole languages by referring to examples by line in the Tar Baby story.

All of the properties listed below are examples of features commonly found in Creole languages.

PHONOLOGY

1. No interdentals. Line (L) 1 *de watuh hole* 'the water hole'
   L3 *turgedder* 'together'
2. final clusters reduced   L1 /læh/ 'land' L1 /watə/ 'water'
3. but note the (unexpected) diphthongs   L1 /dɹay/ 'dry'
   L3 /haws/ 'house'

MORPHOLOGY

1. No plural marking. There is a distinction in single *e* and plural *dem* pronouns. L1 *dem dry up* 'they dried up' and *e ain see Buh Rabbit* 'He hasn't seen Brer Rabbit.' But there is no plural marking on nouns:

   L1 *de creeter* 'the creatures' (note *dem drink*)
   L4 *twix we house* 'between our houses'
   L24 *track* 'tracks'   L50 *dem sperrit* 'the spirit'

   Note that L32 *brains* looks plural, but probably doesn't contrast with *brain*. Note that it refers to a single brain. Similarly L54 *foots*.

2. No possessive *'s*.
   L4 *we house* 'our house'
   L16 *e feeber* 'her fever'
   L24 *Buh Rabbit track* 'Brer Rabbit's tracks'

3. No present tense *s*.
   L6 *befo e git too hot* 'before it gets too hot'

   L16, L18, L20 *tell, say* with 3rd singular subjects and no marker. (These might be past tense forms, however, in which case it's interesting that there is no past tense marking.)

   L14 contains an apparent present tense singular *s, e gots good watuh* 'he has good water' but note that it isn't used consistently. In the same line *e got watuh* 'he has water' shows no marking on the same verb.

4. No past tense *-ed*.
   L1 *drought bin puntop . . . en . . . dem dry up* 'drought was put [on top] . . . and . . . they dried up' We expect a past tense here in the second conjunct because the first conjunct is also about past time.

   L8 *Time e could uh see . . . e staat fuh dig* 'As soon as he could see he started to dig.'

5. No *ing* on verb. L12 *e keep duh tell me* 'she kept telling me,' etc.

6. Regularized forms *say* /se/ for 'said, says'   /sɛd, sɛz/   L20 et passim. L36 *bring* 'brought.'

SEMANTICS

1. Perfective Aspect marked by auxiliary *bin*. L11 *bin ha* 'had'   L13 *bin uh wait* 'had waited'

2. . . . similarly by *done* L32 *done play* 'played'   L46 *done tell* 'told'   The *done* form seems to refer to more recent events.

3. Negative Concord. L1-2 *ain has no watuh* 'didn't have any water'   L27 *din gie um no ansuh* 'hasn't given him any answers'

4. Use of bare noun. L49 *cut me wid knife* 'cut me with a knife'

INTRODUCTION: REGIONAL VARIATION

It is obvious to most people that there is variation among languages — that, for example, English is different from Spanish which is different from Arabic which is different from Russian, and so on. It may not be so obvious, however, that each and every language exhibits internal variation (on all linguistic levels).

Within any particular language there is variation from speaker to speaker, the form of language spoken by one person being known as an *idiolect*. There is also variation from group to group. When a group of speakers of a particular language differs noticeably in its speech from another group we say they are speaking different *dialects*. A dialect, then, is simply any variety of a language, the variety being characterized by systematic differences in pronunciation, grammar and vocabulary from other varieties of the same language. If the variation exists only on the phonological (pronunciation) level then it is termed accent rather than dialect.

How do we know if two (or more) language varieties are different dialects of the same language or if in fact they are separate, distinct languages? One criterion used to distinguish dialect from language is the criterion of *mutual intelligibility;* that is, if speakers of one language variety can understand speakers of another language variety and vice versa, we say that these varieties are mutually intelligible. Suppose you are a native of Brooklyn, New York and you go to visit some friends in Beaumont, Texas. You may notice some differences in the speech of your Beaumont friends (and they in yours) but essentially you will be able to understand each other; your dialect and theirs are mutually intelligible and therefore dialects of the same language.

It is not always easy to decide if two language varieties are different dialects of the same language or different languages just on the basis of mutual intelligibility; other factors (such as cultural or historical considerations) may cloud the issue. In China, Mandarin is spoken in nothern provinces and Cantonese in the southern province of Kwang Tung. Now, even though in spoken form these language varieties are not mutually intelligible, they are considered (by the speakers of these varieties themselves) to be dialects of the same language. Why? One reason is that in written form these two varieties are mutually intelligible, because they use a common writing system. A similar situation exists in the American Southwest between Papago and Pima, two Amerindian languages. These two language varieties are actually mutually intelligible with less linguistic difference between them than between Standard American English and Standard British English. However, because these two tribes regard themselves as politically and culturally distinct, they consider the languages to be distinct as well.

Another complication for the criterion of mutual intelligibility can be found in a phenomenon known as a *dialect continuum*. This is a situation where, in a large number of contiguous dialects, each dialect is closely related to the next but the dialects at either end of the continuum (scale) are mutually unintelligible. Thus, dialect A is related to dialect B which is related to dialect C which is related to dialect D; but D and A are not mutually intelligible. A situation such as this can be found on the border between Holland and Germany, where the dialects on either side of the national border are mutually intelligible. Because of international boundaries, however (and probably political and cultural considerations, as well), speakers of these varieties regard them as dialects of distinct languages. At what point is the line drawn? Clearly, the criterion of mutual intelligibility does not account for all the facts. Indeed, there may be no clear-cut, black-and-white answer to such a question in every case.

From the Family Tree Model in the section on historical linguistics we saw that a parent language may split off and form daughter languages — e.g. Germanic splitting off into English, Dutch and German (among others). This type of split may occur when dialect differences become so great that the dialects are no longer mutually intelligible to the speakers of these language varieties.

A group of people speaking the same dialect is known as a *speech community*. Speech communities are based on a number of different factors, such as age, sex, geography, style and socioeconomic class. When the speech community is based on geography (for instance, when the dialect of a native of New York City is noticeably different from that of a native Alabaman), we identify the dialect spoken in that community as a regional dialect. The study of regional dialects is known as *linguistic geography* or *regional dialectology*. It is this area of language variations which is the subject of Files 131 through 135. File 131 discusses some of the causes of regional variation, such as settlement patterns and natural barriers; File 132 addresses dialect boundaries and isoglosses; and Files 133 through 135 examine regional variation at various linguistic levels (i.e. phonetic, phonological, lexical and syntactic).

REGIONAL VARIATION: SOME CAUSAL FACTORS IN THE FORMATION OF AMERICAN DIALECTS

How did regional variation arise? Some variation can be explained in terms of regional settlement patterns; other variation can be explained in terms of natural barriers to communication. The formation of U.S. regional dialects in part had its beginnings in England as speakers from various regions of England journeyed across the Atlantic and settled the Eastern seabord of the U.S. Thus, from the start, settlers in any given settlement formed heterogeneous speech communities, some perhaps speaking a London dialect, others speaking a southern or northern dialect, etc. In time, because of prolonged contact and necessary communicative compromise (for example, agreeing on a southern English word for small body of water but a northern English word for a water container) the diverse dialects of a particular settlement began to coalesce into a more homogeneous speech community. Compromises would differ, however, from settlement to settlement. Thus, various dialects emerged along the Atlantic seaboard. During this time, some colonial cities such as Boston, Philadelphia and Charleston acquired prestige as a result of becoming centers of trade and culture. The dialects spoken in these cities became prestigious as well and began to exert influence on nearby settlements.

Migration westward to a large extent reflected the settlement patterns of the Atlantic states. Yankees from Western New England and Upstate New York, in moving west, fanned out, settling chiefly in the Great Lakes area; settlers from the Middle Atlantic region (primarily Pennsylvania and Maryland) journeyed west to Ohio, West Virginia and the Mississippi Valley. Influence from the southern Atlantic colonies was felt as speakers from this area settled in the Gulf states. The lines are never clearly drawn, however, because the streams of migration often mingled. Sometimes, New Englanders and speakers from the Middle Atlantic would form compact communities outside their usual area of settlement — e.g. the Yankee enclave of Worthington, Ohio (near Columbus) or the North Carolina Quaker settlement of Richmond, Indiana. Added to these patterns is the influence of the later waves of European immigrants. The spread of migration continued to the Rocky Mountain states, essentially following previously established patterns but with greater mingling and, finally, reaching the West Coast, resulting in even greater crossing of dialect lines. Moreover, the sharp increase in geographic mobility since World War II as a result of transportation technology has contributed greatly to the obscuring of dialect boundaries.

Geographic barriers have also played a role in the formation of regional dialects; that is, regional dialect boundaries often coincide with natural barriers such as rivers, mountains or swamps. For example, speakers of English east of the Alleghenies may use the word *soda* for a non-alcoholic, carbonated beverage while those west of this mountain range use *pop* instead.

REGIONAL VARIATION: MAPS OF AMERICAN ENGLISH REGIONAL DIALECTS

The two following maps show dialect areas in the eastern half of the United States. The map on this pages shows lines, called *isoglosses,* which mark the boundaries of areas where some dialect feature is used by speakers. In this map, each isogloss shows the northern limits of areas in which a particular phrase is used: "sick at the stomach" is used in regions below the dashed line; "barn lot" is used below the dotted line; and "quarter till (two)" is used below the dotted-dashed line. The map on the next page shows five major dialect areas; the boundary lines in this case do not separate single dialect features but rather are a compromise between *bundles of isoglosses* which roughly come together along these lines, separating forms of speech which differ in a number of ways (hence, different dialects).

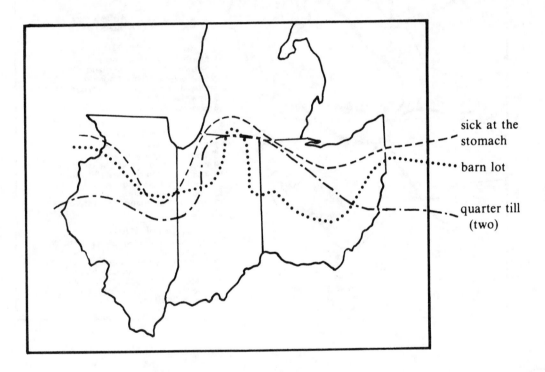

sick at the stomach

barn lot

quarter till (two)

The map on the following page illustrates some regional dialect boundaries of the United States.

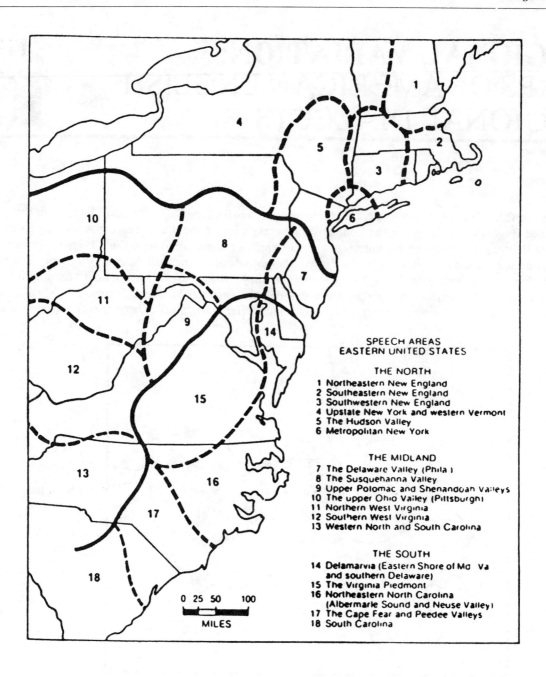

SPEECH AREAS
EASTERN UNITED STATES

THE NORTH

1 Northeastern New England
2 Southeastern New England
3 Southwestern New England
4 Upstate New York and western Vermont
5 The Hudson Valley
6 Metropolitan New York

THE MIDLAND

7 The Delaware Valley (Phila)
8 The Susquehanna Valley
9 Upper Potomac and Shenandoah Valleys
10 The upper Ohio Valley (Pittsburgh)
11 Northern West Virginia
12 Southern West Virginia
13 Western North and South Carolina

THE SOUTH

14 Delamarvia (Eastern Shore of Md Va
   and southern Delaware)
15 The Virginia Piedmont
16 Northeastern North Carolina
   (Albemarle Sound and Neuse Valley)
17 The Cape Fear and Peedee Valleys
18 South Carolina

0 25 50   100

MILES

REGIONAL VARIATION
VARIATION AT DIFFERENT LEVELS OF LINGUISTIC STRUCTURE

While we are all aware that there is some variation in terms of pronunciation and choice of vocabulary item between dialects of the same language, we may be surprised at the extensive variation which exists at *all* levels of linguistic structure. This file is designed to introduce you to different types of variation that exist at each level.

Phonetic Level

I. What the sounds are:

A. In most American dialects [t, d, n, s, z, l] are produced with *alveolar* articulation, but some New York City dialects have *dental* articulation whereby the tongue tip touches the top teeth.

B. Some Black English dialects do not have the sound [θ] ; instead the sounds [f] or [t] are substituted, e.g. *both* [bof], *tenth* [tɛnt] .

Phonological Level

I. What distinctions there are:

A. Most American dialects have one vowel in *caught, dawn,* and *hawk* (something close to [ɔ] but a little lower) and another in *cot, Don,* and *hock* [a] ; but some dialects have the same vowel in all words, and this difference in vowels is not used to distinguish between words, so that in these particular dialects *Don* and *dawn* would be homophonous.

B. In Southern England, words like *flood, but, cup* have the vowel [ʌ] and words like *full, good, put* have the vowel [ʊ] . In Northern English dialects, however, both sets of words have the vowel [ʊ] .

II. Which *combinations of phonemes* can occur:

A. Standard British English does not permit sequences of vowel-*r*-C or V-*r*-#. This is similar to Bostonian English where the sentence *Park the car* would be pronounced [pak ðə ka]

B. Some Black English dialects do not permit sequences of C-*r* or *l*, especially in unstressed syllables, so that the word *professor* would be pronounced [pofɛsə]

III. Which *phoneme* occurs where:

A. Northern and Southeastern British English dialects both have the phonemes [a] and [æ] in their phonemic inventories. In the Southeastern dialects, however, [æ] occurs in *pat, bad* and *cap* but [a] in *path, laugh, grass,* etc., while in the North [æ] occurs in both sets of words.

B. In some southern and midwestern dialects of America there is no distinction between [ɪ] and [ɛ] before nasals; only [ɪ] occurs. So, in the words *pen* and *pin*, which are pronounced [pɛn] and [pɪn] respectively by SAE speakers, the pronunciation is [pɪn] for both words.

Morphological Level

I. What morphemes there are:

A. Some Black English dialects do not have a third person singular present tense -*s*, and say *he kiss, she see,* and *it jump* rather than *he kisses*, etc.

B. In parts of Northern England and Southern Wales -*s* is not just a third singular present tense marker, but a general present tense marker. These speakers say sentences like *I likes him, We goes*, etc.

C. Some root morphemes occur only in some dialects. *Poke* 'a paper bag' occurs in rural western Pennsylvania and Western North Carolina; *been* as a present perfect marker occurs in some Philadelphia dialects (*I been know you* = *I've known you for a long time.*)

II. Where the morphemes occur:

A. Some rural British dialects use the possessive morpheme only with pronouns and not with nouns: *Tom egg* for *Tom's egg*; *the old lady purse* for *the old lady's purse*, but *my life, his dog*, etc.

III. What phonemic shape morphemes have:

A. Most nonstandard dialects of English have *hisself* and *theirselves* for standard *himself* and *themselves*.

B. In Appalachian English the possessive pronouns have an *-n* suffix: *yourn, hisn, hern, ourn, theirn*.

C. In informal styles the auxiliary morphemes have contracted forms. For instance, the word *is* is often pronounced simply [z] in a sentence such as *Who is the new teacher?* Also, *would* often contracts to [d], *will* to [l] and *have* to [v].

Syntactic Level

I. What categories the words are assigned to:

A. For many southern speakers *done* serves not only for a form of *do* but also can be an auxiliary: *She done already told you* rather than *she has*.

B. For many Appalachian speakers *right* can be an adverb as well as an adjective—*A right good meal.*

II. How words are organized into constituents:

A. In some dialects (e.g. Black English and some Southern dialects) combinations of auxiliaries like *might could, might would, may can*, and *useta could* are permitted, and form a single constituent.

III. What syntactic rules there are:

A. Many Appalachian and Midwestern dialects have the construction *The crops need watered* as a variant of *The crops need to be watered.*

B. Many nonstandard dialects have the feature *multiple negation*. For standard English sentences like *Nobody saw it* and *Nobody can touch me*, nonstandard dialects have *Didn't nobody see it* and *Ain't nobody can touch me.*

Semantic Level

I. Different meanings for the same words:

A. *Knock up* means 'rouse from sleep by knocking' in British English, but 'make pregnant' in American.

II. Different words for the same thing:

A. Words for carbonated beverages differ from place to place (*soft drink, soda, pop, soda-pop, coke, pepsi, tonic*, etc.)

REGIONAL VARIATION: VARIATION SAMPLES

I. PRONUNCIATION

Below is a list of·words that have different pronunciations in different dialects. Circle the letter corresponding to the pronunciation you use in relaxed, casual conversation. If you use more than one, circle all the appropriate letters. If· you use an entirely different pronunciation, indicate your pronunciation in the blank at the right. Finally, if you think the pronunciation you use is not the correct or standard one, X out the letter corresponding to the one you consider correct.

1. nucleus: a)[núkyələs], b) [núkliəs].   a   b   _____

2. washing: a)[wɔ́ršɪŋ], b) [wášiŋ].   a   b   _____

3. fire: the vowel is a) [ay], b)[a].   a   b   _____

4. tomato: the second vowel is a)[e], b)[a].   a   b   _____

5. where: begins with a) [ʍ], b)[w].   a   b   _____

6. often: a) [ɔ́fn̩] , b)[ɔ́ftn̩].   a   b   _____

7. greasy: a)[grísi], b)[grízi].   a   b   _____

8. bottle: a[bádl̩], b[báʔl̩].   a   b   _____

9. Columbus: a)[kəlʌ́mbəs], b) [klʌ́mbəs].   a   b   _____

10. police: stressed on a) 1st syllable, b) 2nd syllable.   a   b   _____

II. LEXICAL ITEMS

Here are some sentences containing words and idioms that differ from dialect to dialect. Circle the letter corresponding to the expression you use. If you ordinarily use more than one, circle all the appropriate letters. If you use an entirely different word or idiom, write it in the blank at the right.

1. A large open metal container for water is a: a) bucket, b) pail. a   b   _____
2. To carry groceries, you put them in a paper: a) bag, b) sack, c) poke. à   b   c   _____

3. Window coverings on rollers are: a) blinds, b) shades, c) roller shades, d) window shades, f) curtains
   a   b   c   d   e   f   _____

4. Pepsi-Cola, Coca-Cola, and Seven-Up are all kinds of a) soda, b) pop, c) coke, d) soft drinks, e) soda pop.

   a   b   c   d   e   _____

5. On summer nights when we were kids we used to try to catch a) fireflies, b) lightning bugs, c) fire bugs.

   a   b   c   _____

6. If it's a popular film, you may have to stand a) on line, b) in line.   a   b   _____

7. If your living room is messy, before company comes you a) straighten it up, b) red it up, c) ret it up, d) clean it up.

   a b c d _____

8. If you're talking to a group of friends, you call them a) you guys, b) you all.   a   b _____

9. It's now a) a quarter of 5, b) a quarter to 5, c) a quarter till 5.   a   b   c _____

10. Last night she a) dove, b) dived into an empty swimming pool.   a   b _____

III. SYNTAX

The sentences below were all actually said by some speaker of English. Go through the list of sentences and check, for each sentence, whether you think it is a) natural for you to use in casual conversation; b) something that some people would use but others wouldn't; or c) something that only a foreigner would say. The point is *not* whether you think the sentences are 'correct' or 'incorrect', 'good' or 'bad'. (Based on a questionnaire used by W. Labov.)

	a) natural	b) some	c) foreign
1. The dog is falled asleep.	_____	_____	_____
2. Everyone open their books.	_____	_____	_____
3. My shirt needs cleaned.	_____	_____	_____
4. Ever since he lost his job, he be sleepin' all day long.	_____	_____	_____
5. You shouldn't ought to put salt in your coffee.	_____	_____	_____
6. You usually go to the one you want, but me never.	_____	_____	_____
7. You can see the cops like they're grabbing kids left and right.	_____	_____	_____
8. He didn't have no book.	_____	_____	_____
9. I want for you to go home.	_____	_____	_____
10. Me and Sally played all afternoon.	_____	_____	_____
11. Noodles I can't stand in chicken soup.	_____	_____	_____
12. There's nobody can beat her at telling stories.	_____	_____	_____
13. Of whom are you speaking?	_____	_____	_____
14. Them tomato plants won't live.	_____	_____	_____
15. So don't I.	_____	_____	_____

REGIONAL VARIATION: TRANSCRIPTION OF KEY WORDS ON AMERICAN DIALECT TAPE

135

INTRODUCTION

This transcription accompanies a tape prepared in July 1975. It is composed of sentences read by speakers of various dialects of American English. In order to elicit as natural a pronunciation as possible, the following technique was used: the speakers were presented with each sentence on a card, a blank being placed somewhere in the sentence, and were told to fill in the blank with an appropriate word. This task masked the real purpose, which was to get a natural pronunciation of a key word which was actually elsewhere in the sentence. These key words are presented below in simplified phonetic transcription (some vowel differences are not indicated).

Key Word	Speaker 1 Chicago	Speaker 2 S.E. Ohio	Speaker 3 New Jersey	Speaker 4 Tennessee	Speaker 5 Mass.
1. greasy	[grisi]	[ɡrisi]	[grisi]	[grizi]	[grisi]
2. xerox	[zɪraks]	[ziraks]	[zɪraks]	[ziraks]	[zɪraks]
3. measured	[mɛžərd]	[mežərd]	[mɛžəd]	[mɛžəd]	[mɛžəd]
4. wrestle	[rɛsəl]	[rɛsəl]	[rɛsəl]	[rɛsəl]	[rɛsəl]
5. wash	[wɔš]	[wɔrš]	[wɔš]	[waš]	[wɔš]
6. Ohio	[ohayo]	[ohayo]	[ohayo]	[ohayo]	[ohayo]
7. a. tomato	[tʰəmeDo]	[tʰəmeDə]	[tʰəmeDə]	[tʰəmeDə]	[tʰəmeDo]
b. potato	[pʰətʰeDo]	[pʰətʰeDo]	[pʰətʰeDo]	[pʰətʰeDo]	[pʰətʰeDo]
8. a. roof	[ruf]	[ruf]	[ruf]	[ruf]	[ruf]
b. humor	[hyumər]	[hyumər]	[yũmə]	[hyumə]	[hyumər]
9. calm	[kʰalm]	[kʰalm]	[kʰam]	[kʰam]	[kʰam]
10. fish	[fɪš]	[fiš]	[fɪš]	[fɪš]	[fɪš]
11. push	[pʰuš]	[pʰuš]	[pʰuš]	[pʰuš]	[pʰuš]
12. bag	[bɛæg]	[bæg]	[bæg]	[bæg]	[bæg]
13. syrup	[sɪrəp]	[sərəp]	[sɪrəp]	[sɪrəp]	[sɪrəp]
14. greasier	[grisiər]	[ɡrisiər]	[grisiər]	[grizyər]	[grisiə]
15. a. source	[sɔrs]	[sors]	[suɔs]	[sɔs]	[sɔs]
b. sauce	[sɔs]	[sɔs]	[suɔs]	[sas]	[sas]
16. a. pin	[pʰɪn]	[pʰĩə̃n]	[pʰɪn]	[pʰĩə̃n]	[pʰɪn]
b. pen	[pʰɜn]	[pʰĩə̃n]	[pʰɜn]	[pʰĩə̃n]	[pʰɜn]
17. a. oil	[ɔyəl]	[ɔyl]	[ərəl]	[ɔyl]	[ɔyəl]
b. all	[ɔl]	[ɑl]	[ɔl]	[ɔl]	[ɔl]

351

Key Word	Speaker 1	Speaker 2	Speaker 3	Speaker 4	Speaker 5
18. a. fire	[fayər]	[fayr]	[fayə]	[fayr]	[fayr]
b. far	[far]	[far]	[faə]	[far]	[far]
19. a. Mary	[mɛri]	[mɛri]	[meyri]	[mɛri]	[mɛri]
b. merry	[mɛri]	[mɛri]	[mɛri]	[mɛri]	[mɛri]
c. marry	[mɛri]	[mɛri]	[mæri]	[mɛri]	[mɛri]
20. a. cot	[kʰat]	[kʰat]	[kʰat]	[kʰat]	[kʰat]
b. caught	[kʰɔt]	[kʰat]	[kʰɔt]	[kʰɔt]	[kʰɔt]

INTRODUCTION:
SOCIAL VARIATION

It is important to realize that a person's use of any particular dialect is not a reflection of his or her intelligence or judgment. Linguistically speaking, no one dialect is better, more correct or more logical than any other dialect. A dialect, remember, is simply any variety of a language, and all languages (or varieties of a language) are enormously complex, rule-governed systems and are equally effective systems of communication.

Even though any language is made up of numerous dialects, the popular notion persists that a language can be defined in terms of one "correct" or dominant dialect from which all other "inferior" or "sub-standard" dialects emerge. This dominant dialect is often called the *standard dialect*. It is the variety found in literature and generally used by political leaders, the media and speakers of the higher socioeconomic classes. Moreover, it is the variety taught in schools and to non-native speakers in language classes. Socially speaking, the standard dialect has become the dialect of prestige and power primarily because the prestige of a speech variety is dependent upon the prestige of the speakers who use it. In other words, the prestige of a language variety is wholly determined by society and generally by those in society who enjoy positions of power, wealth and education. But whatever its status in society, linguistically it is still just another dialect.

The standard dialect in the U.S. is called SAE or Standard American English. In actuality, SAE is not a well-defined variety but rather an idealization which even now defies definition due to lack of agreement on what exactly constitutes this variety. Nor is SAE a single, unitary, homogeneous dialect; instead it is comprised of a number of varieties. There are formal varieties, casual varieties, forms spoken with northern accents, midland accents, coastal New England accents and southern accents. As an example of this variety consider the speech of former President Jimmy Carter, who spoke SAE with a Georgia accent. Moreover, consider the "General American" pronunciation of President Reagan, who also speaks SAE. Finally, note the variety of SAE we speak, for example, at a job interview in contrast to the variety we use with close friends (often infused with slang).

In the U.S., where class consciousness is minimal, pronunciation is not terribly important. (After all, Jimmy Carter, as well as John Kennedy of Boston, made it to the White House, and Howard Baker of Tennessee made it to the U.S. Senate). But in Britain, where class divisions are more clearly defined and social mobility is more restricted, standard pronunciation or Received Pronunciation (RP), also known as BBC English or the "Queen's English", takes on the importance of standard grammar and vocabulary. In Britain, one's pronunciation and grammar become a marker of one's social status.

All dialects, then, which are not varieties of the standard are called, simply, non-standard (not substandard or inferior). For examples of some characteristics of one non-standard dialect, consider the following utterances:

> a) I <u>used to could</u> read.
> b) I <u>ain't no</u> girl now.
> c) He had a broken back_____was never set.
> d) Put some bakin' <u>sody</u> on it.
> e) I fell <u>upside of</u> the building.

Clearly, these sentences exhibit features that are non-standard — i.e. features that would disturb many teachers. Note the underlined parts of each sentence: a) a double modal, b) multiple negation, c) relative pronoun deletion, d) substitution of /i/ for the unstressed /ə/ of *soda* (sodi), and e) lexical substitution of 'upside of' for 'up against the side of'.

All of these features have been identified as characteristics of Appalachian English (AE), a dialect which, from its name, appears to be a regional dialect. It will be seen, however, that the description of this variety of English as a regional dialect is not the whole story. In fact, we will see that a dialect is rarely, if ever, just regional, social or ethnic but rather a combination of these factors.

Returning now to sentences (a) - (e): the speaker of these utterances was male, a native of a SE Ohio county which borders several Appalachian counties (and which experienced a post-WWII influx of Appalachian blue-collar workers), of lower socioeconomic status and, at the time of this study, 68 years old. Clearly, where he lives has something to do with his variety of speech. There are other variables, however. It has been determined that the pronunciation of *soda* in (e) represents a dying feature of AE and seems to be limited to older speakers. This feature, then, is not only geographically related but seems to be related to the age of the speaker as well. Moreover, studies indicate that in careful speech men tend to use more non-standard forms than women. So the fact that this speaker is male may also be a factor in his dialect. Finally, AE is a dialect which is related to socioeconomic status as well. That is, it is a dialect spoken primarily by low-income, rural speakers, a group to which our SE Ohio speaker belongs.

So while it is true that AE is a dialect generally restricted to that area designated as Appalachian by the Appalachian Regional Commission, it can also be seen that geographic region overlaps with at least three other (social) factors — age, sex and socioeconomic status. This sort of interaction among social and regional variables appears to be a fact about most, if not all, speech varieties.

The identification of any speech variety as a pure dialect — i.e. purely regional, purely social, etc. — requires the assumption of *communicative isolation* — in which a group of speakers forms a coherent speech community relatively isolated from speakers outside of that community. This type of isolation was perhaps once a possibility but, clearly, today is becoming increasingly rare because of such factors as social and geographic mobility, mass media, etc. What is more likely the case today is that a particular linguistic feature of a speech variety is influenced by not only regional factors but social and/or cultural variables as well — as we saw in the case of AE.

The branch of linguistics which studies linguistic behavior as affected by the interaction of these variables is called *quantitative sociolinguistics*. It makes use of statistical methods (e.g. random sampling) and measures (e.g. chi-square, t-test, analysis-of-variance, etc.) in data collection, analysis and interpretation. Sociolinguistics, in general, is concerned with language as a social and cultural phenomenon.

The files in this section on Social Variation look at the interaction of various social and cultural variables such as ethnicity (File 142 on Black English), social class, prestige and group identification (File 141), social attitudes (File 143), sex (File 144) and styles (File 145), and the effect of this interaction on linguistic features. Finally, File 146 looks at the phenomenon of slang usage in language.

SOCIAL VARIATION:
TWO CASE STUDIES

The following two case studies conducted by the linguist (and sociolinguist) William Labov, illustrate the interaction of regional and social factors in the formation of a speech community. Both studies were conducted in the early 1960s and are considered to be classic studies of the interaction of linguistic behavior and society.

1)   Martha's Vineyard, Massachusetts

In 1961, William Labov conducted a sociolinguistic study on the island of Martha's Vineyard, Dukes County, Massachusetts to investigate the impact of social patterns on linguistic variation or change. The linguistic feature chosen for analysis was centralization of the diphthongs /ay/ and /aw/ as in *why* and *wow,* respectively. That is, the vowel of the diphthongs was becoming centralized to /ʌ/ so that /ay/ was pronounced sometimes as /ʌy/, and /aw/ as /ʌw/ .

In a preliminary investigation Labov discovered that after all phonetic, prosodic and stylistic motivation had been accounted for there was still variation in speakers' use of centralized diphthongs. His subsequent study was designed to discover the motivation underlying this residual variation.

Toward this end, Labov set out to test a number of different variables. Was centralization related to geography? The island was, by universal consensus, divided into up-island (strictly rural) and down-island (consisting of the three small towns where 75% of the population lived). United States Census reports were consulted for information on the population distribution of the island.

Was ethnic group a factor in centralization? Native Vineyarders fell into four ethnic groups: 1) descendents of old English families, 2) descendents of Portuguese immigrants, 3) a small Indian population and 4) a miscellaneous group of a number of origins. Another group, not considered in the study, was the summer population.

Was the economic background and current economic situation of the island in any way correlated with linguistic behavior? In comparison to the rest of the state, the Vineyard had higher unemployment, lower average income, no industry, and thus was heavily dependent on the summer tourist trade. This heavy reliance on tourism was viewed by some islanders as a threat to independence. As a result many islanders displayed resistance to the summer mainlanders and took pride in being different from the tourists, the greatest resistance being felt in the rural up-island areas.

The results of the study revealed that, first of all, centralization was a linguistic feature of Martha's Vineyard, thus *regional* in character; that is, clearly, residents of the island pronounced /ay/ and /aw/ as / ʌy/ and /ʌw/ while summer tourists and mainland residents did not centralize the diphthongs. But within the island population, some residents centralized while some did not. Analysis of centralization by age indicated an increase with age, peaking between 31 and 45 years and then decreasing. This age group seemed to suffer the greatest degree of stress. They had chosen to remain on the island but employment opportunities were not abundant and yet they were expected to support families.

With respect to ethnic group, the Portuguese population which for years had been attempting to enter the mainstream of island life showed a high degree of centralization. Those of Indian descent, having battled discrimination from the other groups for more than 150 years and also desiring acceptance, displayed a high incidence of centralization as well. Additionally, high school students planning to go to college and then return to the island exhibited greater centralization than those going to college but not planning to return to the island.

The conclusion, then, is that the degree of centralization of the diphthongs /ay/ and /aw/ was clearly associated not only with region (i.e. Martha's Vineyard — and even up–island vs. down–island) but with group identification, as well; that is, how closely speakers identified with the island, wanting to remain, wanting to enter into the mainstream, seeing oneself as a Vineyarder and being proud of it, was positively correlated with degree of centralization.

2)   R-lessness in NYC

We have seen, in the study on Martha's Vineyard, how a linguistic feature of a "regional" dialect can be influenced by a social factor such as group identification. In yet another study conducted by William Labov we will see how a linguistic feature of a "regional" dialect, in this case New York City, can be influenced by other social factors — namely social class (or prestige) and speech style (careful or casual).

New York City speech is famous for its r-lessness — i.e. lack of /r/ in words such as *four, card, papers, here, there,* etc. A common misconception holds that there is a total lack of /r/ in such words for speakers of the dialect; yet we will see that this is indeed a misconception.

Labov began his study, on the basis of preliminary investigations, with the assumption that speakers vary in their use of /r/ according to their social status. The use of /r/ is associated with high prestige while the lack of /r/ is associated with low prestige. He set out to interview salespersons from large New York department stores on the further assumption that salespeople tend to reflect the prestige of their customers. If the customers ranked high in prestige, salespeople would "borrow prestige from their customers" *(Labov 1972:45)*. Similarly, if customers ranked low in prestige, salespeople would reflect this as well. Labov's hypothesis, then, was this: Salespeople from the highest prestige store would exhibit the highest incidence of /r/ in their speech while those from the lowest prestige store would exhibit the lowest incidence of /r/.

Labov selected for his study three department stores: Saks 5th Avenue (high prestige), Macy's (moderate prestige) and S. Klein (low prestige). Then, in spontaneous interviews, salesclerks were asked a question which elicited the answer *fourth floor,* this first elicitation representing casual speech. The interviewer then, pretending not to hear the answer, would lean forward asking the clerk to repeat the answer. The clerk repeated the answer but, this time, in careful speech under emphatic stress.

The results of the study showed a clear stratification of /r/ among the salespeople in support of Labov's hypothesis. In Saks 62% of the employees interviewed used all or some /r/, in Macy's 51% and in S. Klein 20%. Thus, the highest incidence of some or all /r/ was, predictably, in the high–prestige store.

What effect did style (careful or casual) have on the use of /r/? In casual response, 63% at Saks pronounced the /r/ of *floor,* 44% at Macy's and 8% at S. Klein; for the /r/ of *floor* in careful speech, 64% at Saks, 61% at Macy's (note the increase from 44%) and 18% at S. Klein. Note the very small difference between casual and careful speech for Saks (a difference of 1%) but the much greater difference between style for Macy's (a difference of 17%) and Klein (a difference of 10%). Moreover, the difference in careful speech between Saks and Macy's (3%) is very slight. This suggests that the /r/ for Macy's employees is the norm or target at which they aim, yet not the one they reach most of the time. Thus, while /r/ may disappear in casual speech it reappears in careful pronunciation. "In Saks we see a shift between casual and emphatic pronunciation but it is much less marked. In other words, Saks employees have more *security* in a linguistic sense." *(1972:52)*

What do these studies show? Essentially they illustrate the interaction of regional and social factors in forming speech communities and, moreover, show the importance of the social function of language behavior in the consideration of linguistic features and variation. These studies by Labov have sparked a great deal more research into the area of social dialects. Further suggested readings are Trudgill's study of English in Norwich (1971), Shuy, Wolfram and Riley's study of social dialects in Detroit (1967) and Labov's study of Black English (1972a).

SOCIAL VARIATION:

DIFFERENCES BETWEEN STANDARD AMERICAN ENGLISH AND BLACK ENGLISH

The aim of this file is to illustrate some of the features of Black English (BE) and to compare these features with Standard American English (SAE). But first we wish to point out several facts which are often overlooked in discussions of BE and its relationship with SAE.

1. The dialect known as Black English is actually an idealization, just as SAE is. BE is a cover term for features found in many different Black English varieties, although one variety may or may not exhibit all of these features. For example, BE is generally said to have the vowel [ə] after vowels where SAE has [r]. Thus SAE speakers would pronounce the word *door* [dor], whereas BE speakers are said to pronounce the same word as [doə]. This is not true of all BE varieties however. In fact in the speech of some Black English speakers there is no vowel [ə] corresponding to SAE [r] post-vocalically. These speakers pronounce the word *door* [do], and it is homophonous with the words *doe* and *dough*, which are also pronounced [do]. Thus we must recognize that there is no homogenous BE dialect, just as there is no homogenous SAE dialect.

2. BE is not (nor is any 'nonstandard' dialect) simply a collection of deviations from SAE. BE is a complete linguistic system itself. It has its own grammar, complete with its own phonological rules, morphological rules, syntactic rules, etc. just as any other dialect of English does.

3. BE does not differ greatly from SAE or from dialects of SAE. In fact, many of the BE features discussed below can be found in other varieties of SAE. Often the difference between BE and other varieties does not lie in a feature of BE that is totally lacking in other dialects, but rather in how *consistently* the feature shows up in each dialect. For example, all dialects of English simplify word final consonant clusters, but BE speakers do it more often and in more situations than, for instance, speakers of SAE.

4. Finally, it is important to note that BE is not spoken by all Blacks. Just as someone born in Boston does not 'automatically' become a speaker of Bostonian English, a Black person is not predestined to be a speaker of Black English. Whether or not a Black person is a speaker of BE depends on his/her environment. In fact, there are many Blacks whose speech is no different from the speech of Non-Blacks around them of the same social class or same region (e.g. Liverpool, England).

PRONUNCIATION DIFFERENCES

A. Reduction of Word-Final Consonant Clusters

All varieties of English may delete the final consonant of words which end in consonant clusters, but different varieties delete the final consonant in *different contexts*. In SAE for example the final consonant of a cluster can be deleted if the next word begins with a consonant, e.g. *best kind* [bɛs kʰaynd]. But if the next word begins with a vowel the final consonant cannot be deleted in SAE, e.g. *cold egg* [kʰoɬd ɛg] but never*[kʰoɬ ɛg]. BE is similar to SAE in that the final consonant can be deleted if the next word begins with a consonant but differs from SAE in that it permits deletion of a final consonant even if the next word begins with a vowel:

	SAE	*BE*
cold cuts	kʰoɬ kʰʌts	kʰoɬ kʰʌts

357

In English, the past tense is formed by the addition of a suffix, [t], [d] or [ə d], depending upon the final sound of the verb base. If the base ends in a consonant, the addition of this suffix may create a consonant cluster. e.g. *bake* [bek] *baked* [bekt]. Consonant clusters which are created by the addition of the past tense suffix are also subject to deletion. Note that this may give BE the appearance of lacking a past tense suffix because BE can delete final consonants in clusters even if they occur before a word beginning with a vowel:

	SAE	*BE*
burned my hand	bṛn may hænd	bṛn may hæn
burned up	bṛnd ʌp	bṛn ʌp
messed up	mɛst ʌp	mɛs ʌp

B. Loss of Final Dental Stop Consonants

Some varieties of BE permit the occasional loss of word-final [t] and [d] (even when not part of a consonant cluster). This occurs most frequently when the following word begins with a consonant:

	SAE	*BE*
good man	gʊd mæn	gʊ mæn
bad kids	bæd kɪdz	bæ kɪdz

C. Monophthongization

Where SAE has the diphthongs [ay] and [aw], BE often has the monophthong [a]. (A *monophthong* is a vowel which is not a diphthong.) The monophthong occurs especially where SAE has a diphthong word-finally (as in *now*) or where a voiced consonant follows (as in *side*), less often where a voiceless consonant follows (*like*). In fact, some BE speakers do not have the monophthong [a] before voiceless consonants at all but have a diphthong like SAE:

	SAE	*BE*
like	layk	layk or lak
now	naw	na
side	sayd	sad
time	tayːn	tam
kite	kayt	kayt or kat

D. Loss of Liquids

Word-initially, liquids are pronounced in all English varieties. In other contexts however, SAE [r] and [ł] correspond to BE [ə]. The most important of these contexts is the position following a vowel:

	SAE	*BE*
steal	stił	stiə
sister	sɪstr̩	sɪstə
nickel	nɪkł̩	nɪkə
here	hɪr	hɪə
dollar	daɫr̩	daɫə
more	mɔr	mɔə

Occasionally, in some BE varieties, [r] is completely eliminated when it occurs between vowels.

	SAE	*BE*
story	stɔri	stɔɪ
merry	mɛri	mɛɪ

E. Interdental Fricatives

The BE sounds which correspond to the SAE interdental fricatives do so in a fairly complex way. What sound occurs in BE depends mainly on the context, that is, the position in a word in which the corresponding SAE interdental fricative would occur.

1. Word-initial position. The initial sound in words like *the, they, that* is frequently pronounced as [d] in numerous BE varieties:

	SAE	*BE*
they	ðe	de
the	ðə	də

BE has numerous sounds corresponding to the SAE word-initial voiceless fricative [θ]. Some varieties have the same sound as SAE, i.e. [θ]. Other varieties vary between the use of [θ] and the dental stop [t].

	SAE	*BE*
think	θɪŋk	θɪŋk or tɪŋk
thin	θɪn	θɪn or tɪn

359

If the following consonant is [r], then there is another possible correspondence in BE, namely [f].

	SAE	BE
three	θri	fri
throat	θrot	frot

2. Medial position (in the middle of a word). Medially, BE [f] and [v] correspond to the SAE interdental fricatives with the following exception: the stop [t] may be substituted for [θ] if the following sound is a nasal consonant:

	SAE	BE
nothing	nʌθɪŋ	nʌfɪn
author	aθɾ	afa
brother	brʌðɾ	brʌvə
bathing	beðɪŋ	bevɪn
arithmetic	ərɪθmətɪk	rɪtmətɪk

3. Word-final position. The word-final correspondences are the same as the medial correspondences *except* that BE may substitute [t] for [θ] if the preceding sound is a nasal consonant.

	SAE	BE
tenth	tɛnθ	tɛnf or tɛnt
month	mʌnθ	mʌnf or mʌnt

DIFFERENCES IN SYNTAX

While the differences between BE and SAE which we have just considered are due to differences in rules of pronunciation, the two varieties of English also show differences in their grammatical systems. Basically, these differences are to be found in the verbal system, the pronominal system, in how sentences are negated, and in how questions are formed.

It is important to point out that some of the differences listed here do not really constitute differences in grammatical systems, because the difference in the use of a grammatical feature is the result of a pronunciation difference.

A. Past Tense

As we pointed out in section A of *Pronunciation Differences*, BE may delete the past tense suffix in a variety of contexts as the result of two pronunciation rules: (1) the reduction of word-final consonant clusters, e.g.,

SAE	*BE*
He walked [wakt] *to town yesterday.*	*He walked* [wak] *to town yesterday.*

or (2) the deletion of final dental stops, e.g.,

SAE	*BE*
Yesterday he played [pʲed].	*Yesterday he played* [pʲe].

B. Deletion of Auxiliary Verbs.

In all varieties of English, the auxiliary verbs *has, have, will, would, is,* and *are* can be contracted to [z, v, ɬ, d, z] and [r] respectively. In BE there are additional rules for removing these contracted auxiliary forms altogether. It is important to note that all the auxiliary verbs of SAE do exist in BE and that there are some contexts in which these auxiliaries *cannot be deleted*. If SAE cannot contract the auxiliary, then BE cannot contract or delete.

	SAE	*BE*
	How beautiful you are.	*How beautiful you are.*
but not	**How beautiful you're.*	**How beautiful you.*

On the other hand, wherever SAE can contract the auxiliary, BE may contract *or* delete:

SAE	*BE*
He's [hʲz] *as nice as Joe is.*	*He's* [hʲ] *as nice as Joe is.*
He's [hʲz] *going.*	*He's* [hʲ] *going.*
I've [ayv] *got it.*	*I've* [ay] *got it.*
He'll [hʲɬ] *miss you.*	*He'll* [hʲ] *miss you.*
He'd [hʲd] *be happy.*	*He'd* [hʲ] *be happy.*

C. Multiple Negation.

If we take a SAE sentence such as:

I had some lunch.

we can note that there are two ways to make this sentence negative. We can negate the verb:

I didn't have any lunch.

or we can negate the word *some*, by changing it to *no*:

>   *I had no lunch.*

While these two sentences may not be exact equivalents stylistically, they mean the same thing. The main point is that in SAE sentences are negated by performing one of these operations, but not both. In BE on the other hand, it is possible to do both in the same sentence. The result is *multiple negation*.

>   *I didn't have no lunch.*

In fact in BE this operation may be performed any number of times in one sentence. Consider, for example, the following SAE sentence:

>   *He doesn't know anything about anything.*

This sentence has been made negative in SAE by negating the verb. In BE it is possible to negate not only the verb but *both anys* in this sentence. As a result the BE equivalent may contain three negatives:

>   *He doesn't know nothing about nothing.*

D. Habitual *be.*

Another grammatical feature of BE which serves to distinguish it from SAE is a particular use of the verb *to be*. Compare the BE use of this form to that of SAE in the examples below:

BE   SAE

1) a. Sometime she *be* angry.   2) a. Sometimes she *is* angry.
   b. Whenever she *be* tired she *be*   b. Whenever she *is* tired she is
      cross.   cross.
   c. The coffee *be* cold.   c. The coffee *is* always cold.
   d. She *be* late everyday.   d. She *is* late every day.

The use of the uninflected *be* in 1) a–d indicates an event, action or state which is habitual or repeatable as opposed to momentary or permanent. Thus, 1) c — The coffee *be* cold — means that this is a recurring property of the coffee — i.e. the coffee is always cold. Notice that in SAE this habitual quality is indicated by adverbials like *always, sometimes, every day, whenever, right now,* etc., and if this adverbial is missing, generally the sentence loses this habitual property. Compare the following two sentences:

>   The coffee is <u>always</u> cold. (Habitual state)
>   The coffee is _____ cold. (Momentary state)

By contrast, in BE the uninflected verb *be* is sufficient for marking the habitual state (although it most often occurs with adverbials). Consider sentence 1)c again — The coffee be cold. With or without the adverbial, *always,* the meaning is clearly habitual because of the uninflected *be*. However, it would not be acceptable in BE to say *The coffee be cold right now* since the *be* conveys habitual while the adverbial *right now* indicates momentary. This is ungrammatical in BE. Rather, the grammatical form would be either *The coffee is cold* (as in SAE) or *The coffee cold* (see B, deletion of auxiliary verbs).

362

SOCIAL VARIATION: A SOCIOLINGUISTIC EXPERIMENT

When we meet a person for the first time, our perceptions of that individual tend to be formed by what we see and hear — i.e. the person's general appearance, facial expressions and gestures as well as speech characteristics like manner, accent, content, rate and voice volume. In other words, we tend to construct our impressions on the basis of all available information.

Numerous studies (Pear, Mehrabian and Weiner, Lambert, etc.) have demonstrated that speech characteristics clearly influence the way one is perceived by others — which is the focus of the following experiment. Based on a person's speech characteristics, we often form judgements about such personal characteristics as intelligence, social status, race, occupation and personality traits.

Instructions: In the tape accompanying this answer sheet you will hear the voices of four speakers. Basing your decision on what the speakers sound like, try to make judgements about them and about their speech by rating them on the following scales.

Speaker 1

a. Circle the number which corresponds most closely to your view of where this *speech sample* fits on each of the following scales:

```
            awkward - 1 - 2 - 3 - 4 - 5 - 6 - 7 - graceful
            relaxed  - 1 - 2 - 3 - 4 - 5 - 6 - 7 - tense
            formal   - 1 - 2 - 3 - 4 - 5 - 6 - 7 - informal
            thin     - 1 - 2 - 3 - 4 - 5 - 6 - 7 - thick
            correct  - 1 - 2 - 3 - 4 - 5 - 6 - 7 - incorrect
```

b. Now rate the *speaker* on each of the following scales:

```
            short    - 1 - 2 - 3 - 4 - 5 - 6 - 7 - tall
            nice     - 1 - 2 - 3 - 4 - 5 - 6 - 7 - nasty
            tough    - 1 - 2 - 3 - 4 - 5 - 6 - 7 - tender
```

c. What do you think this speaker does for a living?

d. What is the race of this speaker?

Speaker 2

a.
```
            awkward - 1 - 2 - 3 - 4 - 5 - 6 - 7 - graceful
            relaxed  - 1 - 2 - 3 - 4 - 5 - 6 - 7 - tense
            formal   - 1 - 2 - 3 - 4 - 5 - 6 - 7 - informal
            thin     - 1 - 2 - 3 - 4 - 5 - 6 - 7 - thick
            correct  - 1 - 2 - 3 - 4 - 5 - 6 - 7 - incorrect
```

b.
```
            short    - 1 - 2 - 3 - 4 - 5 - 6 - 7 - tall
            nice     - 1 - 2 - 3 - 4 - 5 - 6 - 7 - nasty
            tough    - 1 - 2 - 3 - 4 - 5 - 6 - 7 - tender
```

c. What does speaker do for a living?

d. Race of speaker?

Speaker 3

a. Circle the number which corresponds most closely to your view of where the *speech sample* fits on each of the following scales.

```
            awkward - 1 - 2 - 3 - 4 - 5 - 6 - 7 - graceful
            relaxed  - 1 - 2 - 3 - 4 - 5 - 6 - 7 - tense
```

                         formal   - 1 - 2 - 3 - 4 - 5 - 6 - 7 - informal
                         thin   - 1 - 2 - 3 - 4 - 5 - 6 - 7 - thick
                         correct   - 1 - 2 - 3 - 4 - 5 - 6 - 7 - incorrect

b.   Now rate the *speaker* on each of the following scales:
                         short   - 1 - 2 - 3 - 4 - 5 - 6 - 7 - tall
                         nice   - 1 - 2 - 3 - 4 - 5 - 6 - 7 - nasty
                         tough   - 1 - 2 - 3 - 4 - 5 - 6 - 7 - tender

c.   What do you think this speaker does for a living?

d.   What is the race of this speaker?

Speaker 4

             a.   awkward - 1 - 2 - 3 - 4 - 5 - 6 - 7 - graceful
                  relaxed - 1 - 2 - 3 - 4 - 5 - 6 - 7 - tense
                  formal   - 1 - 2 - 3 - 4 - 5 - 6 - 7 - informal
                  thin   - 1 - 2 - 3 - 4 - 5 - 6 - 7 - thick
                  correct - 1 - 2 - 3 - 4 - 5 - 6 - 7 - incorrect

             b.   short   - 1 - 2 - 3 - 4 - 5 - 6 - 7 - tall
                  nice   - 1 - 2 - 3 - 4 - 5 - 6 - 7 - nasty
                  tough   - 1 - 2 - 3 - 4 - 5 - 6 - 7 - tender

c.   What does the speaker do for a living?

d.   Race of speaker?

SOCIAL VARIATION
SEX DIFFERENCES
IN LANGUAGE USE

Differences In How Men and Women Speak: Genderlects

Everyone has intuitive feelings about what sounds "masculine" and "feminine" in speaking, even if s/he cannot point out exactly what it is that assigns the speech to one sex or the other. In certain languages very great differences have become entrenched between the sexes, so much so that speakers of other languages might think that men and women in that society were speaking totally different languages. The term *genderlect* has sometimes been used to refer to the two varieties of speech distinguishing the sexes, and a number of other subtle differences between the male and female genderlects have been noticed and described. For instance, in some languages certain consonants in men's speech correspond to different consonants in women's speech: this is true of Yukaghir, a northeast Asian language, where men use [ty] and [dy] as opposed to the women's use of [ts] and [dz] in the same words. These differences are consciously maintained, as shown by the fact that children of both sexes start out using women's forms, but as the boys reach manhood they switch to the male form.

Besides pronunciation differences, some languages have differences in vocabulary items: men and women use different words to refer to the same thing. In Zulu, for example, the word for "water" is *amanzi* for male speakers, but *amandabi* for females. At least some of these differences arise from *taboos* operating to prevent women from using masculine forms and vice-versa, but others are not so easy to explain. There does seem to be a clear trend in many languages, however, for the women's speech to be more conservative and closer to what is considered to be the "better" form of the language, while men are more *innovative* and make more changes in their speech.

The Speech of American Women

Speakers of American English do not make such noticeable distinctions between the sexes, but many subtle differences do exist. The linguist Robin Lakoff, has compiled a number of linguistic characteristics typical of women's speech, each contributing to various stereotypes that we have about women and their role in society.

If asked whether men or women were more polite, chances are we would answer women. If asked why we have that particular answer, we may say that being impolite is unladylike or we may say that women say 'please' and 'thank you' more often than men do. Linguistically, being polite goes beyond using a few simple words. It may involve avoiding certain words or using longer sentence constructions.

1. Compare:

   Oh, shit, you left the door unlocked again.
   Oh, dear, you left the door unlocked again.

   Who's the asshole who dented my fender?
   Who dented my fender?

2. How would you choose to ask someone to take you to school? How would your brother or sister make the same request?

   a. Take me to school.
   b. Please take me to school.
   c. Will you take me to school?
   d. Will you please take me to school?
   e. Would you take me to school?
   f. Would you please take me to school?

g. Wouldn't you take me to school?
h. Wouldn't you please take me to school?

Associated with the stereotype of politeness, we have the stereotype that women are more prescriptively correct than men are. In school, we tend to assume that boys are better at math and science and girls are better at history and English. Being good at English generally means knowing the prescriptive rules of English grammar.

3. Who do you think would be more likely to utter the following sentences, a man or a woman?

a.   Who are you referring to?
     To whom are you referring?

b.   Sue and I are taking Linguistics 201.
     Me and Sue are taking Linguistics 201.

Because of these stereotypes, many young girls and women suffer from math anxiety. Young boys and men, however, do not suffer from any equivalent "English anxiety". Why? Many men think that prescriptive grammar is trivial and therefore not worth worrying about. Since women worry about such matters, they have been stereotyped as being concerned with the small, unimportant issues in life. Contributing to this notion we find that women make lexical distinctions such as color differences which men might consider ridiculous.

4. Can you imagine two men having the following conversation?

A: I think that the beige curtains would look fine with our new sofa.
B: They look okay, but I think that the ecru ones would be a shade better.

One of the biggest stereotypes that we have about women is that they are indecisive. We can explain the prevalence of this stereotype based on the fact that numerous linguistic traits contribute to this assumption: the use of a question intonation with assertions, the use of tag questions which question a previous claim, the use of hedges which soften the impact of a statement, and the use of "so" instead of "very" to seemingly intensify a sentence.

5. Imagine uttering the following sentence, once using the declarative intonation pattern and once using the interogative pattern. How does the intonation pattern affect the meaning of the sentence?

Dinner will be ready at 6:00 this evening.

Dinner will be ready at 6:00 this evening.

6. Compare:
    a. Reagan is a great president.
    b. Reagan is a great president, isn't he?

7. Which would a women be more likely to utter?

    a. I hate driving across Illinois because it is boring.
    b. You know, I really sort of hate driving across Illinois because it's rather boring.

8. How does the use of "so" instead of "very" change the interpretation of a sentence?

   a. I like him very much.
   b. I like him so much.

Another stereotype that we have about women is that they exaggerate everything. If it is raining outside, we would expect a woman to say that it is pouring. If a child gets an F in some class he has taken, he can expect his mother to get hysterical over the matter as if the world were ending. (How would his father react?)

Exaggeration, however, goes beyond the meaning of sentences. Lakoff claims that women speak in italics, "emphasizing" parts of sentences that men would not ordinarily emphasize. As speculation, we can posit that women do this so that men will pay attention to them. This emphasis could be achieved through more animated intonation patterns or through word choice. We have a class of adjectives called empty adjectives which tell as much about the speaker's reaction to an object as it does about the object itself. Both men and women use these adjectives, but women alone use certain ones, ones which we could describe as more colorful.

9. Examine the following adjectives. Which would be used by women alone? Which by men? Which by both?

great, adorable, divine, charming, terrific, super, cool, sweet, lovely

While these characteristics are representative of women's speech, we should note that they only represent trends. Not all women will use all of these characteristics. Some will use more. Furthermore, some men will use some if not all of them. Because of the distribution of these characteristics across American society, Lakoff has suggested that they reflect power differences rather than gender differences. Think of the type of women likely to use these characteristics, and think of the type of men likely to use these same characteristics. Consider their similarities and differences as well as the relationship between social status and sex. Are these speech characteristics based on sex or power? What do you think?

Sexism and Its Reflection In American English

There is another way in which language reflects sex differences besides genderlects, and that is the way language is used to refer to women as opposed to men. Women have traditionally been considered subordinate to men, and this unequal status has been ingrained in language usage as well. Some specific examples will be described below.

Many terms have different or added connotations (shades of meaning) when used to refer to women as opposed to men, and the more negative meaning usually belongs to the female reference. Likewise, *pairs* of terms which should be equivalent in meaning instead are unequal, with the female term being less positive or simply less important or powerful than the male.

1. See if the following terms have different meanings for you if the blank is filled in with a man's name, rather than a woman's name.

   _____ is loose; _____ is easy; _____ is cold; _____ is fast; _____ is a pro.

2. Compare:
    "He is a tramp."/"She is a tramp."
    "He fought to defend his honor."/"She fought to defend her honor."
    "She mothered him."/"He fathered him."

3. The following terms are not equivalent, or if equivalent in one sense, have an added derogatory meaning possible for the female term, which you should try to identify:

governor/governess	sir/madam
master (mister)/mistress	star/starlet
major/majorette	buddy/sissy
bachelor/spinster	wizard/witch

Another reflection of the status of the sexes in society is that basic or generic terms and those used when sex is not to be specified are all masculine, never feminine.

4. Masculine pronouns are often used to refer to people of unknown sex or to both men and women generally:

> Everyone should do his best. (But note a common usage:
> "Everyone should do *their* best.")
> We will hire the best qualified person regardless of his sex.

5. The following masculine terms can all be generic, referring to people in general, while the feminine counterparts refer only to females:

man	fellowship	man the boats
manhood	masterpiece	you guys (to either men or
brotherhood	man-hours	women, or both together)

(compare woman, womankind, sisterhood, etc.)

6. Masculine words are often the bases from which feminine words are formed (see (3) for examples, and think of others yourself); this applies to proper names as well:

Paul/Paulette	Thomas/Thomasina
George/Georgette or	Robert/Roberta
Georgina	Louis/Louise

7. In married life, it is the man's name which is taken by the woman (though this is changing, and in other societies was never the case):

> Mrs. John Smith, *never* Mr. Mary Smith
> Dr. and Mrs. Smith, *but not (when the wife is a doctor)*
> Dr. and Mr. Smith *or* Mr. and Dr. Smith

A third reflection of sex roles in language involves the existence and interpretation of nouns commonly associated with one sex or another.

8. Some nouns are not specific as to sex, but because of the different roles assigned to men and women they are associated normally with one sex only:

My neighbor is a blonde.	(Is your neighbor male or female?)
My neighbor is a professor.	(Is your neighbor male or female?)

9. Some terms have to be specifically modified to refer to one sex because they are more often connected to the other sex:

nurse/male nurse	doctor/lady doctor
model/male model	career woman, *not* career man
prostitute/male prostitute	family man, *not* family woman

10. There are a number of (mostly derogatory) female terms for which there are no exact male equivalents:

> nymphomaniac (satyr, Don Juan)
> slut (*no* male slut)
> divorcee (*no male equivalent*)
> whore (*no male whore*)
> housewife (*but only recently* househusband)

11. A close look at terms of reference for men and women will reveal some interesting patterns connected to the connotations and values associated with the two sexes. In the two lists below, mark each word according the the "features" characterizing its meaning as follows: A = animal, O = object, F = food, S = explicitly sexual, Y = young, E = elderly, N = neutral connotations, P = positive for personality, activity, and intelligence, and D = derogatory. Some words will have *more than one* feature assigned to them; when you are done, compare the features for men and women and see if any noticeable differences can be found. Also, if any additional terms of reference occur to you, add them to the appropriate list and evaluate them in the same way.

I. Terms for Men

_____ man	_____ bloke	_____ sport	_____ jerk
_____ gentleman	_____ bozo	_____ stag	_____ nerd
_____ gent	_____ chap	_____ stud	_____ cat
_____ boy	_____ codger	_____ hunk	_____ creep
_____ guy	_____ dude	_____ jock	_____ redneck
_____ fellow	_____ galoot	_____ bum	_____ bastard
_____ lad	_____ geek	_____ bud	_____ son-of-a-bitch
_____ laddie	_____ geezer	_____ he-man	_____ prick
_____ brother	_____ old goat	_____ wimp	_____ asshole
	_____ schmuck	_____ m----- f-----	_____ c--- s-----

II. Terms for Women

_____ woman	_____ biddy	_____ skirt	_____ sexpot	_____ sweetie
_____ lady	_____ dame	_____ sugar	_____ bunny	_____ mama
_____ girl	_____ doll	_____ tomato	_____ pussycat	_____ kitten
_____ girlie	_____ damsel	_____ toots	_____ vixen	_____ belle
_____ lass	_____ crone	_____ wench	_____ peach	_____ vamp
_____ lassie	_____ dish	_____ hag	_____ heifer	_____ squaw
_____ sister	_____ honey	_____ tramp	_____ maid	_____ hen
_____ broad	_____ miss	_____ bitch	_____ maiden	_____ angel
_____ chick	_____ pet	_____ whore	_____ fox	_____ nymph
_____ babe	_____ piece	_____ tease	_____ witch	_____ cookie
_____ baby	_____ quail	_____ harpie	_____ catch	_____ hussy
_____ sweetie pie	_____ nympho	_____ darling	_____ dumpling	_____ dog
			_____ tart	_____ chippie

Lakoff, Robin (1975) *Language and Woman's Place*. New York: Harper and Row, Publishers.

SOCIAL VARIATION IN SPEECH STYLES

You probably don't speak to your grandmother exactly as you do to the neighbor's two-year-old, or to your minister as to your roommate. You wouldn't write your reason for requesting a loan in exactly the same terms on a bank form as in a letter to your brother. While you may be aware of making a special effort to produce your best language along with your best manners for some people — a prospective employer, for example, or a prospective in-law — you usually change styles automatically and effortlessly, without giving it a thought. In fact, most people change styles so unconsciously that they may be unaware that they ever do. Some people deny that they *have* different styles, on the grounds that it would be insincere — a form of play-acting — to speak differently to different people. In reality, adapting your spoken style to your audience is like choosing the right tool for a job. You can't eat boullion with a fork or sirloin steak with a spoon. And you may have eaten your peas with a spoon when you were three years old, but you wouldn't feel comfortable doing it a dinner party now. If your four-year-old cousin asks you why your begonia needs light, you can't explain it with the one word "photosynthesis" but you should include that word in your answer to the same sort of question on a botany exam. You may tell your mechanic that one of the wires seems to have come loose from that funny looking black thing, and he may respect the depths of your ignorance by replying to you in similar terms, but if he talks that way to his assistant, you may begin to doubt his competence. Common sense makes you choose simple words to speak to a small child and use appropriate technical words, if you know them, to speak to an expert about his field. "Putting on airs" is not the only way to change your speech style, and it isn't even one of the most common.

Various speech styles differ in at least three major ways: in vocabulary, syntax and phonology. Probably the most obvious of these and the one we are most aware of is vocabulary. Almost everybody learns "bad words" at an early age. Four-year-olds come home proudly from pre-school with brand new words like "son-of-a-bitch," and even if they can be persuaded not to use their store of adult shockers seem endlessly fascinated by their own taboo words like "wee-wee" and "poo-poo." Although nearly everybody outgrows this stage, most of us do occasionally use some kind of "bad language"—some words or expressions we wouldn't want to say in front of the primmest person we know. Because of the forbidden aura around words that have to do with sex and excretion on the one hand and God and religion on the other, we are particularly aware of this part of our vocabulary. We sometimes talk as if it were the whole of speech, in fact, "Watch your language!" usually just means "cut out the naughty words." In practice, however, many other sectors of our vocabulary change with our speech style as well.

In addition to "bad language" we often have a set of words or phrases that belong to "best language," a set we keep for our most formal and impressive occasions as we might keep the best china. Not everybody has best china, of course, but most of us do have best language. You may find that you save your best for formal writing. Look for it in term papers or English compositions or the kind of description of your aims and ambitions you often have to write on college or graduate school applications. Poetic words like *myriad* or scholarly-sounding ones like *multiplicity* might belong to this section of vocabulary.

In between these two levels, nearly everybody uses some technical language, or *jargon*. Many of us are more or less fluent in a number of different jargons. Every job and every field of study has some technical terms of its own. So does every hobby and every sport. Many technical terms escape from their own fields and come to be used generally. The space program has given us all "countdown," "A-ok," and "blast-off," for example, and even people with no interest in baseball know how it feels to "strike out." Within its own area, technical jargon is clear, expressive and economical; for outsiders, much of it usually remains incomprehensible. Both of these characteristics can be useful. Thieves' argot was a technical language invented to keep outsiders from overhearing anything useful. Other professional jargons are sometimes used to confuse or impress people outside the profession. "Rhinitis" sounds a great deal more impressive than "a runny nose." "Rhinoplasty" sounds a lot more complicated and serious than "nose job." When the dermatologist says you have "dermatitis" it sounds like a real diagnosis by an expert; if he called it a "rash" you wouldn't be so sure that he knew more about it than you did.

Besides technical language, most people speak at least two levels of slang: the nearly neutral everyday language that's just a little too informal for letters of application and the like (*fridge* and *t.v.* belong to this vocabulary) and the more specialized, perhaps shorter-lived, "slangier" slang of their own particular group at this particular time. You might call the two sets "common slang" and "in-group slang." "Get off my case" is an example of the latter set where I am now; it means approximately "stop nagging at me." Some slang is very short-lived, like "Twenty-three skidoo!", but some lasts long enough to become accepted in the stuffiest circles. "Fan" appeared as a slangy shortening of "fanatic" in the late 16th Century, and today we have fan letters, fan clubs, and even fan magazines for all kinds of things from baseball stars to rock groups. Slang, like technical language, can be used to keep insiders together and to exclude outsiders.

Pronunciation

We may be less aware of changing our way of pronouncing things than of changing our choice of words, yet our phonology does change with style. A number of studies have been made of "casual" or "fast speech" phonology. For people who are not linguists, the most obvious feature of casual speech is probably "dropping your g's" in words which end in *-ing*. We all know about this, because most of us have had teachers who told us not to do it. Even people who spend their lives telling other people not to, at least occasionally "drop their g's" in expressions like *going fishing*. (Linguists always use quotation marks around that phrase about the g's because what happens phonetically is a change from [ŋ] to [n], with no [g] involved in either pronunciation.) If you listen very carefully, you will find that even people you think *never* drop their g's (you may be one of them) do so sometimes, and even people you think drop them all put in a few. Men are generally said to drop more g's than women, and boys to drop the very most.

People often disapprove officially of casual speech patterns and "sloppy" or "careless" speech, but they're really economical and efficient when used where they belong. With close friends a very careful, formal style is wounding—as rude as the most casual speech style would be addressed to a prospective employer we'd just met. We usually enunciate very carefully with our families only when we're angry and want to show the distance we feel from them.

You may have been taught that it's informal to use contractions, but this is really only true of written style. In speech it is extremely formal, even stilted, not to use contractions. The ordinary contractions like *he'll, she'd, won't*, and *can't* are neutral in style. In tag questions, like "Herbert could do that, couldn't he?", the contraction of *not* is almost obligatory. "You are studying English, are you not?" could only be a non-native speaker's question—or one by a native speaker being extremely highbrow. In really casual speech, we make non-standard contractions, in addition to the ordinary ones. In ordinary fairly careful style, we say "he'd" for "he would" or "he had." In casual speech, we say "he'd've" for "he would have," and in the most informal style, that becomes "he'd'a." A sentence like "It would have been funny" can come out as [ɪD əv bɪn fʌnI], with "it would" reduced to "it'd" and then "id," and "have" reduced to something that sounds just like "of." Children often write *of* for *have* because they sound the same in casual speech.

Syntax

The process of contraction is casual speech leads to syntactic changes as well as phonological ones. Some words seem to be phonologically eroded to almost nothing, and others are deliberately dropped. We use more sentence fragments and leave out more unnecessary words. *I* and *you* as subjects tend to disappear, especially when they would be the first word of a sentence. The verbs *to have* and *to be* drop out, especially when they are auxiliaries, rather than main verbs.

Some types of sentences are usually reserved for casual styles. One process which is characteristically informal is topicalization, which pulls the object to the front of the sentence: "That I'd like to see!" Another is called the *alpha tag*. An ordinary tag question, called a *flip tag,* is a statement with a question "tagged" on: "You know Rosie, don't you?" or "You don't want any more, do you?" These questions have negative tags ("don't you") with positive sentences, positive ones ("do you") with negative sentences. The alpha-tag is a positive tag added to a positive sentence: "You're buying a Borzoi, are you" as opposed to "You're buying a Borzoi, aren't you?" Ordinary tag questions are conversational, but neutral in style. Alpha tags are markedly informal. They may be pointedly sarcastic, or they may just be conversational openers.

In casual speech we may use constructions we would avoid in writing or in speaking to an audience. "Bill and me are going" is normal in casual speech for many people who would write "Bill and I." "Where's it at?" is good casual style for many who would say "Where is it?" if they were speaking carefully. I usually say only "who" in conversation, but I often write *whom*, even in letters to friends.

There may be a number of constructions which we save for writing or for very formal speech, which don't fit our everyday usage. One of these is the subjunctive. The subjunctive is technically a verbal *mood* contrasted with the indicative. The indicative is prescribed for statements of fact, and the subjunctive for wishes, suppositions and other non-factive uses. Many people now don't use the English subjunctive at all, or if they do, reserve it for their most formal style. Only the "contrary-to-fact" subjunctive in clauses like "If I were rich" occurs at all regularly in speech or informal writing, and even that seems to be getting rarer. Forms of the subjunctive other than *were* in *if* clauses usually occur only in fixed phrases of extreme formality, such as a lawyer's "if it please the Court" or a written petition's "we hereby request that this *be* done." Sentences which begin with a subjunctive element—"Be he live or be he dead, I'll grind his bones to make my bread!"—are almost never heard in modern speech, and rarely seen in writing.

The use of passive rather than active constructions is generally formal, and so is a very *nouny* style. For example, that last sentence would sound less formal written this way: When you use passive constructions rather than active ones and write in a very *nouny* style, you usually sound formal. Both passives and nominalizations (nouns made from verbs, as *nominalization* is made from *nominalize*) can be used (a passive) to avoid putting in pronoun agents, which cause trouble of various kinds. The first sentence of this paragraph contains no pronouns and no *agents* or *actors*. Some handbooks and some teachers advise writers to avoid the pronoun *I* in any but the most informal writing. But the "editorial we" can be confusing, especially in articles or books with more than one author, where it might be a real *we*. Writers also sometimes include their readers in a *we* ("As we will see again in a later chapter . . .") and sometimes do not ("We find this solution unsatisfactory, for reasons which we will discuss below."). Writers may eliminate *we* as well as *I* by the extremely formal device of writing third-person phrases like "in the opinion of the present author" to avoid saying "I think." (*I think* that sounds awful, so this is probably a good time to repeat that "most formal" and "best" aren't necessarily the same.)

These are just a few ways in which speech styles can and do differ. To test out the hypothesis that they *do* differ in these ways, try some of the following exercises:

1. Have a friend read the series of numbers 15 — 70 — 21. Then have him/her count from 69 to 80. Use a sheet of paper with columns headed "unassimilated" and "assimilated." For each time your friend says a clear "seventy" with three syllables, a *v*, and an *n*, make a check in the first column; for each time s/he says something different make a check in the second column. Try to describe or transcribe the pronunciation you actually hear.

2. Suppose that you have a very close relationship with someone that you plan to marry. How would you introduce your fiance(e) to the following people under the following circumstances: a) your grandmother, at a family dinner, b) your best friend from high school, at a beer party-picnic; c) the dean of your college, at a reception for a visiting scholar; and d) a group of 8-year-olds in a Saturday morning class you've been working with? See how many differences you can find in the forms of introduction you can come up with. Then compare your list with a friend's to see if they differ significantly.

3. See if you can get through some whole service encounter — buying lunch at a cafeteria, buying a pair of shoes, etc. — without making any requests marked by *please,* but without being rude. Does it make any difference?

SOCIAL VARIATION
SLANG

The very word 'slang' summons up images of four-letter words, of sloppy speech, of admonitions from parents and teachers not to say certain things, of words and expressions you might use with your friends but not with your parents, in your dorm but not in a job interview, and the like. These images give us a good first approximation of what slang is, for they all revolve around language used in particular *contexts,* as defined by the speakers participating in a conversation (e.g. you and your parents versus you and your friends), or by the general situation in which the conversation takes place (e.g. in your room with friends versus in a job interview with someone you have never met before). In a similar way, most speakers of English would agree that *can it!* is a slang way of telling someone to be quiet, or that *beat it!* is a slang expression for telling someone to leave, but at the same time, these expressions have perfectly ordinary and non-slangy uses in different contexts (e.g. *can it* in the context of talking about what to do with a salmon or tuna you have just caught, or *beat it* in a recipe telling you what to do with the egg you have just cracked into a bowl.) Thus context is the key to understanding what constitutes slang usage, with slang essentially being very informal, colloquial language, often marked by highly colorful usage (see the example), metaphorical extensions of meaning and characteristic word formation processes such as *clipping* (i.e. *rents* for *parents, brary* for *library, Trans* for *Trans Am,* etc.)

The context can also refer to a set of shared interests among the participants in a conversation, or more generally in a situation in which there is sustained contact among people. Thus, people who share the same occupation or hobby often develop terms and expressions that outsiders cannot easily interpret. If you have ever overheard two auto mechanics talking about working on a car or two computer hackers talking about their specialty you can understand this aspect of slang. Such occupationally defined slangs are referred to as *jargons.* Often, a word or expression that has an origin in a jargonistic slang escapes from that context into general use; in recent years we have seen that with *bottom line* (originally a technical term in reference to business reports), with *hardware/software/system* (all from computer usage), and less recently with words like *cool* (originally used to refer to a type of jazz).

This side of the phenomenon of slang shows us that it is very much an in-group/out-group phenomenon; slang (and language in general, according to sociolinguists) can serve to define membership in a group, whether it is the group of people in a certain job, on a certain dorm floor, with a particular hobby or interest, of a certain age (as opposed to others of a different age), etc. Learning the appropriate slang is a key to entrance in a particular group, but in order for the group to preserve its closed status, sometimes the slang must change. To a certain extent, this aspect of slang accounts for the fairly high turnover and renewal of slang expressions. Similarly, the fact that slang often injects a bit of color into otherwise ordinary language means that as the color fades, so to speak, new expressions will be needed. In this way, we see that slang in a sense is the linguistic counterpart of fad behavior; just as hula hoops came and went (and perhaps are coming back again), certain slang expressions have come and gone over the years, some to return again, but others never to. At the same time, though, some slang expressions are remarkably resilient and persistent, and survive over long periods of time. The expression *beat it* (for leaving) was used in Shakespeare's time, for instance.

To sum up: slang responds to a need in people to be creative in their language use and to show group membership (often unconsciously) through their language use. These observations, likening slang to some feature in the nature of being human and of interacting with humans, explain why slang is found in all languages and has been found at all times (even in Ancient Greek of 2,500 years ago, for instance). Slang is thus a legitimate sociolinguistic phenomenon and can be studied by linguists as such.

To give you some idea of the richness and variety of slang we give below a collection of terms for two popular activities at many universities: drinking and throwing up. As you look through these lists, compare your own current slang usage with that reported here. Which terms are new to you? Can you see how they may have originated? Why do you suppose there are so many different terms for these activities?

THROWING UP

puke	talk to Ralph	
barf	talk to Earl	
harf	pray to the porcelain god	
yack	kiss the porcelain god	
blow chunks	kneel before the	
blow lunch	porcelain queen	
blow chow	drive the porcelain bus	
chunk cookies	drive the Buick	
fumble	sell the Buick	
boot it	sell the Porsche	
double fault	yawn in technicolor	
play tag		
lose your luggage		
eat backwards		

GETTING DRUNK

get wasted	loose
get stiff	fried
snockered	zoned
crocked	ripped
slushed	buzzed
stoned	tanked
shit-faced	lubered
hazed	rimmed
z'd	aced
plowed	pound a few
blasted	catch a cold
plastered	wear the leash
loaded	

ITEMS FOR DISCUSSION

1. The following are some popular myths about slang. See if you can explain what about them is misconceived especially from the viewpoint established in the above discussion of what slang is:

    a. Slang is bad and degrades the user and the language itself.
    b. Only young people use slang.
    c. There are languages that have no slang.

2. Make up your own list of jargon slang by examining the terms and expressions that are associated with your major (or hobby or whatever). Compare your list with that of someone else in your major (or hobby or whatever) and with someone not in that group. Does the in-group/out-group designation applied to slang hold here?

3. Look through a dictionary of slang (and there are several, for example S. Flexner & H. Wentworth, *A Dictionary of American Slang*) and see what the origins of some of your favorite slang expressions are.

4. We have seen that what is sometimes referred to as sloppy speech is actually a result of the application of natural phonological processes common in fast speech. How might slang likewise be treated as something natural in language?

INTRODUCTION: HUMAN COMMUNICATION BEYOND LANGUAGE

FILE
150

It is easy for us to view human communication as being achieved by language alone. A moment's reflection, however, makes us realize that things are not as simple as that. On the one hand, we may use much more than words when we communicate. We pepper our speech with vocal noises that can hardly be called words. We accompany our speech with various movements of the body, the head, the hands. We also communicate subtle meanings by manipulating the space between us and the other participants in the conversation. On the other hand, we do not have to use words to communicate. We can just gesticulate, use facial expressions and make various types of vocal noises. In extreme cases, we can communicate by not doing anything at all, by silence. Communication by nonlinguistic means we can nonlinguistic communication. We find that nonlinguistic communication either complements language or effects communication on its own.

Despite the prevalence of human nonlinguistic communication, we are most of the time unaware of it. It stays primarily in the background of our communicative situations. Part of the reason for this is perhaps due to its very familiarity. It comes into sharp relief, however, when we observe people from other cultures, who have nonlinguistic communicative behaviors much different than our own. Hindi speakers shake their heads in consent while we nod. The Italian's 'Goodbye' looks like our 'Come here.' Interpretation of space is different for Arabs than it is for Americans, to give just a few examples.

In recent years interest in nonlinguistic communicative phenomena has greatly increased, so much so that they now constitute the domains of systematic investigation in their own rights. The investigation of various vocal noises typically associated with speech falls under the study of *paralinguistic* phenomenon, or *paralanguage*. The study of body movements and gestures is called *kinesics*, or *body language*, in more popular terms. Finally, the study of interpersonal space in communicative situations constitutes *proxemics*. Despite what their names may misleadingly suggest, it is difficult to maintain that all these nonlinguistic ways of communication constitute language in any real sense. Nonetheless, there are several aspects of these phenomena that are shared by human languages, and this fact provides some of the rationale for talking about them in a book about human language. As in the case of animal communication, if we can show in what ways these nonlinguistic ways of communication are similar and in what ways unlike human language, we can learn more about the nature of language itself.

What are some of the things that suggest an affinity between these nonlinguistic communicative phenomena and language? First, there are regular patterns to be observed in these behaviors, just as there are regularities in language. We notice that these communicative behaviors are consistent and predictable to a large extent, both in the same individual and across the same culture. If there were no regularities, there would hardly be any reason to investigate them. Second, these behaviors can hardly be explained purely on behavioristic and physiological grounds. In other words, they are not instinctive responses. In this respect, they differ from the more instinctive animal signals and human vocalisms. Consider the difference between the sounds of sneezing and of expressing surprise. While it is true that both are reponses to something, the former is instinctive and invariant across cultures whereas the latter only looks instinctive and varies from culture to culture. Where in English we say *'Oops'*, in Chinese it is *'Aya'*. In fact, many of the behaviors we are concerned with here are arbitrary and conventional, just as language is arbitrary and conventional. The appearance of instinctiveness and naturalness is quickly dismissed by the realization that different cultures have different behaviors for the same meaning. Just like language, the nonlinguistic behavior we are concerned with here is learned, together with the acquisition of language. Very young children do not have a codified way of expressing surprise as adults do; they do not use the same vocal noise as adults in appreciating food, for example. Indeed, these nonlinguistic behaviors share the feature of traditional transmission with language.

The present section briefly surveys the exciting endeavors in the study of nonlinguistic human communication and reports on some of the major findings that have come out of them. File 151 discusses paralanguage, File 152 deals with body language, and finally, File 153 deals with proxemics.

HUMAN COMMUNICATION BEYOND LANGUAGE: PARALANGUAGE

A. In her book *Paralanguage and Kinesics*, Mary Ritchie Key has defined *paralanguage* as (p. 10):

> . . . . some kind of articulation of the vocal apparatus, or significant lack of it, i.e. hesitation between segments of vocal articulation. This includes all noises and sounds, as well as a large variety of speech modifications, such as quality of voice (sepulchral, whiney, giggling), extra high-pitched utterances, or hesitations and speed in talking.

B. Some examples of various sorts of paralinguistic phenomena:

1. Extra-speech sounds
   a. Hesitation noises: *uh*, *oh*, *ah*
   b. Imitative sounds (onomatopoetic words), primarily of animal sounds — *moo*, *woof* — and noises (*boing*, *pow*)
   c. Interjections of many sorts: *ulp*, *tsk tsk*, *ouch*, *aargh*, *aah*,
      ŏh oh [ˀʌˀo] of dismay, *unhŭnh* [ƛ̃ hƛ̃ˀ], and *um hm* [m̩ hm̩] 'yes', *ununh*
      [ƛ̃ˀƛ̃ˀ] 'no'
   d. Calls: *hey*, *soo-ee* (to pigs)
   e. Non-language sounds: whistles, kisses, yells, hums, laughs, sobs

2. Speech modifications

   a. Tempo, phrasing, and pause: drawled speech, jerky, hesitating.
   b. Loudness: soft, loud, very loud
   c. Pitch levels: high, deep
   d. Vowel quality: whisper, falsetto, breathy voice, adenoidal (denasalized) voice, nasalized speech, labialized 'baby' talk
   e. Expressive intonations: high rise indicating surprise or puzzlement, extended level intonation level indicating unsureness
   f. Clarity of articulation: mumbling, extra-precise speech

C. Paralinguistic phenomena may be:

1. Characteristic of individual speakers (different people have different laughs, some people have a more adenoidal voice quality than others, some use a higher pitch register), or associated with certain group differences (for American males, extra-precise speech is considered effeminate; in different parts of the country, farmers use different calls to cows in the pasture — among them, *boss(ie)* from New England to northern Pennsylvania, *co-ee* from Delaware south along the east coast; *sook(ie)* elsewhere in the east), or common to virtually all speakers of the language (the hesitation noise *uh* is used practically everywhere in the English-speaking world, and it is different from the hesitation noises in French, German, Russian, etc.)

2. Appropriate only in certain contexts or styles (in English, labialized 'baby talk' is appropriate only for affectionate couples, in addressing infants or pets, or as a sarcastic accusation of babyishness; *únhunh* 'no' is used in informal styles and would not be appropriate for, say, job interviews or Presidential press conferences), or widely usable in

different contexts and styles (the hesitation noise *uh* is appropriate on nearly all occasions).

3. Clearly indicative of a specific meaning, in a broad sense of *meaning* (*brr* is used in English to convey that the speaker is cold, *um hm* means 'yes', and some English speakers use nasalization to convey sarcasm), or only vaguely associated with some use or effect (particular laughs do not have an identifiable meaning associated with them, nor does speaking softly or in a low pitch register).

D. Paralanguage is primarily distinguishable from language by being independent of linguistic elements — either occurring separately (*tsk tsk*, calls to animals), interrupting otherwise unified stretches (hesitation noises), or occurring simultaneously with them (speech modifications in general); in each case, some meaning or effect is conveyed *in addition to* that of the linguistic elements that may be present. Typically, the paralanguage associated with a language uses the capabilities of the human vocal tract in ways not exploited in that language; paralanguage may involve combinations of sounds that do not otherwise occur in the language (English *boing*), or sounds that do not otherwise occur in language (English *tsk tsk*; note that some Bantu languages employ the clicks in ordinary words), or even sounds that occur in no known language (whistling does not occur in the ordinary vocabulary of any known language), as well as sounds that do occur in the language but are not phonemes of that language (English *unhunh* [ʌ̃hʌ̃ʔ] always contains [ʌ̃], as in *hunt,* [hʌ̃nt], and [ʔ], as in many speakers' pronunciation of *hatrack* [hæʔræk] — yet in the ordinary English vocabulary the difference between [ʌ̃] and [ə] is not significant, nor is the difference between [ʔ] and [t̸].)

HUMAN COMMUNICATION BEYOND LANGUAGE: KINESICS: BODY LANGUAGE

Recent interest in body language has led many people to want to interpret body movements categorically. That is, every time we see a man or woman cross his or her legs in a certain way, we would like to be able to say "Aha! That person is interested in a 'close encounter of the intimate kind'." We don't know enough about body movements, however, to be able to make such judgments of behavior with any degree of accuracy.

The study of body movements is called *kinesics*. Since body movements always occur in specific contexts, which help determine the meanings of these behaviors, the study of kinesics must take context into account. We can tell very little, if anything, about the meaning of any sort of body movement without knowing such things as: where, when, and with whom the behavior occurred.

Five types of movements have been described in detail. These are: 1) *emblems*, 2) *illustrators*, 3) *affect displays*, 4) *regulators*, and 5) *adaptors*.

Emblems are nonverbal behaviors that translate words or phrases rather directly. In other words, emblems are nonverbal substitutes for specific words or phrases in a language. For example, in our culture we have: an "okay"sign, a "peace" sign, a "come here" sign, a hitchhiker's sign, a "knock on wood" sign, an "up yours" sign, and many others. Emblems may seem inherently meaningful but they are as arbitrary as any word in our language. As a consequence emblems change over time and they differ from culture to culture. Emblems can be used to supplement or reinforce a verbal message or they can be used in place of a verbal message.

Illustrators are nonverbal behaviors that accompany and literally illustrate a verbal message. They include such movements as nodding one's head to indicate "yes", shaking one's head to indicate "no", using one's hand or head in an upward movement to indicate "let's go up", and describing geometric figures like circles or squares while making similar hand movements. Illustrators are so well learned that it can be extremely difficult to reverse them or to use them inappropriately (e.g., try saying "yes, I understand" while shaking your head "no").

Illustrators are somewhat less arbitary than emblems. Many of the same gestures mean the same thing in other cultures but this is not always the case. Illustrators are less subject to change than are emblems. The emblem for "peace" (formerly "victory"), for example, might mean something quite different or nothing at all in a few years since the gesture is already becoming a thing of the past. It is far more difficult to imagine that the meanings associated with nodding or shaking one's head and other illustrators will change in the near future.

Affect displays are movements of the facial area that convey emotional meaning. These are more independent of verbal messages than are emblems or illustrators and are also under less conscious control. Affect displays convey emotions such as anger, fear, happiness, eagerness, fatigue, and many others. They may be used unintentionally (our faces often "give us away") or used intentionally (e.g., most of us have tried to "look surprised" when we aren't surprised at all). While we do not often consciously control our affect displays, they can be controlled. Actors and poker players are often very adept at controlling their facial movements.

Nonverbal behaviors that monitor, maintain, or control the behavior of another individual are called *regulators*. Regulators serve to inform another person what we expect or want them to do. Examples are: nodding one's head, pursing one's lips, adjusting eye focus, using paralinguistic sounds, leaning forward, moving toward the street (to suggest to the person that it is the time to cross the street), or walking away from someone. Frequently we are not consciously aware that we are using regulators or being regulated, though these non verbal behaviors are an important part of communication.

Adaptors are nonverbal behaviors that serve some kind of personal need. Some adaptors involve the manipulation of material things such as movements associated with fixing a car, changing a tire, sewing a dress, cooking a meal, etc. Other adaptors involve using objects as "props" (i.e., the objects are not meant to serve any kind of instrumental function at the moment). Examples would be "toying" with or chewing on a piece of chalk, a pencil, a tie, a cigarette, or a necklace.

Some adaptors like grooming, cleaning, excretory, and autoerotic activities serve very personal needs and are not intended to communicate anything. Examples of these would be: picking one's nose or teeth, scratching various parts of the body, combing one's hair, and similar activities. In public, however, some adaptors cannot be used at all and others must be modified severely. Consider, for example, the lengths one must go to to discreetly scratch certain body parts in public.

Adaptors can be used to communicate things about oneself such as machismo, femininity, social status, group identity and self image. These behaviors are for the most part learned and vary considerably both among and within cultures. Adaptors are perhaps some of the most intriguing non verbal behaviors since they can convey far more about a person than his or her verbal behavior.

Exercises:

Many nonverbal behaviors have not just one possible meaning, but many possible meanings. Meanings vary not only among cultures, but also from one individual to another and from one situation to another.

What *might* each of the following nonverbal behaviors mean? Give as many possible meanings as you can.

1. a smile	12. looking at clock/watch during conversation
2. a frown	13. looking into the distance
3. arms folded	14. standing very close to other person
4. nodding head	15. staring at another person
5. shaking head	16. crying
6. fidgeting in seat	17. flushed face/neck
7. swinging foot	18. avoiding eye contact with other person
8. loud voice	19. turning away from other person(s)
9. soft, low voice	20. leaning forward over desk or table
10. laughing	21. covering eyes with hand
11. speaking very slowly	22. slumping/slouching in seat

HUMAN COMMUNICATION BEYOND LANGUAGE: PROXEMICS: SOCIAL DISTANCE

Birds and mammals not only have territories which they occupy and defend against their own kind but they have a series of uniform distances which they maintain from each other. These have been classified as flight distance, critical distance, and personal or social distance. Man, too, has a uniform way of handling distance. Four of these distances used in social situations are: intimate, personal, social, and public (each with its close and far phases). How people are feeling toward each other is a decisive factor in the distance used. Thus people who are very angry or emphatic about the point they are making will move in close; they "turn up the volume", as it were, by shouting. Similarly — as any woman knows — one of the first signs that a man is beginning to feel amorous is his move closer to her. If the woman does not feel similarly disposed she signals this by moving back.

INTIMATE DISTANCE

At intimate distance, the presence of the other person is unmistakable and may at times be overwhelming because of the greatly stepped-up sensory input and unmistakable involvement with another body.

Close phase (distance: 0 to six inches)

This is the distance of love-making and wrestling, comforting and protecting. Physical contact or the high possibility of physical involvement is uppermost in the awareness of both persons. The detail that can be seen at this distance is extraordinary. Vocalization at intimate distance plays a very minor part in the communication process, which is carried mainly by other channels. A whisper has the effect of expanding the distance. The vocalizations that do occur are largely involuntary.

Far phase (distance: six to eighteen inches)

Much of the physical discomfort Americans experience when foreigners are inappropriately inside the intimate sphere is expressed as a distortion of the visual system. One subject said, "These people get so close, you're cross-eyed. It really makes me nervous. They put their face so close it feels like they're *inside you*." At the point where sharp focus is lost, one feels the uncomfortable muscular sensation of being cross-eyed from looking at something too close. The expressions "Get your face *out* of mine" and "He shook his fist *in* my face" apparently express how many Americans perceive their body boundaries.

The use of intimate distance in public is not considered proper by adult, middle-class Americans even though their young may be observed intimately involved with each other in automobiles and on beaches. Crowded subways and buses may bring strangers into what would ordinarily be classed as intimate spatial relations, but subway riders have defensive devices which take real intimacy out of intimate space in public conveyances. The basic tactic is to be as immobile as possible and, when part of the trunk or extremities touches another person, withdraw if possible. For members of the non-contact group, it is taboo to relax and enjoy bodily contact with strangers!

It should be noted once more that American proxemic patterns for intimate distance are by no means universal. Even the rules governing such intimacies as touching others cannot be counted on to remain constant. Americans who have had an opportunity for considerable social contact with Russians report that many of the features characteristic of American intimate distance are present in Russian social distance. Middle Eastern subjects in public places do not express the outraged reaction to being touched by strangers which one encounters in American subjects.

PERSONAL DISTANCE

"Personal distance" is the term originally used to designate the distance consistently separating the members of non-contact species (those species which do not huddle together and in general avoid touching each other). It might be thought of as a small protective sphere or bubble that an organism maintains between itself and others.

Close phase (distance: one and a half to two and a half feet)

At this distance, one can hold or grasp another person. Where people stand in relation to each other signals their relationship, or how they feel toward each other, or both. A wife can stay inside the circle of her husband's close personal zone with impunity. For another woman to do so is an entirely different story.

Far phase (distance: two and a half to four feet)

Keeping someone at "arm's" length is one way of expressing the far phase of personal distance. It extends from a point that is just outside easy touching distance by one person to a point where two people can touch fingers if they extend both arms. This is the limit of physical domination in the very real sense. Beyond it, a person cannot easily "get his hands on" someone else. Subjects of personal interest and involvement can be discussed at this distance.

SOCIAL DISTANCE

The boundary line between the far phase of personal distance and the close phase of social distance marks, in the words of one subject, the "limit of domination". Intimate visual detail in the face is not perceived, and nobody touches or expects to touch another person unless there is some special effort. Voice level is normal for Americans. There is little change between the far and close phases, and conversations can be overheard at a distance of up to twenty feet. I have observed that in overall loudness, the American voice at these distances is below that of the Arab, the Spaniard, the South Asian Indian, and the Russian, and somewhat above that of the English upper class, the Southeast Asian, and the Japanese.

Close phase (distance: four to seven feet)

Impersonal business occurs at this distance, and in the close phase there is more involvement than in the distant phase. People who work together tend to use close social distance. It is also a very common distance for people who are attending a casual social gathering. To stand and look down at a person at this distance has a domineering effect, as when a man talks to his secretary or receptionist.

Far phase (distance: seven to twelve feet)

This is the distance to which people move when someone says "Stand away so I can look at you." Business and social discourse conducted at the far end of social distances has a more formal character than if it occurs inside the close phase. Desks in the offices of important people are large enough to hold visitors at the far end of social distance. Even in an office with standard-size desks, the chair opposite is eight or nine feet away from the man behind the desk. During conversations of any significant length it is more important to maintain visual contact at this distance than it is at a closer distance.

Proxemic behavior of this sort is culturally conditioned and entirely arbitrary. It is also binding on all concerned. To fail to hold the other person's eye is to shut him out and bring conversation to a halt, which is why people who are conversing at this distance can be observed craning their necks and leaning from side to side to avoid intervening obstacles.

At this distance phase, the voice level is noticeably louder than for the close phase, and it can usually be heard easily in an adjoining room if the door is open. Raising the voice or shouting can have the effect of reducing social distance to personal distance.

The far phase of social distance can be used to insulate or screen people from each other. This distance makes it possible for them to continue to work in the presence of another person without appearing to be rude. Receptionists in offices are particularly vulnerable as most employers expect double duty: answering questions, being polite to callers, as well as typing. If the receptionist is less than ten feet from another person, even a stranger, she will be sufficiently involved to be virtually compelled to converse. If she has more space, however, she can work quite freely without having to talk.

PUBLIC DISTANCE

Several important sensory shifts occur in the transition from the personal and social distances to public distance, which is well outside the circle of involvement.

Close phase (distance: twelve to twenty-five feet)

At twelve feet an alert subject can take evasive or defensive action if threatened. The voice is loud but not full-volume. Linguists have observed that a careful choice of words and phrasing of sentences as well as grammatical or syntactic shifts occur at this distance. Martin Joos' choice of the term "formal style" is appropriately descriptive.

Far phase (distance: twenty-five feet or more)

Thirty feet is the distance that is automatically set around important public figures, but the usual public distance can be used by anyone on public occasions. There are certain adjustments that must be made, however. Most actors know that at thirty or more feet the subtle shades of meaning conveyed by the normal voice are lost as are the details of facial expression and movement. Not only the voice but everything else must be exaggerated or amplified. Much of the nonverbal part of the communication shifts to gestures and body stance. In addition, the tempo of the voice drops, words are enunciated more clearly, and there are stylistic changes as well (Martin Joos' "frozen style" is characteristic). The whole man may be seen as quite small and he is perceived in a setting.

WHY "FOUR" DISTANCES?

The hypothesis behind the proxemic classification system is this: it is in the nature of animals, including man, to exhibit behavior which we call *territoriality* or an ownership-like reaction to space or objects. In so doing, they use the senses to distinguish between one space or distance and another. The specific distance chosen depends on the transaction, the relationship of the interacting individuals, how they feel, and what they are doing. The four-part classification system used here is based on observations of both animals and men. Birds and apes exhibit *intimate*, *personal*, and *social distances* just as man does.

Western man has combined consultative and social activities and relationships into one distance set and has added the public figure and the *public* relationship. "Public" relations and "public" manners as the Europeans and Americans practice them are different from those in other parts of the world. There are implicit obligations to treat total strangers in certain prescribed ways. Hence, we find four principal categories of relationships (intimate, personal, social, and public) and the activities and spaces associated with them. In other parts of the world, relationships tend to fall into other patterns, such as the family/non-family pattern common in Spain and Portugal and their former colonies or the caste and outcast system of India. Both the Arabs and the Jews also make sharp distinctions between people to whom they are related and those to whom they are not.

Until recently man's space requirements were thought of in terms of the actual amount of air displaced by his body. The fact that man has around him as extensions of his personality the zones described earlier has generally been over-looked. Differences in the zones — in fact their very existence — became apparent only when Americans began interacting with foreigners who organize their senses differently so that what was intimate in one culture might be personal or even public in another. Thus for the first time the American became aware of his own spatial envelopes, which he has previously taken for granted. The ability to recognize these various zones of involvement and the activities, relationships, and emotions associated with each has now become extremely important.

Proxemic patterns point up some of the basic differences between people — differences which can be ignored only at great risk. American city planners and builders are now in the process of designing cities in other countries with very little idea of people's spatial needs and practically no inkling that these needs vary from culture to culture. The chances of forcing whole populations into molds that do not fit are very great indeed.

EXERCISES

1. Since what we unconsciously know about proxemics was never directly taught to us by our parents or anyone else, it is interesting that we usually have similar reactions to space. To illustrate this, ask your friends how they would respond in the following situations and compare them to your own responses:

> In a crowded library, there is only one table where you can sit. A member of the opposite sex is sitting in the chair marked with an (x).

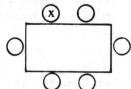

   A. First, assume that (x) is a very attractive person whom you'd like to get to know but have never met. Where would you sit? Why?

   B. Now assume that (x) is an unattractive person you would not like to get to know. Where would you sit?

   C. Where would you sit if (x) is an instructor you have had for a course and liked very much?

   D. Where would you sit if (x) is an instructor you have had for a course and disliked very much? The instructor gave you an unfair grade.

2. Territoriality or the possessive reaction we have to space or to objects is also not directly taught to us. We are usually unaware of our feelings of territoriality until "our space" or "our objects" are violated by another person. Notice the reactions of others if you do any of the following:

   A. In an uncrowded bus, you sit next to a person who has put some object on the seat that he/she must move when you attempt to sit down.

   B. When there is only one person in an elevator, you stand right next to that person.

   C. In a class that has been meeting for several weeks, you sit in the seat where one particular person has sat everyday.

   D. In a library that is not crowded, you deliberately move someone's books and sit down while the person is away from the table.

   E. In your home or dorm, you occupy someone else's "special" chair, desk, or room.

For more information on proxemics see *The Hidden Dimension* by Edward Hall (1966).

Computational linguists use computers to deal with language in some way. In particular, there are a number of things that humans do with language that can be automated to some degree on a computer — translating from one language to another, recognizing the words in speech, pronouncing these words, understanding sentences and larger texts, and producing text that conveys meaning or information. (Each of these tasks is discussed below.) The fact that programming a computer requires that all details of an operation be explicitly specified makes computers an ideal environment for linguists (including theoretical linguists, psycholinguists, and sociolinguists) to test their theories and models.

Machine translation is the use of computers to translate one language to another. Some machine translation programs rely on a "dictionary look-up" method combined with some simple rules of syntax which switch and modify words. For example, *white house* in English would first be translated into the Spanish phrase *blanco casa*. Then, syntactic rules would add gender agreement and switch the words in order to translate it into the correct Spanish phrase *casa blanca*. The translated text is somewhat awkward, but the results are good enough that the text is intelligible and useful for most technical applications. As for translating literary text such as novels or textbooks, machine translation still cannot come close to human translators.

Speech recognition involves the use of computers to transform spoken language into written language. There are obvious uses for such a device — e.g. voice controlled typewriters, games, and other machines. You may have already used a speech recognition system if you have been polled by a computer over the telephone or if you have a home computer with such capabilities. One system of speech recognition uses sound templates (or sound patterns) of individual words which are matched to the incoming words through a microphone. This process, however, is slow and limited, requiring the speaker to teach the computer the words before any translations can be performed. A more linguistic approach to speech recognition involves combining all the levels of linguistic knowledge (e.g. phonology, syntax, semantics, and pragmatics) in order to allow speaker-independent understanding of continuous speech. Speech recognition of this type has been the focus of a lot of time, money, and research, yet the results are still less than satisfying. Today's commercial speech recognition systems still use some sort of template matching, can only recognize words in isolation (spoken separately one at a time) and have a vocabulary of about 100 to 5,000 words. The most ambitious effort to date using template matching techniques is the Kurzweil VoiceWriter which can have a user-specific vocabulary of 7,000 to 20,000 words and can translate words spoken one at a time by using many powerful micro-chips working at the same time.

Speech generation (or speech synthesis) is the use of computers to produce human-like speech. Today, telephones, cars, elevators, and even soft drink machines talk to us, in varying degrees of naturalness. This variation in naturalness stems from the fact that speech generation ranges from the use of simple "recordings" of actual human speech which has been digitized by a computer, to the use of phonemes and phonological rules to produce speech. Speech generators that use phonemes and phonological rules can "pronounce" most words and phrases by rule, thus enabling computers to read free text aloud. Such machines are now in use for reading to the blind. Speech generators which use linguistic rules of pronunciation are flexible and understandable, yet they still lack naturalness.

Text understanding involves the use of computers that can be programmed to analyze sentences syntactically, that is, to parse sentences. There are, however, two problems with automated parsing. First, parsing is extremely slow even with modest-sized grammars. Second, syntactic rules alone are not sufficient to guide the parsing process. Semantics, pragmatics, context, and world knowledge must play a role as well. The applications for this research are numerous: programs that allow users to communicate with computers using natural language, programs that take text and create databases of information, programs that summarize and index, and programs that correct grammar.

Text generation involves the use of computers to create sentences from abstract knowledge and to respond to humans using human language (whether it be spoken or written). Just as with text understanding, syntactic rules alone are not sufficient to generate meaningful text. A text generation program must first know what real world knowledge is relevant for a specific text before it decides on such things as the type of sentence it wants to generate (e.g. question, statement), or what tenses, order, and types of words it wants to use. Applications in text generation include answering questions about a database, summarizing text, creating fluid, natural language from outlines, generating stories, and generating translations of foreign languages.

In this section on language and computers, we will examine speech synthesis in greater detail (see File 161) as well as various other tasks like machine translation, text understanding and speech recognition (File 162).

Speech Synthesis

Not too many years ago the only talking machines you would be likely to run into were in science fiction stories. Computers like HAL in *2001: A Space Odyssey* were fun to think about, but also very far removed from normal life. Now, instead of reading about them in science fiction, you can read about talking machines in car advertisements and newspaper stories. In fact, you may have grown up playing with toys (like See'N Say) that talk. Machines that talk are especially interesting to linguists because they provide an opportunity to *apply* the knowledge gained by linguistic investigation.

Phonetics and Speech Synthesis

The application of the **source-filter theory of speech production** to speech synthesis is one example of the use of phonetic knowledge for a practical purpose. The central idea of the theory is that the acoustic qualities of speech sounds result from the interaction of a sound source (vocal cord vibration) and an acoustic tube with particular filtering qualities (the vocal tract). Thus, the sound made by our vibrating vocal cords is modified by the acoustic filtering properties of the vocal tract.

This model of speech production has been used as an approach for speech synthesis. A computer is made to synthesize speech by simulating the human production of speech as it is described in the source-filter theory of speech production. Just as the source-filter theory uses two basic components in the description of what goes into human speech production (a sound source and a filter) so also the computer's algorithm for speech synthesis is divided into two parts — the synthesis of a sound source and then the simulation of the vocal tract's filtering function.

The sound source is the computer's version of the vibrating vocal cords. Most synthesizers simply use sawtooth waves as the sound source as illustrated in Figure 1A. The difference between the waveforms in Figure 1A (the synthetic sound source) and 1B (the natural sound source) illustrates one reason for the unnatural sound of some synthesized speech. Although the speech produced by a system using a sawtooth wave as its voice source is understandable, it usually sounds somewhat unhuman. One reason for using a sawtooth wave rather than a more natural sounding source is that the algorithm which generates the sawtooth wave is much simpler and faster than the complex type of algorithm which is necessary for the more natural sounding voice source.

Figure 1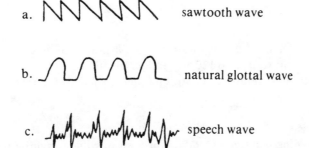

a. sawtooth wave

b. natural glottal wave

c. speech wave

After producing a sound source the filter function must be simulated. There are two standard ways of modeling the filtering properties of the vocal tract. These will be discussed in the paragraphs below.

The first approach models the filtering properties in strictly acoustic terms. The filter's characteristics are specified in terms of the frequencies, band widths and amplitudes of formants. This approach to speech synthesis is called **formant synthesis.** Formant synthesis is done without any reference to the articulation of speech. The filtering characteristics of the vocal tract are specified in terms of the acoustic output which is desired (the sound that the synthesizer is supposed to make), and without any regard for the positions of the articulators which might be involved in the human production of the sounds. The information which is necessary in order for formant synthesis to succeed is the type of information which is gathered in acoustic phonetics. The phoneticians who record and analyze the acoustic properties of speech sounds provide the information which is necessary for formant synthesis.

The second method of providing a filter for the speech sound source is called **articulatory synthesis.** In this method of synthesis the area of the vocal tract is modeled by the computer and from that model a filter function is computed. The information which is required for articulatory synthesis is physiological in nature. The quality of the synthesized speech which results from articulatory synthesis depends on the accuracy of the vocal tract simulation which is used by the synthesizer. Thus, the success of the synthesizer is tied very directly to the extent and accuracy of our knowledge of the anatomy and mechanics of the human vocal tract (things like the shape of the tongue during vowels, how fast the tongue moves from one place of articulation to another, the relative timing of different coordinated actions in articulation, and so on).

In this section we have been concerned primarily with the phonetics of speech synthesis (i.e. with getting human sounding noise to come from machines). In the section to follow we will discuss some problems which have to do with the application of phonology to speech synthesis. Before going on though we should describe briefly how the time dimension is incorporated into speech synthesis.

One crucial characteristic of speech sounds is that their acoustic qualities are not stationary in time. By this we mean that the source function and the filter function (using once again the terminology of the source/filter theory) change over time. Thus, the source function may change due to the fact that the rate of vocal fold vibration (pitch of voice) may go up or down during an utterance. The filter function also changes as the speaker moves his mouth to make the different sounds of an utterance.

This variation over time is incorporated into speech synthesis by the use of a sequence of control parameters. The sequence of parameters functions as a list of instructions to be carried out by the synthesizer at regular intervals of time over the course of synthesizing an utterance. For instance, if the sequence of control signals which is shown in Table 1 were used to control a formant synthesizer, the following instructions would be issued:

Table 1

Time (in milliseconds)	F0	F1	F2
0	0	0	0
5	120	300	900
10	130	300	900
15	135	300	1000
20	140	300	1100

At time 0 set all of the parameters of the synthesizer to 0. At time 5 milliseconds set the fundamental frequency (F0 equals the rate of vibration of the source) to 120 Hz, and set the filter function to have spectral peaks (formants) at 300 Hz (F1) and 900 Hz (F2), etc. With a table of control parameters like this the synthesizer can simulate the changes in speech sounds that happen when we move our mouths.

Phonology and Speech Synthesis

Using one of the types of synthesis systems just described it is possible to synthesize human speech. However, it is very tedious and time consuming work to specify the control parameters for an entire sentence (for instance) when the entire set of parameters must be specified every five milliseconds. That would be 200 lines of parameter specifications for every one second of speech. This is also quite an uneconomical way of storing the information which is used to synthesize speech.

This basic problem in speech synthesis can be resolved by turning to linguistic theory for an answer. In particular, the concept of the phoneme which is central to the study of phonology, provides a way of specifying speech sounds which is much easier and more economical to use than are parameter lists. Rather than specifying a full list of control parameters for a sound, it is simpler to specify only one set of typical parameters (with some indication of the typical duration and pitch of the item). From this typical set of parameters the synthesizer can then compute the full list of control parameters taking into account the possible influences of the surrounding sounds.

For instance, if we wish to synthesize the sequence /an/ the synthesizer would look up the typical control parameters for the vowel /a/ and the nasal /n/. It would then take into account the fact that the vowel will be in utterance initial position and adjust the vowel's typical parameters so that an abrupt glottal stop type of start is synthesized. In view of the fact that the consonant following /a/ is nasal the synthesizer will also change the vowel's neutral parameters to reflect the nasalization that is usually found on vowels before nasals in English (this effect may be constrained to only take place after a certain portion of the vowel has been synthesized without nasalization). Finally, the synthesizer will adjust the duration of the vowel segment to reflect the fact that it is being produced before a voiced consonant. Thus, three phonological processes are incorporated into the synthesis of this simple sequence:

1) glottalization of an initial vowel
2) nasalization of a vowel when a nasal consonant follows it
3) lengthening of a vowel when a voiced consonant follows it

All three of these phonological processes (plus many more) are absolutely necessary if natural sounding speech is to be synthesized from phoneme specifications. Thus, a basic knowledge of how phonology works makes it possible to greatly simplify and economize speech synthesis.

Conclusion

In this file we have seen how linguistic knowledge and theories make it possible to synthesize speech. Beyond just a description of some of the typical techniques used in speech synthesis, it is important to see the connection between linguistic knowledge and successful speech synthesis. Without basic phonetic and phonological knowledge the task of speech synthesis would be hopeless.

from "Computer Software for Working with Language" by Terry Winograd.

In the popular mythology the computer is a mathematics machine: it is designed to do numerical calculations. Yet it is really a language machine: its fundamental power lies in its ability to manipulate linguistic tokens—symbols to which meaning has been assigned. Indeed, natural language (the language people speak and write, as distinguished from the artificial languages in which computer programs are written) is central to computer science. Much of the earliest work in the field was aimed at breaking military codes, and in the 1950s efforts to have computers translate text from one natural language into another led to crucial advances, even though the goal itself was not achieved. Work continues on the still more ambitious project of making natural language a medium in which to communicate with computers.

Today, investigators are developing unified theories of computation that embrace both natural and artificial languages. Here I shall concentrate on the former, that is, on the language of everyday human communication. Within that realm there is a vast range of software to be considered. Some of it is mundane and successful. A multitude of microcomputers have invaded homes, offices and schools, and most of them are used at least in part for word processing. Other applications are speculative and far from realization. Science fiction is populated by robots that converse as if they were human, with barely a mechanical tinge to their voice. Real attempts to get computers to converse have run up against great difficulties, and the best of the laboratory prototypes are still a pale reflection of the linguistic competence of the average child.

The prospect that text might be translated by a computer arose well before commercial computers were first manufactured. In 1949, when the few working computers were all in military laboratories, the mathematician Warren Weaver, one of the pioneers of communication theory, pointed out that the techniques developed for code breaking might be applicable to machine translation.

At first the task appears to be straightforward. Given a sentence in a source language, two basic operations yield the corresponding sentence in a target language. First the individual words are replaced by their translations; then the translated words are reordered and adjusted in detail. Take the translation of "Did you see a white cow?" into the Spanish "Viste una vaca blanca." First one needs to know the words 'did' and 'you' are not translated directly but are expressed through the form of the verb 'viste.' The adjective 'blanca' follows the noun instead of preceding it as it does in English. Finally, 'una' and 'blanca' are in the feminine form corresponding to 'vaca.' Much of the early study of machine translation dwelt on the technical problem of putting a large dictionary into computer storage and empowering the computer to search efficiently in it. Meanwhile the software for dealing with grammar was based on the then current theories of the structure of language, augmented by rough-and-ready rules.

The programs yielded translations so bad that they were incomprehensible. The problem is that natural language does not embody meaning in the same way that a cryptographic code embodies a message. The meaning of a sentence in a natural language is dependent not only on the form of the sentence but also on the context. One can see this most clearly through examples of ambiguity.

In the simplest form of ambiguity, known as lexical ambiguity, a single word has more than one possible meaning. Thus "Stay away from the bank" might be advice to an investor or to a child too close to a river. In translating it into Spanish one would need to choose between 'orilla' and 'banco,' and nothing in the sentence itself reveals which is intended. Attempts to deal with lexical ambiguity in translation software have included the insertion of all the possibilities into the translated text and the statistical analysis of the source text in an effort to decide which translation is appropriate. For example, 'orilla' is likely to be the correct choice if words related to rivers and water are nearby in the source text. The first strategy leads to complex, unreadable text; the second yields the correct choice in many cases but the wrong one in many others.

In structural ambiguity the problem goes beyond a single word. Consider the sentence "He saw that gasoline can explode." It has two interpretations based on quite different uses of 'that' and 'can.' Hence the sentence has two possible grammatical structures, and the translator must choose between them.

An ambiguity of deep structure is subtler still: two readings of a sentence can have the same apparent grammatical structure but nonetheless differ in meaning. "The chickens are ready to eat" implies that something is about to eat something, but which are the chickens? One of the advances in linguistic theory since the 1950s has been the development of a formalism in which the deep structure of language can be represented, but the formalism is of little help in deducing the intended deep structure of a particular sentence.

A fourth kind of ambiguity—semantic ambiguity—results when a phrase can play different roles in the overall meaning of a sentence. The sentence "David wants to marry a Norwegian" is an example. In one meaning of the sentence the phrase 'a Norwegian' is referential. David intends to marry a particular person, and the speaker of the sentence has chosen an attribute of the person—her being from Norway—in order to describe her. In another meaning of the sentence the phrase is attributive. Neither David nor the speaker has a particular person in mind; the sentence simply means that David hopes to marry someone of Norwegian nationality.

A fifth kind of ambiguity might be called pragmatic ambiguity. It arises from the use of pronouns and special nouns such as 'one' and 'another.' Take the sentence "When a bright moon ends a dark day, a brighter one will follow." A brighter day or a brighter moon? At times it is possible for translation software to simply translate the ambiguous pronoun or noun, thereby preserving the ambiguity in the translation. In many cases, however, this strategy is not available. In a Spanish translation of "She dropped the plate on the table and broke it" one must choose either the masculine 'lo' or the feminine 'la' to render 'it.' The choice forces the translator to decide whether the masculine 'plato' (plate) or the feminine 'mesa' (table) was broken.

In many ambiguous sentences the meaning is obvious to a human reader, but only because the reader brings to the task an understanding of context. Thus "The porridge is ready to eat" is unambiguous because one knows porridge is inanimate. "There's a man in the room with a green hat on" is unambiguous because one knows rooms do not wear hats. Without such knowledge, virtually any sentence is ambiguous.

Although fully automatic, high-quality machine translation is not feasible, software is available to facilitate translation. One example is the computerization of translation aids such as dictionaries and phrase books. These vary from elaborate systems meant for technical translators, in which the function of looking a word up is made part of a multilingual word-processing program, to hand-held computerized libraries of phrases for use by tourists. Another strategy is to process text by hand to make it suitable for machine translation. A person working as pre-editor takes a text in the source language and creates a second text, still in the source language, that is simplified in ways facilitating machine translation. Words with multiple meanings can be eliminated, along with grammatical constructions that complicate syntactic analysis. Conjunctions that cause ambiguity can be suppressed, or the ambiguity can be resolved by inserting special punctuation, as in "the [old men] and [women]." After the machine translation a post-editor can check for blunders and smooth the translated text.

The effort is sometimes cost-effective. In the first place, the pre-editor and post-editor need not be bilingual, as a translator would have to be. Then, too, if a single text (say an instruction manual) is to be translated into several languages, a large investment in pre-editing may be justified because it will serve for all the translations. If the author of the text can be taught the less ambiguous form of the source language, no pre-editor is needed. Finally, software can help in checking the pre-edited text to make certain it meets the specifications for input to the translation system (although this is no guarantee that the translation will be acceptable).

A machine-translation system employing pre- and post-editing has been in use since 1980 at the Pan-American Health Organization, where it has translated more than a million words of text from Spanish into English. A new system is being developed for the European Economic Community, with the goal of translating documents among the official languages of the community: Danish, Dutch, English, French, German, Greek and Italian. Meanwhile the theoretical work on syntax and meaning has continued, but there have been no breakthroughs in machine translation. The ambiguity pervading natural language continues to limit the possibilities, for reasons I shall examine more fully below.

Is there software that really deals with meaning—software that exhibits the kind of reasoning a person would use in carrying out linguistic tasks such as translating, summarizing or answering a question? Such software has been the goal of research projects in artificial intelligence since the mid-1960s, when the necessary computer hardware and programming techniques began to appear even as the impracticability of machine translation was becoming apparent.

There are many applications in which the software would be useful. They include programs that accept natural language commands, programs for information retrieval, programs that summarize text and programs that acquire language-based knowledge for expert systems.

No existing software deals with meaning over a significant subset of English; each experimental program is based on finding a simplified version of language and meaning and testing what can be done within its confines. Some investigators see no fundamental barrier to writing programs with a full understanding of natural language. Others argue that computerized understanding of language is impossible. In order to follow the arguments it is important to examine the basics of how a language-understanding program has to work.

A language-understanding program needs several components, corresponding to the various levels at which language is analyzed. Most programs deal with written language; hence the analysis of sound waves is bypassed and the first level of analysis is morphological. The program applies rules that decompose a word into its root, or basic form and inflections such as the endings -s and -ing. The rules correspond in large part to the spelling rules children are taught in elementary school. Children learn, for example, that the root of 'baking' is 'bake,' whereas the root of 'barking' is 'bark.' An exception list handles words to which the rules do not apply, such as forms of the verb 'be.' Other rules associate inflections with 'features' of words. For example, 'am going' is a progressive verb; it signals an act in progress.

For each root that emerges from the morphological analysis a dictionary yields the set of lexical categories to which the root belongs. This is the second level of analysis carried out by the computer. Some roots (such as 'the') have only one lexical category: others have several. 'Dark' can be a noun or an adjective; 'bloom' can be a noun or a verb. In some instances the morphological analysis limits the possibilities. (In its common usages 'bloom' can be a noun or a verb, but 'blooming' is only a verb.) The output of the morphological and lexical analysis is thus a sequence of the words in a sentence, with each word carrying a quantity of dictionary and feature information. This output serves in turn as the input to the third component of the program, the parser, or syntactic-analysis component, which applies rules of grammar to determine the structure of the sentence.

Two distinct problems arise in designing an adequate parser. The first problem is the specification of a precise set of rules—a grammar—that determines the set of possible sentence structures in a language. Over the past 30 years much work in theoretical linguistics has been directed toward devising formal linguistic systems: constructions in which the syntactic rules of a language are stated so precisely that a computer could employ them to analyze the language. The generative transformational grammars invented by Noam Chomsky of the Massachusetts Institute of Technology were the first comprehensive attempt; they specify the syntax of a language by means of a set of rules whose mechanical application generates all allowable structures.

The second problem is that of the parsing itself. It is not always possible to tell, when a part of a sentence is encountered, just what role it plays in the sentence or whether the words in it go together. Take the sentence "roses will be blooming in the dark gardens we abandoned long ago." The words 'in the dark' might be interpreted as a complete phrase; after all, they are grammatically well formed and they make sense. But the phrase cannot form a coherent unit in a complete analysis of the sentence because it forces "Roses will be blooming in the dark" to be interpreted as a sentence and therefore leaves "gardens we abandoned long ago" without a role to play.

Parsers adopt various strategies for exploring the multiple ways phrases can be put together. Some work from the top down, trying from the outset to find possible sentences; others work from the bottom up, trying local word combinations. Some backtrack to explore alternatives in depth if a given possibility fails; others use parallel processing to keep track of a number of alternatives simultaneously. Some make use of formalisms (such as transformational grammar) that were developed by linguists. Others make use of newer formalisms designed with computers in mind. The latter formalisms are better suited to the implementation of parsing procedures. For example, *augmented-transition networks* express the structure of sentences and phrases as an explicit sequence of *transitions* to be followed by a machine. *Lexical-function grammars* create a functional structure in which grammatical functions such as head, subject, and object are explicitly tied to the words and phrases that serve those functions.

Although no formal grammar successfully deals with all the grammatical problems of any natural language, existing grammars and parsers can handle well over 90 percent of all sentences. This is not entirely to the good. A given sentence may have hundreds or even thousands of possible syntactic analyses. Most of them have no plausible meaning. People are not aware of considering and rejecting such possibilities, but parsing programs are swamped by meaningless alternatives.

The output of a parsing program becomes the input to the fourth component of a language-understanding program: a semantic analyzer, which translates the syntactic form of a sentence into a logical form. The point is to put the linguistic expressions into a form that makes it possible for the computer to apply reasoning procedures and draw inferences. Here again there are competing theories about what representation is most appropriate. As with parsing, the key issues are effectiveness and efficiency.

Effectiveness depends on finding the appropriate formal structures to encode the meaning of linguistic expressions. One possibility is predicate calculus, which employs the quantifiers $\forall X$ to mean 'all' and $\exists X$ to mean 'there exists.' In predicate calculus "Roses will be blooming . . . " is equivalent to the assertion "There exists something that is a rose and that is blooming . . ." This entails a difficulty. Is one rose adequate to represent the meaning of "roses will be blooming" or would it be better to specify two or more? How can the computer decide? The dilemma is worsened if a sentence includes a mass noun such as 'water' in "Water will be flowing . . ." One cannot itemize water at all. In designing a formal structure for the meaning of linguistic expressions many similar problems arise from the inherent vagueness of language.

Efficiency must also be considered, because the computer will employ the logical form of a sentence to draw inferences that in turn serve both the analysis of the meaning of the sentence and the formulation of a response to it. Some formalisms, such as predicate calculus, are not directly amenable to efficient computation, but other, more procedural representations have also been devised. Consider the efforts to answer the question "Are there flowers in the gardens we abandoned long ago?" The computer needs to know that roses are flowers. This knowledge could be represented by a formula in predicate calculus amounting to the assertion "Everything that is a rose is a flower." The computer could then apply techniques developed for mechanical theorem-proving to make the needed deduction. A different approach would be to give certain inferences a privileged computational status. For example, basic classificational deductions could be represented directly in data structures. Such deductions are required constantly for reasoning about the ordinary properties of objects. Other types of fact (for example that flowers need water in order to grow) could then be represented in a form closer to predicate calculus. The computer could draw on both to make inferences (for example that if roses do not get water, they will not grow).

A good deal of research has gone into the design of representation languages that provide for the effective and efficient encoding of meaning. The greatest difficulty lies in the nature of human commonsense reasoning. Most of what a person knows cannot be formulated in all-or-nothing logical rules; it lies instead in normal expectation. If one asks, "Is there dirt in the garden?" the answer is almost certainly yes. The yes, however, cannot be a logical inference; some gardens are hydroponic, and the plants there grow in water. A person tends to rely on normal expectations without thinking of exceptions unless they are relevant. But little progress has been made toward formalizing the concept of relevance and the way it shapes the background of expectations brought to bear in the understanding of linguistic expressions.

The final stage of analysis in a language-understanding program is pragmatic analysis: the analysis of context. Every sentence is embedded in a setting: it comes from a particular speaker at a particular time and it refers, at least implicitly, to a particular body of understanding. Some of the embedding is straightforward: the pronoun 'I' refers to the speaker; the adverb 'now' refers to the moment at which the sentence is uttered. Yet even these can be problematic: consider the use of 'now' in a letter I write today expecting you to read it three or four days hence. Still, fairly uncomplicated programs can draw the right conclusions most of the time. Other embedding is more complex. The pronoun 'we' is an example. 'We' might refer to the speaker and the hearer or to the speaker and some third party. Which of these it is (and who the third party might be) is not explicit and in fact is a common source of misunderstanding when people converse.

Still other types of embedding are not signaled by a troublesome word such as 'we.' The sentence "Roses will be blooming . . ." presupposes the identification of some future moment when the roses will indeed be in bloom. Thus the sentence might have followed the sentence "What will it be like when we get home?" or "Summer is fast upon us." Similarly, the noun phrase "the dark gardens we abandoned long ago" has a context-dependent meaning. There may be only one instance of gardens in which we have been together; there may be more than one. The sentence presupposes a body of knowledge from which the gardens are identifiable. The point is that a phrase beginning with 'the' rarely specifies fully the object to which it refers.

One approach to such phrases has been to encode knowledge of the world in a form the program can use to make inferences. For example, in the sentence "I went to a restaurant and the waiter was rude" one can infer that 'the waiter' refers to the person who served the speaker's meal if one's knowledge includes script, so to speak, of the typical events attending a meal in a restaurant. (A particular waiter or waitress serves any given customer.) In more complex cases an analysis of the speaker's goals and strategies can help. If one hears "My math exam is tomorrow, where's the book?" one can assume that the speaker intends to study and that 'the book' means the mathematics text employed in a course the speaker is taking. The approach is hampered by the same difficulty that besets the representation of meaning: the difficulty of formalizing the commonsense background that determines which scripts, goals and strategies are relevant and how they interact. The programs written so far work only in highly artificial and limited realms, and it is not clear how far such programs can be extended.

Even more problematic are the effects of context on the meaning of words. Suppose that in coming to grips with "the dark gardens we abandoned long ago" one tries to apply a particular meaning to 'dark' of "those dark days of tribulation" or that of "How dark it is with the lights off!" or that of "dark colors?" Although a kernel of similarity unites the uses of a word, its full meaning is determined by how it is used and by the prior understanding the speaker expects of the hearer. "The dark gardens" may have a quite specific meaning for the person addressed; for the rest of us it is slightly mysterious.

At first it might seem possible to distinguish literal uses of language from those that are more metaphorical or poetical. Computer programs faced with exclusively literal language could then be freed from contextual dilemmas. The problem is that metaphor and poetic meaning are not limited to the pages of literature. Everyday language is pervaded by unconscious metaphor, as when one says, "I lost two hours trying to get my idea across." Virtually every word has an open-ended field of meanings that shade gradually from those that seem utterly literal to those that are clearly metaphorical.

The limitations on the formalization of contextual meaning make it impossible at present—and conceivably forever—to design computer programs that come close to full mimicry of human language understanding. The only programs in practical use today that attempt even limited understanding are natural-language front ends that enable the user of a program to request information by asking questions in English. The program responds with English sentences or with a display of date.

A program called SHRDLU is an early example. Developed in the late 1960s, it enables a person to communicate with a computer in English about a simulated world of blocks on a tabletop. The program analyzes requests, commands, and statements made by the user and responds with appropriate words or with actions performed in the simulated scene. SHRDLU succeeded in part because its world of conversation is limited to a simple and specialized domain: the blocks and a few actions that can be taken with them.

Some more recent front-end interfaces have been designed with practical applications in mind. A person wanting access to information stored in the computer types natural-language sentences that the computer interprets as queries. The range of the questioning is circumscribed by the range of the data from which answers are formulated; in this way, words can be given precise meaning. In a data base on automobiles, for example, 'dark' can be defined as the colors black and navy and nothing more than that. The contextual meaning is there, but it is predetermined by the builder of the system, and the user is expected to learn it.

The main advantage of a natural-language front end is that it presents a low initial barrier to potential users. Someone invited to pose a question in English is usually willing to try, and if the computer proves unable to handle the specific form of the question, the user is probably willing to modify the wording until it works. Over time the user will learn the constraints imposed by the system. In contrast, a person who must learn a specialized language in order to formulate a question may well feel that an inordinate amount of work is being demanded.

The most obvious prediction about the future of computer software dealing with language is that the decreasing cost of hardware will make applications that are possible but impractical today available quite widely in the future. Software that mimics the full human understanding of language is simply not in prospect. However, some specific trends can be noted.

The first is that spoken language will get more emphasis. To be sure, the computerized understanding of spoken language presents all the difficulties of written language and more. Merely separating an utterance into its component words can vex a computer; thus hopes for a voice typewriter that types text from dictation are just as dim as hopes for high-quality machine translation and language-understanding. On the other hand, many useful devices do not require the analysis of connected speech. Existing systems that can identify a spoken word or phrase from a fixed vocabulary of a few hundred items will improve the interface between users and machines; the recent emergence of inexpensive integrated-circuit chips that process acoustic signals will facilitate the trend. Speech synthesizers that generate understandable utterances (although not in a natural-sounding voice) will also play an increasing role. Improved speech compression and encoding techniques will make acoustic messages and acoustic annotation of computer files commonplace.

A second trend in software dealing with language is that constraints on linguistic domain will be handled with increasing care and theoretical analysis. At several points in this article I have noted instances in which computers deal with meaning in an acceptable way because they operate in a limited domain of possible meanings. People using such software quickly recognize that the computer does not understand the full range of language, but the subset available is nonetheless a good basis for communication. Much of the commercial success of future software that deals with language will depend on the discovery of domains in which constraints on what sentences can mean still leave the user a broad range of language.

A third trend lies in the development of systems that combine the natural and the formal. Often it is taken for granted that natural language is the best way for people to communicate with computers. Plans for a fifth generation of intelligent computers are based on this proposition. It is not at all evident, however, that the proposition is valid. In some cases even the fullest understanding of natural language is not as expressive as a picture. And in many cases a partial understanding of natural language proves to be less usable than a well-designed formal interface. Consider the work with natural-language front ends. Here natural language promotes the initial acceptance of the system, but after that the users often move toward stylized forms of language they find they can employ with confidence, that is, without worrying about whether or not the machine will interpret their statements correctly.

The most successful current systems facilitate this transition. Some systems mix the natural and the formal: the user is taught to recognize formal properties of utterances and include them explicitly in messages. Thus the computer handles formal structures, while people handle tasks in which context is important and precise rules cannot be applied. Other systems incorporate a highly structured query system, so that as the user gains experience the artificial forms are seen to save time and trouble. In each case the computer is not assigned the difficult and open-ended tasks of linguistic analysis; it serves instead as a structured linguistic medium. That is perhaps the most useful way the computer will deal with natural language.

One of the difficult things about confronting a new discipline such as linguistics is that there is new terminology to learn and get used to. New terminology can take two forms. First, there are words which are used only within that particular discipline, such as *quark* in physics or *phoneme* in linguistics. For such words you simply have to learn the meaning and usage and in doing so you acquire a new vocabulary item in your mental dictionary. Somewhat trickier, though, is the second type of new terminology, that is, familiar words which have a special technical sense when used in the context of a certain discipline. For example, in ordinary usage, most of us use *velocity* as if it meant exactly the same thing as *speed*; in physics, however, the two are not synonymous in their technical senses, velocity being the time rate of linear motion in a given direction while speed is the rate of motion irrespective of direction, the magnitude of velocity expressed as a particular relationship (definitions from *Webster's Third International Dictionary*).

Throughout this course, you will be encountering many brand new terms, such as phoneme, but in addition you will also run into many familiar words which have a somewhat different, more specialized and technical sense in linguistics. Some of these are listed below with a contrast drawn between the popular sense and the technical sense of the word.

1. **Linguist** — Someone who studies the structure of language and its use, *not* someone who speaks many languages (a person who speaks many languages is a polyglot).

2. **Languages** — Systems of signs and constructs used by people as a primary form of communication, *not* specialized vocabulary (e.g., *medical language, the language of dance*).

3. **Dialects** — Varieties of a language used in different geographical and/or social areas (e.g. Southern English, British English, Cockney English, etc.), *not* foreign languages.

4. **Phonetic** — Of or relating to speech sounds and their representation via special symbols (c.f., the *phonetic alphabet,* a set of symbols that maintain a one-to-one correspondence with speech sounds), *not* a spelling system that corresponds closely to pronunciation. (*Spanish is a phonetic language).*

5. **Meaning** — That which is signaled or conveyed by a word or a phrase (*'unhappy' means not happy*), *not* intent or indication (e.g., *she meant to hurt him, smoke means fire*).

6. **Argument** — A reason put forth in support of (or against) a particular theory or belief, *not* 'disagreement' or 'quarrel.' Also used to refer to the elements of a sentence that combine with other elements to form larger semantic units. For example, the direct object of a verb is one of its *arguments.*

7. **Prediction** — A fact that is consistent with or entailed by a certain set of assumptions, *not* something that is forseen or prophesized.

8. **Inflection** — Modification of a word to express grammatical relationship (e.g., *The plural ending is an inflectional affix*), *not* modulation of voice or characteristic vocal quality (e.g., *He has a Southern inflection, From the change in his inflection we could tell his feelings were hurt.*).

9. **Logical** — Following from the rules of logic, *not* 'reasonable' or 'natural.' For example, if a claim is *logically valid,* it follows from the rules of scientific reasoning.

The above are just a few examples of common words which have a special sense when used in linguistic discussions. Such words are particularly common in linguistics because language, unlike physics, is something ordinary people frequently discuss. Be on the alert for other examples of this type throughout the course. Do not allow the layperson's definition of a word to interfere with its *linguistic* use.

APPENDIX: TEN COMMONLY SPOKEN LANGUAGES

This tape exemplifies ten of the most widely spoken languages in the world. Below is the text of the tape in each speaker's native language, along with an English translation. (For languages whose writing system differs from ours, a transcription of the text into the Roman alphabet is also provided.) Speakers were asked to talk spontaneously about American food.*

I. MANDARIN CHINESE

Mandarin is a dialect of northern mainland China; but since it is used as a standard language, it is spoken, either natively or as a second language, by about two thirds of China's population of 750 million.

總的來講，美國菜不大用調料。比如說牛排吧。

烤的時候什麼也不擱，要吃了才撒上鹽和胡椒，頂

多再放些蕃茄醬或 A-1 sauce 等。漢堡包也差不多。

中國人做牛肉可要放很多佐料，或者把肉用調料拌

好了，或者在煮的時候一點一點放。做中國菜比較

費事，可吃中國菜是一種享受。

Zong de lai jiang, mei guo cai bu da yong tiao liao. Bi ru shuo niu pai ba. Kao de shi hou shen me ye bu ge, yao chi le cai sa sang yan he hu jiao, ding duo zai fang xie fan qie jiang huo A-1 sauce deng. Han bao bao ye cha bu duo. Zhong guo ren zuo niu rou ke yao fang hen duo zuo liao; huo zhe ba rou yong tiao liao ban hao le, huo zhe zai zhu de shi hou yi dian yi dian fang. Zuo zhong guo cai bi jiao fei shi, ke chi zhong guo cai shi yi zhong xiang shou.

Generally speaking, American cooking does not use too much seasoning. Take beef steaks for example. You put nothing on them when you broil them. It is only when you eat them that you put some salt and pepper; at most you put some more ketchup and A-1 sauce. It is pretty much the same with hamburgers. When Chinese cook beef, however, they use a lot of seasoning. They may marinate it long before cooking or put in various seasoning in the process of cooking. Cooking Chinese is a little time-consuming, but eating Chinese food is an enjoyable thing.

II. ENGLISH

The English language is spoken natively by about 300 million people in the British Isles, North America, Australia, and many other parts of the world.

For instance, pizza. You're not likely to find pizza like Americans make it in Italy or just about anyplace, except in the United States. And that's pretty good stuff.

III. RUSSIAN

The Russian language is spoken either natively or as a second language by nearly 190 million people in the Soviet Union.

*Estimates of the number of speakers for each language are from Kenneth Katzner's *The Languages of the World* (Funk & Wagnalls, 1975).

Сравнительно с русской пищей американская пища мне нравится очень. Особенно полуфабрикаты. Нигде- в России нельзя найти такого количества вкусной, прекрасной, чистой пищи, как здесь - в таких местах, как Макдональд, Венди и так далее.

Sravnitel'no s russkoj piščej amerikanskaja pišča mne nravitsja očen'. Osobenno polufabrikaty. Nigde v Rossii nel'zja najti takogo količestva vkusnoj, prekrasnoj, čistoj pišči, kak zdes'—v takix mestax, kak Makdonal'd, Vendi i tak dalee.

I like American food very much, certainly more than Russian. I especially like fast food. Nowhere in Russia can one find such abundance of tasty, fresh food as in this country, in places like McDonald's, Wendy's, etc.

IV. SPANISH

The Spanish language is spoken natively by about 200 million people in Spain, South America, Central America, Mexico, the Caribbean islands, and many other places, including parts of the United States.

Yo pienso que es fantastico! Además, bueno hay gente que se preocupa mucho de "gourmet cooking," esa clase de alimentos requiere mayor trabajo. Esto me recuerda más, la forma de alimentación en mi país, donde se gartan muchas horas en la cocina y donde tenemos cuatro comidas al día.

I think it is fantastic! Besides, there are people who care a lot about gourmet cooking, that kind of food whose preparation requires more work. This reminds me of the way we prepare food in my country, where many hours are spent in the kitchen because we have four meals a day.

V. HINDI

The Hindi language was originally from north central India; but since it is widely used as a standard language, it is now spoken either natively or as a second language by about 180 million people throughout India.

अमरीकी खाना और भारतीय खाना.... इन दोनों की तुलना की ही नहीं जा सकती। ... ये तो मेरा खयाल है।

अगर सोचने लगो तो पहले पहले ध्यान में आता है कि जहांपर हिन्दुस्तानी खाने में ज्यादातर मसालों का बहुत ही इस्तेमाल होता है अमरीकी खाने में मसाले बहुत ही कम इस्तेमाल कीये जाते हैं। ये बात और की अमरीकी खाने में युरोपीय खाने से ज्यादा मसाले इस्तेमाल कीये जाते है फिर भी भारतीय खाने की इससे कोई तुलना हो ही नहीं सकती।

amariki khana aur bharatiy khana—in donõ ki tulna ki ̃ hi nahĩ ja sakti. ye to mera khayal hai. agar socne lago to pahale dhyanamẽ ata hai ki jahãpar hindustani khanemẽ jyadatar masalõ ka bahut hi istemal hota hai amariki khanemẽ masale bahut hi kam istemal kiye jate hai. ye bat aur ki amariki khanemẽ yuropiy khanese jyada masale istemal kiye jate hai phir bhi bharatiy khane ki usse koi tulna ho hi nahĩ sakti.

American food and Indian food—these two cannot be compared. That is what I think. If you start thinking, first you realize that whereas in Indian food a lot of spices are used, in American food spices are used to a very small extent. That American foods have more spices in them than European food is another thing. Yet it cannot be compared to Indian food.

VI. BENGALI

The Bengali language is spoken natively by nearly 120 million people in northeastern India and Bangladesh.

অ্যামেরিকান খাদ্য সাধারণত: আস্বাদহীন
ও গন্ধহীন, তাই ক্ষুধা না থাকলে অ্যামেরিকান
খাবার খাওয়া বেশ দুঃসাধ্য, আমি কয়েকদিন
ম্যাকডোনাল্ড-এর বিগ ম্যাক খাওয়ার চেষ্টা করেছি,
কিন্তু আমি কখনই পুরোটা খেতে পারিনি।

ʌmerikan khaddo sadharanataḥ aswadahin o gandhahin. tai ksudhã na khakale ʌmerikan khabar khaoya beš duḥsaddho ami kayekadin maekḍonald-er big maek khaoyar ceṣṭa karechi, kintu ami kakhanai puroṭa khete parini.

American foods are usually tasteless and odorless. Thus it is difficult to eat it unless one is hungry. On occasions I tried to eat a Big Mac at McDonald's but I could never eat all of it.

VII. ARABIC

The Arabic language is spoken natively by about 115 million people throughout the Middle East and Northern Africa.

ولكن إذا نظرنا إلى الطعام العربي
فأحبه جداً. فمنه الكبّه ومنه الحمّص والفول
والفلافل وأنا أحب هذا الطعام كثيراً
وآكله كل يوم.

wa-lākin ᵓidẖā naẓarnā ᵓilā ṭ-ṭaᶜāmi l-ᶜarabī fa- ᵓuḥibbuhu jiddan. fa-minhu l-kubbah wa minhu l-ḥummuṣ wa-l-fūl wa-l-falāfil wa ᵓanā ᵓuḥibbu hāḏā ṭ-ṭaᶜām kaẖīran wa ᵓakuluhu kulla yawm.

But if we looked to Arabic food, which I like very much—like *kubba* [meat pies], also *hummus* [chickpeas] and *ful* [beans] and *falafel*. I like this food a lot and I eat it every day.

VIII. JAPANESE

The Japanese language is spoken natively by over 100 million people on the island of Japan.

アメリカの料理ってのは、あれですね、あんまり味付けに凝らないんですよね、フランス料理とか中国料理とか日本料理みたいに比べて。だからテーブルの上でそのまま塩をかけて食べちゃうとか、そういう、ちょっと原始的なところがあって、で、結構いいレストランへ行ってもそんな感じなんですよね。だから肉とかそういうものをあらかじめ下ごしらえを十分にするとか、そういうことにあんまり気を使わないみたい。

Amerika no ryooritteno wa, aredesune, anmari azituke ni koranain desu yone, Huransu ryoori toka Tyuugoku ryoori toka Nihon ryoori mitai ni kurabete. Dakara teeburu no ue de sonomama sio o kakete tabetyau toka, sooiu, tyotto gensi teki na tokoro ga atte, de, kekkoo ii resutoran e ittemo sonna kanzi nandesuyone. Dakara niku toka sooiu mono o arakazime sitagosirae o zyuubun ni suru toka sooiu koto ni anmari ki o tukawanai mitai.

American cooking, it seems to me, doesn't bother much about seasoning, as compared with French cooking, Chinese cooking, or Japanese cooking. So, you just put some salt at the table and eat the meal, which seems a little bit primitive to me. This is so even in a modest restaurant. So, it seems that people don't care much about pre-seasoning of meat or other things.

IX. GERMAN

The German language is spoken natively by about 100 million people in Germany, Austria, and Switzerland, as well as other parts of the world.

Was sofort einem Deutschen auffällt, ist, dass hier die Brotsorten sehr viel anders sind als in Deutschland. Und anders ist eigentlich etwas höflich ausgedrückt, denn das amerikanische Brot ist für meinen Geschmack sehr weich und mit wenig Geschmack.

What someone from Germany notices right away is that the bread eaten here is much different from German bread. And to say that it's different is to put it politely, because American bread is in my opinion too soft and is almost completely tasteless.

X. PORTUGUESE

The Portuguese language is spoken natively by more than 100 million people in Portugal, Brazil, and other parts of the world.

Com excessão das comidas do sul dos Estados Unidos eu acho que a comida americana é muito diferente da comida brasileira em geral. Eu falo a comida do sul porque eu tive acesso a alguns pratos que parecem muito com os pratos baianos e eles levam todos os tipos de ingredientes como quiabo, camarão, azeite de dendê. Não sei se realmente eles usam azeite de dendê, mas fica com a mesma cor que os pratos baianos.

With the exception of the food of the southern United States, I think American food is very different from Brazilian food in general. I say food from the South because I have had access to some dishes which look like dishes from Bahia and they take all types of ingredients like okra, shrimp, palm oil. I don't know if they really take palm oil, but they have the same color as the dishes from Bahia.

APPENDIX: WRITING SYSTEMS

Many different writing systems have been devised to render human language into a form that allows messages to be preserved over time. But these writing systems differ greatly from one another with respect to the appearance of the graphic symbols (or "characters") that they utilize. There are in fact only *three* basic ways of using characters that have been employed in any of the writing systems that people have adopted.

The system of writing used to render English is, as you know, called an *alphabet*. But not all languages are written in alphabets. *Alphabet* has come to be used as a technical term which refers to only one of the three basic types of writing systems. The other two types are called *logographic systems* and *syllabaries*. It is easiest to talk about the three basic types of writing by defining the foregoing terms.

THE BASIC TYPES

LOGOGRAPHIC WRITING

In *logographic writing systems* each character that is used represents a separate morpheme. (For this reason, they are also called *ideographic*). The term *logographic* is derived from the Greek word *logos*, meaning 'word.' Since the words of any language are structural elements which represent concepts, the written symbols of a logographic system are equivalent to words. Thus each character used stands for a word as a whole, and not for any of the sounds that make up the word.

Logographic writing systems have been developed independently in separate parts of the world, and are the oldest type of writing. The "hieroglyphic" writing of Ancient Egypt, the "cuneiform" writing of Ancient Mesopotamia, and the Chinese writing system were all logographic in their earliest form, although they each became modified as they were utilized by succeeding generations. All three of these writing systems were invented at least five thousand years ago, and survived for thousands of years. The Chinese logographic system is, of course, still in use wherever Chinese is spoken.

An example from Chinese will suffice to demonstrate how a logographic system works. In the following sentence, each symbol stands for a word.

他 是 中 國 人   'He is a Chinese.'
he   be   center - country   person

A logographic system has the great disadvantage that an enormous number of symbols must be memorized, since each word has its own equivalent symbol. It has been estimated, for example, that a person must learn approximately 5000 characters in order to read a newspaper printed in Chinese, and as many as twice that number to read a college-level textbook. China has a highly literate population; therefore, it is obvious that it is not a task beyond the capacity of most people to learn such a large number of characters, although the task requires years of schooling.

On the other hand, a logographic system has the great advantage that it is not necessary for a person to know how to pronounce the language represented by the writing system in order to learn to read the messages written in it. This is because the characters represent concepts directly, and have little or nothing to do with their pronunciation. Persons who speak different dialects of Chinese — like Mandarin and Cantonese — which are so different that they can be considered different languages, can still read the same books and newspapers because of this fact.

Syllabic Writing

A second type of writing system is one in which each symbol represents a syllable that is used in composing words of the language being written. This is called a *syllabic writing system*. The total set of characters which are used for a given language is referred to as a *syllabary*. Syllabaries have been used for several languages, including Ancient Persian, Sanskrit, Japanese, and Cherokee.

The following Japanese example illustrates the way in which words are represented in a syllabary.

コレ　ワ　ホン　デ　コザイマス　　'This is a book.'
ko-re　wa　ho-n　de　go-za-i-ma-su

Each unique syllable of a language is represented by a unique character in a syllabary.

Each syllable in a language is either a vowel sound or a combination of consonants with a vowel sound. Since the pronunciation of each word in a language is composed of a single syllable or a sequence of syllables, you can see that a syllabic writing system requires far fewer symbols than a logographic writing system. Therefore, a syllabary has the advantage that it is more economical, in the sense that it requires far less memorization and learning time. Any word in the Japanese language, for example, can be written with a combination of the characters in the following syllabary, called *katakana*.

ア a	イ i	ウ u	エ e	オ o

カ ka	ガ ga	キ ki	ギ gi	ク ku	グ gu	ケ ke	ゲ ge	コ ko	ゴ go

| サ sa | ザ za | シ ši | ジ dži | ス su | ズ zu | セ se | ゼ ze | ソ so | ゾ zo |

| タ ta | ダ da | チ tši | ヂ dži | ツ tsu | ヅ dzu | テ te | デ de | ト to | ド do |

| ナ na | ニ ni | ヌ nu | ネ ne | ノ no |

| ハ ha | バ ba | ヒ çi | ビ bi | フ ɸu | ブ bu | ヘ he | ベ be | ホ ho | ボ bo |

| パ pa | ピ pi | プ pu | ペ pe | ポ po |

| マ ma | ミ mi | ム mu | メ me | モ mo |

408

ヤ
ya

ユ
yu

ヨ
yo

ラ
Da

リ
Di

ル
Du

レ
De

ロ
Do

ワ
wa

ヲ
wo

ン
n

Alphabetic Systems

The third major type of writing system is the type we use to write English, called an *alphabetic writing system*. An alphabetic system employs a character or combination of characters to represent each speech sound used by the language which is written. Each of the syllables which make up the words of a language is, in turn, composed of one or more speech sounds. Since there are just a limited number of speech sounds used by any given language, there are fewer unique speech sounds than unique syllables in a language. Therefore, it stands to reason that an alphabetic writing system requires even fewer characters than a syllabic writing system. Following is a list of the symbols of the Cyrillic alphabet used to write Russian.

А а	Л л	Х х
Б б	М м	Ч ч
В в	Н н	Ц ц
Г г	О о	Ш ш
Д д	П п	Щ щ
Е е Ё ё	Р р	Ъ ъ
Ж ж	С с	Ы ы
З з	Т т	Э э
И и Й й	У у	Ю ю
К к	Ф ф	Я я

There are two types of alphabetic writing systems that have been developed. One is the *consonantal alphabet*, in which only the consonants in words are written, with the vowels left out. Both the Hebrew and Arabic alphabets are of this type. An example of this type of writing is shown in the following Hebrew words. (Note: Hebrew is written from right to left.)

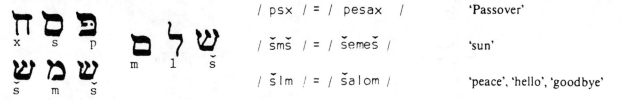

פ ס ח
p s x

ש ל מ
š l m

ש מ ש
š m š

/ psx / = / pesax /   'Passover'

/ šmš / = / šemeš /   'sun'

/ šlm / = / šalom /   'peace', 'hello', 'goodbye'

Notes: [š] represents a voiceless palato-alveolar fricative.

        [dž] represents a voiced palato-alveolar fricative.

        [tš] represents a voiceless palato-alveolar fricative.

        [c] represents a voiceless palatal fricative.

        [φ] represents a voiceless bilabial fricative.

        [D] represents a voiced alveolar tap.

It might at first seem such writing would be very difficult to read. But the fact that one's knowledge of the language allows one to 'fill in' the vowels by observing the overall context of a sentence is illustrated by using the following example from English, in which only the consonants are written. *Ths sntnc s wrttn wth th vwl smbls lft t.* The second type of alphabetic system, in which the vowels are represented as well as the consonants is referred to as a *true alphabet*.

THE HISTORICAL EVOLUTION OF WRITING SYSTEMS

As was stated above, logographic writing systems were the first type developed. The first characters developed for such systems were simple *pictograms*. Pictograms are merely stylized drawings of concrete objects. The Ancient Egyptian, Ancient Mesopotamian, and Ancient Chinese writing systems used the following pictograms.

	Sumerian	Egyptian	Chinese
'man'			
'ox'			
'star'			
'sun'			
'water'			
'road'			

A refinement that was soon made in each of the ancient writing systems named above was the *semantic extension* of the original pictograms. This means that the original pictograms came to be used not just to refer to concrete objects, but also to refer to activities and abstract concepts associated with the objects originally pictured. For instance, the following Ancient Egyptian hieroglyphs were used to refer to activities or concepts which were not directly picturable.

	Original Significance	Extension
	'knife'	'to cut, slay'
	'fire'	'to cook, burn'
	'sail'	'wind, air'
	'man with arms down'	'submission'
	'man with arms raised'	'to pray, praise'
	'men grasping hands'	'friendship'

At the point where such semantic extension has taken place, the characters of a writing system are considered *logograms*, rather than pictograms, because they are used to represent all types of words — abstract nouns, verbs, adjectives, etc., as well as concrete nouns.

It is thought that syllabic writing systems and alphabetic writing systems were developed from logographic writing systems. Although at first logographic characters symbolized entire words, as time went on, the conventional symbols used as logograms came to be associated more closely with the pronunciations of the words which they represented. This meant that the symbols began to represent sequences of sounds in the minds of their users. Consequently, the people used the symbols as characters to write sequences of sounds, or syllables, rather than whole words. For example, the Egyptians used the following hieroglyphs to represent syllables.

Also, some logographic characters were used to refer to sequences of sounds in an abbreviated fashion. That is, they came to represent the first sound in the pronunciation of the word to which they originally referred. For example, the Egyptians originally used the symbol,

to represent an owl, the word for which was pronounced something like / mu loč /. Eventually this hieroglyphic character came to indicate the sound / m /.

There were similar developments in other originally logographic writing systems, including the Mesopotamian cuneiform system, and the Chinese systems, to a limited extent.

The Semitic tribes living in the Sinai developed a system of writing based on the Egyptian usage of symbols to represent the first sound in the pronunciation of the word represented by the character. This eventually gave rise to the consonantal alphabets used by the Hebrews and the Arabs. For example, in the Semitic writing system, the character ⱦ represented an ox's head, and the character ⧧ represented a house. The Semitic words for these objects were pronounced something like /ʔalef/ and / bet /, respectively. Therefore, the Semites used ⧧ to write the glottal stop consonant / ʔ / which began the word for 'ox' and ⧧ to write the bilabial stop consonant / b / which began the word for 'house'. (All the characters in this alphabet were called by the names of the objects which they originally represented.)

The Phoenicians who used the Semitic consonantal alphabet, taught it to the Greeks, who adapted it for use in writing the words of their own language. Since Ancient Greek did not possess some of the consonants used in the pronunciation of Semitic languages, the Greeks began employing some of the borrowed characters to write vowel sounds of their language. For example, since the glottal stop / ʔ / was not used in the pronunciation of any Greek words, the symbol ⱦ came to represent the vowel / a / at the beginning of the borrowed word / ʔalef /, which the Greeks pronounced / alpʰa /. The Greeks borrowed all the names for the Phoenician characters along with the characters, pronouncing them each with a Greek accent. They referred to the whole list of symbols by the Greek version of the names of the first two symbols in the list, namely, / alfa / and / beta /, which is the source of the term *alphabet*.

APPENDIX: TAKING EXAMS

In the examinations you will be taking in this course, you will encounter several different types of questions. While some may be quite familiar types to you and thus pose no real difficulties in terms of your strategy for completing the exam successfully (for example, true-false or multiple choice questions), others may prove somewhat more difficult. Two types of questions which prove especially troublesome for students are *definitions* and *essay questions*. Below are some hints regarding each of these types as well as some pointers on exam taking in general.

A. DEFINITIONS

Most people have a hard time giving good, concise, and informative definitions for the technical terms that come up in a beginning linguistics class. The reason for this is not just that the terms are quite new, but also that the act of defining is actually not something one is commonly called upon to perform in ordinary everyday language use. As an exercise in what constitutes a good definition, consider the following task: define what an *orange* is (notice that this is parallel to tasks on linguistics exams, such as "Define *dissimilation*").

Let's see what a good answer to this question would be: that is, what a good definition of an orange *would* be. Consider the following possible definitions:

1. An orange is when there is a fruit which is colored orange and you squeeze it to make juice; it comes from a tree.

2. An orange is a round, orange-colored citrus fruit which yields a sweet or bitter acidic juice.

Clearly the second definition is preferable to the first. Why? Both definitions give information about oranges and how one might identify such a fruit, but the second is structured in a much better way than the first. The second definition starts out by classifying *orange*, i.e. identifying as narrowly as possible that class of objects to which it belongs, thereby reducing the range of possible fields a reader has to consider when trying to determine what an orange is. Then it gives some salient characteristics of an orange which help to differentiate it from other members of its class, i.e., from other citrus fruits like the grapefruit or tangerine. By contrast, the first definition does none of that, and moreover, by using the construction "an orange is when . . .," it is considering an orange to be an event, something that happens, rather than an object, or something that is.

Let's apply this strategy of defining terms to a linguistic example now, namely *dissimilation*. A definition parallel to the first for *orange* would be:

3. Dissimilation is when there are two sounds in a word which become less like one another.

Compare that with a definition parallel to the second one for *orange*:

4. Dissimilation is a type of phonological process in which one sound in a word becomes less like another sound in the same word with respect to one or more phonological features.

The second definition again is to be preferred, in part because it locates dissimilation in its proper class, namely that of phonological processes, and then goes on from there to specify the features which distinguish it from other members of that class. In contrast, the first definition (3) does not give this "genus and species" information, and a teacher grading such an answer would have to ask him/herself whether the student understood just what type of thing *dissimilation* actually is.

Finally, it is often a good idea to give an appropriate example, either real if possible, or made-up if necessary, to indicate that you really do understand just what it is you are defining; thus a fully complete answer to the question "Define dissimilation" would be:

5. Dissimilation is a phonological process in which one sound in a word becomes less like another sound in the same word with respect to one or more phonological features; for example, the Latin word *peregrinus* turned into French *pelerin* 'pilgrim' and the -r- changing to an -l- is a case of dissimilation.

B. ESSAY QUESTIONS

The purpose of essay questions is to allow an instructor to find out whether the student understands the course material well enough to see the relationships among the data and to create some synthesis in his own mind, rather than to just regurgitate a more or less random collection of ideas. Thus essay questions test the *depth* of a student's knowledge. In order to do this you must be able to present the required information in an organized, logical way. The following are some suggestions to aid you in this endeavor.

1. *Know* the material. For instance, a typical essay question a linguistics instructor may ask is: *Is language more iconic than arbitrary? Support your answer with illustrations from human language.*

   To study for questions such as this, you should not simply memorize all the terms you have heard your instructor mention in class. Rather you should learn the terms *in relation to language* and why such distinctions are important. For this particular example you should discuss both the iconic and the arbitrary features of language. Be prepared to give specific examples of each type of feature. Based on your observations you should determine which feature seems to be more dominant in characterizing the system of language as a whole.

2. *Read* the questions. This may sound trivial, but it's incredible how many people blow exams simply because they don't take the trouble to be sure of what they're being asked to do. If you can't understand the question after reading it carefully, for heaven's sake ask the instructor what he or she is asking you to do. For example, failing to take note of the crucial words *more . . . than* in the example given above, you may give examples of arbitrariness and iconicity in language without ever addressing the question of which term more obviously characterizes language—an oversight on your part which will probably result in the loss of most of the points for the question.

3. *Plan* your answer. Once you know what the instructor wants, take a little time to figure out how to give the answer. What are the main points you are trying to make? How can you support them? For instance, if you decide that language is more arbitrary than iconic, you've done the easy part and answered the first part of the question. However, now comes the hard part, backing up your claim with actual facts from English or other languages. The main point you want to make is that language is *mostly* arbitrary. Before you start writing your answer you should think of and jot down data which support this claim. For example:
   —the same object in nature is referred to with different sequences of sounds in different languages. For instance, in English we call paper, bound together with writing on it, a *book*; in French it is a *livre*, and in Russian *kniga*.
   —the fact that there is no intrinsic reason for calling a dog in English *dog*. It just so happens that at one time speakers agreed upon a sequence of sounds to represent such an object, and we have inherited, in a somewhat changed phonetic form, this verbal label.

4. *Don't pad your answer.* You don't have the time to wander off into irrelevance, and your instructor doesn't have the time to read it. So, all other things being equal (accuracy, clarity, completeness), the shorter answer is better than the longer answer. If your points are *substantial* and *relevant*, extra words are unnecessary and potentially confusing.

5. *Pace* yourself. Remember that you're working against the clock, and don't spend half your time on a question worth ten percent of your grade. If the exam allows you to choose questions, don't spend a lot of time deciding: if one is clearly easier for you, answer it, and if two are of about the same difficulty, pick the first one. If the questions are worth different numbers of points spend proportionally more time on the more heavily weighted ones. If you get stuck go on to the next question and come back later.

6. *Proofread* your answer. If you have a few extra minutes, use them to make sure that you (a) said what you meant to say and (b) said it clearly (most teachers will take points off if you make it difficult to figure out what you're talking about). Proofreading may prove even more valuable in the question above if, for instance, you inadvertently confused the terms *iconic* and *arbitrary* and have them completely backwards!!

SAMPLE ESSAY

The following provides you with a sample essay based on the question above. Read the essay carefully and note how it addresses the question with clear and concise details. Immediately after the essay is a sample outline which shows the organization of the essay. You will probably not have enough time to make an outline quite this complete in an actual test situation, but even a rough sketch of the points you want to make (written as you think of them) will be of great use when organizing your answer.

> *Although natural language contains elements of both arbitrariness and iconicity, it is beyond a doubt more arbitrary than iconic.*
>
> *The term **arbitrariness** refers to the fact that in human language there is not necessarily a connection between the sound symbol (word) which stands for an object and the object itself. **Iconicity**, on the other hand, assumes that there is a very close relationship between the verbal label for an object and the object itself. Onomatopoetic words (words that sound like what they name, for example **hiss** for the sound a snake makes) illustrate the iconic nature of language. The arbitrary nature of language can be more easily illustrated. For example, in the word **stereo** there is no clue as to the nature of the object referred to. The same object could just as easily have been called a **frimble**. Nor in the case of the word **sincerity** is there any clue as to the nature of the concept.*
>
> *One reason why language is more **arbitrary** than **iconic** is somewhat obvious: there are many, many more examples of arbitrary words than iconic words. In fact, after a few minutes you would probably run out of examples of iconic words in any particular language. However, arbitrary words which are arbitrarily related to the thing they name are endless.*
>
> *A second reason which leads us to argue that language is mostly arbitrary is that we use **different** arbitrary sequences of sounds to name the same object cross-linguistically. For example, the word **book** in English names an object which is 'paper bound together with writing on it' in a purely arbitrary manner. In French, however, a different arbitrary word names this object, namely **livre**, and in Russian in the same way **kniga**. Therefore, even the choice of arbitrary symbols to refer to objects and concepts is arbitrary!*
>
> *For these two reasons, then, it is clear that language is a predominantly arbitrary system of communication. Most of language is arbitrary, and things in nature are given arbitrary labels cross-linguistically.*

OUTLINE

A. Introduction
  1. Introducing the terms *arbitrary* and *iconic*
  2. Language is more arbitrary than iconic
B. Defining arbitrary and iconic
  1. Example of iconicity in English
  2. Examples of arbitrariness in English
C. Why language is more arbitrary than iconic
  1. More examples of arbitrary words
  2. Cross-linguistic evidence
D. Conclusion—restating evidence
  1. Most of language is arbitrary
  2. Things in nature are given arbitrary labels cross-linguistically

C. ADDITIONAL INFORMATION

Unfortunately, knowing *how* to apply the techniques discussed in parts A and B is not enough; you must also know *when* each type of answer is appropriate. For example, the clearest definition in the world is not going to help you much if the question is really asking you to do something else. This mistake is particularly common when students are asked to compare and contrast terms. First impulse tells us to simply define the two terms and go on, but if we think a minute about what 'compare' and 'contrast' *mean* we see that this really isn't sufficient. Compare and contrast questions are asking you to go beyond definitions, to *synthesize* what you know about the material. To satisfactorily answer a compare and contrast question you must make *explicit* the properties or features that the two items share and the properties or features that distinguish them. Simply defining the two terms achieves neither of these goals. This brings up a point that is relevant to other types of questions as well: if there is a conclusion to be made, make it! Do not expect your instructor to read between the lines to figure out what your conclusion is. It is *your* job to make what you mean clear.

A similar point can be made about essay writing. It is a waste of time and effort (especially time) to develop an elaborate response for a simple short answer question. On the other hand, you want to be certain that your answer is complete enough. One clue to the degree of depth expected is the relative point value of the question. The more the question is worth, the more detailed your answer should be. Another indication is the amount of time spent on the topic. If the issue was not addressed in detail in class or in the readings, then your instructor probably won't expect a very detailed answer either. Finally, the phrasing of the question itself can be a clue. General, open-ended questions, such as *Discuss the phenomenon of dissimilation* or *Argue for or against the view that language is more arbitrary than iconic*, require more detailed answers than questions like *What is dissimilation?* or *Give an example of arbitrariness in human language.* The latter pair explicitly ask for a particular piece of information, the former merely supply the topic to be expanded upon. It is up to *you* to determine what or how much needs to be said. All of these factors—point value, degree of emphasis and phrasing—should be taken into consideration *before* you begin your answer so that you can budget your time wisely. If you have any doubts at all as to how much is expected of you *be sure to ask your instructor.* After all, s/he is the one who will be judging your work.

In closing, let us emphasize again an important general strategy mentioned above in regard to taking an examination (and this holds, by the way, for any exam, not just those in linguistics classes and for any type of exam question, not just essays): allot your time according to the relative importance of the questions. Thus, if one question is worth only 10 points, don't spend 20 minutes on it in a hour-long exam. Since many universities' class 'hours' are 48 minutes in length and exams are often calculated on a scale of 100 points, it is a good rule of thumb to allow yourself no more than one-half as many minutes as the points the question is worth. For example, a ten point question should at first occupy you no more than five minutes, a twenty-pointer no more than ten minutes. Once you have made an attempt to answer all the questions, you can go back (time permitting) to work on ones you were not able to complete at first.

APPENDIX:
INDEX

—Notes—

—Notes—

—Notes—

—Notes—

—Notes—